SLAVERY IN THE AMERICAN REPUBLIC

SLAVERY IN THE AMERICAN REPUBLIC

Developing the Federal Government, 1791–1861

David F. Ericson

 University Press of Kansas

Published by the University Press of Kansas (Lawrence, Kansas 66045), which was
organized by the Kansas Board of Regents and is operated and funded by Emporia
State University, Fort Hays State University, Kansas State University, Pittsburg State
University, the University of Kansas, and Wichita State University

Library of Congress Cataloging-in-Publication Data

Ericson, David F., 1950–
   Slavery in the American republic : developing the federal government, 1791–1861 /
David F. Ericson.
      p.   cm.
   Includes bibliographical references and index.
   ISBN 978-0-7006-1796-8 (cloth : alk. paper) 1. Slavery—Government policy—United
States—History. 2. Slavery—Political aspects—United States—History. 3. Federal
government—United States—History—18th century. 4. Federal government—United
States—History—19th century. 5. United States—Politics and government—1783–1865.
6. Sectionalism (United States)—History. 7. Slavery—Southern States—Justification.
I. Title.
   E449.E733 2011
   973.4—dc23
                                                                                    2011033175
British Library Cataloguing-in-Publication Data is available.

Printed in the United States of America

10 9 8 7 6 5 4 3 2 1

The paper used in this publication is recycled and contains 30 percent postconsumer
waste. It is acid free and meets the minimum requirements of the American National
Standard for Permanence of Paper for Printed Library Materials Z39.48-1992.

CONTENTS

Preface   vii

1. Slavery in a "House Divided"   1

2. Slavery and Controlling the National Borders   25

3. The First American Colony   53

4. The Slave-Catching Republic   80

5. The Slavery Garrisoned State   107

6. Free Labor Not Preferred   135

7. The "House Divided" Revisited   164

Appendix A   187

Appendix B   188

Appendix C   189

Notes   191

Index   275

PREFACE

Believe it or not, this project began while I was giving a test in an Introduction to American Politics course in April 2001 at Wichita State University. I had finished my second book the previous year and ever since I had been attempting to figure out what that next big project would be. My first stab, a project on Hobbes and liberalism, had turned out to be a dead end. Knowing that I would have some time to think about such matters during the hour I gave the test, I was determined to conjure up that next project. Well, to my own surprise, I did. How about exploring how slavery influenced the development of the federal government, not with the usual broad brush strokes typical of the literature on the history of American slavery but in concrete detail? Of course, this epiphany was not without some long roots.

The longest roots went back to a course I took as a graduate student at the University of Chicago, on Jacksonian Politics, taught by J. David Greenstone. I found this course fascinating, and not only because of the eccentricities of the instructor. It was this course that turned me from the history of political philosophy, strictly speaking—though not completely (hence the Hobbes project)—to more American matters. As the course progressed, I became more and more convinced that slavery was the defining issue of American history, which may or may not have had something to do with the question that made the course famous, at least among my cohort of graduate students. In which "Greenstone box" would you place historical figure X (e.g., John Quincy Adams, Daniel Webster, etc.)? Arminian or antinomian? Individual or community? The class exploded the day $X =$ Captain Ahab.

My dissertation (and later, first book) and second book had both explored the slavery issue in American politics as important pieces of intellectual history. I, however, was very dissatisfied with the way that I had connected that intellectual history to events on the ground. In the meantime, I had begun to read the literature on American political development, not yet enough to redefine myself as an APD scholar but enough to find a lacuna in the literature with respect to the relationship between the continuing presence of slavery on American soil and American state development during the long stretch from the framing of the U.S. Constitution to the beginning of the Civil War. Those two lacunae sparked my epiphany.

As typically happens, the more research I did on the relationship of slavery to the development of the federal government, the more research I discovered I needed to do. What began as a project somewhat narrowly focused on aggregating federal expenditures on such slavery-related spending items as fugitive-slave returns and slave-trade interdiction, (thankfully) broadened out to explore the full range of the relationship between the presence of slavery and American state development. I also discovered how much research had already been done in this field of study and yet how extremely fragmented the research remained. Don Fehrenbacher's magisterial book on the slaveholding republic pulls together many of those fragments, enough to make a convincing case on just how much the presence of slavery influenced public policy during the pre–Civil War period, but not enough to make the same case for American state development. To say that the federal records relevant to this topic are also extremely fragmented is, of course, a gross understatement.

Nine years and three universities later, I can claim to have pulled together many of those fragments, certainly not all, but enough, I believe, to make a convincing case about just how much the presence of slavery influenced American state development. It is no false humility to claim that, nor, alternately, to emphasize how much more still needs to be done in this field of research.

To acknowledge all the people who have helped me along the way would make for a very long list. Special mention, however, must go to Peter Breiner, Ira Katznelson, and Bruce Miroff for their especially careful readings of drafts of the first chapter as well as to Mark Graber, who started out as an anonymous reviewer of the book manuscript and then became its improver-in-chief. I would also like to thank the other (still) anonymous reviewer of the manuscript for very helpful suggestions. Archivists Walter B. Hill and John VanDereedt offered invaluable assistance in searching for the needles among the haystacks at the National Archives. I am extremely grateful to the James Madison Program on American Ideals and Institutions at Princeton University for funding a very productive year of writing and research as well as providing a very stimulating intellectual climate in which to pursue those tasks.

Earlier versions of the argument of this study appeared as a research note, "The Federal Government and Slavery: Following the Money Trail," *Studies in American Political Development* 19, 1 (Spring 2005): 105–116, and as a book chapter, "Slave Smugglers, Slave Catchers, and Slave Rebels: Slavery and American State Development, 1787–1842," in *Contesting Slavery: The Politics of Slavery in the New American Nation,* ed. John Craig Hammond and Matthew Mason (Charlottesville: University Press of Virginia, 2011). I would like to thank the editors of that book (Craig and Matt) and that journal (Karen Orren and Stephen Skowronek) for their assistance and comments, as well as the University Press of Virginia and

Cambridge University Press for the use of material from those works. Finally, very special mention must go to the person who planted the kernel, Chicago Bulls fan *extraordinaire,* J. David Greenstone. I am sure this would be a better book if he were still alive.

SLAVERY IN THE AMERICAN REPUBLIC

1. Slavery in a "House Divided"

In the long stretch of U.S. history from the beginning of the new federal government under the Constitution to the Civil War, the American state was uniquely a "house divided" between slavery and freedom. The continuing presence of slavery in the Southern states did not affect the development of only one side of that house. It affected the development of both sides, as well as of the house itself. It also shaped the initial construction of the house. Slavery was in the walls and in the woodwork, and, as it turned out, the institution could not be eradicated without destroying the house.[1]

This study explores how the presence of slavery influenced the development of the American state during this long stretch of U.S. history. It is a study of American state development during a period when the politics and history literature argues that little state development occurred and that the development that did take place occurred for reasons other than the presence of slavery. In fact, the literature suggests that the presence of slavery depressed early American state development because a politically privileged group of Southern slaveholders blocked state development out of fear that a strong state would act to abolish the institution. This study shows the converse. It demonstrates how the presence of slavery contributed to early American state development, not only in opposition to the demands of Southern slaveholders but sometimes in response to their demands. The claim that the federal government would have developed very differently than it did in the absence of slavery may seem obvious, but unfortunately it is a claim that many prominent studies of American state development fail to make except, possibly, in a negative sense.[2]

To the contrary, the presence of slavery influenced the development of the early American state in many positive ways. The enforcement of the constitutionally authorized slave-import ban first involved the federal government in border control and eventually led to a significant reallocation of its naval forces. The federal government partnered with the American Colonization Society (ACS) in founding the nation's first overseas colony in Liberia, establishing an early model of public-private partnerships. Over time, the enforcement of fugitive-slave law produced dramatic changes in federal law-enforcement practices. The presence of slavery also spurred the development of the U.S. army through its many slavery-related deployments, in particular, in prosecuting the Second Seminole War (1835–1842). The federal government's slave rentals added to its state capacities as well as influenced its labor-management practices. The politics and history

1

literature has largely ignored these policy areas. As a result, it has buried one of the principal stories of early American state development. This study unearths that story.

Before discussing at greater length how this study contributes to the politics and history literature, it will be useful to briefly review that literature. Three major fault lines have emerged in the literature. First, different studies use different standards of comparison to measure American state development. Second, different studies rely on different definitions of the state. Third, different studies offer different conceptions of state development.

FRAMING ISSUES

In the politics and history literature, the American state has been compared to itself over time, to other states, both over time and at one point in time, and to its own member-states, either individually or as a whole. Most studies compare the earlier to the later American state. Stephen Skowronek adopts this approach in showing how an early American state of "courts and parties" developed into a modern, administrative state in the late nineteenth and early twentieth centuries.[3] Karen Orren also adopts this approach in demonstrating how the American state gradually shed its feudal lineages and emerged as a definitively modern, liberal state only in the 1930s.[4] Richard Bensel epitomizes this approach in positing the existence of as many as five different American states over the course of the last half of the nineteenth century.[5]

Nevertheless, the standard of comparison in many studies of American state development is, at least implicitly, other Western states, especially Great Britain, France, and Prussia (Germany).[6] In these cross-national comparisons, the American state is typically found to be underdeveloped or weak compared to other Western states. Daniel Rodgers details how the development of social-welfare programs during the Progressive Era was stunted in the United States, compared to their development in other Western nations.[7] Theda Skocpol and her colleagues reach similar conclusions relative to other periods of U.S. history.[8] Even Skowronek, Orren, and Bensel import from European contexts notions of what modern states look like.

These cross-national comparisons, again at least implicitly, reassert the case for American exceptionalism. Ira Katznelson takes the next step. He argues that because historically the American state has been exceptionally liberal, it has followed an exceptionally liberal path of development. Katznelson notes that the American state experienced less of the military-driven development that European states did because for most of its history it fought wars with citizen soldiers, not professional armies. He claims that this difference did not necessarily make the

American state less developed or weaker than European states; it merely made it different.[9]

Another type of "across space" comparison is the federal-state comparison within the United States. William Novak chronicles how active the state and local governments were during the nineteenth century in using their police powers to regulate the conduct of their citizens. He concludes that if the nineteenth century was the golden age of "laissez-faire," it was *not* at the subnational level.[10] His work dovetails with a long tradition of "commonwealth studies" that document how, in comparison to the federal government, the state and local governments were very active during the nineteenth century in promoting economic development by building roads, canals, railroads, and other improvements.[11] The thrust of these federal-state comparisons is that the American state was underdeveloped or weak at the turn of the twentieth century not only relative to European states but to its own member-states.[12]

A second major fault line has emerged in the literature over different definitions of the state. One type of definition of the state is functional. Publics establish states to accomplish a common set of objectives that any public wishes to accomplish, such as providing personal security and building economic infrastructure. A public then assigns a group of people, through birth, civil-service tests, or elections, and supplies them with the necessary resources, through property seizures, user fees, or taxation, to accomplish those objectives. Stronger states accomplish those objectives more effectively than weaker ones, presumably because stronger states have greater capacities (human and fiscal resources) to accomplish them. In the politics and history literature, Bensel, again, epitomizes this functional, or state-capacities, approach.[13]

In contrast, many politics and history scholars define the state in terms of a common set of political institutions. Skowronek pioneered this structural or institutional approach, which has now become the most common approach.[14] The contrast between the functional and structural approaches is not an either/or. In fact, the two approaches are often combined. Publics establish particular institutions to accomplish particular purposes. Scholars who adopt a more structural approach are, however, more likely to emphasize how institutions become independent of the purposes and publics they ostensibly serve.

A structural approach may also offer a different assessment of state strength than a functional approach. Indeed, the "new institutionalists," such as Orren and Skowronek, encounter major difficulties in measuring the strength of a state as a whole or the strength of any particular political institution within the state.[15] One solution has been to attempt to measure the degree of institutional autonomy, which assumes that institutions are strong to the degree that they do not merely respond to public demands. This solution only relocates the problem to another level, of how to measure institutional autonomy. Daniel Carpenter measures institutional autonomy in terms of the continuity of the "mezzo-level" management of an institution and its ability to cultivate its own supportive constituencies.[16] A well-entrenched bureaucracy can often define a common set of public policies that are relatively impervious to at least short-term changes in public opinion as well as in executive and legislative leadership. The ability of bureaucrats to "lock in" policy programs is also central to Paul Pierson's concept of path dependency.[17]

Other scholars emphasize other aspects of states. In his comparative study of war and state development, Sheldon Pollack borrows Max Weber's famous definition of the state as possessing a "monopoly of the legitimate use of physical force within a given territory."[18] Presumably, under this definition, the state is the collection of people or institutions that possesses such a monopoly. Weber's definition is structural, but it also includes a functional aspect in explaining what states "do": They coerce people. In the American case, this definition points directly to different levels of government sharing coercive powers. According to Novak, state and local governments extensively used police powers in the nineteenth century to coerce people, while the federal government coerced people, if it coerced them at all, almost exclusively through its military powers.[19] The state and local governments were stronger than the federal government during the nineteenth century if one considers only this aspect of states.

The other side of coercion is legitimacy. Under Weber's definition, the acceptance of a state by the people it may coerce decreases the need for the state to coerce them. More broadly, this aspect of states implies that whatever entity a public acknowledges as its state is its state. It also implies that most members of the public feel that the specific actions their state performs are appropriate actions for a state to perform, even if they do not necessarily agree with those actions. This psychological aspect of states underscores Katznelson's claim that liberal states can be weak in terms of coercive powers, institutional autonomy, and state capacities but still be strong in terms of legitimacy. For example, when a liberal state goes to war, volunteer soldiers and citizen militia lessen its need for a professional army or compulsory draft.[20]

Finally, Orren and Skowronek propose "governing authority," "durable shifts in governing authority," and "intercurrences" among governing authorities as the key concepts of state development.[21] These concepts introduce an explicitly normative dimension. A public authorizes a state to do certain things, and, presumably, not to do other things. Once again, under this aspect a liberal state is the model of a state. In liberal states, publics have the ability to de-authorize, re-authorize, and further limit or expand the authority of the state to act on their behalf. In the American case, this ability has been enshrined in amendable constitutions on both the federal and state levels. On this aspect, the federal government compares more favorably to the state and local governments during the nineteenth century to the extent that the U.S. Constitution authorized several major shifts in governing authority from the state to the federal level.

Based on this abbreviated literature review, a good working definition of the state would be a public entity that has adequate capacities (money and manpower) to provide an agreed-upon set of collective goods (personal security and economic infrastructure) and that has developed political institutions (courts, legislatures, and executives) with the requisite autonomy to accomplish the objectives the public has authorized it to accomplish. A state also possesses the power to coerce people who attempt to thwart the accomplishment of its assigned objectives, while enjoying legitimacy among those who have authorized it to act on their behalf sufficient to allow it to act on their behalf without excessive use of force.[22] Within this working definition, a state could be simultaneously stronger and weaker than other states, or, in a federal system, its own member-states, depending on the object of comparison. Similarly, a state could be both stronger and weaker than itself in any over-time comparison. The historical evidence does not suggest any single teleological path of development toward stronger states.[23] States experience both short- and long-term fluctuations on various measures of state strength as well as undergo general processes of growth, stasis, and decay. States can also fail and perhaps be reborn in some other form.

The third major fault line that has emerged in the literature involves different measures of state development. Obviously, different definitions of the state will generate different measures of state development. Yet, just as one can broadly categorize different definitions of the state into functional and structural definitions, one can broadly categorize different conceptions of state development into society-centered and state-centered conceptions.[24] This distinction involves the difference between models of state development that stress exogenous social forces as the primary engines of development and those that emphasize endogenous bureaucratic processes. Again, this difference is not an either/or. Functional definitions of the state are, however, clearly more congenial to society-centered models of state development and structural definitions, to state-centered models. Bensel, for example, contended that the development of the modern, administrative American state was primarily a response to the industrial revolution, which outstripped the capacities of the earlier Gilded Age state to provide minimal levels of economic security for millions of Americans.[25] On the other hand, Pierson's "path dependency" model is a good example of a state-centered model of state development in assuming that prior policy choices "lock in" later ones.[26] Walter Dean Burnham's influential work on "critical elections" provides one way of operationalizing how transformative political events can "unlock" policy paths.[27] In their "state of the field" essay, Orren and Skowronek attempt to balance state-centered and society-centered models of state development in claiming that the fit between state structures and societal demands determines which demands are most likely to be translated into public policy at any given moment.[28]

Without denying the virtues of other research approaches, I believe that some approaches offer more promise than others when applied to the study of early American state development. I have framed my own study accordingly.

This study is an over-time comparison of the development of the American state during the pre–Civil War period, as opposed to a cross-national or federal-state comparison. I believe that the over-time comparison tells us more about the nature of the early American state and how it developed over time, while the other two comparisons tell us more about how it did *not* develop. The important truth behind Skowronek's "courts and parties" view of the early American state is that the federal government was, in many respects, a shell of a government during the pre–Civil War period.[29] Still, the early American state was not inert. It developed in certain respects, and its unique "house divided" nature helps explain the ways in which it did and did not develop.

Similarly, I have adopted a society-centered model of state development that explores how the presence of slavery affected the development of the early American state. I believe that state-centered models are more appropriate for heavily bureaucratized states, which the early American state was *not*.[30] I also believe that the effects of the presence of slavery on the development of the early American state have not been as fully explored as other societal factors, such as the market revolution, frontier settlement, and interstate wars.

In examining how the presence of slavery affected the institutional development of the federal government, my approach is structural. The presence of slavery affected the institutional development of the federal government in several important cases. The Second Seminole War, which was, alternately, a slave roundup and a slave revolt, represented a pivotal event in the development of the U.S. army, as regular army units replaced the militia and volunteer units that the American state had traditionally depended on to fight its wars.[31] The suppression of American participation in the international slave trade was a major episode in the development of the U.S. navy following President Buchanan's 1858 decision to reinforce both the African and Home squadrons for that purpose.[32] The enforcement of the Fugitive Slave Law of 1850 prompted the federal government to strengthen its own law-enforcement agencies instead of relying on those of the state and local governments.[33] I also examine how the presence of slavery affected other, noninstitutional aspects of the development of the federal government, which were at least equally important in increasing its state capacities.

Across a broad spectrum of policy areas, the early American state employed private agents to perform state functions. This practice both compensated for and contributed to its lack of institutional development. Despite its increasing professionalization, the U.S. army heavily depended on auxiliary forces to complete its assigned tasks. The authorized peacetime force of the army did not exceed 12,000 men until 1855. In "Bleeding Kansas," the federalization of the territorial militia was still critical to its success.[34] In slave-trade and fugitive-slave cases, the federal government also continued to rely heavily on private agents. Private citizens were deputized as marshals to seize alleged slave smugglers, fugitive slaves, and slave rescuers, private attorneys were hired to prosecute them, and private jailers and doctors were paid to care for them when they were taken into custody. Whatever advantages and disadvantages "outsourcing" may have, states in general and the American state in particular have always employed private agents to perform state functions. No matter how bureaucratized states may become, state officials will never be able to anticipate every task they must perform, nor would it make sense to hire employees in anticipation of every task they might have to perform.

Furthermore, at least in liberal democracies, private citizens *should* perform state functions. Voters choose officeholders, political activists petition legislative assemblies, army reservists assist regular soldiers, and jurors assess the guilt and innocence of those accused of violating state laws. In every society, a wide range of people perform state functions, often without any self-awareness of that fact. In the early American republic, many of those people were slaves whom federal officials had rented or themselves leased to the federal government to perform particular state functions. The federal employment of slave labor changed the way that the American state relied on private agents to perform state functions as the micromanagement structures federal officials established to supervise their slave employees were applied more generally to other employees.[35]

HISTORICAL NARRATIVES

In order to further justify my "slavery-centered" model of the development of the early American state, it will be useful to compare my model to other society-centered models of early American state development. This comparison demonstrates how society-centered models of early American state development that emphasize factors other than the presence of slavery do not sufficiently recognize how slavery affected those other factors. It also shows how other society-centered models of early American state development that recognize the importance of slavery either recognize only its negative influences on state development or recognize its positive influences only in insufficient ways. In making these comparisons, my premise is not that the presence of slavery was the only societal factor that shaped the development of the early American state but rather that its significance in shaping early American state development has been seriously discounted in the past.

One longstanding narrative of American state development is the frontier thesis. In its original, Turnerian form, the thesis is not really about state development. Private initiative was the principal agent of westward expansion.[36] Later versions have, however, "brought the state back in." Federal, state, and local governments built the infrastructure that facilitated westward expansion. The federal government played a more exclusive role in removing Native Americans and selling their vacated lands, not to mention in acquiring new territories from France, Spain, and Mexico. These activities, in turn, "thickened" the American state. Army engineers built frontier outposts and surveyed lands preceding European American settlement, land and post offices then followed the main routes of European American settlement, and, finally, army engineers returned to oversee internal improvement projects even when they were constructed under other auspices.[37]

Slavery is absent in both versions of the frontier thesis. The original version does not explore the role that Southern slaveholders and their slaves played in conquering the frontier. The newer versions overlook the role that slaveholders played in lobbying the federal government to remove Native Americans. Slaveholders demanded removal not only because they wanted Native American lands but also because they wanted to better secure their slaveholdings against slave runaways to Native American lands as well as against Native American slave raids on their plantations. In their analysis of the congressional vote on the Indian Removal Act of 1830, Leonard Carlson and Mark Roberts found, even after controlling for party and section, that the larger the percentage of slaveholders in a congressional district, the more likely the member of Congress from that district was to vote for the act. Adam Rothman recently reasserted the general argument that southwest expansion was slavery expansion, though neither Rothman nor Carlson and Roberts looped their findings back to state development.[38] In all probability, the frontier would have been conquered anyway, in both the trans-Appalachian North and South, without federal direction and without the involvement of Southern slaveholders and their slaves. Yet, if timing issues are crucial to plausible counterfactual histories, then federal direction was crucial to westward expansion because without it the process would not have occurred in the same time frame.[39] In Southern states and territories, the presence of slavery played a similar role in quickening the pace of frontier settlement, both on the private level in actually settling former Native American lands and on the state and territorial level in encouraging federal intervention to facilitate that process.

The "market revolution" is another major narrative of American state development. As Charles Grier Sellers stresses in his version of this narrative, the

American state, through its various levels of government, strongly supported the market revolution by building economic infrastructure and establishing a favorable legal environment. He also emphasizes the ways that the presence of slavery propelled the market revolution, at least in the Southern states and territories.[40] In the South, an interstate market in slave labor competed with local labor markets, and the capital market in slave property often dwarfed the capital markets in other forms of property.[41] What is left out of the "market revolution" narrative is the way that the federal government provided additional support for slave markets. The federal government created more secure and stable slave markets by removing Native Americans, deterring slave revolts, and recovering fugitive slaves. It created more profitable and national slave markets by enacting a ban on slave imports and by *not* enacting a ban on the interstate slave trade.[42] It even entered the market by renting slave labor. In the process of implementing these slavery-friendly policies, the federal government increased its state capacities. It reinforced navy squadrons to interdict illegal slave trading, hired deputy marshals to capture alleged fugitive slaves and slave rescuers, and deployed army soldiers to remove Native Americans and deter slave rescues and revolts. Again, a "market revolution" narrative that places slavery more at the center of the narrative is a richer narrative.

A third major narrative of American state development assumes that wars drive state development. This type of narrative is a common narrative of European state development. Charles Tilly is the main proponent of the thesis that wars drove state development in early-modern Europe because they required central agencies to aggregate the human and fiscal resources necessary to fight them.[43] Initially, politics and history scholars saw the United States as the exception that proved the rule to this model of state development. The United States was spared major wars with major powers because of its relative isolation in the New World. As a result, the early American state experienced little military-driven development and remained relatively weak. This aspect of American exceptionalism has been subject to increasing scrutiny. Max Edling contends that the early Federalist administrations mimicked the major European powers in constructing an embryonic "fiscal-military" state that could expand as needed during wartime precisely because the Federalists did not feel isolated from European affairs.[44] David Mayhew claims that subsequent wars with Great Britain and Mexico, however minor they may have seemed from a European perspective, caused spurts in American state development. The War of 1812 ushered in the "American System" of protective tariffs, internal improvements, and a second national bank, while the Mexican-American War produced a new policy regime pivoting on the issue of slavery in the nation's new territories.[45] Francis Paul Prucha suggests that frontier conflicts with Native Americans, especially the protracted Second Seminole War, also fit this model of military-driven state development.[46] Of course, Americans fought one major war during the nineteenth century and, as Bensel shows, the Civil War spawned two strong military states within the territorial limits of the once and future United States.[47]

The role that the presence of slavery played in this military-driven state development remains relatively unexplored. Though the presence of slavery was not a proximate cause of the War of 1812, it affected how the war was fought. The governors of at least one lower-South state (Georgia) and territory (Mississippi) refused to allow their militia to be deployed elsewhere for fear that slaves would exploit the opportunities of war to revolt or escape to freedom.[48] In the case of the Mexican-American War, slavery was at least a proximate cause of the war. While the war still might have occurred in the absence of slavery, the expansion of slavery into Texas launched a chain of events that resulted in war with Mexico and, eventually, civil war among the no-longer-united states.[49] The causal nexus from the presence of slavery to war was even tighter in the case of the Second Seminole War, the nation's longest war of the nineteenth century. In territorial Florida, European American slaveholders insisted on Seminole removal to better secure their slaveholdings against Seminole "depredations"; Black Seminoles, in particular, resisted removal for fear that they would lose their freedom in the process.[50] In comparison to the Mexican-American War, the Second Seminole War is less vulnerable to the counterfactual argument that the war would still have occurred in the absence of slavery. During the entire pre–Civil War period, the presence of slavery steered American state development even further in a military direction than otherwise would have been the case. It also contributed to several related, long-term political dynamics during the period, toward executive and judicial, as opposed to congressional, policy-making; toward federal, as opposed to state and local, powers; toward closed, as opposed to open, government; and toward decision-making on the periphery as opposed to at the center.[51]

The influence of slavery did not overwhelm the influence of the other developmental factors identified in these three major narratives of early American state development. Nevertheless, a revision that integrates slavery more into each narrative enriches the narrative. The presence of slavery was one strand in a web of developmental factors, both society-centered and state-centered, that were constitutive of early American state development in the sense that one cannot imagine the American state developing in the way that it did in their absence. A grand narrative of early American state development would explore the influence of each of those factors on state development as well as how they interacted with one another to affect it together. This study makes no pretense of being such a grand narrative, but it adds greatly to our understanding of one critical component of any such narrative.[52]

Other narratives of early American state development place slavery more at the center of the narrative but either only in a negative way or in a positive way that is inadequate. Many scholars claim that the presence of slavery negatively affected early American state development because Southern slaveholders feared that a strong state might act to abolish the institution. Bensel, David Brion Davis, Robin Einhorn, Ronald Formissano, Michael Holt, James Huston, Richard John, Orren, Sellers, and Skowronek are among the leading politics and history scholars who make this claim.[53] The claim is, however, somewhat incidental to their studies. In contrast, it is central to Anthony Marx's comparative study of post-emancipation societies in Brazil, South Africa, and the United States. Marx argues that, in the United States, because Southern slaveholders represented a greater threat to regime stability in the minds of Northern elites than Southern slaves did, Northern elites accepted the otherwise undesirable combination of the continuing existence of slavery and a weak state as the price of regime stability. After the Civil War, Southern elites, despite losing their slaveholdings as well as the war, remained a major threat to regime stability. It was thus not surprising that Reconstruction ended with a renewed cross-sectional, bipartisan commitment to a weak state and white hegemony. According to Marx, a stronger American state could emerge in the twentieth century only when the Southern elite threat to regime stability had significantly receded as a result of both targeted policies of national (white) integration and long-term social changes that worked toward that same end. This stronger state could then begin to address the long-suppressed demands of African Americans, who, not coincidentally, had now transformed themselves into a greater threat to regime stability through civil-rights protests and urban unrest.[54]

What Marx leaves out of his account is the way that Southern slaveholders wanted a strong state to help them control their slaves, who represented the greatest threat to their own regime stability. The Fugitive Slave Law of 1850 was the most unequivocal congressional response to their demands but, as Carlson and Roberts demonstrate, those demands also factored into the passage of the Indian Removal Act of 1830. The truism is that Southern slaveholders, like most other Americans, supported federal action when federal action served their interests and federal inaction when federal inaction served their interests. Except for a small, ideologically committed minority, their commitment to states rights was pragmatic.[55] Southern slaveholders were also not a homogenous group. Some slaveholders would enjoy greater benefits or, alternatively, suffer lesser harms from proposed federal actions than others would. The debate over the slave-trade clause at the Constitutional Convention was only the first in a series of proposed federal actions that exposed a diversity of interests among Southern slaveholding elites.[56]

The same deficiency appears in more focused studies of how the presence of slavery negatively affected early American state development. Einhorn details how federal officials were extremely reluctant to levy direct taxes after their first attempt to levy such taxes in the late 1790s imploded because of the resistance of Southern slaveholders. They, in particular, resisted direct taxation because it required someone to assess the value of their slaves, which they saw as a threat to their political hegemony.[57] Other than a second, short-lived direct tax to fund the War of 1812 debt, the federal government relied almost exclusively on tariffs for its revenues during the pre–Civil War period. Customs duties accounted for nearly 90 percent of federal revenues over that time.[58]

Einhorn's study is very persuasive, but I wonder about the counterfactual argument. If federal officials had been more desperate more often for revenues, if tariffs had been less productive of revenue, and if the nation had been involved in more wars, would they not have turned more often to direct taxes?[59] Einhorn herself admits that the productivity of the tariffs is a key variable. She also identifies other reasons for the failure of the first direct tax, such as disputes over how to fairly assess and tax the value of houses.[60] Her study adds an important factor to the explanation of why tariffs were the tax of least resistance and direct taxation the tax of last resort. However, at most, it demonstrates how the presence of slavery was one factor that depressed early American state development in one policy area.[61]

Politics and history scholars who contend that the presence of slavery depressed early American state development most often refer to internal improvements as the one policy area where it had this effect. They typically cite the opposition of the Southern-based "Old Republicans," such as Senators John Randolph (Virginia) and Nathaniel Macon (North Carolina), to a national system of internal improvements in the post–War of 1812 years on the grounds that it created a slippery slope of loose constructionism that would culminate in a federally mandated emancipation of their slaves. As Randolph warned during the debate over the General Survey Act of 1824, "[i]f Congress possesses the power to do what is proposed by this bill . . . they may emancipate every slave in the United States—and with stronger color of reason than they can exercise the power now contended for."[62] Southern presidents James Madison and James Monroe delivered one blow to this policy initiative by insisting that it required the sanction of a constitutional amendment; Southern President Andrew Jackson then delivered a second and final blow with his Maysville Road veto. Pamela Baker convincingly retells this narrative in a recent study.[63]

The internal-improvements narrative is vulnerable at several points. First, the "Old Republicans" were a minority even among the Southern members of the Democratic-Republican caucus. Southern Democratic Republicans actually provided some of the strongest supporters of a national system of internal improvements, such as Secretary of War John C. Calhoun (South Carolina) and House Speaker Henry Clay (Kentucky).[64] Even the "Old Republicans" were not averse to a little loose constructionism when it served Southern interests, as in turning aside constitutional objections to the Louisiana Purchase.[65] Second, if there was a decline in support for internal improvements, it was a gradual decline. In fact, Congress passed the General Survey Act of 1824 despite the "Old Republican" opposition, and federal spending on internal improvements peaked during the Jackson administration, despite his Maysville Road veto.[66] Third, factors other than Southern anxieties over slavery contributed to the subsequent decline in federal spending on internal improvements. Carter Goodrich suggests that internal improvements constituted a classic log-rolling policy and therefore were very vulnerable to interstate and interregional rivalries.[67] Stephen Minicucci claims that the failure of Congress to institutionalize log-rolling within the committee structure made internal improvements especially vulnerable to such rivalries.[68] John Lauritz Larson finds a general decline in public spending on internal improvements at all levels of government in the 1840s as internal improvement projects were privatized in reaction to growing public indebtedness and the belief that private firms could build them better or, at least, cheaper.[69] None of these scholars deny that Southern anxieties over slavery were one factor in this decline.[70] Yet each broadens the internal-improvements narrative to demonstrate, once again, that the presence of slavery is, at most, one factor in depressing early American state development in one policy area.

Many politics and history scholars who argue that the presence of slavery negatively affected early American state development present this case as their sole evidence for that general argument. Whatever the validity of the evidence, it is an extremely slender foundation on which to build such an argument, even if one buttresses it with Einhorn's excellent research on tax policy. The argument appears all the weaker when one considers the evidence on the other side, of how the presence of slavery positively affected early American state development.

Don Fehrenbacher's posthumously published work, *The Slaveholding Republic: An Account of the United States Government's Relation to Slavery,* marshals the evidence on the other side. Fehrenbacher examines the governance of the nation's capital, foreign relations, interdicting illegal slave trading and smuggling, recovering fugitive slaves, and territorial policy as five policy areas in which the presence of slavery strongly influenced public policy. He acknowledges that many of the specific policies enacted in these five areas were not proslavery in nature but rather the results of intersectional compromises, such as the three-fifths and slave-trade clauses of the U.S. Constitution, the Missouri Compromise, and the Compromise of 1850. He also acknowledges that some policies, such as the series of congressional statutes sanctioning American participation in the slave trade, can reasonably be interpreted as antislavery in nature. Nonetheless, Fehrenbacher insists that even those policies were implemented with a Southern, proslavery bias,

as in the attempt to make Kansas a slave state, the lax enforcement of the nation's slave-trade laws, and the extra-constitutional reach of the Fugitive Slave Law
of 1850.[71]

Fehrenbacher's explanation for this proslavery bias is that Southern politicians
dominated the executive departments of the federal government for most of the
pre–Civil War period through their dominance of the Democratic-Republican and
Democratic coalitions that ruled the nation for most of the period. A Southern
slaveholder was president of the United States for 49 of the 72 years from 1789 to
1861. The slave states also enjoyed parity with the free states in major cabinet and
diplomatic appointments and held a two-to-one advantage over the free states in
the appointment of federal clerks, auditors, and controllers, despite the fact that
their percentage of the total white population dropped further below 50 percent
with each census.[72] In addition, 24 of the 35 presidents pro tem of the Senate, 23 of
the 35 speakers of the House, and 19 of the 34 Supreme Court justices, including
the chief justice from 1801 to 1861, were from slave states.[73] Though Fehrenbacher
is careful not to frame his "slaveholding republic" argument as a "slave power conspiracy" argument, the two arguments converge to a considerable degree.[74]

Fehrenbacher's book is a tour de force. However, it largely ignores several slavery-
influenced policy areas that I cover in detail in this study. African colonization,
military deployments, and federal employment practices were each strongly influenced by the presence of slavery.[75] More important, this study connects slavery-
influenced policy areas more explicitly to early American state development, a
connection that remains largely implicit in Fehrenbacher's book. I also attempt
to trace the amount of money and manpower the federal government devoted
to slavery-influenced policy areas more thoroughly than he does, as one way of
showing more precisely how the presence of slavery positively affected state development. I, finally, demonstrate that the presence of slavery positively affected state
development in part because of the routine decisions federal administrators made
in implementing policies that were not directly related to slavery. For instance,
the civil engineer in charge of building new dry docks at the Gosport (Norfolk)
Navy Yard in the late 1820s and early 1830s rented slave labor because he sought to
accommodate the interests of local slaveholders and also because free labor was
scarce and slave labor cheap. In making this decision, Loammi Baldwin acted au-
tonomously because the federal government had no formal policy against the use
of slave labor on construction projects.[76] When the free white laborers who were
working or had worked on the project complained to Baldwin's superiors at the
Department of Navy about his use of slave labor, he unapologetically defended his
employment practices. His superiors supported him even after the white workers
wrote a letter of protest to President Jackson. The case was deeply ironic. Baldwin was anything but a slave-power conspirator. He was from Boston, and he had

initially decided not to use "inferior" slave labor on the project. Yet, over time, he became a very strong supporter of its use.[77]

Far removed from the great sectional and partisan debates over the fate of slavery in Congress, federal administrators enjoyed the bureaucratic autonomy to make such decisions.[78] They made such decisions not as slave-power conspirators but as public officials who, regardless of their own sectional and partisan backgrounds, were sensitive to local milieus. In the Southern states and territories, they made decisions that they would not have made in the absence of slavery and, in their cumulative effects, those decisions influenced not only public policy but also state development. This administrative terrain escapes Fehrenbacher's attention because his focus is on federal policy-making, and federal policy-making at the center, not on the periphery. Indeed, the presence of slavery was one of the major factors pushing federal policy-making to the periphery because of the political paralysis it frequently created at the center. Federal employment policy was, for example, effectively made on the ground by the middle- and low-level federal officials who made the actual hiring decisions, not by Congress or the cabinet-level officials who formulated general employment policies.

From Fehrenbacher's work, we gain a wonderful sense of how much the continuing presence of slavery shaped the public face of the American regime, both domestically and internationally, during the pre–Civil War period. But beyond its public face, the presence of slavery permeated the whole regime, including the more subterranean processes of policy formation, implementation, and legitimation that undergird state development.

In terms of early American state development, a number of studies explore how the presence of slavery influenced the development of specific institutions at the Constitutional Convention, including congressional apportionment, the electoral college, and the division of powers among various departments and levels of government.[79] Some studies also examine how the continuing presence of slavery influenced subsequent institutional development. Richard Newman demonstrates how an informal gag rule emerged in the first Congress in response to the early Quaker antislavery petitions, more than forty years before the House formalized the rule.[80] Richard John shows how the abolitionist mailings controversy undermined the bureaucratic autonomy of the Post Office during Jackson's second administration.[81] Barry Weingast chronicles how the admission of California as a free state in 1850 abrogated the informal congressional convention of maintaining sectional parity in the Senate by admitting free states and slave states in tandem.[82]

This prior research does not, however, indicate how the presence of slavery positively affected American state development over the entire pre–Civil War period. Nor does it investigate state development in terms of other, noninstitutional forms of development. This study does those things. More specifically, it demonstrates how the federal government fulfilled such traditional state functions as policing the national borders in interdicting slave smuggling, an early and often unnoticed form of immigration control; how it enhanced its governing authority in recovering fugitive slaves, though at some cost to its legitimacy in many of the Northern states and territories; and how it increased its state capacities in forcibly removing the Seminoles from Florida, now at some gain to its legitimacy in several of the Southern states and territories. In its largest slavery-related expenditure, the federal government spent an estimated $30 million and deployed an estimated 40,000 soldiers to remove approximately 3,000 Seminoles from Florida during the Second Seminole War.[83] I highlight these and other major slavery-related allocations of federal resources as measures of how the presence of slavery positively affected early American state development. These measures have the virtue of quantifiability. They also have the virtue of exposing areas in which the presence of slavery positively affected state development when the effect did not become official policy (African colonization) and even when it violated official policy (slave rentals at navy yards).

I follow the trail of federal spending and hiring decisions as one way of exposing specific cases in which the presence of slavery positively affected early American state development. The fiscal and employment data that I present in this study is a simulacrum of a larger whole, both in the sense that the data itself is incomplete and in the sense that it points to other ways that the presence of slavery positively affected state development.[84] In tracing how the presence of slavery influenced federal expenditure and employment levels, my goal is not merely to add up totals and subtotals—though sometimes those are important indicators of state capacities and how the federal government deploys them—but also to indicate how the presence of slavery caused changes in state behavior which, in turn, led to state development. Building on the research of many other politics and history scholars, I offer a much more complete picture of how the presence of slavery positively affected early American state development than they have offered, either individually or collectively.

Much work remains to be done. Still more complete pictures of how the presence of slavery positively affected early American state development await further research. Given the state of government records from the pre–Civil War period, I have no confidence that our still more complete pictures of how the presence of slavery positively affected state development will ever be complete, or even close to it.[85] In this sense, previous work at this research site exposed a fossil and excavated some of its bones. I have now excavated enough of its bones to provide a good sense of what the creature looked like. But we need to continue the excavation work so that, over time, our picture of what the creature looked like will become ever more refined.

In revising the traditional narrative that the presence of slavery had little to do with the development of the early American state or, at most, negatively affected it, we, furthermore, should be careful not to over-revise. In transitioning from narratives of state development in which slavery is (almost) nowhere, we do not want to end up with narratives in which slavery is (almost) everywhere.[86] We must be able to discriminate cases when the presence of slavery affected state development, either positively or negatively, from those when it did not. We also must be able to determine what it was specifically about the presence of slavery that caused the observed effect as we, counterfactually, imagine how the early American state might have developed in the absence of slavery.

COUNTERFACTUAL HISTORY

Counterfactual history helps us accomplish these tasks.[87] For each case, we must ask the question whether the case would have occurred, with a high degree of probability and within a similar time frame, in the absence of slavery. Some cases are relatively easy. Particular instances of federal officials renting slave labor and returning fugitive slaves would not have occurred in the absence of slavery. Counterfactual history also helps us determine what specifically about the presence of slavery contributed to state development. In these cases, the contributions were the micromanagement structures that federal officials established to supervise slave labor, which they would otherwise not have established, and the law-enforcement agencies that they strengthened to return fugitive slaves, which they would otherwise not have strengthened.

One could always argue that in the absence of slavery federal officials would simply have hired free labor in the cases where they rented slave labor and it would have had the same effect on federal expenditure and employment levels. The problem with this counterfactual is that, in the absence of slavery, it is unlikely that federal officials would have established, the same micromanagement structures that they established to supervise temporary employees or that they would have engaged in the same covert hiring practices. Similarly, one could argue that, in the absence of slavery, federal officials would have engaged in the extradition of fugitive slaves to other countries where the institution still existed (assuming that it still existed in other countries). The problem with this counterfactual is that it seems improbable that federal officials would have expended as much effort extraditing fugitive slaves to other countries as they expended returning fugitive slaves from one member-state to another or that they would have developed the same law-enforcement tools to extradite fugitive slaves as they developed to return fugitive slaves.[88]

Other cases are more difficult. If, in an inspired effort to erase the hypocrisy of the continuing presence of slavery in "an empire of liberty," the American states had jointly issued an emancipation proclamation as the final act of the American Revolution that had immediately, or, more likely, gradually, abolished slavery throughout the nation, they almost certainly would also have enacted comprehensive slave-trade legislation. In this counterfactual history, the United States would have been in a similar situation to the one Great Britain eventually was in, as a former slaveholding "empire."[89] Federal officials might then have sought to place the United States in competition with Great Britain for "liberator nation" status not only by enacting but by vigorously enforcing legislation against American participation in the slave trade (again assuming slavery still existed in other countries).[90] Another scenario, though, is at least as probable. Without the continuing presence of slavery on American soil, the pressure on the federal government to enact slave-trade legislation might have decreased, rather than increased, and federal officials, confronting other, more insistent priorities, might have made only token efforts to enforce any such legislation. In the nation's real history, American enforcement efforts could (and should) have been much greater, but they were not token, at least not after 1842. Moreover, those efforts were the result of two regional pressures, from Northern, free states and from upper-South, slave-exporting states, which would not have existed, at least not in the same form, in the absence of slavery.[91]

The African colonization movement also might have been more successful if all the American states had abolished slavery in the late eighteenth century. The express purpose of the American Colonization Society (ACS) was to colonize free African Americans in Africa with their own consent and, in this counterfactual history, a target population of 760,000 free (or to be freed) African Americans would have existed.[92] Yet few free blacks volunteered for colonization. The ACS colonized only 4,541 free blacks in the first 50 years of its existence, from 1817 to 1867, or approximately 90 per year. It is hard to imagine why a greater number of free blacks would have volunteered for colonization if they were no longer in any danger of re-enslavement. As it was, approximately 75 percent of the Liberian colonists were either liberated slaves or Africans seized from suspected slave ships and transported to Liberia at federal expense.[93] One, if not both, of those population pools would have shrunk in the absence of slavery. On the European American side, the presence of slavery increased the pressure on federal officials to aid the ACS, just as it increased the pressure on them to enact and enforce slave-trade legislation. By promoting African colonization, federal officials could claim that they were placing the institution of slavery in the course of ultimate extinction on the logic that the policy encouraged Southern slaveholders to emancipate their slaves by establishing a safely distant repository for their freed slaves, which was one of the official claims of the society that resonated with more gradualist antislavery sentiment in the lower North and upper South.[94] By promoting African colonization, federal officials could, alternately, claim that they were protecting the institution of slavery by dissipating the threat free blacks represented to the institution, a threat that the society stressed in its appeals to more proslavery audiences.[95]

On the other hand, two of the ACS's claims with broad-based, cross-sectional appeal would have retained, even increased, their vigor in the absence of slavery and the presence of 760,000 free (or to be freed) African Americans. These claims were the alleged threat that free blacks posed to the public safety and morals of the American people and the supposed impossibility of creating a biracial society where blacks and whites lived together as equals.[96] The issue of African American consent would, however, have remained. The extent to which the freed slaves defied the society's predictions that they would vote with their feet for Liberia after the nation's real Emancipation Proclamation suggests that this issue would also have retained its full vigor.[97] If in this counterfactual history the federal government coerced African Americans to emigrate, then the comparison to the nation's real history has shifted to a comparison where at least two key variables are different. Whether or not this shift in the terms of comparison is legitimate, it suggests that an "early" abolition of slavery in the United States would have resulted either in an even less successful or nonexistent colonization movement or in a more successful movement of a more explicitly coercive character.[98] An "early" abolition would certainly have made it more difficult for any colonization society to finesse the feasibility issue.[99]

Counterfactual history can also help us exclude cases that might seem like they belong. The Mexican-American War was the consequence of a chain of events unleashed by the expansion of slavery into Texas. But the causal chain from the presence of slavery to the Mexican-American War was an extended one. If we counterfactually remove the presence of slavery from that chain, the Mexican-American War still might have occurred within a similar time frame. In the absence of slavery, Texas would probably still have been settled by Americans, just as they settled the free territory of Oregon, which also did not clearly belong to the United States at the time.[100] The American settlement of Texas would probably have been slower in this counterfactual history. The Texas revolution, though, did not occur until 1835. It still might have occurred within a similar time frame based on the widespread separatist sentiments among the American settlers of Texas, even without the special threat the Mexican abolition of slavery posed to their slaveholdings.[101] The U.S. annexation of Texas also still might have occurred absent the desire of Southern slaveholders to add a slave state (or two or more) since Northern Democrats also strongly supported annexation. In fact, without the presence of slavery, Texas annexation would probably have enjoyed strong support from both sectional wings of both major parties and might have occurred sooner rather than later.[102] The final result then still may have been a war with Mexico to acquire more Mexican lands. Many Americans, in the North as well as the South, considered continental expansion part of the nation's manifest destiny independent of its effects on the future of slavery in the country.

This counterfactual history is far from conclusive. After all, the Polk administration fought for all-Texas but not all-Oregon. Polk's prioritizing of southwest over northwest expansion can be explained, however, on other grounds than the strong Southern presence in his administration. Mexico was a much weaker power than Great Britain. Great Britain also seemed much more likely to negotiate a border dispute that might shrink a lightly settled part of a very distant colony than Mexico was to negotiate its own dismemberment. Scholars can present and have presented plausible scenarios on both sides of this case.[103]

If one compares the Mexican-American War to the Second Seminole War, the connection between the presence of slavery and war appears less proximate in the latter case than in the former. The Seminoles would probably have been eventually removed from Florida, as other Native American nations were removed from other states and territories, in the North as well as the South. Seminole removal, though, would probably not have required seven years of warfare and $30 million in federal expenditures without the presence of slavery. On the Seminole side, the Black Seminoles fiercely resisted removal for fear of (re-)enslavement. On the European American side, local slaveholders in Florida and the surrounding states insisted that the Black Seminoles whom they claimed as their slaves should be surrendered to them before the other Seminoles were removed and that the other Seminoles should be removed to stanch the flow of their slaves to Seminole lands. The Seminoles were the only Native American nation to violently resist removal for an extended period of time.[104] It is unlikely that they would have resisted so long and so violently without the special slavery-related factors that affected them more than other Native American nations. It is also unlikely that local European American settlers would have been so insistent on their removal in the mid-1830s, given that they had already been pushed onto less desirable lands, farther from European American settlements, during the First Seminole War.[105] As General Thomas S. Jesup (Kentucky) told his superiors at the Department of War in 1836, the Second Seminole War was a "negro war," not an "Indian war."[106]

A counterfactual history in which all the American states had abolished slavery in the late eighteenth century and a very long, expensive war of removal between the U.S. army and the Seminoles occurred in the 1830s is not implausible. The Black Seminoles were not the only Seminoles who resisted removal, nor were local slaveholders the only European Americans who wanted them removed.[107] Nonetheless, such a counterfactual history is less plausible than one in which all the American states abolished slavery in the late eighteenth century and the U.S.

army removed the Seminoles in the 1830s through the less violent means that it employed to remove the other four major Native American nations in the southeastern United States.[108] The fact that those four nations—Cherokees, Chickasaws, Choctaws, and Creeks—were also slaveholding nations again introduces a second variable to consider in comparing alternative histories. What if the United States and the five "civilized" nations had abolished slavery in similar time frames? From the European American perspective, the southeast removals would probably have seemed less urgent and proceeded more smoothly in the absence of disputes over slaves and slavery expansion.[109]

Counterfactual history is an inexact science. Most historical cases are ambiguous and provide fertile ground for speculation but little for closure. I was cautious in the cases I considered slavery-related, including, for instance, the Second Seminole War but not the Mexican-American War. In part, I followed the scholarship in my inclusions and exclusions. No scholarly consensus exists that the presence of slavery directly influenced the initiation and conduct of the Mexican-American War, but such a consensus exists in the case of the Second Seminole War.[110]

It is important to bear in mind that a counterfactual claim is not a causal claim. The claim is not that one event or condition caused another but rather that in the absence of the first, the second would not have occurred.[111] Of course, some direct influence of the first event or condition on the second must be present, or we end up with such silly counterfactuals as that if Charles Dickinson had killed Andrew Jackson instead of only wounding him in their 1806 duel, then the Second Seminole War would not have occurred because Jackson would not have been elected president in 1828, the Indian Removal Act of 1830 would not have been enacted, and the Seminoles would not have been a removal target in 1835. The presence of slavery in Florida and the surrounding states had a direct influence on the initiation and conduct of the Second Seminole War; the Dickinson-Jackson duel did not.

TIME FRAME

The time frame of this study is from 1791 to 1861. This period forms a discrete period in U.S. history when the republic was divided into free states and slave states. This factor strongly influenced the framing of a new federal government at the Constitutional Convention. It also strongly influenced the functioning of that government until the republic was no longer a house divided.

The 1791 starting point is simply a matter of data availability. The new Congress first convened on March 4, 1789, but some time was required before Congress could begin functioning and appropriating money, and before the executive departments could begin spending it.[112] The Census Bureau retrospectively combines 1789–1791 into one fiscal year in reporting its "historical statistics." I followed that decision in reporting my findings. The end point is the last fiscal year before the beginning of the Civil War, FY1861 (July 1, 1860–June 30, 1861).[113] This end point is not simply a matter of data availability. The Civil War marked the demise of a republic divided into free states and slave states.[114] Bensel details how the war led to the creation of two new, stronger American states, one in the Union and one in the Confederacy. The result is exactly what one would expect if war is the primary engine of state development. Bensel also argues that the antebellum American state differed from its predecessor and successor states not because it was necessarily weaker but because its weakness was centrally defined by its division into free states and slave states.[115] Recent works by John Craig Hammond, Matthew Mason, and George William van Cleve show how the division between free states and slave states also centrally defined the American state in the early republic.[116] My own research supports the view that the United States, in both the early-republic and antebellum periods, was not stateless (Burnham) but rather governed by a distinctive type of state (Orren and Skowronek). It was a distinctive type of state not because it was weak (Bensel) or because it was a state of "courts and parties" (Skowronek) or "belatedly feudal" (Orren) or even because it was liberal (Katznelson). It was distinctive because of its division into free states and slave states, which both depressed (Einhorn) and accelerated (Fehrenbacher) state development.[117] In Abraham Lincoln's prophetic words, the nation was "a house divided against itself" that could not stand. It could not stand because, as Lincoln explains in his "House Divided" speech, Southern slaveholders and Northern "doughfaces" had increasingly steered American state development in a proslavery direction, and the new Republican Party was determined to reverse course.[118]

HISTORICAL AND CONTEMPORARY SIGNIFICANCE

In placing slavery more at the center of early American state development, this study is important for both historical and contemporary reasons.

First, it is important "to get it right." We cannot remove slavery from the history of the early American state. A slavery-centered narrative of early American state development enriches our understanding of U.S. history even as we recognize that the existence of slavery was not the only factor driving state development and that state development was not the only factor perpetuating slavery. The history of the American state and of American slavery are each important because of the way that both institutions affected the life-chances of Americans—red, white, and black. The fate of Tocqueville's "three races in America" was intertwined through the institution of slavery.[119] The fates of the American state and of American slavery were also intertwined. Since so much of the history of the relationship between the two institutions remains invisible, any effort to expose that relationship is an important historical enterprise.

Second, some of the social forces that drove American state development after the Civil War were strongly related to those that drove American state development before the Civil War. While the Civil War ended slavery-driven state development, it did not end race-driven state development. As Michael Brown, Eric Foner, Carol Horton, Ira Katznelson, Desmond King, Philip Klinkner, Daniel Kryder, Robert Lieberman, Rogers Smith, and Richard Valelly chronicle in various ways, race remained central to American state development throughout the rest of the nineteenth century and into the twentieth and now twenty-first centuries.[120] Providing a long, comparative perspective on race, Anthony Marx demonstrates how European Americans saw race control, whether in the form of slavery or Jim Crow, as critical to their own cross-sectional alliances in both the pre– and post–Civil War periods. From his perspective, race control was less about controlling African Americans than about uniting European Americans.[121] Examined from any number of perspectives, race-driven and slavery-driven state development share common motives.

More specific programmatic and institutional analogues bridge the pre– and post–Civil War periods. The federal ban on slave imports was an early form of immigration control that targeted a group of (to most European Americans) undesirable people, whether defined as slaves or blacks or both.[122] In the late nineteenth and early twentieth centuries, the American state targeted other "undesirable" peoples. Recent immigration policies have been more universalistic but probably no more effective in excluding the "unwanted" than the slave-import ban, despite the greatly increased capacities of the modern American state.[123] Liberia was the nation's first overseas colonial project and was partially justified by the "civilizing inferior peoples" trope used to justify later imperialistic ventures.[124] It was also an early example of a mixed public-private enterprise, which federal officials have continued to find an attractive vehicle for pursuing controversial purposes.[125] President George W. Bush's "faith-based initiative" is a good recent example of this policy approach, and one with religious overtones similar to those that characterized African colonization. Along with sanctity of contract cases, fugitive-slave cases constituted one of the two earliest examples of federal efforts to enforce a constitutional right against the state governments. In this sense, these cases served as ironic precedents for the federal efforts to enforce the new constitutional rights of the freed slaves against the states during Reconstruction.[126] In enforcing the constitutional rights of slaveholders to the return of their fugitive slaves during the 1850s, the federal government also relied on its own law-enforcement agencies, as it did again during both the first and second "reconstructions" to enforce the constitutional rights of the freed slaves and their descendants.[127] Only in the Reconstruction case was the analogue actually appealed to as a precedent despite the very different motives behind fugitive-slave returns and civil rights acts. The other cases, in contrast, show a precedent of motive that state actors found it politically inexpedient to acknowledge.

Third, this study has more direct contemporary significance. It makes us more aware of how central slavery was to early American state development and therefore more aware of how and why slavery is not merely our past but our present. Placing slavery more at the center of early American state development may also strengthen the case for slave reparations.[128] I myself am ambivalent about the issue because of the length of time that has passed and the challenge of arbitrating eligibility and desert. Slave reparations would have been very good public policy in 1870 or even in 1900 but probably not in 2011.

In 2011, it is clear that African Americans are disproportionately poor.[129] It is also clear that federal policies, both before and after the abolition of slavery, contributed to that result. But it is not clear what the proper governmental response is, beyond official recognition of the terrible injustices of those policies. In the following chapters, I show how the policies, practices, and institutions of the early American state functioned to protect slavery, to the detriment of the vast majority of African Americans who were slaves. Even state actions that seemed antislavery in intention were intermixed with proslavery or racist motives. In this respect, the slave-trade clause of the U.S. Constitution is an appropriate starting point for a study of the relationship between the presence of slavery and early American state development because prominent politics and history scholars have interpreted it both as a blow against racial slavery and as a blow for racial exclusion.[130]

2. Slavery and Controlling the National Borders

Federal efforts to interdict illegal slave trading and smuggling represent a major episode in the development of the U.S. navy. They also represent the first federal efforts to control the national borders. Even though the trend from 1791 to 1861 was toward more, and more expensive, enforcement activities, the trend was discontinuous. Five decision points divide the 1791–1861 period into shorter discrete periods of relative federal activity or inactivity in this policy area, 1791–1807, 1808–1819, 1819–1842, FY1843–FY1859, and FY1860–FY1861. Federal officials made a substantial commitment of resources to interdicting illegal slave trading and smuggling only during the last two years of the Buchanan presidency.[1]

The Constitutional Convention was the first decision point. In the face of the strenuous opposition of the lower-South delegates, the convention did not authorize Congress to enact an immediate ban on slave imports into the United States. Instead, the convention delegates compromised on authorizing Congress to enact such a ban with the earliest possible effective date of January 1, 1808. From 1791 to 1808, the state governments had primary responsibility for interdicting slave smuggling, and the state laws prohibiting slave imports provided the legal structure for prosecuting slave smugglers. All the states had such laws, at least for part of the period. Yet even during this early period, Congress passed several laws that barred the participation of American citizens, ships, and flags in the international slave trade, whether the destination was the United States or some other country. At this time, the bifurcation between slave trading and smuggling was legally a federal-state bifurcation. Federal efforts to deter either activity were, however, haphazard at best.[2] The period closed with a second decision point. On March 2, 1807, Congress acted upon its constitutional authority to enact a federal ban on slave imports, with a January 1, 1808, effective date. The ban ended the legal bifurcation between slave trading and smuggling.

Beginning in 1808, the federal government assumed primary responsibility for interdicting both slave smuggling into the United States, in violation of its new ban on slave imports, and suppressing American participation in the slave trade, in violation of its existing slave-trade laws. The record of the federal government improved only marginally on either front from 1808 to 1819. This second period was also a period of relative inactivity in interdicting illegal slave trading and smuggling, not unlike the first period, despite the additional authority the federal government had assumed in this policy area. Nonetheless, federal authorities raided several infamous slave-smuggling operations along the Southern frontier and captured several slave-laden ships in the Gulf of Mexico during this period. The period closed with a third decision point that promised to realize the potential of the first two. In March 1819, Congress enacted new slave-trade legislation and, for the first time, appropriated money to implement its provisions.

From 1819 to 1843, the federal government devoted more resources to interdicting illegal slave trading than it had during the first two periods. Many of those resources, though, were diverted to helping the American Colonization Society (ACS) found a colony for expatriated African Americans on the west coast of Africa, including most of the initial $100,000 slave-trade appropriation. Coincident with the founding of Liberia, the U.S. navy was active off the African coast against slave traders. Navy vessels captured nine suspected slave ships in African waters during 1820 and 1821. However, after 1821, navy slave-trade patrols became more and more sporadic, and American participation in the trade experienced no apparent diminution. Similarly, the federal government remained relatively inactive in enforcing its ban on slave imports during this third period but for a very different reason. Beginning with the U.S. occupation of Spanish East Florida in 1821, there was a precipitous decline in the number and scale of efforts to smuggle slaves into the country. This third period closed with a fourth decision point. Under the terms of the Webster-Ashburton Treaty (1842), the United States finally agreed to establish its own permanent African squadron, as Great Britain had done as early as 1808.

For many years, the post-treaty period was not much different than the pre-treaty period. The new African Squadron enjoyed an initial success in capturing the *Pons* with approximately 900 Africans aboard in December 1845. Yet the squadron did not capture another suspected slave ship with Africans aboard until 1860. Part of the problem was that the squadron was small—typically four ships—and it was slow—no steamships. In contrast, the British West African Squadron averaged nineteen ships, with an increasing number of steamships, during the 1843–1859 period.[3] Toward the end of the period, in August 1858, the Home Squadron captured the *Echo* off the coast of Cuba with 318 Africans aboard. This fourth period closed with the fifth, and final, decision point. Soon after the *Echo* capture, President James Buchanan decided to enlarge both the African and Home squadrons with steamships. His decision made the suppression of the slave trade a national priority.

In the twelve months from April 26, 1860, to April 21, 1861, the fortified African and Home squadrons together seized nine slave-laden ships with a total of more than 5,300 Africans aboard.[4] The Civil War began shortly after this surge in slave-ship seizures. At the beginning of the war, the bulk of the African Squadron was reassigned to Union blockade duty. Then in 1862, the United States signed a mutual search and seizure treaty with Great Britain that signaled a cessation of U.S. efforts to suppress the slave trade. Though this fifth period was short-lived, lasting only two fiscal years, the navy captured more slave-laden ships, with more Africans aboard, than it had during the first four periods combined. Compared to the first four periods, the federal government also spent far more resources on slave-trade suppression. The Civil War abruptly ended this policy episode. It nevertheless represents a major episode in the development of the U.S. navy as new resources flowed to both the African and Home squadrons. It also prepared the navy for its wartime responsibilities; the navy's search-and-seizure duties shifted from capturing suspected slave ships to capturing suspected contraband ships.[5]

My estimate of the total costs associated with the federal efforts to interdict illegal slave trading and smuggling from 1819 to the end of FY1861 is $8,710,200.[6] This estimate covers the time frame from the first congressional appropriation to support the suppression of the slave trade to the beginning of the Civil War. It includes the costs of navy patrols for illegal slave trading off the west coast of Africa, which for FY1843–FY1861 would include the operating costs of the African Squadron. It also includes the $25 per capita bounties navy crews received for the Africans they seized from suspected slave ships, a new provision of the 1819 slave-trade law. Most of these slave-trade expenditures occurred after 1842, when the navy finally established a permanent African Squadron, and especially in FY1860 and FY1861, after the Buchanan administration had enlarged the squadron. My estimate for 1819–1842 is $480,000, based on averaging the navy's reported slave-trade expenditures of $200,000 during the first ten years of the period over the full twenty-four-year period.[7] My estimate for FY1843–FY1859 rises to $6,566,500, based on the 1850 navy estimate of $384,500 for the annual operating costs of the African Squadron as well as an estimated $30,000 in bounties for the *Pons* and *Echo* captures.[8] Finally, my estimate for FY1860–FY1861 is $1,663,700, based on doubling the $384,500 estimate of the annual operating costs of the African Squadron for each of those two fiscal years to reflect the costs of its larger size.[9] The FY1860–FY1861 estimate also includes $125,700 in bounties that navy crews received for the Africans they seized from suspected slave ships during those two fiscal years.[10]

During a period when annual federal expenditures were minuscule by contemporary multi-trillion-dollar standards, totaling $21,464,000 in 1819 and reaching only $66,547,000 in FY1861, $8,710,200 was a significant amount of money.[11] The scholarly consensus, though, is that the federal government's enforcement of its own slave-trade laws was very lax and that it could, and should, have spent more money in this policy area. I agree with that consensus. In comparison to Great Britain, which was the acknowledged international leader in this policy area, the U.S. effort was relatively insignificant.[12] The British government spent $48,884,640 on slave-trade suppression during the 1819–1861 period, almost six times as much as the U.S. government did. On average, the British navy assigned almost five times as many ships to its African squadron as the U.S. navy did. Only in FY1860 did the U.S. navy begin to make a comparable commitment. Finally, the British navy captured 1,340 suspected slave ships, including 443 slave-laden ships with a total of approximately 131,600 Africans aboard, from 1821 through 1860. The U.S. navy captured 67 suspected slave ships, including 13 slave-laden ships with a total of approximately 6,900 Africans aboard, from 1819 through FY1861. Again, only in FY1860 did the U.S. navy begin to compile a record comparable to that of the British navy.[13]

Of course, Great Britain was the wealthiest nation in the world at the time and the most proficient at raising revenues. It also possessed the largest navy. The British government could better afford a more robust commitment to the suppression of the slave trade, which was one of the arguments it made to other parties in offering them bribes to sign bilateral slave-trade treaties.[14] When one compares the United States and Great Britain in terms of the percentage of public expenditures each devoted to slave-trade suppression, the United States figure (0.61 percent) was actually higher than the British figure (0.41 percent) for the 1819–1861 period. By dividing the 1819–1861 period into smaller periods, we can more accurately track the comparable efforts of the two nations. The comparable figures are 0.01 percent (US) to 0.30 percent (GB) for 1819–1842, 0.82 percent (US) to 0.55 percent (GB) for 1843–1859, and 1.28 percent (US) to 0.32 percent (GB) for 1860–1861. It is also valuable to compare each nation's expenditures on slave-trade suppression as a percentage of total navy expenditures. These figures are 0.46 percent (US) to 2.89 percent (GB) for 1819–1842, 3.93 percent (US) to 4.21 percent (GB) for 1843–1859, and 6.95 percent (US) to 1.94 percent (GB) for 1860–1861. We can also compare the number of ships each navy assigned to its African squadron as a percentage of its total fleet. These figures are 12.1 percent (US) to 4.01 percent (GB) for 1843–1859 and 14.7 percent (US) to 2.27 percent (GB) for 1860–1861. Last, we can compare the manpower each navy assigned to its African squadron as a percentage of its total manpower. These figures are 7.5 percent (US) to 7.26 percent (GB) for 1843–1859 and 12.9 percent (US) to 3.1 percent (GB) for 1860–1861.[15]

Percentage comparisons can be misleading, especially when the percentages are very small. It seems best to conclude that American efforts to suppress the slave trade lagged far behind the British efforts until the Webster-Ashburton Treaty and matched the British efforts only on the eve of the Civil War, almost exactly at the point that they ceased.

This conclusion becomes clearer if we also track the relative success over time of the two navies in seizing suspected slave ships and recaptured Africans. The annual averages for ship seizures were 0.63 (1819–1842), 1.41 (FY1843–FY1859), and 6.0 (FY1860–1861) for the U.S. navy compared to 14.6 (1821–1840) and 7.05 (1841–1860) for the British navy. The annual averages for recaptured Africans were 13 (1819–1842), 72 (FY1843–FY1859), and 2,673 (FY1860–FY1861) for the U.S. navy, compared to 3,720 (1821–1840) and 2,835 (1841–1860) for the British navy.[16] Given the relative capacities of the two states, the American state actually out-achieved the British state in its efforts to suppress the slave trade.

In thinking about this case counterfactually, I would argue that, *pace* W. E. B. Du Bois, the continuing presence of slavery did not act as a significant drag on American efforts to suppress the slave trade and that other factors were much more important.[17] The most important factor was probably the fact that such efforts were very expensive, as they ultimately proved to be during the last two years of the Buchanan administration. Slave-trade suppression lost out in the competition for scarce federal resources because it was not a high priority for any major issue bloc in the nation until an unusual convergence of factors made it one for the Buchanan administration.[18] Absent slavery, federal officials might have been more ideologically committed to slave-trade suppression, but fiscal barriers would still have existed to pursuing such a commitment. In fact, federal officials might have been even less committed to slave-trade suppression in the absence of slavery because many Southern slaveholders strongly supported the policy. The geographic division on the slave trade was as much an upper South–lower South division as it was a North-South division. The upper South was a slave-exporting region whose slaveholders had an economic interest in decreasing the supply of African slaves, while the lower South was a slave-importing region whose (potential) slaveholders had the opposite interest. Antislavery sentiment was also more prevalent in the upper than lower South, and antislavery sentiment was anti–slave trade sentiment, though the reverse was not always the case. Much of the political pressure for suppressing the slave trade originated in the upper South, not the North. Absent slavery, that pressure would not have existed or would at least have been much less.[19]

Yet even in the lower South, the opposition to federal efforts to suppress the slave trade was relatively weak because a unique natural increase in slaves and a thriving domestic slave trade greatly diminished the demand for further slave imports.[20] Anti–slave trade sentiment was also relatively widespread, even if antislavery sentiment was not. The suppression of the slave trade was generally not a sectional or partisan issue. Even the abolitionists targeted the domestic much more than the international slave trade.[21] Slave smuggling into the United States might have been a more divisive issue if more smuggling had occurred. Otherwise, the slave trade seemed distant to most Americans, except for those who illegally profited from the trade or who hoped to directly profit from its revival. In short, it is just as likely that the presence of slavery acted to increase federal efforts in this policy area during the 1791–1861 period as to decrease them.

By 1819, the federal government seemed to have settled on a policy of devoting some but not many resources to the suppression of American participation in the slave trade. Federal expenditures in this policy area reached an elevated level only in the last two fiscal years before the Civil War, when several factors combined to make it more of a national priority, or at least more of one to President Buchanan. Still, the slave-trade policy area had contributed to American state development during the preceding years in several important ways. It produced a durable shift in authority over border control from the state governments to the federal government. It also strongly affected U.S. relations with Great Britain, the nation's primary foreign adversary for most of the period. In both respects, the American state added capacities in order to compete on a global stage. The Department of Navy was the principal beneficiary.

JOINT AUTHORITY, FEDERAL INACTIVITY (1791–1807)

In framing a new federal government, one of the most contentious issues the Constitutional Convention delegates debated was whether to grant Congress the power to prohibit or otherwise restrict slave imports. The debate over slave imports had to surprise most of the delegates because the issue was central neither to the structure of the new federal government nor to the division of powers between it and the state governments. The strong proslavery and antislavery statements that the debate provoked also had to surprise most of the delegates, given that none of them seemed to believe that either the convention or the new federal government would, or even could, act to abolish slavery.[22] The convention was emblematic of early American politics in that slavery entered into disputes over seemingly tangential issues.[23]

John Rutledge (South Carolina) instigated the convention debate over the slave trade when he was able to insert a clause into the report of the Committee of Detail that barred Congress from prohibiting or otherwise restricting slave imports.[24] The committee report precipitated a heated debate over the desirability of a federal ban on slave imports, which, in turn, prompted general attacks on and defenses of slavery. While Northern delegates joined the debate, the exchanges between upper-South and lower-South delegates generated most of the heat. In fact, the Northern delegates generally counseled compromise, in effect siding with the lower-South delegates.[25]

On August 21, 1787, Luther Martin (Maryland) launched the upper-South attack on the slave-trade clause in the committee report. He claimed that "it was inconsistent with the principles of the revolution and dishonorable to the American character to have such a feature in the Constitution."[26] Rutledge responded acerbically, declaring that "religion and humanity had nothing to do with this question—interest alone is the governing principle with nations." He went on to threaten disunion if the new constitution allowed Congress to restrict slave imports as well as to appeal to the commercial interests of the Northern states in carrying the products of slave labor.[27] Charles Pinckney (South Carolina) soon seconded Rutledge's threat of disunion. He also predicted that South Carolina would eventually follow the lead of Maryland and Virginia in prohibiting slave imports on the state level.[28]

When the debate over the clause resumed the next day, George Mason (Virginia) went well beyond Martin in attacking both the slave trade and slavery. In his long list of the evils of slavery, he included its discouragement of arts and manufactures, its disincentive to the immigration of much-needed European (white) laborers, and its pernicious effects on Southern manners. Echoing Thomas Jefferson, he declared that "every master of slaves is born a petty tyrant." Mason concluded that the federal government should at least be able to prevent an increase in the number of slaves in the country.[29] Now, Charles Pinckney reacted angrily, asserting that "if slavery be wrong, it is justified by the example of all the world."[30] The other Pinckney, Charles Cotesworth, then sought to reduce the position of the upper-South delegates to naked self-interest. He insinuated that the slaveholders of the upper-South states wanted to restrict slave imports only in order to make more money selling their surplus slaves to the slaveholders of the lower-South states.[31] Abraham Baldwin (Georgia) joined the South Carolina delegates in making the issue the *sine qua non* of continued union and in predicting that his state would also eventually prohibit slave imports on its own.[32]

The debate had a somewhat skewed character because no delegate defended the slave trade *per se*. It also had a somewhat surreal character because every state but Georgia had already acted to prohibit or otherwise restrict slave imports.[33] The debate concluded with the "dirty compromise" between the South Carolina and New England delegations not to allow Congress to prohibit slave imports before 1808 but to allow it to pass navigation acts by simple majorities.[34] Since the general expectation was that Congress would act to prohibit slave imports when it could, the result left open a twenty-year window for the lower-South states to import more slaves.[35] Whether or not this result was a major victory for those states, as Paul Finkelman has argued most vehemently, it brought the slave trade within the powers of Congress, something which Rutledge had clearly sought to prevent.[36]

During the ratification debates, Federalists defended the slave-trade clause on various grounds. In the Northern states, they defended it as a blow against slavery. In Pennsylvania, James Wilson even claimed that a federal ban on slave imports would lay "the foundation for banishing slavery out of this country."[37] In the lower South, Federalists defended the clause as an important victory for their states because it delayed any federal slave-import ban. In South Carolina, Charles Cotesworth Pinckney even claimed that the clause "secured an unlimited importation of negroes for twenty years. Nor is it declared that the importation shall be then stopped; it may be continued."[38] In the upper South, Federalists defended the clause as a blow against the slave trade but *not* against slavery. In Virginia, James Madison insisted that the proposed constitution granted the federal government "no power . . . to interpose with respect to the property in slaves now held by the states" even as he applauded the slave-trade clause as "a great point gained in favor of humanity."[39] The clause was, however, not a major issue during the ratification debates. The Anti-Federalists certainly did not make it a major point of attack on the proposed constitution.[40]

Early in the first session of the first Congress under the new constitution, Josiah Parker (Virginia) introduced a motion to impose the constitutionally authorized $10 per capita duty on slave imports. James Jackson (Georgia) badgered him into withdrawing it. Jackson contended that such a duty would be discriminatory and, again, disparaged the motives of Virginia politicians who sought to restrict slave imports.[41]

During the next session of Congress, the Pennsylvania antislavery society as well as two Quaker yearly meetings petitioned the body, praying that it deploy the full extent of its powers against both the slave trade and slavery.[42] These petitions provoked another strong reaction from lower-South congressmen. In the process of denying that Congress had any powers to accomplish the objects of the petitions, at least not until 1808, William Loughton Smith (South Carolina) unapologetically defended slavery in a style prescient of the antebellum "positive good" school. Smith maintained that "the slaves in South Carolina were a happier people than the lower order of whites in many countries he had visited." He also excoriated "a misguided and misinformed humanity" which failed to realize that "if it [slavery] be a moral evil, it is like many others which exist in all civilized countries, and which the world quietly submit to."[43]

Although the Senate refused to consider these early antislavery petitions, the House appointed a select committee to investigate the substance of their pleas. Even the creation of the committee infuriated Smith and his lower-South colleagues, and they refused to serve on it. In the end, only one Southern state (Virginia) was represented.[44] The committee report, authored by Abiel Foster (New Hampshire), suggested both that slavery was an evil institution and that individual states should at least act to limit its evils. The report also concluded that Congress could pass laws against American participation in the slave trade, even if it could not prohibit slave imports until 1808 or otherwise interfere with the existence of slavery in the states where it already existed.[45] The Committee of the Whole toned down this relatively strong antislavery report but apparently not enough to appease an increasingly united Southern congressional delegation. Madison's compromise proposal to insert both committee reports into the *House Journal*, which would, in effect, table the petitions but also accord them official recognition, passed on a close 29–25 vote. The regional breakdown of the vote was lower North, 13–2, and New England, 9–6, in favor; upper South, 9–7, and lower South, 8–0, in opposition.[46]

Four years later, Congress took action against the slave trade when it enacted a law outlawing American participation in the trade. In 1800, it passed new, stronger slave-trade legislation that also prohibited U.S. citizens from owning interests in foreign slave-trading ventures.[47] Federal officials, however, made no concerted effort to enforce these early slave-trade laws.[48] During the embargo years, Treasury Secretary Albert Gallatin (Pennsylvania Democratic Republican) instructed customs collectors to concentrate their efforts on catching embargo runners, not slave smugglers.[49] In the ten years from 1798 to 1808, navy vessels seized only six ships on the suspicion that they were slave ships, none with Africans aboard.[50] In 1831, Congress appropriated $1,000 to pay the creditor of one ship owner for the losses that the latter had sustained from one of those seizures.[51]

While prohibiting slave imports and interdicting slave smuggling into existing states remained a state responsibility until 1808, they were a federal responsibility in the territories. The first Mississippi territorial constitution (1798) contained a ban on slave imports.[52] The first Louisiana territorial constitution (1804) went further. It prohibited bringing slaves into the territory, both from other countries and from other states and territories, except when they were brought by *bona fide* settlers for their personal use.[53] In the meantime, the Louisiana Purchase had prompted the South Carolina legislature to allow its ban on slave imports to lapse in 1803 in order to take advantage of the demand for slaves in the new southwestern territories.[54] The Louisiana Purchase had also opened a vast new frontier for slave smuggling into the United States. Yet again, federal officials made no concerted effort to enforce these territorial bans on slave imports.[55]

This first period of relative federal inactivity against the slave trade closed with congressional passage of the constitutionally authorized federal ban on slave imports. President Thomas Jefferson had encouraged Congress to act early on the matter in his 1806 annual message to the body. In his most exalted language, Jefferson advocated proscribing "all further participation in those violations of human rights which have been so long continued on the unoffending inhabitants of Africa, and which the morality, the reputation, and the best interests of our country, have long been eager to proscribe."[56] The ensuing debate revealed nearly unanimous congressional sentiment favoring the enactment of a federal slave-import ban. The final vote was 103–5, with only three Southern dissenters. Sectional differences, though, emerged over the enforcement of the ban in intercoastal waters, the severity of the criminal penalties for violating the ban, and the disposition of any Africans seized in the process of enforcing it. Congress fashioned Southern-leaning compromises in all three cases. The new law regulated the intercoastal slave trade only in ships of less than forty tons; established five- to ten-year penalties for slave-trade violations rather than, as James Sloan (New Jersey Democratic Republican) had proposed, death; and, for the lack of one vote, permitted state officials to determine whether recaptured Africans should be freed, sold into slavery, or kept as public slaves rather than uniformly freed. John Randolph (Virginia Democratic Republican) led the opposition to placing any restrictions on intercoastal slave shipments as a violation of the rights of property. Somewhat hyperbolically, he warned that such restrictions would establish "the pretext of universal emancipation."[57]

The state development inherent in the passage of a federal ban on slave imports was an authority shift from the state to the federal level. For the first time, the federal government had authority over all aspects of this policy area. It could make laws against both slave trading and smuggling and enforce them through interdiction activities, both internationally and domestically. The fact that the federal government now had this plenary authority, though, did not mean that federal officials would use it.

UNIFIED AUTHORITY, CONTINUED INACTIVITY (1808–1819)

This second period was also one of relative federal inactivity against illegal slave trading and smuggling as the potential effects of the federal ban on slave imports remained largely unrealized. While Great Britain established an African squadron to interdict illegal slave trading off the west coast of Africa in 1808, the United States did not.[58] The British West African Squadron was soon called into duty against France with the resumption of the Napoleonic Wars and then against the United States during the War of 1812. The Treaty of Ghent (1814) obligated Great Britain and the United States to undertake more strenuous efforts to interdict illegal slave trading, but again it was only Great Britain that implemented the treaty article by re-establishing its West African Squadron in 1816.[59]

On the domestic front, the federal government moved more aggressively against slave smuggling during this period. In 1811, Orleans territorial Governor William C. C. Claiborne dispatched Captain Andrew Hunter Holmes (Virginia) and forty dragoons to shut down slave-smuggling activities in the bayou country south of New Orleans. Future war hero Jean Lafitte was but one of many slave smugglers who operated out of the area. Holmes took Lafitte into custody, but Lafitte was released on bond and, in the end, the Holmes mission proved ineffectual.[60] In 1814, the U.S. army and navy launched a more concerted and successful effort to shut down slave-smuggling operations in the area, which was the occasion for Lafitte's "volunteering" to help defend New Orleans from imminent British invasion.[61] After the War of 1812, he, however, resumed his slave-smuggling activities on the other side of the state, where he teamed with another frontier hero of questionable stature, Jim Bowie. Finally, the Department of Navy dispatched the USS *Enterprise* in 1820 to shut down their highly successful Galveston operation. Lafitte simply disappeared early the next year, while Bowie went on to use his slave-smuggling earnings to speculate in Texas lands en route to his fabled death at the Alamo.[62]

In 1817, the U.S. army and navy also combined to (illegally) invade Amelia Island, in Spanish East Florida, to shut down slave-smuggling operations on that frontier.[63] Creek Indian agent and former Georgia governor David B. Mitchell had allegedly profited from those operations. Even though Mitchell was never prosecuted, the evidence against him was strong enough for President James Monroe to dismiss him from federal service in 1821.[64] The military invasion was only a temporary success. Slave smuggling continued in the area until the United States occupied Florida in 1821 under the terms of the Adams-Onís Treaty.[65]

On the other side of the Florida peninsula, U.S. army, navy, and treasury personnel combined to capture three American ships, the *Louisa, Merino,* and *Constitution,* carrying slaves near Pensacola in June 1818. Spanish colonials had hired the ships to transport their slaves from Cuba to Pensacola, which at the time was still part of Spanish East Florida. The USS *Surprise* seized the *Louisa* and *Merino* on June 21. A Treasury revenue cutter seized the *Constitution* eight days later. The seizures were subject to lengthy litigation until the U.S. Supreme Court finally decided in 1824 that the owners of the 84 slaves seized from the *Constitution* were owed restitution. In an opinion written by Associate Justice Bushrod Washington (Virginia Federalist), the court ruled in favor of the appellants on the grounds that the *Constitution* had first been seized not in international waters by the revenue cutter but in Pensacola harbor by American soldiers, who were (illegally) occupying the town at the time and, after seizing the ship, had released it for recapture by the awaiting revenue cutter.[66]

U.S. authorities had seized a total of 109 slaves from the three ships, but their final disposition is unclear.[67] Apparently, 40 slaves either died in or escaped from U.S. custody in Mobile, where they had been landed, or else ended up in the hands of local slaveholders. Of the 69 remaining slaves, the federal district court allotted 54 for sale to reimburse the *Constitution* claimants and 15 to the disposition of the state of Alabama. The state also auctioned the latter, pursuant to the provisions of the federal slave-import ban, despite the fact that another one of the new provisions of the 1819 slave-trade law required recaptured Africans to be resettled outside the territorial limits of the United States.[68] The federal government spent $12,450 on their care during the six years of litigation. This sum included reimbursements to three separate U.S. marshals as well as jail and medical fees.[69] In 1825, the federal government spent another $16,156 to reimburse the *Merino* and *Louisa* claimants for their losses under an adverse Florida territorial court ruling.[70]

By 1819 then, federal officials had moved to control the national borders more effectively. In fact, the presence of slavery inspired the first concerted efforts to fulfill that traditional state function as the Departments of Navy and Treasury began to enforce the federal slave-import ban. Those efforts required greater state capacities. The Department of Navy procured gunboats explicitly to chase slave smugglers in low tidal waters.[71] The Department of Treasury purchased revenue cutters and opened customs stations explicitly to deter slave smuggling.[72] By 1819, federal officials had also heavily sanctioned American participation in the slave trade and seized several American ships carrying slaves in the Gulf of Mexico. The lacuna in the federal efforts in this policy area was a failure to interdict slave traders off the west coast of Africa. As ACS officials argued in one of their early memorials to Congress, the best way to attack the slave trade was to attack it at its source.[73] In 1819, Congress sought to remedy this situation by passing a new law sanctioning American participation in the trade and, for the first time, appropriated money to enforce its provisions. The law would lead to the initial U.S. naval efforts to interdict illegal slave trading off the African coast, though, at first, only incidentally.

THE FIRST SLAVE-TRADE APPROPRIATIONS (1819–1842)

The 1819 slave-trade law represented the third decision point in the federal commitment to interdicting illegal slave trading and smuggling.[74] Given the largely symbolic nature of the first two decision points, the new slave-trade law promised a significant expansion in federal efforts to suppress the trade. Yet, once more, the potential impact of the law went largely unrealized, at least until 1843, when the U.S. navy finally established a separate African squadron.

Instead, President Monroe diverted the initial $100,000 slave-trade appropriation to the ACS to help it found a colony for expatriated African Americans on the west coast of Africa. Monroe's diversion was not unreasonable, given that the new law required Africans seized from suspected slave ships to be resettled outside the territorial limits of the United States rather than remaining subject to the disposition of state officials. The ACS's prospective African colony could serve as a resettlement site.[75] Society officials also promised that the existence of such a colony would act to depress the African slave trade.[76] The effect of Monroe's decision, though, was that the money was not spent to finance regular navy patrols off the coast of Africa or to establish a separate African squadron. Federal efforts to interdict illegal slave trading during this third period remained sporadic and ineffective.

During the early years of this period, U.S. navy vessels were active off the west coast of Africa while assisting the ACS in founding its African colony. In 1820 and 1821, the *Alligator, Cyane,* and *Hornet* seized nine suspected slave ships off the African coast, though none with Africans aboard.[77] Navy crews sailed six of the nine ships back to the United States to be libeled.[78] In the case of the French ship *La Jeune Eugénie,* Associate Justice Joseph Story (Massachusetts National Republican), sitting on the Massachusetts circuit, ultimately decided that the ship had been illegally seized and remanded it to French authorities.[79] Then in late 1821, the *Hornet* seized the French ship *La Pensée,* with 220 Africans aboard, from a Columbian privateer in the Caribbean. In this case, the Monroe administration decided to turn both the ship and recaptured Africans over to French authorities, bypassing any legal proceedings. The cost of caring for the Africans while they were in U.S. custody in New Orleans was $4,247.[80]

In 1820, Congress passed a new slave-trade law that declared participation in the trade a form of piracy, which was a capital offense.[81] The barriers to slave-trade convictions were, however, quite steep, even absent the piracy charge. Typically, U.S. attorneys decided to merely libel the ship (assuming that it had been confiscated) and not prosecute the captain, crew, or owners (assuming that they had been taken into custody) or to prosecute them on lesser charges than piracy. They were rarely convicted in any case, especially if their ships had been captured without any Africans aboard.[82]

The early years of this period also witnessed a sharp decrease of slave smuggling into the United States. One of the last authenticated cases of a large-scale attempt to smuggle slaves into the United States occurred in 1820. This case involved the Spanish slave ship *Antelope,* which the revenue cutter *Dallas* captured near

Amelia Island on June 29, 1820, with 281 Africans aboard. All signs pointed to the fact that John Smith, the American captain of the ship, was attempting to smuggle slaves into the United States, though Smith insisted that he was only seeking food and water for his crew and the Spanish- and Portuguese-owned slaves aboard the ship. Again, the seizure led to lengthy litigation and, again, the Supreme Court partially sided with the Spanish (but not Portuguese) claimants and remanded a portion of the recaptured Africans to their custody. The case was complicated by the fact that Smith was a privateer who had captured the *Antelope* as it loaded slaves on the west coast of Africa.[83] In the end, the Supreme Court accepted the finding of the federal district court in Savannah that the Spanish claimants, who financed the *Antelope's* original slave-trading expedition, had substantially proven their ownership to 39 of the recaptured Africans. It then awarded the rest to the U.S. government for resettlement in Liberia, pursuant to the 1819 slave-trade law.[84]

In July 1827, after seven years of litigation, the ACS transported to Liberia the approximately 130 surviving *Antelope* Africans whom the court had awarded to the U.S. government.[85] The 37 surviving Africans whom the court had awarded to the Spanish claimants were sold to Congressman Richard Wilde (Georgia Democratic Republican) for $11,700 to pay the costs the claimants had incurred during litigation, including U.S. Marshal John Morel's $6,347 fee for their care.[86] In the meantime, Morel had employed many of the recaptured Africans on his own plantation and rented others to various third parties in the Savannah area to, in effect, pay for their own care. He had, nevertheless, received an additional $20,287 from the federal government for their care, until Navy Secretary Smith Thompson (New York Democratic Republican) uncovered his scheme and stopped payment early in 1823.[87] The navy disbursed another $5,500 in bounty money, though the captain of the *Dallas,* John Jackson (Georgia), received only $400 of that money. Senator John M. Berrien (Georgia Democratic Republican), who had acted as Jackson's counsel in persuading the court to award him the money, received the rest in legal fees.[88]

The next authenticated case of a large-scale attempt to smuggle slaves into the United States did not occur until 1858.[89] The occupation of Spanish East Florida made slave-smuggling on the southeastern frontier more difficult. The emergence of a relatively autonomous slaveholding region and then republic in Texas reversed the flow of slaves on another frontier where slave-smuggling activity had been prevalent. The natural increase of slaves in the Southern states and the strong interstate market in slaves meant that the demand for new African slaves was relatively weak. Finally, moral censure against slave smuggling probably had some deterrent effect, especially because the profits to be made from smuggling slaves into the United States were much more uncertain than the profits to be made from carrying slaves to Brazil or Cuba, where the demand for new African slaves was much stronger and the sanctions against slave trading much weaker.[90] As a result, the federal ban on slave imports was largely self-enforcing. It was not a major source of state development.

On the other hand, the federal laws against American participation in the slave trade were not largely self-enforcing. The "frontier" for slave trading was much larger than for slave smuggling. Any moral censure against slave trading was also less effective because of the great profits to be made from the trade. According to eyewitness reports from Liberia, American participation in the African slave trade had returned to pre-colonization levels by 1830.[91] The enforcement of the federal laws against that participation could have been a major source of state development because it would have required a substantial commitment of resources. The 1819 slave-trade law portended such a commitment, but no substantial commitment of resources to interdicting illegal slave trading occurred until much later.

Following the founding of Liberia, navy activity along the west coast of Africa dwindled to occasional visits to the colony of ships assigned to the Pacific Squadron.[92] The Missouri Crisis and the reemergence of partisan and sectional divisions during Monroe's second administration seemed to dissipate the political will for a major commitment of resources to interdicting illegal slave trading. At times it appeared as if Congressman Charles Francis Mercer (Virginia National Republican), who had shepherded both the 1819 slave-trade and 1820 piracy laws through Congress, was a lone voice in the wilderness in calling for more strenuous efforts to enforce the nation's slave-trade laws.[93] Instead, the U.S. navy adopted the minimalist policy of timing slave-trade patrols along the west coast of Africa to the occasional visits of its ships to Liberia. This policy did not require much additional spending. It also did not require the reallocation of existing navy ships or the construction of new navy ships, as a separate African squadron might have required. Consequently, the seizure of suspected slave ships was infrequent and almost accidental in nature during this period.

From 1823 through 1842, the U.S. navy captured only three suspected slave ships and only one with Africans aboard.[94] The latter was, once again, a Spanish ship. In 1830, the USS *Grampus* inadvertently captured the *Fenix* with 82 Africans aboard when it came to the aid of the *Kremlin*, an American ship that was in distress off the coast of Haiti and that, unbeknownst to the *Grampus* crew, was being plundered by the *Fenix*.[95] In this case, the federal district court justice in New Orleans took a more askance view of the Spanish claimants. He ruled that all the surviving Africans should be resettled in Liberia. It cost a total of $6,000 to care for the recaptured Africans the five years that the case was in litigation and to then transport to Liberia those who had not died, escaped, or ended up in the hands of local slaveholders.[96]

Another slave-trade case that generated significant federal expenditures during this period was not strictly speaking a slave-ship seizure. In 1827, both the Spanish slave ship *Guerero* and the HMS *Nimble,* which was pursuing it, shipwrecked in the Florida Keys. Samuel Sanderson loaded his wrecker with 121 of the 561 Africans who were aboard the *Guerero*.[97] He transported them to Key West, where they were placed in the custody of U.S. Marshal Waters Smith. In 1829, Congress appropriated a total of $16,000 to pay Smith for the costs of their care and transportation to Liberia.[98] Eight years later, Sanderson received $3,025 in bounty money for the 121 Africans whom he had "recaptured." In recommending that Sanderson receive the money, Congressman Philo Case Fuller (New York Whig) of the Committee of Claims noted how the committee had stretched the law to fit the case.[99] No one stretched the law to prevent Smith from leaving the recaptured Africans in the hands of local slaveholders instead of arranging for their transportation to Liberia.[100]

The suppression of the slave trade did not, however, incur many significant federal expenditures during the 1819–1842 period. The U.S. government spent an estimated $480,000 in this policy area during the period and the British government, an estimated $18.4 million. The U.S. navy captured two slave-laden ships with a total of 302 Africans aboard during the period, while the British navy captured 292 slave-laden ships with a total of approximately 74,500 Africans aboard during a somewhat shorter 1821–1840 period.[101] The most significant effect of this policy area on state development was its effect on Anglo-American relations. British officials wielded the slave-trade issue as an ideological weapon against the United States in international contexts, testing both the intentions and capacities of American officials to respond with interdiction efforts.[102]

Near the end of the period, President Martin Van Buren responded to this British diplomatic pressure by instituting more regular navy visits to the west coast of Africa in 1839.[103] During the negotiations that culminated in the Webster-Ashburton Treaty (1842), the British government pressed for more, and Secretary of State Daniel Webster (Massachusetts Whig) agreed that the United States would finally establish its own permanent African squadron. The treaty committed the United States to a squadron of at least 80 guns, minimally two frigates.[104]

Partisan and sectional differences in this policy area emerged during the 1819–1842 period, which witnessed the birth and maturation of the second-party system. A Northern Democratic president (Van Buren) surpassed his Southern Democratic predecessor (Jackson) in committing resources to the suppression of the slave trade, and a Northern Whig Secretary of State (Webster) surpassed both.[105] Still, international factors could also explain these policy initiatives. They were ways for U.S. officials to respond to the continuing British diplomatic pressure to engage in more strenuous efforts to deter American participation in the slave trade short of signing a mutual search and seizure treaty with Great Britain. U.S. presidents, secretaries of state, and foreign ministers, regardless of their partisan or sectional affiliations, had consistently resisted taking this step ever since John Quincy Adams's tenure as Secretary of State.[106] In addition to sharing a general skepticism of international treaties as putative violations of national sovereignty, U.S. officials were especially reluctant to grant the British navy the power to search and seize American ships because of past conflicts over the practice. Slave-trade suppression was simply not a major partisan or sectional issue during the period.

The Webster-Ashburton Treaty represented a fourth decision point in the federal commitment to the suppression of the slave trade. Once more, the nation seemed poised for a substantial increase of federal activity in this policy area.

AFRICAN SQUADRON: THE EARLY YEARS
(FY1843–FY1859)

During this fourth period, the federal government committed a higher level of resources to the suppression of the slave trade, but the level could easily have been higher. Indeed, President John Tyler's Navy Secretary, Abel Upshur (Virginia Democrat), reassured Congress in January 1843 that the new African Squadron would require only a reallocation of existing navy vessels and resources to meet the minimum Webster-Ashburton Treaty obligations.[107] The creation of the African Squadron was another decision point that proved less than decisive in its implementation. Perhaps if President William Henry Harrison had not died or if Webster had remained Tyler's Secretary of State, the Webster-Ashburton Treaty would have had more immediate results.[108] Such a counterfactual history, however, seems implausible, given how subsequent events converged to over-determine Buchanan's decision to finally commit a substantial level of resources to slave-trade suppression.[109]

Initially, the U.S. navy met its treaty obligations by reassigning four vessels, with a total of 94 guns, from the Pacific Squadron to the African Squadron.[110] While the navy built new ships during this fourth period, it is highly unlikely that they were built because the navy fleet was stretched thin by its new squadron, especially when the United States only sporadically fulfilled its treaty obligations during the period.[111]

Upshur's assertion that the African Squadron would not require new money is more debatable. Even at its initial, small size, the new squadron was relatively expensive because of the logistics of supplying its African base of operations. The squadron's estimated annual costs were $384,500, which was 10.3 percent of total navy expenditures in 1843 ($3,728,000). This sum was an additional fixed cost that the navy would have to absorb every year that the squadron existed at its current size.[112]

The African Squadron's success rate in capturing suspected slave ships with Africans aboard is the easiest way to measure its performance. From FY1843 through FY1859, its success rate was exactly one slave-laden ship with approximately 900 Africans aboard. The squadron's success in capturing the *Pons* in 1845 was not repeated for another 15 years. In comparison, the British Navy captured 151 slave-laden ships with a total of approximately 56,700 Africans aboard during a slightly longer 1841–1860 period.[113]

Given the African Squadron's relative lack of success in capturing slave-laden ships, both Du Bois and Fehrenbacher have claimed that its primary mission was to protect American commerce, especially from possible British searches and seizures.[114] Based on the number of the squadron's ship seizures during this period, it would be difficult to prove them wrong. Upshur's initial instructions to squadron commanders expressly state that protecting American commerce was one of its two main missions.[115] Another one of Tyler's five navy secretaries, John Y. Mason (Virginia Democrat), further downplayed the squadron's slave-trade mission, stating that "the rights of our citizens engaged in lawful commerce are under the protection of our flag, and it is the chief purpose as well as the chief duty of our naval power to see that those rights are not improperly abridged or invaded." Later, he adds that "while the United States sincerely desire the suppression of the slave trade . . . they do not regard the success of their efforts as their paramount interest nor as their paramount duty."[116] The fact that Tyler refused to release these instructions to Congress and that they were not released until 1859, when Buchanan finally decided to make slave-trade suppression a national priority, is also relevant to assessing the squadron's mission. Still, it is not clear that squadron commanders ever perceived that protecting American commerce was its primary mission. As Judd Harmon has argued most vigorously, many factors could explain the squadron's relative lack of success in capturing slave-laden ships during this period other than a lack of commitment on the part of its commanders to slave-trade suppression.[117] Two critical factors were its relatively small size and the relative slowness of its ships. These factors point more to fiscal constraints than mission ambivalence as an explanation for the squadron's failures. Another factor was that seizures of suspected slave ships rarely produced convictions and opened navy captains to countersuits for illegal seizures. During this period, Congress, in fact, compensated two squadron captains for their legal fees in libel suits, appropriating a total of $1,713 in the two cases.[118] Weighing the arguments on both sides, "lack of resources" seems the more compelling explanation for the squadron's failures. Both sides agree, however, on one point, that before the Buchanan administration, the suppression of the slave trade was not a priority to American presidents and their mostly Southern navy secretaries.[119]

Near the end of the FY1843–FY1859 period, the USS *Dolphin,* which was assigned to the Home Squadron, captured the American slave ship *Echo* with 318 Africans aboard on August 21, 1858, off the coast of Cuba.[120] The recaptured Africans were placed in the custody of U.S. Marshal Daniel Hamilton in Charleston to await transport to Liberia. More than 100 of the Africans died either in custody or in transit to Liberia because of their weakened condition at the time of capture and their less than adequate care in Charleston.[121] Despite the overwhelming evidence against the crew, local jurors found them innocent of the piracy charges that U.S. District Attorney James Connor had lodged against them. South Carolina Attorney General Isaac W. Hayne, who assisted Connor in this unsuccessful prosecution, received $1,500 for his services. Hamilton himself received at least $7,328 for the care of the recaptured Africans placed in his custody.[122] The captain of the *Echo,* Edward N. Townsend, was tried separately on Key West and also acquitted.[123]

Later that same year, the first authenticated case of a large-scale attempt to (successfully) smuggle slaves into the United States since 1820 occurred.[124] On November 28, 1858, the crew of the *Wanderer* landed 407 Africans near Savannah, Georgia. The co-owner of the ship was a prominent Savannah businessman, Charles Lamar, who had conspired to violate the federal ban on slave imports in the past. Treasury Secretary Howell Cobb (Georgia Democrat) had stymied Lamar's first attempt to defy the ban by refusing to grant his own ship, the *Richard Cobden,* clearance to sail to Africa to transport "emigrants" back to the United States. Lamar then bought a share of the *Wanderer* from William C. Corrie to more covertly smuggle African slaves into the country. But his involvement in the case was hardly a secret to either local residents or federal authorities. He even bought back the *Wanderer* at the libel auction.[125]

The *Wanderer* case generated eleven separate indictments, five trials, and zero convictions. The U.S. district attorney in Savannah, Joseph Ganahl, initially charged three members of the *Wanderer* crew with piracy. To assist Ganahl with these prosecutions, Attorney General Jeremiah S. Black (Pennsylvania Democrat) appointed a prominent Savannah attorney, Henry Rootes Jackson, as his own special assistant in the case. Ganahl and Jackson took the case to trial, but, again, local jurors refused to convict any of the three crew members.[126] At that point, both Ganahl and Jackson quit the case, with Jackson receiving as much as $6,000 for his services.[127] The new U.S. district attorney, Hamilton Couper, shifted tactics and, in eight separate indictments, charged Lamar and seven other men with harboring smuggled slaves. Juries also refused to convict the first two men Couper brought to trial even on this lesser charge.[128] The fourth *Wanderer* trial involved a mysterious fourth crew member, J. Egbert Farnum, who had originally escaped arrest.

After the initial indictments, Jackson had hired Lucien Peyton, a local Patent Office employee, to locate Farnum in New York and escort him back to Savannah to stand trial for piracy as well as to testify against Lamar and the other remaining defendants. Peyton received $900 for his services. Farnum was, however, also acquitted.[129] At that point, Couper decided to drop the charges against Lamar and the other remaining defendants.[130] The fifth and final *Wanderer* trial occurred in Charleston. U.S. District Court Justice Andrew G. Magrath short-circuited the trial of *Wanderer* captain and part owner Corrie by effectively nullifying the 1820 federal piracy law on the grounds that international trafficking in Africans who were already enslaved was commerce, not piracy. Confronted with such an obtuse ruling, District Attorney Connor decided not to proceed with his case against Corrie.[131]

In the meantime, President Buchanan had decided to fortify both the African and Home squadrons for slave-trade suppression. By the summer of 1859, his Northern secretary of the navy, Isaac Toucey (Connecticut Democrat), had reshuffled the navy fleet to increase the size of the African Squadron from four to eight ships and the Home Squadron from five to thirteen ships. Most of the new ships were steamships.[132]

Buchanan had multiple motives for this decision. The primary factor was probably the growing evidence of American involvement in the Cuban slave trade. Buchanan also had partisan motives for his decision. He hoped that the decision would help shore up the Northern wing of the Democratic Party in the face of the continued erosion of its popular support to the Republican Party by demonstrating that his party was committed to attacking the slave trade, if not slavery itself. The vocal efforts of a group of Southern fire-eaters who favored rescinding the federal ban on slave imports increased Buchanan's determination to show Northern (and Southern) constituencies that he would not allow any slippage on the ban. The *Echo* and *Wanderer* cases undoubtedly added to this determination. On a more personal level, Buchanan was also committed to a more rigorous enforcement of the nation's slave-trade laws. His tenures as secretary of state and U.S. minister to England had certainly exposed him to incessant British complaints about the lack of enforcement efforts. British diplomatic pressure on the State Department to engage in more strenuous enforcement efforts continued during his presidency. It was now coupled with a threat to unilaterally search and seize suspected American slave ships in Cuban waters. This last factor also strongly influenced Buchanan's decision.[133]

As the nation headed toward civil war and partisan divisions began to map onto sectional divisions, the enforcement of the nation's slave-trade laws became more of a political issue. As early as 1854, Democratic Senator John Slidell (Louisiana) crafted a resolution to abrogate the eighth article of the Webster-Ashburton

Treaty under which the African Squadron had been created, though his resolution was never brought to a vote.[134] An 1856 House resolution condemning the slave trade passed, 152–57, but with 55 of the 73 Southern congressmen who voted on the resolution in opposition.[135] This vote stands in sharp contrast to the nearly unanimous Southern congressional support for a federal slave-import ban in 1807. In the Senate, Democrats rebuffed Republican senators William Seward (New York) and Henry Wilson (Massachusetts) in their efforts to commit the federal government to more strenuous enforcement of the nation's slave-trade laws, prompting them to lobby Buchanan to accomplish the task on his own authority.[136]

Yet, as Ronald Takaki argued in his study of the slave-trade revival movement, Southern support for the movement was relatively isolated.[137] Most Southern fire-eaters opposed the movement as a threat to sectional unity and a distraction from their own secessionist efforts. Even the efforts of the Southern activists who supported the movement seemed more symbolic than indicative of a serious policy initiative. The movement also found little support in the upper South, re-creating the original upper South–lower South division on the slave trade that had been evident at the Constitutional Convention. Indeed, an upper-South congressman, Emerson Etheridge (Tennessee Whig), had introduced the 1856 House resolution condemning the trade. Of the eighteen Southern congressmen who voted for the resolution, all but one was from the upper South.[138] While fifty-five Southern congressmen voted against the resolution, their vote appeared to be more of a show of sectional solidarity than an endorsement of the slave trade. Accordingly, Congressman James L. Orr (South Carolina Democrat), who had himself voted against the Etheridge resolution, introduced a new resolution declaring it inexpedient to revive the trade at this time immediately after the vote on the Etheridge resolution. His resolution passed overwhelmingly, 183–8.[139] On the state level, no Southern state, not even South Carolina, ever took official action to nullify a federal slave-trade law.[140] The lower-South states also agreed to place a slave-import ban in the Confederate constitution, though, admittedly, strategic motives were strongly implicated in this decision, including a desire to entice the upper-South states that had not yet seceded from the union to secede.[141] A final piece of evidence pointing to the relative political insignificance of the slave-trade revival movement was the fact that the president who made the first substantial commitment of resources to the suppression of the trade was the proverbial "doughface," a Northern Democrat whose electoral support came predominantly from the South and whose domestic policies bore an unmistakably Southern stamp. Given his "doughface" reputation, it is not surprising that Buchanan rarely receives the credit he deserves in this policy area.[142] But his strong commitment to slave-trade suppression also demonstrates that the issue was one that generally transcended sectional and partisan divisions.

Regardless of the motives behind Buchanan's decision to enlarge the African and Home squadrons and of how broadly his decision was supported, it represented the single most significant increase in the federal commitment to interdicting illegal slave trading and smuggling. Even if the decision meant only a reallocation of existing ships within the navy fleet, the expenses that resulted from the decision required sizable new slave-trade appropriations. For the next two fiscal years, the business of the U.S. navy was slave-trade suppression.

AFRICAN SQUADRON: THE LATER YEARS (FY1860–FY1861)

During the next two fiscal years, the African and Home squadrons combined to capture nine slave-laden ships with a total of at least 5,346 Africans aboard.[143] The number of seizures of slave-laden ships was more than two times the total for the previous forty years. The number of Africans seized was more than three times the total for those forty years. The performance of the U.S. African Squadron finally approached the performance of its British counterpart, though the latter still enjoyed a 19–12 advantage in capturing suspected slave ships in 1860–1861.[144] Only the Civil War halted this major escalation in the federal commitment to slave-trade suppression.

To meet the expenses of this upsurge in ship seizures, Congress appropriated a total of $2,050,000 in new money in FY1860–FY1861.[145] As we will see in the next chapter, much of the money went to other parties than to the U.S. navy for slave-trade suppression. Still, the operating costs of the African and Home squadrons had increased substantially, as had the bounty money for recaptured Africans. These increases were all the more significant because they occurred at a time of budget retrenchment. Both total navy and federal expenditures decreased in FY1860 and only partially rebounded in FY1861. The estimated operating costs of the enlarged African Squadron accounted for 6.85 percent of total navy expenditures in FY1860 ($769,000 of $11,515,000) and 6.35 percent in FY1861 ($769,000 of $12,421,000).[146]

This fifth period also saw the first and only execution of an American citizen for piracy because of his slave-trade activities. Nathaniel Gordon was the captain of the *Erie*, one of the four slave-laden ships that the African Squadron captured in 1860. He was prosecuted, twice, in federal district court in New York in 1861. The first trial ended in a hung jury but in the second the jury returned a guilty verdict. U.S. District Court Justice William Davis Shipman then sentenced Gordon to hang until death. He was executed on February 21, 1862.[147]

Although I found no records of the costs associated with this case, they must have been considerable. Gordon, unlike Lamar in the *Wanderer* case, was not free on bail while he awaited trial. He spent a total of fifteen months in jail, from October 1860, when he was first taken into custody in New York, to his execution.[148] The new Republican U.S. district attorney in New York, E. Delafield Smith, also hired private investigators to find the four *Erie* crew members whose testimony was crucial to the different result of the second trial.[149] After they had been located in Boston and escorted to New York, Smith incurred additional expenses when he decided to sequester them for three months while he prepared the case for retrial.[150]

Together, the *Wanderer* and Gordon cases were indicative of the continuing presence of partisan and sectional differences over the enforcement of the nation's slave-trade laws. While Gordon's prosecution had begun under a Democratic administration, the new Republican administration and its new district attorney in New York were determined to convict Gordon in a city where Tammany Hall had made slave-trade convictions very difficult.[151] But even if the pre-Gordon record on slave-trade cases was abysmal in heavily Democratic New York, it was still better than the record in the South. The *Wanderer* case was anomalous in many respects but not in its results. No American citizen was convicted by any Southern jury of any slave-trade violation after 1846.[152]

On the other hand, Gordon's conviction occurred after the Civil War had begun, and that changed context was undoubtedly also an important factor in the different results of his two trials.[153] The war also meant that any partisan and sectional differences between the Lincoln administration and its predecessors could not play themselves out under "normal" circumstances. After all, the Buchanan administration had shown some determination in prosecuting Lamar. It may have shown an equal determination in prosecuting Gordon if it had continued. Following Takaki's interpretation of the Southern slave-trade revival movement, the lack of slave-trade convictions in the region may have been more a case of sectional solidarity against any federal action that intruded on its "domestic affairs" than a positive affirmation of the slave trade or even of slavery itself.

Further evidence that the Buchanan administration took the *Wanderer* case seriously was its commitment to slave-smuggling espionage. Attorney General Black authorized Peyton not only to seize Farnum as a *Wanderer* witness and co-defendant but also to investigate other possible slave-smuggling incidents along the eastern seaboard.[154] In September 1859, Buchanan's secretary of interior, Jacob Thompson (Mississippi Democrat), dispatched Benjamin F. Slocumb (Indiana) on a two-month espionage mission to the Southern interior. Slocumb's report discussed many rumored slave-smuggling incidents but dismissed them all as merely rumors.[155] The commitment to slave-smuggling espionage continued in the early months of the Lincoln administration. Under its new secretary, Caleb

B. Smith (Indiana Republican), the Interior Department paid U.S. marshals extra money to engage in such espionage. It paid Marshal Charles Clark in Maine $400 to watch for slave-smuggling activities, Marshal James Aiken in Delaware a "small amount" for the same purpose, and Marshal Robert Murray in New York $300 to inspect a suspected slave ship.[156] This slave-smuggling espionage made sense of Buchanan's 1858 decision to consolidate the federal efforts in this policy area in the Department of Interior, which was a major boost to the development of a fledgling department.[157]

The federal government also paid the transportation and living expenses of a number of witnesses in slave-trade cases in the years immediately preceding the Civil War. A lengthy 1860 congressional report on the slave trade indicates that the federal government paid the expenses of several witnesses to testify in cases involving slave-ship seizures in Cuban waters during the late 1850s. In the *C. Perkins* seizure, it paid two witnesses $30 for their transportation from Havana to New York. It also paid them $1.50 per day for the time their services were required, which may have been as long as nine months. In the *Haidee* seizure, it paid two witnesses $25 for their transportation from Havana to Boston, as well as $25.50 in board for one witness and $8.50 for another.[158] Department of Interior records show that in February 1861 it paid a witness $209.15 for his travel expenses to testify in an unidentified slave-trade case.[159]

By February 1861, seven Southern states had seceded from the union. The Civil War began a few months later. The war closed an important episode in the development of the U.S. navy even as it opened another, more important episode. The war brought the African Squadron home for Union blockade duty.[160] On April 7, 1862, the United States signed a mutual search and seizure treaty with Great Britain.[161] This treaty culminated four decades of British diplomatic pressure on American officials to sign such a treaty. By these two actions, the United States effectively ceded the enforcement of its own slave-trade laws to the British navy, something which had been anathema to American officials for those forty years. The U.S. navy's recent enforcement efforts had, nonetheless, prepared it for its wartime duties as navy crews shifted their search-and-seizure routines from international to intercoastal waters. The skills they had learned capturing slave-laden ships were directly transferable to capturing Confederate contraband ships, a task at which they were surprisingly successful.[162]

CONCLUSION

From 1791 to 1861, the federal government committed an increasing level of resources to the suppression of the slave trade. The pattern was not one of steadily increasing resources indicative of a constant rise in infrastructure costs or bureaucratic capture. Rather, the pattern was one of step increases, in 1819, 1842, and, most significantly, 1859.

The relative timing and magnitude of these step increases suggests that partisan and sectional divisions over slavery were the primary causal factors. The increasing, and increasingly overlapping, partisan and sectional divisions over slavery were important causal factors, certainly in the case of Buchanan's decision to enlarge the African and Home squadrons. The first step increase was also timed to a period of elevated sectional tensions associated with the Missouri crisis and the second to the hyper-partisanship of Tyler's "accidental" presidency. Yet other factors played at least as important a role in these step increases. Buchanan's decision was over-determined by a confluence of political, diplomatic, and personal factors. The first step increase was probably primarily a response to the organization of the ACS, not the Missouri crisis, and the second to a number of ongoing disputes with Great Britain that begged for settlement, not Tyler's "accidental" presidency.[163] One constant factor was the British diplomatic pressure on U.S. officials to interdict illegal slave trading more actively, particularly when American citizens, ships, or flags were involved. The ebb and flow of demand in the major slave markets of Brazil and Cuba and of American participation in those markets were additional factors. Finally, a general moral censure against the slave trade formed a baseline for committing at least some resources to suppression efforts, once the American state had acquired sufficient capacities to engage in such efforts.[164]

The suppression of the slave trade involved a number of state functions and capacities. First, it involved an attempt to control the national borders against smuggling activities. This function required a minimal commitment of state capacities because the federal slave-import ban was largely self-enforcing. Second, the suppression of the slave trade involved an attempt to restrict immigration into the United States. In a deeply ironic sense, African slaves were the nation's first proscribed immigrant group.[165] This function was also largely self-enforcing because after 1807 African slaves could enter the United States only illegally, as smuggled slaves. Third, the suppression of the slave trade involved navy interdiction of an illegal activity in international waters. This function eventually led to a significant commitment of state capacities because the nation's slave-trade laws were not largely self-enforcing. Fourth, the suppression of the slave trade involved the application of coercive measures against both American citizens and foreign nationals who participated in the trade, whether as slave procurers, traders, smugglers, dealers, or purchasers. This function required the activation of the extensive latent capacities of the American state because it required the cooperation of federal, state, and local officials to enforce the nation's slave-trade laws and prosecute those who had allegedly violated them. It also required the cooperation of private citizens in support of these law-enforcement efforts.

In the course of performing their other duties, a variety of federal employees were involved in interdicting illegal slave trading and smuggling. U.S. customs officials assisted in identifying alleged slave smugglers, arresting them, and libeling their ships. U.S. marshals took alleged slave traders and smugglers into custody and investigated their activities. Assuming they were not granted or could not meet bail, U.S. marshals also arranged for their imprisonment with state and local officials while they awaited trial. U.S. attorneys gathered evidence against them and sometimes brought them to trial. Federal justices oversaw their trials, and, if they were convicted, sentenced them to pay fines, serve time in prison, or, in one case, face execution. Navy crews captured suspected slave ships and received bounties for the number of Africans they seized from such ships. U.S. marshals arranged for the care of these recaptured Africans in cases where they were not transported directly to Liberia.

Interdicting illegal slave trading and smuggling not only required state and local officials to cooperate with federal officials; it also required private citizens to perform state functions. The federal government paid private investigators to track down alleged slave traders and smugglers and those who had witnessed their activities. It paid deputy marshals to help arrest and imprison alleged slave traders and smugglers. It paid private attorneys to prosecute them. It paid witnesses to testify against them and jurors to weigh their guilt and innocence. It paid doctors and jailers to help care for them during the time they were in custody and, if convicted, while they were in prison. It also paid private parties to help care for recaptured Africans, and it paid a private organization to resettle them in Liberia. My estimate of the total federal expenditures in this policy area includes very few of these specific costs. In most cases, the costs were undocumented and, individually, quite small, but they obviously could have accumulated to significant amounts of money over the course of the seven decades from 1791 to 1861.[166]

The cooperation that federal officials received from other state actors as well as non-state actors in this policy area meant that the number of federal employees who were engaged in various slave-trade suppression activities was not indicative of the total number of people who were engaged in such activities. Nor was the number of navy personnel assigned to the African Squadron indicative of the total number of federal employees who were engaged in various slave-trade suppression activities, given the number of other federal employees who were engaged in such activities on an incidental basis. Through these cooperative efforts, the federal government was able to coerce a number of American citizens as well as foreign nationals to desist from illegal slave trading and smuggling. These cooperative efforts reflected the growing authority and legitimacy of the American state. The federal government proved itself capable of performing a number of state functions through its own efforts to suppress the slave trade. By finally demonstrating a capacity to suppress the trade, the U.S. navy, in particular, was rewarded with sizable new congressional appropriations. On the other hand, the failure of the federal government to enforce territorial slave-import bans in Mississippi and Louisiana probably actually enhanced its legitimacy among local residents, though that failure was also a sign of its initial lack of governing authority and state capacities in those territories.[167] Much later, as private citizens and local, state, and even some federal officials in the Southern states refused to cooperate in federal efforts to suppress the slave trade during the 1850s, both the legitimacy and authority of the federal government suffered. This lack of cooperation was a prelude to civil war.[168]

Du Bois was certainly correct to argue that the federal government should and could have committed more resources, to the suppression of the slave trade than it did. Yet it still committed considerable resources, and, as a result, the early American state developed differently from how it would have developed in the absence of such a commitment. By the beginning of the Civil War, slave-trade suppression had made an important contribution to the development of the U.S. navy. In FY1860, the African Squadron absorbed 13.5 percent of navy personnel (approximately 1,300 of 9,884 men), 18.8 percent of the navy fleet (nine of 48 ships), and 6.9 percent of navy expenditures (approximately $769,000 of $11,515,000).[169] The American state (finally) committed a substantial amount of human and financial resources to slave-trade suppression. This policy area also made significant contributions to the development of the Departments of Interior, State, and Treasury, all of which (eventually) shared authority with the navy over slave-trade suppression.[170] Slave-trade cases precipitated a number of domestic and international political disputes, the latter particularly with Great Britain. One or more of those four departments—Navy, Interior, State, and Treasury—had to commit resources to address such disputes, as did the Attorney General's office in cases requiring litigation.

In terms of its long-range consequences, the slave-trade policy area contributed to a growing tendency toward executive policy-making during the 1791–1861 period.[171] Congressional divisions over slavery created opportunities for executive initiatives, such as Buchanan's 1858 decision to substantially boost federal enforcement efforts in this policy area. The slave-trade policy area also contributed to the growth of federal powers during the period, as the delegates to the Constitutional Convention had envisioned in authorizing Congress to enact a federal slave-import ban. After 1807, no states-rights argument against federal powers emerged in this policy area, perhaps not surprisingly, given its strong connection to foreign relations and border control, which were increasingly viewed as the "natural" provenances of not only the federal government but its executive departments.

While partisan and sectional differences existed on the implementation of the nation's slave-trade laws, a state commitment to implement those laws, at least at minimal levels, had emerged by 1819. Thereafter, this state commitment fluctuated with the different priorities of key federal decision-makers. But it also transcended such individual variances.

In this case, several factors generated the commitment of the American state to the suppression of the slave trade. One factor was the relative lack of partisan, ideological, and regional differences over the venality of the trade.[172] The presence of slavery did not depress state development in this case because of bitter sectional proxy disputes, as it may have in the cases of federal taxation and internal improvements. Another factor was the commitment of prominent upper-South politicians, such as Jefferson, Mercer, and Monroe, to the suppression of the slave trade. This commitment had both moral and economic dimensions, and at least the latter would not have existed in the absence of slavery. A third factor was that even in the lower South, opposition to slave-trade suppression was weak. Lower-South cabinet officers Cobb (Treasury) and Thompson (Interior) fully participated in the Buchanan administration's enforcement initiatives. A final factor was Great Britain's state-to-state pressure on the United States to more effectively enforce its own slave-trade laws. Again, key federal decision-makers varied in their susceptibility to this pressure, but none could afford to totally ignore it in light of the power of the British navy.

Yet another reason that the American state remained committed to slave-trade suppression during the 1819–1861 period was that it remained committed to African colonization. From the very inception of the ACS, both society and federal officials—who were frequently the same people—declared slave-trade suppression one of the many virtues of that policy.

3. The First American Colony

The American Colonization Society (ACS) may have been a private organization, but its African colonial enterprise was not a private project.[1] Almost from its very inception, the society enjoyed the financial support of the federal government. Liberia became the nation's first overseas colonial venture, with significant consequences for early American state development. The public-private partnership established to pursue the project was not only one of the first of its kind in the history of the American state; it was the longest lasting and most well-funded partnership during the 1791–1861 period. American state actors, even those ostensibly opposed to the venture, proved to be remarkably resilient in assisting the ACS's colonial enterprise.

The relationship between the ACS and federal government followed three different trajectories from 1819 to 1861. Depending on the type of support, federal support of the society declined to zero after an initial peak, remained relatively stable, or rose steeply near the end of this period.[2]

The first trajectory is the most familiar. At its origins, the ACS attracted the support of the "Washington Community." The society held its initial meeting at the Davis Hotel in the nation's capital on December 21, 1816. The society's founding members appointed one distinguished committee, including prominent Washington lawyer Francis Scott Key, Attorney General Richard Rush, and Associate Supreme Court Justice Bushrod Washington, to draft a constitution. They appointed another distinguished committee, including Key, Rush, and Congressmen John Randolph and Robert Wright, to draft a memorial to Congress requesting federal support. The society reconvened a week later in the chambers of the House of Representatives to adopt a constitution with a veritable who's who in attendance. Among the signers of its original constitution were House Speaker Henry Clay, Treasury Secretary William Crawford, former Senator John Taylor, Congressman Daniel Webster, as well as Key, Randolph, and Washington.[3]

On January 1, 1817, the ACS reconvened at the Davis Hotel to hold its first annual meeting. The main purpose of this meeting was to elect a slate of officers. Washington was elected the society's first president and Clay, Crawford, General Andrew Jackson, Rush, and Taylor were among its first thirteen honorary vice presidents.[4] For its first anniversary annual meeting, held exactly a year later, the society returned to the House chambers to renew its call for federal support.[5] In 1819, the society's pleas were answered when it received a $100,000 federal endowment at the initiative of President James Monroe to found a colony for expatriated

African Americans on the west coast of Africa. However, during the next decade, the society's colonization project became the target of increasing partisan (Democratic) and sectional (Southern) opposition until President Jackson, a Southern Democrat and former ACS vice president, cut off its federal funding.[6]

The second trajectory is the least familiar. Even after the Jackson administration cut off its federal funding, the ACS's colonization project continued to receive support from the federal government. As it had during Liberia's founding period, the U.S. navy continued to protect the colony and supply it with arms and other in-kind subsidies. The federal government also continued to share a colonization agent in Liberia with the ACS, both organizations partially paying his $2,400 annual salary.[7] After Liberia declared independence in 1847, the federal government appointed its own commercial agent to the new nation. Because the United States refused to recognize Liberian independence until 1862, this commercial agent functioned as an unofficial ambassador to Liberia in the interim, drawing a $1,000 annual salary and adding *counsel general* to his title in 1856.[8] At least from the American perspective, Liberia retained its colonial status under the joint custody of the ACS and federal government. In addition to whatever other purposes the Liberian enterprise may have served for society officials, it served several national purposes that motivated federal officials to continue to support the project over these years. Obviously, this second trajectory was not cost-free for the federal government, even if the costs were less visible and harder to measure than under the first trajectory.

The third trajectory was the most expensive. This trajectory followed the connection between African colonization and the suppression of the slave trade. As we have seen, even the ACS's initial $100,000 federal endowment was part of that connection because the money was appropriated under a 1819 law to enforce the nation's slave-trade laws more effectively. Monroe diverted the money to the society under the rationale that its projected African colony would serve as the entrepôt for Africans seized from suspected slave ships, who, according to the provisions of the new law, would no longer be left to the disposition of state officials. As we have also seen, the connection between African colonization and slave-trade suppression was sporadic over the next three decades because the navy's efforts to suppress the trade were sporadic, even after a separate African squadron was finally established in 1843. However even during the "unfriendly" Jackson administration, the ACS continued to receive federal funds to resettle and care for recaptured Africans in Liberia. President James Buchanan then formally entered into an agreement with the society in 1858 to pay it $150 for each recaptured African whom it resettled in Liberia.[9] When Congress approved this arrangement in 1860, it was the first time that it explicitly authorized the disbursement of federal funds to the ACS. Even though the Senate reduced Buchanan's $150 per capita figure to $100, a surge in slave-ship seizures sent federal money flowing through the society's treasury at an unprecedented pace.[10] Federal support for the ACS actually peaked in 1861.

From the beginning of its existence, the ACS saw federal support as the *sine qua non* of its success.[11] Yet the society sent mixed signals about how exactly to measure success. Different society officials at different times—and sometimes the same official at the same time—defined success differently. The ACS's stated goals included establishing an independent Christian republic in Africa that would "civilize" the whole continent, attacking the slave trade at its source, protecting the public safety and morals by removing "degraded" free African Americans from the United States, offering "oppressed" free African Americans a refuge where they could enjoy the prospect of elevating themselves and demonstrating their capacity for self-government, protecting the institution of Southern slavery by removing "incendiary" free African Americans from the country, and encouraging Southern slaveholders to emancipate their slaves by providing a safely distant site for their removal (perhaps) coincident to a very gradual abolition of slavery in the United States.[12] There was an obvious sectional bias among ACS officials in how they defined success, but that bias was far from absolute.[13] Concretely, these different measures of success had different implications as to the target population for removal, the expected volume of removal, and, correspondingly, the aggregate costs.[14] Officially, the society discredited none of these measures of success because it wished to remain a "big tent" that attracted broad support throughout the nation as well as within the halls of Congress.[15]

While the ACS regularly appealed for federal support, it did not regularly receive federal support, at least not in a monetary form. Over time, society officials lowered their expectations. They claimed that their Liberian project had at least proven that a private benevolent organization could establish an African American colony in Africa.[16] This measure of success was not only attractive in terms of its apparent feasibility but also in terms of its consensual nature.[17] ACS officials from both the North and South could agree on the importance of "Americanizing" Africa, especially because they agreed that African Americans and European Americans could not live together as equals in the same society.[18] Society officials also began to place greater emphasis on other measures of success, such as Liberia's value in deterring the African slave trade by offering more legitimate avenues of commerce to Africans, in specifically promoting American commerce to and from Africa, and in checking British influence on the continent.[19] The ACS's appeals for federal support now took the form of arguing that its Liberian project had shown that it was possible to establish an African American colony in Africa but that federal support was necessary to take the enterprise to the next level, whatever that level might be.[20] Again, it made sense politically to leave the project's ultimate goal indeterminate.

It is impossible to accurately measure the exact value of the federal assistance that the ACS received because it received three different types of federal assistance. The indirect ways that the society received most of its federal support not only obscured the amount of support that it received but the very fact that it received support. Even society officials sometimes seemed to forget the federal support that their Liberian project had received and often portrayed it as a strictly private enterprise.[21]

In his valedictory address at the 1853 annual meeting of the society, ACS Vice President Charles Fenton Mercer, who had been the society's most vocal congressional supporter, sought to set the record straight.[22] One of the targets of his lengthy address was fourth auditor Amos Kendall's 1830 report on colonization expenditures, which had played a pivotal role in the loss of the society's federal funding.[23] In the course of the report, Kendall had asserted that the use of public funds to help found the ACS's Liberian colony was a misuse of public funds. Mercer argued, to the contrary, that the use of public funds for that purpose was entirely appropriate under Monroe's interpretation of the 1819 slave-trade law and that Congress had acquiesced in that interpretation of the law for more than a decade prior to Kendall's audit. In response to Kendall's suggestion that, however worthy the Liberian enterprise was, it should have been pursued solely by private means, Mercer insisted that the colony would never have been established or continued to survive without federal support. His $350,000 estimate of the value of that support was actually a very good to-date estimate.[24]

My calculation of the value of the federal support that the society received for the whole 1819–1861 period is $627,689, which would represent more than one third of the society's total receipts ($1,739,645) over those years.[25] The amount would also represent more than twice the value of the federal support that any other private organization received during this period. The next largest "social welfare" subsidy was the $300,000 that the Connecticut Asylum for the Education and Instruction of Deaf and Dumb Persons netted from its 1819 federal land grant of 23,000 acres.[26] The ACS subsidies also differed qualitatively from other early federal subsidies to private organizations in not being a one-time land grant and in establishing a continuing relationship between the federal government and the recipient organization. The ACS–federal government relationship was a public-private partnership that lasted for more than four decades.

The three types of federal assistance that the ACS received are comparable to three types of federal grant programs today. Under trajectory one, the society received executive set-asides to spend at its own discretion in pursuing its primary purpose of founding a colony for expatriated African Americans on the west coast of Africa. Even though Congress never explicitly authorized this funding, the money, which totaled approximately $250,000 from 1819 to 1830, was clearly a federal subsidy to the ACS. Under trajectory two, it received in-kind subsidies to maintain its Liberian colony. Like most in-kind subsidies, the value of this type of support is impossible to measure with any degree of accuracy, but it may have been essential nonetheless. Under trajectory three, the society received congressionally approved categorical grants for the specific purpose of resettling Africans seized from suspected slave ships in Liberia. This assistance also totaled approximately $250,000 from 1859 to 1861. It was explicitly connected to the suppression of the slave trade, which was one of the auxiliary purposes of African colonization. In fact, Congress appropriated almost all the federal money the ACS received under that purpose. The official conflation of the two policies of African colonization and slave-trade suppression further complicates the task of determining the exact amount of federal support that the society received.[27]

In weighing the connection between the continuing presence of slavery in the Southern states and federal support for African colonization, two factors are important. First, the presence of slavery was one factor that motivated the founders of the ACS to dedicate themselves to colonizing African Americans in Africa. Though the exact way that they connected African colonization to the presence of slavery differed, society officials continually made that connection. Second, the federal government would probably not have spent any money on African colonization without the existence of a private organization dedicated to that purpose. Counterfactually, the federal government could have established its own African colony. This possibility, however, seems remote given how much controversy was created merely by its indirect subsidization of the ACS's colonization project.

Members of Congress who were strong supporters of African colonization could pursue the project by forming and indirectly funding a private organization dedicated to establishing an unofficial African colony more effectively than they could by attempting to establish an official colony. Using a fiscal mechanism that was later used to fund many internal-improvement projects, African colonization was a mixed public-private enterprise that allowed federal officials to accomplish controversial public purposes that would have been difficult to accomplish in other ways.[28] From the perspective of ACS officials, federal support, however indirect and unofficial it might have been, made their cause seem more authoritative. From both perspectives, the mixed nature of the enterprise was a means of stretching scarce resources.

This policy episode has fascinated politics and history scholars because so many prominent people were members of both the ACS and federal government and therefore had stakes on both sides of the public-private equation.[29] It is also a fascinating policy episode because once the ACS and federal government had established an African colony, a separate state interest in its survival emerged and convinced even federal officials who were not strong supporters of the enterprise to assist it. This development, in turn, prompted ACS officials to emphasize the ways that African colonization served state purposes in their appeals for federal support, purposes that the society's founders had not emphasized or even articulated in their initial appeals for support. At least rhetorically, this shift in emphasis connected the venture more intimately to state development. Eventually, it had significant practical effects in steering additional public resources toward the project.

DECLINING FEDERAL SUPPORT

The who's who of early ACS supporters includes prominent politicians from the North and South as well as Democratic Republicans, Federalists, and future Democrats and Whigs. If one combines the former, present, or future members of Congress, the cabinet, and Supreme Court who were signers of the society's original constitution with its first vice presidents, the list includes Clay (Kentucky Democratic Republican/Whig), Crawford (Georgia Democratic Republican), John Carlyle Herbert (Maryland Federalist), John E. Howard (Maryland Federalist), Jackson (Tennessee Democratic Republican/Democrat), Robert Bland Lee (Virginia Federalist), Charles Marsh (Connecticut Federalist), Thomas Patterson (Pennsylvania Democratic Republican), George Peter (Maryland Federalist/Democrat), Randolph (Virginia Democratic Republican), Rush (Pennsylvania Democratic Republican), Samuel Smith (Maryland Democratic Republican/Democrat), Taylor (Virginia Democratic Republican), Washington (Virginia Federalist), Webster (Massachusetts Federalist/Whig), and Peter Hercules Wendover (New York Democratic Republican).[30] During the next decade, Congressman Mercer (Virginia Federalist/Whig), who had led the fight for colonization in the Virginia legislature and was now leading it in Congress, was added to the list of honorary vice presidents, along with former Senator Robert Goodloe Harper (Maryland Federalist), Congressman Isaac McKim (Maryland Democratic Republican/Democrat), and Supreme Court Justice John Marshall (Virginia Federalist).[31] Harper, Howard, Jackson, Smith, and Taylor were no longer on the list; Harper, Howard, and Taylor because of death.[32]

This distinguished group of twenty early ACS supporters was disproportionately from the upper South; fourteen were from Kentucky, Maryland, Tennessee, or Virginia.[33] If there was a partisan bias, it was Federalist since half the group was Federalist at a time when the party was a small congressional minority.[34]

Although the society's early supporters were disproportionately from the upper South, the new organization still seemed to enjoy broad-based support for its goal of colonizing African Americans, both free blacks and slaves emancipated on the condition of emigration, in a colony to be established on the west coast of Africa.[35] This goal carried with it others from which potential supporters could pick and choose to ensure that the ACS remained a "big tent." As those goals were articulated during the early years of the society, they included offering free blacks who faced deep-seated racial prejudices in the United States a chance to elevate themselves in their "natural" home, excising an "unwelcome" portion of the population that was allegedly undermining good government as well as the public safety and morals of the American people, facilitating a gradual, voluntary abolition of slavery by providing Southern slaveholders who wished to emancipate their slaves with a safe haven for their emancipated slaves, protecting the Southern institution of slavery by removing a potentially rebellious free African American population, curtailing the slave trade, and spreading the "blessings" of Western civilization, Christianity, and republicanism to the African continent.[36]

With respect to the institution of slavery itself, the ACS disclaimed any intention of interfering with the institution in the states where it already existed.[37] Society officials claimed that the society offered only a means of facilitating the manumission process for those slaveholders who were disposed to pursue it, either immediately or by testament. The ACS attempted to appeal to antislavery politicians by offering a possible vehicle for a very gradual abolition of slavery in the Southern states while attempting to avoid antagonizing proslavery politicians by attacking the institution in only very general terms, as a national evil that would perhaps be extinguished at some time in the indefinite future.[38] In 1851, long-time ACS President Clay counseled patience. He noted that "[i]t took two centuries and more to bring from the shores of Africa her sons now existing in a state of slavery in the United States. It may take two centuries, more or less, to transport their descendants to such an extent as no longer to create any solicitude or anxiety about the few that may linger and remain behind."[39] Even Randolph's speech at the initial meeting of the society, which was later to cause such controversy for its strong proslavery tone, espoused a belief in the general desirability of emancipation. After contending that the removal of free African Americans "must materially tend to secure the property of every master in the United States over his slaves," Randolph predicted that "if a place could be provided for their reception and a mode of sending them hence, there were hundreds, nay thousands of citizens" who would emancipate their slaves.[40]

By colonizing free African Americans, the ACS promised to at least diminish a population group that all society members, whether from the North or South, found especially troublesome. Randolph called this group, alternately, "a great

evil," "a nuisance," and "a bug-bear to every man who feels an inclination to emancipate his slaves."[41] Society officials also stressed that emigration was to be completely voluntary on the part of both the potential African American emigrant,
whether presently free or enslaved, and the potential European American emanci-
pator.[42] They invoked the seemingly universal prejudices of whites against blacks
as a rationale for the latter to emigrate and for the former to help them do so.[43] It
was then with a great deal of optimism that ACS officials memorialized Congress
in the early years of the society to solicit financial support for their cause.[44]

Partly in response to these early ACS memorials, Congress passed a new slave-
trade law in 1819. The new law appropriated $100,000 to fund federal efforts to
suppress American participation in the slave trade and also authorized the federal government to resettle Africans seized from alleged slave traders and smugglers outside the territorial limits of the United States rather than leaving their
fates to the discretion of state authorities.[45] In fact, Georgia's practice of selling
recaptured Africans into slavery and the ACS's "rescue" of a group of thirty-four
recaptured Africans before Georgia sold them into slavery was one of the catalysts
for the new law.[46] Clearly, Monroe had cogent reasons for placing the $100,000
slave-trade appropriation at the disposal of the society to help it found a colony
on the west coast of Africa for resettling recaptured Africans as well as any African American emigrants whom it might "recruit." For the remainder of Monroe's
two administrations and into the John Quincy Adams administration, Congress
did not attempt to block this practice of indirectly subsidizing the ACS's colonial enterprise, perhaps not surprisingly given how many members of Congress
were also members of the society. Accordingly, the House Select Committee on
the Colonization of Free People of Colour, chaired by ACS Vice President Mercer,
commended Monroe's "just and liberal construction" of the 1819 slave-trade law
in its 1827 report.[47]

However by the time of the Mercer report, the congressional climate had
changed dramatically, and for the worse for the ACS. Partisan divisions, which had
been suppressed during "The Era of Good Feelings," began to reemerge during
Monroe's second administration. These divisions centered on candidates competing to succeed Monroe but also involved competing visions of government that
were either more or less sympathetic to the practice of indirectly subsidizing private organizations, especially organizations that had any relation to slavery. Three
of the five leading candidates to succeed Monroe were or had been vice presidents
of the society: Clay, Crawford, and Jackson. The fact that Jackson formally resigned his ACS vice presidency in 1822 was not coincidental. Nor was the fact that
Crawford and Randolph stopped attending society meetings at this time. These
were signs of the society's increasingly politicized future.[48]

John Quincy Adams' presidential election in 1825 fanned the partisan flames, particularly in light of his opponents' allegations of a corrupt bargain with Clay to secure it. Given that Clay had staked a substantial amount of political capital on the ACS, the emerging Democratic coalition of Jackson and Van Buren adopted a more oppositional stance toward the society. The emerging Democratic coalition was also anchored in the South, and Southern politicians, even those from the upper South, had become more suspicious of the ACS because of its general antislavery stance, however mild that stance might have been. In the wake of the Missouri Crisis and Denmark Vesey conspiracy, Southern members of Congress had also become even more sensitive about any discussion of slavery in Congress, which ACS requests for federal support inevitably provoked. Some Southern members of Congress were also opposed to strengthening the federal government for fears that a stronger federal government would act to abolish slavery. The practice of indirectly subsidizing the ACS looked like an action a stronger federal government would take. Federal retrenchment became the new watchword of many Southern politicians, especially those who joined the new Democratic coalition. The ACS proved to be an easy Democratic target because its success in resettling African Americans in Liberia and in raising money from private sources was not very impressive. Meanwhile, in this increasingly hostile political environment, the Adams administration continued the previous administration's policy of indirectly subsidizing the society's colonization project.[49]

With the opposition firmly in control of Congress after the 1826 midterm elections, the Senate Committee on Foreign Relations, chaired by Senator Littleton Waller Tazewell (Virginia), wrote a decidedly more negative report on African colonization than the Mercer report of the previous Congress. Without mentioning Monroe's "just and liberal construction" of the 1819 slave-trade law, the Tazewell report questioned how the federal government could constitutionally aid African colonization in any form. Sounding the watchwords of limited government, enumerated powers, and states rights, this 1828 report insisted that "the framers of the Constitution most wisely abstained from bestowing upon the [federal] government . . . any power whatever over the coloured population of the United States . . . whether this population was bond or free." In its conclusion, the report drew attention to the apparent conflict of interest created by the fact that so many members of the federal government were also members of the ACS.[50]

The next year Jackson succeeded John Quincy Adams as president of the United States. He cut off the ACS's federal funding after Kendall's 1830 audit found that the federal government had spent $264,710 over the previous decade to help the society resettle 260 recaptured Africans in Liberia, which seemed, at least to Kendall, a prodigious waste of money. Kendall also explicitly criticized Monroe for his diversion of slave-trade appropriations to the society. He praised the society's benevolent purposes in attempting to lessen the evils of slavery and suppress the slave trade, but he believed that it should pursue those purposes by strictly private means. Kendall went on to characterize Liberia as an official American colony, and inappropriately so. He argued that "the terms of the [1819 slave-trade] act were hardly sufficient to authorize the *establishment of a colony*, owing allegiance to the United States, and entitled to [its] protection." Kendall then listed the many ways that the federal government had assisted the society's colonization project as he questioned the authority of its agent for recaptured Africans to "*colonize them, to build houses for them, to furnish them with farming utensils, to pay instructers* [sic] *to teach them, to purchase ships for their convenience, to build forts for their protection, to supply them with arms and munitions of war, to enlist troops to guard them, or to employ the army or navy in their defense.*"[51]

Clay and Mercer, now members of the emerging anti-Jackson Whig coalition in Congress, continued to introduce bills to indirectly fund the ACS in ever more innovative ways. None of those attempts succeeded. In 1833, with the Whigs holding a congressional majority, Congress approved a Clay-sponsored bill that would have linked state funding of African colonization to the redistribution of the surplus revenues from public-land sales. Jackson vetoed the bill.[52]

By the mid-1830s, the congressional efforts to fund the ACS had ceased, and the society had decided to stop asking for federal support because such efforts seemed so futile.[53] When Clay became the society's president in 1836, he could not even convince Congress to grant it a federal charter.[54] Robert Strange (North Carolina Democrat) strongly opposed Clay's motion to refer a memorial to that effect to the Committee on the District of Columbia because it would "hold out to the slave population a desire to become free." While John C. Calhoun (South Carolina Democrat) initially supported the motion, he hoped the committee would not act on the memorial because "the prevailing opinion of the great body of the people of the South was against it." In the end, Calhoun voted with the majority not to take up the memorial. It was tabled, 25–16, in a highly partisan and sectional vote. Whigs voted 10–3 in favor of the motion and Democrats 22–6 in opposition; Northern senators voted 12–9 in favor and Southern senators 16–4 in opposition. All four of the supportive Southern senators represented upper-South states, and three of the four were Whigs.[55]

The rapidly expanding list of ACS vice presidents had also taken on a more partisan cast. In addition to Clay, Mercer, and Webster, several prominent Whig members of Congress were now on the list, including Theodore Frelinghuysen (New Jersey), William C. Rives (Virginia), and Samuel Southard (New Jersey), who had been Monroe's secretary of navy when the navy had offered the society's Liberian colony critical assistance in the early years of its existence.[56] On the

Democratic side, only former Senator Louis McLane (Delaware), who had rotated from Treasury Secretary to Secretary of State, remained an ACS vice president but, unlike most of the Whig vice presidents, he was not active in society affairs.[57]

Outside Congress, public support for the ACS was also on the decline. In the 1820s and into the early 1830s, the society had attracted the support of many of the most powerful antislavery voices in the nation because of its gradualist emancipation rhetoric and also because it seemed "the only game in town" for those opposed to slavery. James Birney, William Lloyd Garrison, William Jay, Amos Phelps, Gerrit Smith, Arthur Tappan, and Theodore Weld all supported African colonization before they became abolitionists.[58] But in 1832 Garrison strongly attacked the colonization movement in his *Thoughts on African Colonization* as a Southern plot to perpetuate the institution of slavery.[59] In 1833, Garrison, Phelps, and Tappan helped organize the American Anti-Slavery Society (AASS) dedicated to the principle of immediate emancipation. Almost overnight, the AASS replaced the ACS as the major antislavery vehicle in the Northern states. Weld and Jay followed Garrison in strongly attacking the colonization movement, the former during the celebrated debates over the expediency of abolitionism at Lane Seminary in Cincinnati in 1834 and the latter in his *Inquiry into the Character and Tendency of the American Colonization and the American Anti-Slavery Societies* in 1835.[60] Under Weld's influence, Birney, a Kentucky slaveholder and the ACS's traveling agent for the lower Mississippi valley, converted to abolitionism. In 1834, he freed his slaves and resigned his position with the society.[61] Birney, in turn, cajoled Gerrit Smith, who had been an ACS vice president and its largest private donor, into leaving the society the next year.[62]

Almost simultaneously, the ACS was also attacked from the other extreme. William & Mary Professor Thomas R. Dew dismissed African colonization as a totally visionary scheme in his review of the historic 1831–1832 debate in the Virginia legislature over the future of slavery in the state. During that debate, the Virginia opponents of slavery, or at least of the disproportionate power of eastern Virginia slaveholders, pushed colonization as their favored antislavery vehicle. The legislature ultimately agreed that the state should promote colonization. It did not, however, immediately appropriate any money for that purpose, nor adopt any other measure to ease manumissions in Virginia.[63] Dew not only insisted that African colonization was a deeply flawed project; he defended slavery in the process as an institution that, at least under the present circumstances, benefited both whites and blacks.[64]

Clay, among other ACS leaders, began to lament the fact that the society was under attack from both extremes and to emphasize the society's neutrality between them. He portrayed its "middle" position as an advantage to the ACS in attracting the support of the vast majority of people in both sections of the coun-try who were neither abolitionists nor defenders of slavery.[65] Yet that advantage was not necessarily an advantage when each extreme claimed that the society was a covert operation of the other. The ACS response was to temper its already tem-perate antislavery rhetoric, which, by its own admission, undercut its appeal in the North without necessarily increasing it in the South, certainly not in the lower South. In 1837, the society's Board of Managers despaired of the future of an orga-nization that "is assaulted by the concentrated power of the Abolitionists on the one side, and very inadequately defended and sustained by its southern friends on the other."[66]

The free African American community played a major role in the transition from colonization to abolition for the Garrison circle.[67] David Walker had pre-ceded Garrison in attacking the ACS in print as a Southern plot to perpetuate slavery.[68] Free blacks were dissuaded from supporting African colonization not only by the fact that Southern slaveholders, such as Clay, Mercer, and Washington, held such prominent positions within the society but by the high mortality rates among the colonists and the negative eyewitness reports that they received regard-ing conditions in Liberia. Few African Americans seemed to consider Africa their natural home. Many still had relatives in slavery whom they would be abandoning if they emigrated to Liberia. Free blacks also seemed disinclined to abandon all hope that slavery would be abolished during their lifetimes.[69]

Some free African Americans supported colonization, beginning with Paul Cuffee, whose explorations of the west coast of Africa as a colonial site had strongly influenced the ACS founders in choosing such a site. More free blacks would probably have emigrated to Liberia if the society had possessed more resources. During the antebellum period, some black leaders, such as Alexander Crummell, Martin Delaney, and Henry Highland Garnet, supported colonization, though not necessarily the ACS's project.[70] Still, by all accounts, including the so-ciety's own, most free blacks did not support colonization.[71] Frederick Douglass, James Forten, and Abraham D. Shadd were among the black leaders who vigor-ously opposed it.[72]

The generally negative response of the free African American community to colonization restricted one potential source of recruits. The other projected source also proved unreliable. Slaves were an unreliable source not only because slaveholders were extremely reluctant to emancipate them under any condition but because even when slaveholders did offer to emancipate them on condition of emigration to Liberia, some refused to accept that Hobson's choice.[73] By the mid-1830s then, with heavy debts, few colonists, and declining public, congressional, and executive support, the ACS seemed a moribund organization.[74] By all appear-ances, the Jackson administration had delegitimized the society's colonization project by cutting off its federal funding, leaving it to languish as a strictly private enterprise. Those appearances were deceptive.

CONTINUING FEDERAL SUPPORT

The ACS and its Liberian colony survived the loss of federal funding, though with tempered expectations of the future. Official society reports of a thriving colony were a case of "it doth protest too much," especially when combined with desperate pleas for private donations to remedy its deteriorating financial situation. The ACS was even placed in the ironic situation of refusing what it once so desperately desired, free African American emigrants. The society simply could not afford to charter any more ships to transport them to Liberia and provide them with subsistence for the six-month "settling in" period.[75] Liberia's African neighbors, who did not always welcome this early instance of Yankee Protestant imperialism, also constantly threatened and occasionally attacked the colony.[76]

Federal assistance helped Liberia through these troubled times. The federal government had a stake in the survival of the colony because it provided a commercial and diplomatic foothold on the west coast of Africa to counteract British influence in the area. Potentially, it could also serve as a point of attack on the slave trade, if the federal government ever decided to make the suppression of the trade a higher priority. Humanitarian reasons and a concern for national reputation also probably carried some weight with federal officials who decided to support a struggling colony of former American slaves. For multiple reasons, Jackson therefore did not follow Kendall's advice to sever all ties with the ACS.[77] His administration continued the practice of partially paying the salary of a colonial agent in Liberia, though at a somewhat reduced rate. It also continued the practice of paying the ACS for resettling recaptured Africans in Liberia. When available, naval vessels protected the colony from attack. Subsequent administrations also provided in-kind subsidies to the colony. Even during this ebb in relations between the federal government and ACS, executive officials still deployed state capacities on behalf of the society's colonization project.

This federal support was particularly significant because while the Jackson and Van Buren administrations were assisting the ACS's colonial project, they were not assisting other private organizations.[78] The Democratic Party's limited-government strictures applied to the ACS and African colonization but apparently in a less holistic way than to other private organizations and purposes because the society's purposes were more directly connected to state purposes. African colonization was another policy area where states rights proved to be a permeable barrier to federal action.

The colonial agent in Liberia was both an ACS and a federal employee. As a federal employee, he supervised the settlement of recaptured Africans in Liberia. In this role, he reported to the Secretary of Navy. As an ACS employee, he supervised the settlement of the other colonists and was also *de facto* governor of the colony. In this role, he reported to the society's Board of Managers and oversaw a locally elected colonial assembly.[79] For performing these roles, he received $800 from the ACS and $1,600 from the federal government.[80] Over time, as the local assembly acquired more authority, the agent's role evolved into a more administrative one. When colonial agent Thomas Buchanan, who was the brother of the future president of the United States, died in 1841, the society appointed Joseph Jenkins Roberts to replace him. Roberts was the first African American colonist to hold the post on a permanent basis.[81] At that point, the federal government saw no need for a colonial agent in Liberia, especially because so few recaptured Africans had been resettled in the colony during the previous decade. The fact that Roberts was black may also have been a factor in this decision. With Liberian independence looming, the ACS urged the federal government to at least appoint a commercial agent to Liberia.[82] After Liberian independence, the federal government appointed such an agent. This agent unofficially served as the American ambassador to Liberia from 1848 until the United States officially recognized its independence in 1862. However, in the interim, both the ACS and federal government remained heavily involved in Liberian affairs, presumably to ensure that "their" colonists were properly treated.[83]

The U.S. navy also remained heavily involved in Liberian affairs, as it had from the very beginning of the colony. Indeed, the colony would not have been established, at least not within the same time frame, without its intervention.

The first group of eighty-six colonists sailed to the west coast of Africa in 1820 aboard the *Elizabeth,* which the Monroe administration had chartered and provisioned with $33,000 in cash from the initial $100,000 slave-trade appropriation. The USS *Cyane* escorted the *Elizabeth* to Africa. Malaria and other tropical diseases took a heavy toll on this first expedition at its temporary location on Sherbro Island. Fifteen colonists died, as did the two U.S. agents and the one ACS agent who headed the expedition. The *Cyane* and another navy vessel, the USS *John Adams,* transported the surviving colonists to the shelter of the British free-black colony of Sierra Leone.[84]

The next year the federal government chartered another ship, the *Nautilus,* to transport a second expedition of thirty-three colonists to Africa along with two new ACS agents and two new U.S. agents. The mission of the two ACS agents was to find and purchase a healthier, permanent colonial site on the mainland and then settle the first two groups of colonists, now both temporarily housed in Sierra Leone, on that site. The agents proceeded to negotiate a treaty with local

African leaders to cede land for a colonial site, but the society's Board of Managers rejected the treaty because of its provisions for a $300 annual tribute to those leaders.[85]

Later that same year the ACS's Board of Managers sent another agent, Eli Ayres, to secure a colonial site. The U.S. navy was integral to his success. Ayres traveled to Africa aboard the USS *Shark,* under the command of a young Lieutenant Matthew Perry (Rhode Island). Once in Sierra Leone, Ayres encountered a group of very restive colonists and was unable to enter into any negotiations to secure a colonial site.[86] Finally, in late 1821 Lieutenant Robert T. Stockton (New Jersey), who had taken a personal interest in the project, convinced the Secretary of Navy, Smith Thompson (New York Democratic Republican), to send him to Africa aboard the USS *Alligator* to secure a colonial site. Together, Ayres and Stockton were able to purchase land in what is now Liberia in exchange for goods valued at a mere $300. The deal was consummated at the point of Stockton's gun.[87]

During the initial years of the colony, U.S. navy vessels remained active in the area, protecting the colony from attack and supplying it with goods from the ACS's $100,000 federal endowment because the society had little money to supply the colony itself.[88] Within a few years, the navy presence in the area dwindled to occasional visits of vessels assigned to the Pacific Squadron en route to and from the Indian Ocean, but even those occasional visits were indicative of the colony's special status in the eyes of federal officials.[89] In 1822, several of the local African leaders who had agreed to the treaty of acquisition seized the opportunity presented by the absence of navy ships to attack the colony. With the colony in imminent danger of destruction, the new colonial agent, Jehudi Ashmun, appealed to both the British and U.S. navies for help.[90] Fortunately for Ashmun and the colonists, a British man-of-war was in the area. British navy personnel joined the colonists in repelling the attackers.[91] Upon receiving word of the attack, Captain Robert T. Spence (New Hampshire) of the *Cyane,* which had recently left Liberia at the end of a long tour of duty, turned the ship around and sailed it back to the colony. By the time the *Cyane* arrived, British navy officers had negotiated a truce, but Spence and his crew built fortifications in Liberia to protect the colony from further attack. The estimated cost of the fortifications was $27,211 in labor and materials.[92]

Navy protection of the colony continued over the next two decades, though without a permanent African squadron, it remained sporadic. When the United States finally agreed to establish such a squadron under the terms of the Webster-Ashburton Treaty in 1842, the ACS was especially well-connected. Both Secretary of State and treaty negotiator Webster and Navy Secretary Upshur were ACS vice presidents, and President John Tyler had been active in the ACS as a delegate from his state society.[93] While initially the squadron was relatively small and had very limited success in capturing suspected slave ships, its presence undoubtedly had some effect not only in inhibiting slave traders and protecting American commerce but also in deterring attacks on Liberia.[94]

The U.S. navy's actions in supplying Liberia with goods and building fortifications in the colony were clear cases of federal in-kind subsidies. In-kind subsidies were a less frequent type of federal assistance than navy protection and government agencies, but they continued nonetheless. The colony received shipments of arms and naval stores in 1839 and 1840 during the Van Buren administration.[95] In 1843, the Tyler administration shipped $1,500 worth of goods for the benefit of the recaptured Africans who lived in their own separate settlement in Liberia, though unfortunately the ship carrying the goods was wrecked at Cape de Verde, where it had first landed to deliver supplies to the African Squadron.[96] These in-kind subsidies occurred during the time of the ACS's greatest financial need, as the Panic of 1837 had sunk the society deeper into debt.[97] The subsidies demonstrated that federal officials, both Democrats and Whigs, had defined the survival of the colony as a national interest. However low a priority they might have given that interest, they assisted the colony, at least when they could and when it did not cost too much. Until independence, the ACS's Liberian colony benefited from this type of indirect federal support. Again, it is impossible to assign an exact value to this support, but the monetary value is not necessarily a true measure of its significance. At the time of his death, the ACS's Board of Managers formally recognized Stockton's inestimable role "in meeting and successfully surmounting the bitter opposition of the natives" to acquire "the territory upon which has arisen . . . the Liberian Republic."[98]

In light of this more favorable political climate, the ACS renewed its appeals for federal support in 1842, ending a twelve-year hiatus. These new appeals placed a greater emphasis on the colony's role in suppressing the slave trade. They also emphasized that the colony served an important national purpose in offering a point of entry to Africa's growing commerce, which, in the ACS's view, the benighted policies of the U.S. government had allowed British merchants to engross at the expense of their American counterparts. Minimally, the society called for appointing a commercial agent to Liberia.[99]

The ACS's new appeals to Congress netted $5,000 in supplemental appropriations for the support of recaptured Africans in Liberia.[100] They also prompted a very sympathetic, and very long, House report.[101] The 1843 report of the House Committee on Commerce, chaired by John Pendleton Kennedy (Maryland Whig), stresses the diplomatic value of the ACS's Liberian colony in countering British (and French) influence in the area and in deterring the slave trade. The report also portrays the colony as a mixed public-private enterprise, "[f]ounded partly by the private enterprise of American citizens and partly by the aid of the Federal and

State authorities."[102] Kennedy acknowledges that "the idea of an American colony is a new one" but, unlike Kendall, he could find "nothing in our Constitution to forbid it." He cited Native American removals as a precedent, noting that "Indian tribes had already been placed beyond the limits of the States, on the purchased territory of the Union." In conclusion, the Kennedy Report recommended that the United States at least establish a commercial agency in Liberia.[103]

Liberia's transition from colony to nation did not materially affect the ACS's agenda. From the society's perspective, it merely signified the difference between a foreign colony and a client state. On behalf of the new nation, society officials thus urged Congress not only to recognize its independence but also to grant it special trading privileges, if for no other reason than to match British initiatives in those areas.[104]

By the time Liberia declared independence, the ACS had retired its old debts under a policy of paying its creditors only half of what they were owed. In fact, the society was in the process of acquiring new debts because of an increase in emigrant applications and a new policy of not refusing them.[105] The early 1850s were the society's halcyon days. The Fugitive Slave Law of 1850 produced a spike in free African American emigration.[106] As an increasing number of the ACS's early supporters died, the society benefited from their monetary bequests and testamentary manumissions.[107] President Millard Fillmore, Secretaries of State Webster and Edward Everett (Massachusetts Whig), Associate Supreme Court Justice James Wayne (Georgia Democrat), Senators Clay and Stephen A. Douglas (Illinois Democrat), and former Secretary of Treasury Robert J. Walker (Mississippi Democrat) were among the dignitaries who attended its annual meetings.[108] Secretary of Treasury Thomas Corwin (Ohio Whig) and Attorney General John Crittenden (Kentucky Whig) were also active in the society.[109] The new "friendly" Secretary of Navy was John Pendleton Kennedy.[110]

When Franklin Pierce succeeded Fillmore as president of the United States in 1853, the new Democratic administration remained friendly to the ACS, though not as friendly as the previous Whig administration. Pierce himself became a life director of the ACS in 1854 when $1,000 was donated to the society on his behalf. Secretary of State William Marcy (New York Democrat) was a longtime ACS vice president.[111] Revenues and emigrant applications also continued to rise.[112] More state governments became active in funding various colonization projects. By the end of the Pierce administration, a total of eight state governments—Maryland, Virginia, Connecticut, Pennsylvania, Indiana, New Jersey, Missouri, and Kentucky—had appropriated funds either to establish a separate colony or settlement in Liberia or to defray the costs of colonizing African Americans from their own states. Six of those initiatives were launched during the Fillmore and Pierce administrations.[113]

At the 1854 annual meeting, Associate Supreme Court Justice and ACS Vice President Wayne delivered a full-blown constitutional defense of African colonization. In his speech, Wayne contends that the United States had colonized Africa under its powers to suppress the slave trade and regulate interstate commerce and that it could acquire territory for such a colony under either the treaty-making or war powers. He finally invokes the general welfare clause of Article I, section 8, as the broadest constitutional warrant for African colonization.[114] Voicing assumptions widely shared among the ACS membership, the former Democratic congressman explains that "there is a great constitutional conservative obligation upon the National Government to remove a national evil [free blacks], when it presses upon the general welfare of the United States, and when it can be done without interfering with the rights of private property, or with those institutions [slavery] allowed by the states, and which were meant to be guarded by the constitution of the United States." Repeating an analogy that by 1854 was well tested, Wayne insists that the federal government had exactly the same authority to colonize African Americans as it had to remove Native Americans.[115]

Yet, beneath the surface, the ACS confronted some perennial problems. In 1844, the House Committee on Foreign Affairs responded very differently to a new round of colonization memorials from the society and "other parties" than the Committee on Commerce had the previous year. Chaired by South Carolina Democrat Robert Barnwell Rhett, the committee not only tabled the memorials but begged to be relieved of considering any future ones.[116] The ACS did not formally petition Congress again until the Civil War.[117] The United States also did not recognize Liberian independence or grant it special trading privileges until the war, though it did (belatedly) appoint a commercial agent in 1848.[118] Even more than Haiti, the other black republic that the United States refused to recognize, Liberia remained in official limbo.[119] In 1852, Liberian President Roberts acknowledged the reality that formal American recognition of his nation was unlikely as long as the institution of slavery continued to exist in the United States, though he had once hoped that "notwithstanding the peculiar institution of that country, that it would have been among the first . . . to welcome Liberia among the family of nations."[120]

The ACS attempted to inoculate itself from the divisive effects of the broader public disputes over slavery by professing an apparent neutrality on the issue. At its 1852 annual meeting, the Reverend Philip Slaughter, representing the Virginia state society, introduced a resolution "that the publication of schemes of emancipation, and arguments in their favor, in the *African Repository,* and other official documents of this Society, is a departure from our fundamental law, and should be excluded from such documents." The resolution was adopted.[121] At the 1855 annual meeting, Slaughter introduced a further resolution that the ACS's Board

of Managers should preapprove speakers at the society's annual meetings in order
to exclude "all suggestions and discussions of schemes of emancipation" from its
proceedings. This resolution was also adopted.[122] Such efforts were pyrrhic. When
Senator and future ACS Vice President Douglas pushed his Kansas-Nebraska bill
through Congress in 1854, the ensuing political realignment sent the society into
another tailspin.[123] Ironically, it was the slave-trade connection that temporarily
revived the ACS's flagging fortunes.

INCREASING FEDERAL SUPPORT

The connection between African colonization and the suppression of the slave
trade was indirectly the predominant source of the ACS's federal funding.[124] Monroe's interpretation of the 1819 slave-trade law had forged that connection and initially sent money flowing through it. The establishment of the African Squadron
in 1843 had reforged the connection. Buchanan's midterm decisions to enter into a
formal agreement with the ACS to resettle and care for recaptured Africans in Liberia and to fortify the African and Home squadrons for slave-trade suppression
sent new money flowing through it. Federal officials were reminded of the reasons
that the federal government had originally supported the society's colonization
project as a repository for recaptured Africans.[125] The United States thus resuscitated its tripartite colonial relationship with the ACS and Liberia, at least until
the end of the Civil War, which Lincoln's wartime decision to finally recognize
Liberian independence did nothing to belie.

In his 1830 audit, Kendall claimed that 260 recaptured Africans had been resettled in Liberia during the 1820s at a cost of $264,710. In making that calculation,
he did not try to separate the costs of resettling recaptured Africans in Liberia
from the costs of assisting the ACS's colonization enterprise in other ways, nor
did he try to separate expenditures on African colonization from expenditures on
the navy's efforts to suppress the slave trade off the west coast of Africa. Even if he
had attempted to distinguish those different types of federal expenditures, Kendall
would have found it very difficult to do so. The two policies of African colonization and slave-trade suppression were and would remain so interconnected that
he would have found it difficult to distinguish their costs. Given that the ACS and
federal government did not establish any specific arrangement to pay any specific amount for resettling recaptured Africans in Liberia until 1858, he would have
found it impossible to calculate those precise costs. Of course, it made good press to
declare, as former newspaper editor Kendall did, that they were $1,000 per capita.[126]

Beginning in the early 1820s and continuing into the 1840s, navy activity off the
west coast of Africa remained sporadic. The U.S. navy captured only one suspected

slave ship, with no Africans aboard, off the African coast from 1823 through 1844.[127] Two sets of Africans seized elsewhere were, however, resettled in Liberia over those years. In 1835, the ACS received $4,400 for the thirty-six recapturedAfricans from the *Fenix* who were resettled in the colony, slightly more than $120 per capita.[128] The other case involved two African children whom a navy captain, Caleb Miller (Connecticut), had attempted to smuggle into the United States, apparently for his own personal use. In 1836, the ACS received $200 to resettle them in Liberia.[129] Interestingly, both these federal payments occurred during the "unfriendly" Jackson administration.

The creation of a permanent African Squadron promised to end this period of relative inactivity. The new squadron enjoyed an initial success in 1845 when it captured the *Pons* with approximately 900 Africans aboard. In this case, the ACS had to petition Congress repeatedly to be reimbursed the costs of the care of the 756 *Pons* Africans who were resettled in Liberia. The society finally received $37,800 in 1852, only $50 per capita.[130]

The U.S. navy did not seize another slave-laden ship until 1858. By then, the ACS was in the midst of another downturn. Despite its increasingly ecumenical rhetoric, the sectional divisions over slavery had crippled its fundraising efforts. The society no longer had any active agents in the South.[131] Only seven state auxiliaries were represented at its 1858 annual meeting. Three of those auxiliaries were from New England (Connecticut, Massachusetts, and Maine), three from the lower North (New Jersey, New York, and Ohio), and only one was from the (upper) South (Virginia).[132] The last state to fund a colonization initiative was Kentucky in 1856.[133] Both free blacks and white slaveholders in the Southern states were proving increasingly reluctant to employ the ACS's "services."[134] The geographic base of the society had shifted dramatically within a relatively short period of time. Whatever future prospects the society had, they now seemed dependent on the support of blacks and whites who were most removed from the effects of slavery.[135]

This downturn ended when the Home Squadron's USS *Dolphin* captured the *Echo* off the coast of Cuba with 318 Africans aboard in August 1858 and landed them at Charleston. By the close of the year, President Buchanan had entered into a formal arrangement with the ACS to reimburse it for the costs of resettling the *Echo* Africans in Liberia and appointed the society's colonial agent, John Seys, the new U.S. agent for recaptured Africans.[136] Buchanan had also decided to reinforce both the African and Home squadrons for slave-trade suppression, at least doubling the size of each squadron.[137]

As we saw in the last chapter, a number of political, diplomatic, and personal factors motivated Buchanan's decision to make the suppression of the slave trade a national priority. One personal motive was directly related to the African colonization movement. Buchanan's brother had literally dedicated his life to the movement. Buchanan's Secretary of Navy, Isaac Toucey (Connecticut Democrat), was another "friendly" Navy Secretary who had been active in the ACS as a delegate from his state auxiliary as well as a member of its Board of Managers.[138] The African Squadron's longest-serving Northern navy secretary, Toucey, may also have influenced Buchanan's decision. Regardless of his motives, the effects of Buchanan's decision were almost immediate. Within a one-year period, from April 26, 1860, to April 21, 1861, navy vessels assigned to the African and Home squadrons combined to capture nine slave-laden ships with a total of more than 5,300 Africans aboard.[139]

The Civil War ended this activity as abruptly as it began. However, throughout the war, the Africans who had been seized from these nine ships and resettled in Liberia were a financial boon to the ACS because of the federal contracts it received for their first year's care. In fact, the Liberian government thought that the arrangement was so profitable to the ACS that it pressured the society into transferring the responsibility for fulfilling the contracts to it.[140] Under this new arrangement, the ACS became, in effect, a third-party auditor of the contracts, transmitting the money it received from the U.S. government to the Liberian government on satisfaction that the latter was properly caring for the recaptured Africans. The society charged Seys with monitoring the performance of the Liberian government in this regard.[141] In return, the ACS received 2.5 percent of the transferred funds in fees.[142] On the federal side, this new arrangement entailed more money and greater responsibilities for the Department of Interior, which oversaw the disbursement of the funds and monitored Seys's performance of his own duties. Whether or not the arrangement was profitable to either the ACS or Liberia or advantageous to the United States, it was a perfect demonstration of how even after Liberian independence the three parties remained locked together in an unofficial colonial relationship.

The process of financing this massive resettlement of recaptured Africans in Liberia was not only very complicated but expensive.[143] The federal government owed the ACS $150 per capita for the first year's care of the *Echo* captives under the original arrangement with Buchanan. Though Congress reduced that sum to $100 per capita for the subsequent captures, the initial three Home Squadron seizures proved more expensive because the recaptured Africans were first landed on Key West to await transport to Liberia.[144] To cover the costs associated with the *Echo* capture, Congress appropriated $30,000 in FY1859.[145] After the first Home Squadron seizure in FY1860, Congress appropriated another $250,000.[146] It also mandated that in the future recaptured Africans should be transported directly to Liberia in order to save money.[147] Home Squadron vessels had, however, already seized two more slave-laden ships in Cuban waters and landed the recaptured Africans on Key West. The African Squadron then began to seize slave-laden ships with alacrity, a total of six with more than 3,900 Africans aboard during FY1861. Congress made two appropriations of $900,000 each in FY1861 to cover the costs of this second round of seizures and any shortfall from the earlier seizures.[148]

Congress did not earmark the FY1860–FY1861 appropriations solely to pay the ACS and Liberian government for the care of recaptured Africans. As had been the case since the beginning of its relationship with the federal government, the federal funds that the society received for the care of recaptured Africans were appropriated to support the suppression of the slave trade. Congress thus intended the FY1860–FY1861 appropriations to cover all the costs associated with the multiple slave-ship seizures during those two fiscal years, including the increased operating costs of the African and Home squadrons, the costs of caring for the Key West Africans before they were transported to Liberia, the costs of transporting them to Liberia, the costs of the bounties navy crews received for recaptured Africans, as well as the costs of the first year's care of the surviving recaptured Africans in Liberia.[149]

Once again, the now-official connection between African colonization and the suppression of the slave trade makes it difficult to track the amount of money that the federal government spent on each purpose. Because many of the recaptured Africans, especially the *Echo* and Key West Africans, died at various points along the time line between when they were captured and what would have been the end of their first year in Liberia, it is not even clear how much money the federal government owed the ACS. Tragically as many as 1,000, or more than one sixth, of the FY1859–FY1861 recaptured Africans died before they could be landed in Liberia.[150] If one calculates how much the federal government owed the society based on how many recaptured Africans were landed in Liberia, the society should have received approximately $30,000 for the approximately 200 surviving *Echo* Africans and approximately $450,000 for the approximately 4,500 surviving Africans from the nine FY1860–FY1861 seizures, for a total of roughly $480,000.[151] The ACS actually received $32,500 for the *Echo* Africans and $349,823 for the remainder, an apparent shortfall of roughly $100,000.[152] By the end of 1861, it had received $201,303 of that total. The ACS also received an additional $54,351 for transporting the Key West Africans to Liberia. From the beginning of 1859 to the end of 1861, the society's federal receipts were $255,654.[153]

Regardless of how much more federal money the ACS and Liberian government deserved for resettling recaptured Africans in Liberia from 1859 through 1861, the two parties received a substantial amount. The $255,654 total represented 63.2 percent of the society's receipts for those three years and 14.7 percent of its receipts for the whole 1819–1861 period.[154] From the standpoint of ACS officials, recaptured Africans became an unexpectedly large source of colonists, surpassing the number of free African American emigrants and almost equaling the number of African Americans who immigrated to Liberia as a condition of their emancipation. The society's fiftieth anniversary figures were 5,722 recaptured Africans, 4,541 free blacks, and 5,957 liberated slaves.[155] More than three quarters of the first group were from the nine FY1860–FY1861 seizures.

This transatlantic financial arrangement resuscitated, at least temporarily, the colonial relationship that had long existed between the United States and Liberia. It was a relationship that ACS officials had not only strongly promoted but also personally mediated. During the Civil War, Seys was the pivot of that triad as he took his responsibilities seriously—some would say too seriously—in monitoring the performance of the Liberian government in its treatment of its new residents.[156] His intrusiveness into the affairs of an independent nation (which was finally recognized by the United States as such in 1862) hardly befitted its sovereignty. Imagine the consequences if Liberia had assigned an agent to the United States to monitor its treatment of African Americans on grounds that they were potential émigrés, especially if that agent had been granted the power to withhold foreign aid. But then Liberia was still considered an American dependency.

CONCLUSION

The American state's episode with African colonization would have been less likely if, counterfactually, slavery had been abolished in the United States prior to the formation of the ACS in 1816. In this alternative history, any African American removal policy would have seemed overwhelming for either private or public resources or even both together. The marginal removal policy that the early American state pursued through a mixture of private and public resources made the most sense to a group of racially prejudiced state actors in a country where slavery continued to exist, where there were relatively few freed slaves, and where they could frame the policy, to themselves and others, as part of a benevolent enterprise to establish an overseas colony on behalf of those freed slaves.[157]

In the nation's real history, Monroe's interpretation of the 1819 slave-trade law initiated the special relationship that would develop between the federal government and the ACS's colonization project. The consequences of that special relationship were profound. Unofficially, Liberia was the first U.S. overseas colony; that fact alone dwarfs in significance the amount of money that the federal government spent on the enterprise. Under the ACS's tutelage, Liberia's colonial government mimicked the U.S. territorial structure. Like territorial governors, the society's colonial agent had veto power over laws passed by the local assembly and was responsible to an outside authority, in his case both the society and federal government.[158] Under the ACS's tutelage, Liberia's colonial government evolved toward independence in the same way that U.S. territories evolved toward state-hood, with the local assembly acquiring more powers, including the power to override gubernatorial vetoes, and the local electorate gaining the ability to se-lect a wider range of local officials.[159] Not surprisingly, the first national Liberian constitution was modeled after the U.S. constitution, even adopting its federal structure.[160]

Early in the history of the colony, former Senator and ACS Vice President Harper explained its special status. He insisted that "I do not wish to see in Af-rica a colonial government, permanently attached to the United States . . . but I wish to see the paternal arm of authority stretched out for the protection of this colony, until it shall be able to manage its own affairs, legislative, judicial, and executive."[161] According to Harper, the final result was to be independence, not statehood, but until then the paternal model applied with even more force in the Liberian case than it did in the case of official U.S. territories.[162]

Prior to independence, supportive federal officials indirectly funded the ACS as their colonial mechanism, just as supportive European officials indirectly funded private companies as their colonial mechanisms.[163] This mixed public-private model offered federal officials a means to stretch tight resources as well as to pursue controversial projects. The least controversial rationale for African colonization was to connect the enterprise to the suppression of the slave trade, which was why society officials increasingly stressed that rationale.[164] After ACS President Clay declared at the 1851 annual meeting that "all hearts are united—not only all American hearts, but all the hearts of Christendom are united on the pro-priety of suppressing that odious traffic in slaves with Africa," he thus congratu-lated the society that "we have shown the most effectual and complete method by which there can be an end put to that abominable traffic, and that is by Coloniza-tion."[165] African colonization also advanced several other national purposes that sustained the special relationship between the federal government and the ACS's colonization project when sectional and partisan divisions had blocked further federal funding for the project and federal officials did not consider slave-trade suppression a priority.

The multiple rationales for African colonization make this a complicated case. Yet two conclusions seem warranted. First, without the slave-trade connection, the project would have enjoyed less federal support. Second, without African colo-nization fulfilling other national purposes, the project would have enjoyed less sustained federal support.

The special relationship that was cemented between the United States and Li-beria before the Civil War continued after the war. While that relationship ap-pears to have seriously deteriorated in recent decades, former President George W. Bush still visited Liberia on his 2008 African tour. ACS and federal officials did not envision that Liberia would become a permanent American colony, much less an American state, but they did envision that Liberia would be permanently attached to the United States as a former colony. Liberian colonization also anticipated subsequent American colonial efforts. Hawaii was a later case where private entrepreneurs pressed federal officials into an overseas colonial venture, though in this case statehood was, somewhat unexpectedly, the final result.[166]

The African colonization policy area also demonstrates that the interests of state actors are not necessarily coincident with the interests of the private actors that their actions are intended to promote. From this perspective, the case is a complicated one because the relevant state actors and private actors were often the same people. The Tazewell report depicts this interpenetration of state and society as a conflict of interest. Still, in this policy area, all the relevant state actors and private actors had to converge on a common subset of rationales for African colonization, despite the very real partisan and sectional differences that existed over the issue. Furthermore, the interpenetration of state and society in this policy area was hardly unique during a period of time when the institutional development of the American state was only beginning and public and private business were not clearly distinguished. We observe the same interpenetration in the slave-trade policy area, as when politically well-connected lawyers profited shamelessly from litigating slave-trade cases. Even in the highly institutionalized American state of the twenty-first century, this interpenetration occurs, as when Department of Defense officials hire politically well-connected private contractors to rebuild occupied nations.

Together, the slave-trade and African-colonization policy areas show that the federal government was involved both in encouraging black emigration from the United States and in discouraging black immigration into the United States during the 1819–1861 period. In opposing continued federal support of the ACS's colonization project, the Tazewell report suggests that "if Congress were now . . . to invite and encourage the emigration or transportation of that particular class of persons [slaves], whose introduction into the States they were at first expressly prohibited from preventing," it would violate not only states rights but common sense.[167] Retrospectively, it is very difficult not to see racism as the "common sense" behind both policies, in addition to whatever humanitarian purposes they were intended to serve.[168] The strong racist overtones of the ACS's colonization project explains why state actors have not appealed to it as a precedent for later public-private ventures, any more than they would appeal to Native American removal as a precedent for later rural-development programs.

The African colonization policy area did not have as great an impact on state development during the 1791–1861 period as the slave-trade policy area did. Nevertheless, to the extent that the U.S. navy was involved in founding, protecting, and populating Liberia, the early American state deployed its capacities on behalf of a private organization. Federal employees, goods, and dollars also helped the ACS maintain its Liberian colony. The project had, in turn, measurable effects on the development of both the Departments of Navy and Interior. The U.S. navy first became involved in the suppression of the African slave trade at its source because of the ACS's colonial enterprise. The Interior Department then took over the primary responsibility for this policy area in 1858, including responsibility for the disposition of the Africans whom navy crews seized from suspected slave ships. African colonization was part of an effort not only to control the nation's borders but to shape its domestic population. While the effects were minimal with respect to the second purpose, the society certainly had grandiose designs as to how it wanted to shape the domestic population. The ACS's goal of creating a "whites only" republic is now hopelessly anachronistic, and thankfully so.

The African colonization policy area also had a different impact on federal authority and legitimacy during the 1791–1861 period than the slave-trade policy area did. As both the Tazewell and Kendall reports underscored, the authority of the federal government to assist the ACS in its colonization efforts always remained suspect. The slave-trade policies of the American state were much different in this respect because they were matters of constitutional authorization. Not coincidentally, those policies were probably also viewed as more legitimate policies by a broader spectrum of the American public, even in the lower South. This difference helps explain why the African colonization policies of the early American state were even more executive-driven than its slave-trade policies were. Congress did not finally establish an official African-colonization policy until 1860, almost exactly forty years after federal money had first begun flowing to the ACS and more than sixty years after it had passed its first slave-trade legislation. Even then, colonization subsidies were indirect subsidies. Partisan and sectional differences were clearly much stronger in this policy area than in the slave-trade policy area, which helps explain why executive officials used slave-trade suppression as a means to subsidize African colonization.

Despite the controversial nature of the ACS's Liberian enterprise, the federal government eventually deployed its coercive powers on behalf of the project. The U.S. navy transported recaptured Africans to Liberia whether they desired to settle in Liberia or not. Again in relation to the slave-trade policy area, the effects of these coercive efforts might seem modest. Liberia had no "fugitive African" laws. Recaptured Africans could always filter back to their native lands or settle elsewhere. On the other hand, the Liberian government did offer $3 rewards for recovering recaptured Africans who had fled their host families during the 1860–1861 surge in their numbers.[169]

The United States, of course, had fugitive-slave laws. Fugitive-slave laws seemed to work at cross-purposes both with slave-trade laws and African colonization in keeping blacks "in" rather than keeping or pushing them "out." From the standpoint of Southern slaveholders, the common sense behind these three policies was that they targeted different blacks to keep "in" than they targeted to keep or push "out."

4. The Slave-Catching Republic

Federal officials actively assisted Southern slaveholders in recovering their fugitive slaves or in receiving compensation for their slave losses during the 1791–1861 period. By focusing only on fugitive-slave renditions that fell under fugitive-slave law, politics and history scholars, such as Stanley Campbell, Thomas Morris, and Karen Orren, miss the full significance of this policy area for early American state development.[1] Long before the 1850s, when federal officials first became active in fugitive-slave renditions under the Fugitive Slave Law of 1850, they had been active in assisting Southern slaveholders in recovering their fugitive slaves or in receiving compensation for their slave losses in other ways. After all, slaves did not only escape to other American states or territories. They also fled to other nations, including Native American nations, and to the colonies of other nations.

Fugitive-slave recoveries involved federal officials in disputes not only with state and territorial officials but also with the leaders of other communities to which the slaves of Southern slaveholders had fled or been taken by the members of those communities. International fugitive-slave disputes were sometimes settled by public diplomacy and sometimes by armed conflict, and sometimes they were not settled at all. Regardless of the outcome, federal officials marshaled human and fiscal resources to attempt to settle them. The federal government acted as the extended arm of Southern slaveholders in both domestic and international fugitive-slave disputes during the 1791–1861 period as U.S. attorneys, justices, commissioners, marshals, diplomats, soldiers, and Indian agents became increasingly active in recovering fugitive slaves and in ensuring compensation in cases where they were not recovered.

This policy area has multiple dimensions with multiple chronologies. Somewhat artificially, I divide my discussion of the policy area into fugitive-slave renditions under fugitive-slave law and fugitive-slave recoveries by other, extralegal means. I then subdivide the latter discussion into fugitive-slave recoveries involving relations with European nations and colonies or former colonies and those involving relations with Native American nations, particularly the five "civilized" nations of the American South. Each of those five nations—Cherokees, Chickasaws, Choctaws, Creeks, and Seminoles—were slaveholding nations and were encouraged by federal officials to mimic the slaveholding patterns of the European Americans who were settling on their lands as one mark of their "civilization." For example, acting Indian agent Captain John R. Bell (New York) reported to Congressman Thomas Metcalfe (Kentucky Democratic Republican) in 1822 that the

Seminoles owned approximately 300 slaves, adding that "the duties of this agency will be, among other things, . . . to use, in the best possible manner, every means that shall tend to make them cultiv[at]ors assisted by their slaves."[2]

This policy area was the site of major federal activity and state development. Again, we miss the full significance of the policy area if we focus only on its domestic, legal dimensions. The fugitive-slave clause of the U.S. Constitution signaled a shift in authority from the state governments to the federal government, but that authority shift was ineffectual until it received the strong statutory support of the Fugitive Slave Law of 1850. In the meantime, U.S. attorneys, justices, commissioners, marshals, diplomats, soldiers, and Indian agents were active in fugitive-slave cases involving other nations. Private citizens also served the American state in this policy area as auxiliary soldiers, deputy marshals, legal counsel, jurors, witnesses, jailers, doctors, as well as members of mixed commissions and armed posses. Like slave-trade cases, fugitive-slave cases affected U.S. relations with major European colonial powers, particularly Great Britain and Spain. They also precipitated military conflicts with powerful Native American nations.

When Congress enacted the Fugitive Slave Law of 1850, it strengthened the offices of U.S. marshals and commissioners. In 1853, it then transferred the supervisory authority over marshals from the Department of State to the Attorney General's office, an important step in their transition from clerks to lawmen.[3] This policy episode was also an important step in the creation of autonomous federal law-enforcement agencies. It curtailed the need for federal officials to rely on the police powers of state governments and the "self-help" efforts of private citizens.[4] During the 1850s, federal law-enforcement officials vigorously enforced the new law. Yet well before then, the federal government had projected the image of a strong state in this policy area in pursuing fugitive-slave and slave-loss cases with other nations.

The durable shift in governing authority in this policy area did not only involve the constitutional powers of Congress under the fugitive-slave clause of the U.S. Constitution. It also involved the constitutional powers of the executive departments over military affairs and foreign relations, including relations with Native American nations.[5] Throughout the 1791–1861 period, federal officials asserted those powers to protect slavery. The implementation of the Fugitive Slave Law of 1850 was only the pinnacle of that effort.

This policy area is also significant because it directly contravenes the traditional view that Southern slaveholders desired a weak state. To the contrary, Southern slaveholders insisted on adding a fugitive-slave clause to the proposed constitution in 1787. Southern slaveholders demanded statutory action that obligated state officials to extradite fugitive slaves in 1793 and again in 1817. Southern slaveholders protested the Jay Treaty in 1795 when John Jay (New York Federalist) abandoned their Revolutionary War slave claims against the British in the treaty negotiations. After the War of 1812, Southern slaveholders exhorted the federal government not to abandon their slave claims against the British from that war. Southern slaveholders pressured federal officials, in turn, to pressure British officials in Canada and the West Indies, Spanish officials in Florida and Mexico, and then Mexican officials in an independent Mexico to extradite fugitive slaves who had escaped to their lands. Southern slaveholders secured fugitive-slave clauses in treaties with Native American nations that obligated the members of those nations to return slaves who had fled to their lands. Southern slaveholders lobbied federal officials to enforce those treaty obligations even to the point of armed conflict and westward removal. Southern slaveholders pushed for a stronger federal fugitive-slave law during the 1840s. After Congress passed such a law in 1850, Southern slaveholders urged federal officials to vigorously enforce it in a way that seemed to violate not only due process but also states rights. When they felt that federal officials were not adequately fulfilling their constitutional obligations under the law, Southern slaveholders strongly supported the secession of their states from the union in 1860.[6] However else Southern slaveholders might have been champions of states rights and a weak central state for fear that a powerful federal government would act to abolish slavery, they were *not* champions of states rights and a weak central state when a powerful federal government could act to protect slavery.

In the fugitive-slave policy area, Southern slaveholders betrayed little heterogeneity of interest.[7] They demanded the extraterritoriality of state laws that established their rights as slaveholders. While scholars have long recognized this demand in the unsuccessful Southern campaign for a territorial slave code, they have not sufficiently recognized it in the case of fugitive-slave law.[8] In this policy area, Southern slaveholders were much more successful. At least from the perspective of federal officials, Southern law followed Southern slaves wherever they escaped, whether to Northern states, U.S. territories, European colonies or former colonies, or Native American lands. Ironically, Southern law did not follow Southern slaves wherever they moved with their masters, though the *Dred Scott* decision portended such a result.[9]

Given the legal, political, and diplomatic significance of this policy area, the total federal expenditures on fugitive-slave renditions and recoveries grossly undervalues its importance. Most of the expenditures were on a case-by-case basis and, individually, quite small. Moreover, I was able to find records of such expenditures only in a limited number of cases, so that it made little sense to aggregate the expenditures I found or could reasonably estimate. Still, those expenditures suggest that the total was not insignificant.[10]

Federal officials would probably not have been active in this policy area if slavery had not continued to exist in the United States. They might have been active in returning fugitive slaves who had fled from places where slavery still existed (assuming it still existed in other places), but, even then, they might have adopted the attitude of British colonial officials and refused to return fugitive slaves. In either case, fugitive-slave renditions and recoveries would have been, at most, incidental forms of federal activity and peripheral to state development. With the continuing existence of slavery in the United States, the case was different. Taken in the aggregate, fugitive-slave renditions and recoveries were not incidental forms of federal activity. They prompted the development of executive and judicial institutions that would probably not have developed in the absence of slavery, at least not within the same time frame. They also had significant effects on both the authority and legitimacy of the federal government. Finally, they strongly influenced the ways that the federal government deployed its coercive powers and other state capacities.

FUGITIVE-SLAVE RENDITIONS

In 1787, the delegates to the Constitutional Convention added a fugitive-slave clause to the proposed constitution near the end of their proceedings, almost as an afterthought, at the insistence of South Carolina delegate Pierce Butler. Unlike the slave-trade clause, the fugitive-slave clause was subject to hardly any convention debate, perhaps because Congress had recently included a similar clause in the Northwest Ordinance.[11] Roger Sherman (Connecticut) objected to Butler's original motion because he "saw no more propriety in the public seizing and surrendering a slave or servant than a horse." James Wilson (Pennsylvania) objected on the grounds that it would be expensive for the state governments to enforce.[12]

Butler's original motion had analogized fugitive slaves to criminals.[13] The placement of the clause in the Constitution immediately following the section on criminal extraditions from one state to another also suggests that the convention delegates thought the process would work the same way in the two cases. Butler's amended motion that fugitive slaves should not be discharged from labor "in consequence of any regulation subsisting in the state to which they escape" signaled the intent of the clause.[14] He sought to establish a constitutional norm against the interference of either the officials or residents of free states with the efforts of Southern slaveholders to recover fugitive slaves on the grounds that slavery had no legal existence in their states. The convention delegates approved Butler's amended motion without objection.[15] The question of how active the state governments should be in helping slaveholders recover their fugitive slaves was apparently an open question in the minds of most of the delegates, though Wilson's initial objection assumed that they would be active in enforcing the clause.

However, it is highly unlikely that the delegates contemplated any active federal role in the process.[16]

The fugitive-slave clause also generated less debate in the state ratifying conventions than the slave-trade clause did. Both James Madison in Virginia and Charles Cotesworth Pinckney in South Carolina pointed to the clause as reassurance to Southern slaveholders that they had nothing to fear from the new federal government. Pinckney noted that "we have obtained a right to recover our slaves in whatever part of America they may take refuge, which is a right we had not before."[17]

Congress enacted a fugitive-slave law on February 12, 1793, that reflected an expansive interpretation of the fugitive-slave clause of the Constitution, but only after both houses of Congress had rejected bills that reflected much more expansive interpretations of the clause.[18] The new law was a response to a political impasse that included both criminal-extradition and fugitive-slave aspects. This impasse occurred when Virginia Governor Beverley Randolph refused to honor a request from Pennsylvania Governor Thomas Mifflin to extradite three Virginians charged with kidnapping John Davis from Pennsylvania and returning him to slavery in Virginia.[19] After failing to resolve the impasse, President Washington turned the matter over to Congress for statutory clarification.

The resulting law contained sections on both fugitive slaves and criminal extraditions. In fact, the initial House bill treated the two cases as identical. The bill would have required state and local officials to assist in the recovery of persons fleeing from either justice or slavery on the request of either governors or slaveholders. The bill, though, failed to receive a third reading in the House, and legislative activity shifted to the Senate.[20] The initial Senate bill was similar to the failed House bill. However, before it was finally approved by the chamber, the Senate bill was heavily amended to strip it of any implication that state and local officials had to assist slaveholders in recovering their fugitive slaves. These amendments opened a gap between fugitive-slave and criminal-extradition cases. In its final form, as approved by both houses of Congress, the new law left the recovery process largely in the hands of slaveholders themselves. The only stipulation was that they or their agents had to secure a court-approved certificate of removal before transporting the person they claimed as a fugitive slave from one state to another. Members of Congress envisioned a largely passive role for both the federal and state governments in the recovery process, which was one of the suppositions of a final Senate amendment that added penalties for state and local officials who interfered with the efforts of Southern slaveholders to recover fugitive slaves.

The Fugitive Slave Law of 1793 certainly "leaned South" in favoring the claims of slaveholders over the rights of African Americans, whether escaped slaves or not. Nevertheless, the law leaned less South than both the original House and

Senate bills, and over time slaveholders were to find its "self-help" provisions unsatisfactory.

In 1817, Southern congressmen attempted to change this situation. Again, legislative action started in the House. A special committee consisting of Richard Clough Anderson (Kentucky Democratic Republican), Philemon Beecher (Ohio Democratic Republican), and James Pindall (Virginia Federalist) reported a bill that not only obligated state officials to assist slaveholders in their own efforts to recover fugitive slaves but also provided that the judicial determination of the status of alleged fugitive slaves should occur in the state of residence rather than the state of seizure.[21] The bill survived strong objections from Charles Rich (Vermont Democratic Republican) that it violated due process, from Arthur Livermore (New Hampshire Democratic Republican) that court action should occur in the state of seizure because Northern judges were more likely to render impartial decisions in fugitive-slave cases than Southern judges were, and from Clifton Clagett (New Hampshire Democratic Republican) that the federal government should not dragoon state officials into enforcing its own laws.[22] Southern congressmen, including Thomas Wills Cobb (Georgia Democratic Republican), Pindall, and John Rhea (Tennessee Democratic Republican), strenuously defended the bill in the face of these objections.[23] The House approved the bill on an 84–69 vote early the next year. The vote revealed an emerging pattern of greater Southern than Northern congressional unity. Southern congressmen voted almost unanimously in favor of the bill (64–2); Northern congressmen much less solidly in opposition (67–20).[24]

When legislative action shifted to the Senate, William Smith (South Carolina Democratic Republican) treated his colleagues to another proslavery jeremiad. Smith echoed his predecessor, William Loughton Smith, in unapologetically defending slavery and attacking those who criticized the institution as possessing "a total want of knowledge of the comfortable condition of the slaves."[25] David Lawrence Morril (New Hampshire Democratic Republican) responded in measured tones, offering a detailed constitutional argument against requiring state officials to enforce federal laws.[26] In the end, the Senate amended the bill to (marginally) strengthen its due-process protections.[27] On the strength of the tie-breaking vote of Vice President Daniel D. Tompkins (New York Democratic Republican), it also attached a four-year sunset provision to the bill.[28] These amendments were apparently "killer amendments" for Southern congressmen because when the bill was sent back to the House, the chamber tabled it and took no further action on the matter.[29] The debate was also a harbinger of the nation's future politics, of how during the antebellum period Northern politicians would wrap themselves in the mantle of states rights in this policy area and Southern politicians in the mantle of federal powers.

Fugitive-slave renditions were handled differently in the territories. With the Northwest Ordinance and U.S. Constitution as precedents, the federal government accepted responsibility for fugitive-slave renditions in the territories. For example, Secretary of War John C. Calhoun (South Carolina Democratic Republican) authorized Florida territorial Governor William Du Val to organize a military expedition to recover fugitive slaves who had formed a maroon community on Pine Island, near Coral Gables, in September 1823.[30] The District of Columbia was also directly under federal jurisdiction, and federal officials pursued fugitive-slave cases in the district. One indication of such activity was a report that U.S. Marshal Tench Ringgold submitted to Congress on the number of slaves who had been temporarily housed in Washington County prison from January 1, 1826, to January 1, 1829. His report shows that seventy-eight "runaways" had been held in the prison during that three-year period. Of this group, Ringgold had returned sixty-six to their masters, released eleven as free persons, and sold one to a private party to cover the costs of his maintenance.[31] Despite a number of fugitive-slave cases in the nation's capital and U.S. territories, the federal government remained relatively inactive in this policy area until the Supreme Court decision in *Prigg v. Pennsylvania* (1842).[32]

In the *Prigg* decision, the Supreme Court provides an expansive interpretation of the Fugitive Slave Law of 1793 and its expansive interpretation of the fugitive-slave clause of the U.S. Constitution, though at least one justice argued for a much more expansive interpretation. The circumstances of the case were similar to those surrounding the 1793 law. Acting on behalf of Maryland slaveholder Margaret Ashmore, slave catcher Edward Prigg crossed the Pennsylvania state line, seized Margarette Morgan and her two children, and returned them to Ashmore's custody in Maryland. A Pennsylvania jury convicted Prigg *in absentia* of violating the state's anti-kidnapping statute.[33] After the Pennsylvania Supreme Court affirmed Prigg's conviction, the Maryland and Pennsylvania legislatures agreed to jointly appeal the case to the U.S. Supreme Court in order to test the constitutionality of the Pennsylvania statute. The court overturned Prigg's conviction as well as the Pennsylvania statute on the grounds that the statute infringed on an area of exclusive federal jurisdiction. The court also ruled that state and local officials were not obligated to assist slaveholders in recovering fugitive slaves and that federal officials could not compel them to do so. The decision established the supremacy of federal over state law but not of federal over state officials.[34]

Associate Justice Joseph Story (Massachusetts National Republican) wrote the majority decision in the case. Eight justices agreed to overturn Prigg's conviction, but only three concurred with Story's reasoning. In a separate opinion, Chief Justice Roger B. Taney (Maryland Democrat) argues that the U.S. Constitution obligated state and local officials to assist federal officials in enforcing federal

fugitive-slave law. Taney thus retrospectively provides his constitutional imprima-
tur to the line of argument that Southern legislators had unsuccessfully pressed in
their 1793 and 1817 efforts to first enact and then strengthen federal fugitive-slave
law. Tacking back toward states rights, he insists that the federal government did
not have exclusive jurisdiction in this policy area. But, according to Taney, state
governments could use their concurrent authority only in one direction, to enact
their own fugitive-slave laws, not to enact "personal liberty" laws that provided
various legal protections for African Americans claimed as fugitive slaves.[35] Interestingly, Taney's future *Dred Scott* foil, Associate Justice John McLean (Ohio
Democrat), accepts his major premise in this case. McLean agrees that fugitive-
slave law was one of the few areas of law in which federal officials could compel
state and local officials to perform certain actions. In his view, Prigg was culpable
for bypassing the legal processes that both the federal and state governments had
established for recovering fugitive slaves.[36]

In principle, the decision should not have materially affected the fugitive-slave
recovery process because the 1793 law had placed that responsibility in the hands
of slaveholders themselves, not in the hands of either federal or state officials. Yet,
in practice, the decision had a dramatic impact on the recovery process. This impact arose from the fact that the "self-help" provisions of the 1793 law were only as
effective as the ability of slaveholders to find a court of law, either on the federal or
state level, that was at least not unfriendly toward the recovery process. Northern
state legislatures interpreted the *Prigg* decision as an invitation to establish unfriendly legal processes. From 1843 to 1848, eight Northern states—Connecticut,
Massachusetts, New Hampshire, New Jersey, Ohio, Pennsylvania, Rhode Island,
and Vermont—either enacted or strengthened "personal liberty" laws that provided various legal protections for African Americans claimed as fugitive slaves.[37]
(This, of course, was *not* the direction in which Taney had coached them to use
their concurrent authority.) In reaction, Southern slaveholders urged Congress to
establish a stronger, friendlier federal legal process to assist in fugitive-slave recoveries and counteract the increasingly unfriendly state processes.[38] *Prigg* seemed to
invite this step as well.

Southern congressmen were, however, not immediately successful in their
campaign to strengthen federal fugitive-slave law. In the intervening years, the
federal government continued to prosecute fugitive-slave cases in areas under its
exclusive jurisdiction.

In 1844, Jonathan Walker agreed to sail a group of seven runaway slaves from
Pensacola, Florida, to the Bahamas on his ship.[39] Though Walker was originally
from Massachusetts, he apparently acted more from humanitarian motives than
abolitionist sympathies. Unfortunately, the captains of two wreckers, who had become suspicious of Walker's African American "crew," intercepted his ship as it

neared the Florida Keys.[40] They handed Walker over to federal authorities on Key West and transported the seven slaves back to Pensacola to claim a $1,000 reward. A navy vessel transported Walker himself back to Pensacola, where U.S. Marshal Ebenezer Dorr placed him under arrest.[41] U.S. District Attorney Walker Anderson prosecuted Walker on three separate indictments of slave "stealing." A local jury found him guilty on all counts. It sentenced Walker to an unusual, if not cruel, set of punishments: a $150 fine, fifteen-day jail sentence, one hour on the pillory, and branding as a slave stealer.[42] Dorr executed the latter sentence by burning an "SS" into Walker's hand. Because Walker was indigent, he spent nearly a year in prison before an *ad hoc* coalition of Northern abolitionists raised sufficient funds to pay his fines as well as legal fees and prison costs.[43] Prior to his release, the Florida legislature passed a new law making "slave stealing" a capital offence.[44]

Four years later, Northern abolitionists lent a more direct hand to an attempted slave escape from the District of Columbia. Mary and Daniel Bell recruited William L. Chaplain, a local attorney who was active in freedom suits and a close friend of the prominent New York abolitionist Gerrit Smith, to help them and several other African American families flee to Philadelphia.[45] Chaplain approached Daniel Drayton for his assistance in securing a captain and ship to sail the group to Philadelphia, offering Drayton $100, which the Bells had provided him for that purpose.[46] Drayton, in turn, hired Edward Sayres, captain of the *Pearl*. Almost immediately after the *Pearl* embarked, a local posse sequestered another ship, which soon intercepted the *Pearl*.[47] U.S. District Attorney Phillip Barton Key indicted Drayton, Sayres, and Chester English, who was the third member of the crew, on 110 counts of "stealing, taking, and carrying away" slaves.[48] Key dropped the charges against English when he became convinced that English had no knowledge of the plan. Apparently, neither did Sayres, at least not the full extent of it, but Key prosecuted both him and Drayton anyway.[49] After several trials and retrials, local juries eventually convicted Drayton of multiple counts of stealing slaves and Sayres of carrying them away. U.S. District Court Justice Thomas Hartley fined Drayton $10,360 and Sayres $7,400.[50] Neither could pay their hefty fines and, as a result, they remained in prison.

Drayton and Sayres served four years in prison until President Millard Fillmore finally pardoned them in 1852. Even at that point they might have remained in prison if not for the quick work of Senator Charles Sumner (Massachusetts Whig), who had persuaded Fillmore to issue the pardons. After Fillmore pardoned them, his Secretary of Interior, Alexander H. H. Stuart (Virginia Whig), immediately ordered Drayton and Sayres held for possible extradition to Virginia to face charges in state court.[51] Sumner, however, convinced their guard to release them on the strength of Fillmore's pardons and then helped them flee to their original destination, Philadelphia. Though I have been unable to find any records of how much Key earned prosecuting the case, he could have earned as much as $3,300 because, in lieu of a salary, U.S. district attorneys at the time received $10 per indictment.[52] The lengthy trials and prison times as well as retention of outside counsel would have added considerably to the costs of the case.[53] The case might well have incurred further federal costs because the escape attempt precipitated widespread anti-abolitionist rioting in Washington. President James K. Polk was forced to take the unusual step of ordering federal employees not to participate in the rioting and to instead join the local citizen patrols that were attempting to quell it.[54]

Meanwhile, Congressman Joshua R. Giddings (Ohio Whig) had made the case another antislavery *cause célèbre*. After the *Pearl* slaves were taken into custody, Giddings visited them in prison. The next day he attempted to introduce a resolution to establish a select committee to investigate the practice of holding "runaways" in Washington prisons. The shouted objections of Southern congressmen prevented him from introducing the resolution. John Gorham Palfrey (Massachusetts Whig), in the House, and John Parker Hale (New Hampshire Free Soil), in the Senate, then took up the cause, inciting increasingly vitriolic responses from their Southern colleagues. Calhoun (South Carolina Democrat), Jefferson Davis (Mississippi Democrat), Henry Foote (Mississippi Whig), and Alexander Stephens (Georgia Whig) were among those who were incited.[55]

The *Pearl* case deepened the sense of sectional crisis in the late 1840s. It also added urgency to the Southern demand for a new federal fugitive-slave law as part of any possible solution to the crisis. Calhoun's 1849 "Southern Address" made the growing resistance Southern slaveholders encountered in the Northern states when they attempted to recover their fugitive slaves the first of its two indictments against the North. He called that resistance "one of the most fatal blows ever received by the South" and could not recall "a more flagrant breach" of the Constitution.[56] From the other side of the spectrum, antislavery lawyer and future senator Salmon P. Chase presented a sweeping argument against the constitutionality of the Fugitive Slave Law of 1793 in the case of *Jones v. Van Zandt* (1847). Though the Taney Court unanimously upheld the constitutionality of the law, the court could not vouch for its efficacy.[57]

As a compromise package began to emerge in Congress in 1850, Southern lawmakers rallied behind the demand for a more stringent federal fugitive-slave law. In the Senate, John M. Mason (Virginia Democrat) introduced such a bill and defended it against a phalanx of Northern senators, most notably Chase (Ohio Democrat), William L. Dayton (New Jersey Whig), and Robert Winthrop (Massachusetts Whig). Mason defended the bill as particularly important to the upper-South states, such as his own Virginia, but more generally he stated that "it is putting too grievous a burden upon the people of the slaveholding States to require them to submit to the loss of hundreds of thousands of dollars yearly, because the general government either will not or dare not carry into effect the provisions of the Constitution."[58] When Dayton unsuccessfully attempted to attach a jury trial provision to the bill, Chase bitterly commented that "it seems to be taken for granted that but one class of rights is to be regarded at all in this controversy—the rights of masters."[59] Ultimately, Congress approved Mason's bill as part of the Compromise of 1850. The vote was, not surprisingly, a sectional one. In the Senate, only 3 of the 15 Northern senators who voted on the new law voted in its favor and in the House, only 31 of the 107 Northern congressmen who voted on the law voted in its favor. In addition, all the Northern members of the Senate and all but three of the Northern members of the House who voted for the law were Democrats.[60]

The Fugitive Slave Law of 1850 created the stronger, friendlier federal legal process that Southern slaveholders had sought to counteract the increasingly antagonistic state processes in the Northern states. The new law also completed the process of severing fugitive-slave from criminal-extradition cases and significantly strengthened federal police powers. It provided for court-appointed U.S. commissioners to grant certificates of removal in fugitive-slave cases, authorized U.S. marshals to appoint deputies and organize posses to secure the return of fugitive slaves in the face of local resistance, obligated the federal government to pay the costs for the protection and transportation of fugitive slaves in cases where such resistance was anticipated, and made marshals liable to a $1,000 fine for failing to enforce the law.[61] Obviously, the new law was only as strong as the will of federal officials to enforce it. The law had been enacted as one of the pro-Southern measures of the Compromise of 1850 package. Thereafter, even many Southern moderates supported a platform that made its enforcement the *sine qua non* of continued union.[62] Throughout the rest of the decade, both Northern Whig and Democratic presidents were determined to enforce the law.[63] Despite several celebrated slave rescues, it was enforced.

In his study of the enforcement of the Fugitive Slave Law of 1850, Stanley Campbell found 332 fugitive-slave recovery cases from 1850 through 1860. In these 332 cases, 141 alleged fugitive slaves (42.5 percent) were reclaimed without any federal court proceedings, meaning that they were essentially kidnapped. The remaining 191 cases involved federal court proceedings. In these 191 cases, 157 alleged fugitive slaves were remanded to their claimants (82.8 percent), 11 were released (5.8 percent), 22 were rescued (11.5 percent), and only 1 escaped (0.5 percent). In 68 of the 157 cases (43.4 percent) where alleged fugitive slaves were remanded to their claimants, the federal government paid protection and transportation costs.[64] In one of the most expensive of those 68 cases, Campbell reported federal expenditures of $14,166 to seize Anthony Burns in Boston in 1854 and return him to slavery in Virginia.[65] Treasury Department ledgers recorded protection and trans-portation costs in 23 other cases, ranging from $25 to $745 per case.[66] If we add the costs of those 23 cases to the costs of the Burns rendition, then documented federal expenditures in fugitive-slave cases totaled $18,759 during the decade.

This figure, however, represents only the proverbial tip of the iceberg. It does not include any costs for the 44 other cases in Campbell's population that involved federal protection and transportation costs, and it includes court costs only for the Burns case, not for the 190 other cases in Campbell's population that involved federal court proceedings. The total costs in the Thomas Sims (Boston 1851) and Margaret Garner (Cincinnati 1856) renditions have been estimated at, respectively, $20,000 and from $30,000 to $40,000.[67] Nor does the $18,759 figure include federal costs in fugitive-slave cases that fell outside Campbell's population or in the slave-rescue cases that did occur in the 1850s.[68] Contemporary estimates of the federal costs associated with the unsuccessful prosecution of Castner Hanway for his al-leged role in the Christiana (Pennsylvania) slave rescue in 1851 range from $50,000 to $70,000.[69] If we add these estimated costs to the $18,759 in documented costs, then federal expenditures in fugitive-slave and slave-rescue cases were at least $118,759 during the decade; a decade that also saw a traditionally underfunded and understaffed Attorney General's office expand its staff from three to eight people and its payroll from $5,300 to $14,367.[70]

The total is, however, still incomplete because of the lack of records or estimates of the prosecution and prison costs associated with other celebrated slave rescues. The federal government also prosecuted the rescuers in the Shadrach Minkins (Boston 1851), Jerry McHenry (Syracuse 1851), Joshua Glover (Racine, Wisconsin, 1854), June Johnson (Philadelphia 1855), and John Price (Oberlin, Ohio, 1858) cases as well as the attempted rescuers in the Burns case.[71] In the Johnson and Price cases, the rescuers spent considerable time in prison before they were either re-leased or acquitted or, alternatively, after they had been convicted.[72]

The most celebrated of the cases associated with these slave rescues was the prosecution of Sherman Booth for his role in the Glover rescue. The Booth case produced dueling legal proceedings in federal and state courts. A federal jury con-victed Booth and his co-defendant, Ryan Ryecraft, of interfering with the legal process in the Glover rescue but they were able to avoid their jail sentences and fines by successfully asserting their *habeas corpus* rights in state court.[73] The legal side of the case culminated in the *Ableman v. Booth* (1859) decision in which Taney, whose states-rights principles never seemed much in evidence when the interests of slaveholders were at stake, asserted the supremacy of federal fugitive-slave law over Wisconsin's "personal liberty" law.[74] The Civil War intervened to prevent any constitutional crisis over the case.[75] Private attorney Edward V. Ryan, who had successfully prosecuted the federal cases against both Booth and Ryecraft, later wrote Attorney General Caleb Cushing (Massachusetts Democrat) requesting $1,000 in legal fees, but there is no indication that he was ever paid.[76]

The authority shift in this policy area was not a wholesale one. As in the Booth case, the Northern states continued to assert concurrent authority in this area of law, and they continued to be partially successful in opposing federal authority.[77] Slave rescues also continued to occur, which undermined federal authority on a more individual level. Yet, for the most part, the federal government successfully enforced the Fugitive Slave Law of 1850, notwithstanding its general unpopularity in the North.[78] The law signaled a substantial shift in governing authority from the state governments to the federal government that persisted into the Civil War.[79] It was an authority shift that Southern slaveholders eagerly supported. Legal nationalization in this area of law was clearly in their interests.

FUGITIVE-SLAVE RECOVERIES: EUROPEAN AMERICAN CASES

Even if we could document the total federal costs in fugitive-slave and slave-rescue cases for the 1850–1861 years or even for the whole 1791–1861 period, the figure would still represent only a fraction of the total federal costs in this policy area. The federal government also assisted Southern slaveholders in recovering their fugitive slaves or in receiving compensation for their slave losses in other ways.

During the Revolutionary War, at least 20,000 American slaves fled to freedom, many behind British lines.[80] The Treaty of Paris (1783) prohibited British forces from "carrying away any negroes or other property of the American inhabitants," but the British army departed New York harbor with as many as 4,000 former American slaves.[81] The issue remained on the table for the Jay Treaty negotiations in 1794. In the face of the British refusal to negotiate the issue, Jay decided to focus on settling what he considered more pressing issues, such as the British navy's seizure of American ships engaged in trade with France and other combatants, the British army's continued occupation of fortifications on the northwestern frontier, and the British government's prohibitive restrictions on trade with its West Indian colonies. Jay's "concession" became one of the major points of controversy in the Senate debate over the treaty. Though the Senate eventually approved the treaty, the key vote to reject a Democratic Republican substitute motion was the minimum two thirds necessary for treaty approval, 20–10. Aaron Burr (New York) had introduced the substitute motion, which, among its other revisions to the treaty, included an article on the Revolutionary War slave claims. The vote on his motion was strongly indicative of the emerging partisan and sectional divisions in

Congress. Only two of the twelve Democratic Republican senators voted against the motion and only five of the twelve Southern senators did, all Federalists, who were unanimous in their support of the treaty.[82] Much later, Congress agreed to settle one Revolutionary War slave claim itself. In two separate appropriations during the 1850s, it awarded the grandson of Major William Hazard Wigg a total of $38,757 in compensation for the ninety-six slaves whom Wigg had lost during the war while he was a British prisoner of war in occupied South Carolina.[83]

The War of 1812 scenario was similar but concluded differently. Again, the second article of the Treaty of Ghent (1814) obligated the British government to compensate Americans for the property, including slaves, that its forces had "carried away."[84] And again, the British government initially refused to pay any claims for slave losses. Under continuing pressure from Secretary of State John Quincy Adams (Massachusetts), who had been one of the five American treaty negotiators, British officials finally agreed to submit the matter to Tsar Nicholas I for arbitration in 1818. In his 1822 ruling, the tsar sided with the American interpretation of the article, at least to the extent that individual slaveholders could prove that their slaves had been "carried away." The two governments appointed a mixed commission to decide on the legitimacy of individual claims for slave losses under the tsar's guidelines as well as the amount of money each successful claimant should receive. This commission deadlocked. In 1826, British officials then set aside $1,204,960 to cover the claims, allowing American officials to decide how to distribute the money among the claimants. At that point, President John Quincy Adams appointed a second, all-American commission to accomplish the task. The cost of these two commissions to the federal government was $56,887.[85]

In 1853, British and American officials appointed another mixed commission to settle all the outstanding claims of the citizens of their two nations against each other. Of the forty American claims that the commission considered, I could identify thirteen as slavery related. Of the twelve American claims that the commission approved, I could identify six as slavery related. These six claims total 92 percent of the money awarded on the American side, $300,561 of $329,734. All but one of the thirteen slavery-related claims and all six of the successful slavery-related claims involve either British seizures of American ships on suspicion that they were slave ships or seizures of slaves from American ships that had sought shelter in British Caribbean ports. The latter category includes the $110,330 awarded to the insurers of the *Creole*, which had sought shelter in Nassau harbor after a successful slave revolt aboard the ship.[86] The cost of this mixed commission to the federal government was $36,526.[87] On the British side, I could identify only one successful claim as slavery related. This claim also involved the seizure of a ship on the suspicion that it was a slave ship, this time of a British-owned ship by the U.S. navy. The commission awarded the ship owner $20,000 in this case.[88]

American officials also long sought a slave-extradition treaty with British colonial officials in Canada, where many slaves escaped through the underground
railroad.[89] In one celebrated case, Arkansas Governor Archibald Yell successfully
lobbied British officials in Canada for the return of an Arkansas fugitive slave,
Nelson Hackett, who was accused of stealing a horse in order to make his escape
in 1841.[90] One of the less-known articles of the Webster-Ashburton Treaty (1842)
required extraditions in cases in which fugitive slaves were accused of committing crimes, though not in other cases.[91] Still, British officials refused to extradite
seven slaves who were accused of murdering a Florida resident and then fleeing
to Nassau in 1842. In response to a formal protest from Secretary of State Abel
Upshur (Virginia Democrat) two years later, British officials claimed that the men
had not been positively identified in Nassau.[92] The continuing presence of slavery
did not affect Anglo-American relations only in slave-trade cases. Nor were slave-
smuggling cases the only reason for American officials to assert control over U.S.
borders, even if in fugitive-slave cases the objective was to keep blacks "in" rather
than "out."

Local disputes over slaves and slavery similarly affected U.S. relations with the
other imperial power that had colonies on or near its borders. Until the United
States acquired Florida in 1819, Georgia citizens engaged in constant controversies with Spanish colonial authorities over fugitive slaves who had allegedly fled
to Spanish East Florida. American incursions into Florida in 1812–1814, 1814, 1816,
and 1817–1818 were at least partly slave-catching expeditions.[93] Under the terms of
the Adams-Onís Treaty (1819), the federal government agreed to pay the claims of
Florida residents who had suffered property losses, including slave losses, during
those incursions. It eventually paid $1,199,669 to cover such claims.[94] Unfortu-
nately, the official records of the payments indicate only how much each claimant received, without indicating specific amounts for specific items. It is therefore
impossible to determine exactly how much of the total was paid for slave losses.
I would estimate 20 percent, roughly $240,000.[95] The claimants included many
American nationals who had settled in Florida before its acquisition and even
some who had participated in one or more of the incursions.[96]

Texas spawned many disputes over slaves and slavery as the area transitioned
from Spanish rule to American statehood. While Texas remained part of Spanish
Mexico, the disputed border region with Louisiana was the locus not only of slave
smuggling into the United States but of slave escapes from the United States. In
one early case, Orleans territorial Governor William C. C. Claiborne engaged in
a lengthy correspondence with Spanish provincial officials to ensure the return
of a group of fugitive slaves.[97] Once Mexico achieved independence, the United
States unsuccessfully sought a slave-extradition treaty with the new nation.[98] The
primary locus of disputes over slaves and slavery in the area, however, shifted to

disputes between Texas slaveholders, who sought to protect and even expand their slaveholdings, and Mexican officials, who sought to limit and possibly extinguish them. Those disputes provided one rationale for Texas's declaration of independence in 1835.[99]

With Texas independence, the locus of disputes over slaves and slavery in the area shifted once again, to the U.S. Congress and American presidential politics. President John Tyler's determination to annex Texas sparked bitter partisan and sectional disputes in Congress over the advisability of annexing a slaveholding republic. The issue also played a pivotal role in the 1844 presidential elections, with dark-horse candidate Polk (Tennessee Democrat) riding it all the way to the White House.[100]

After the United States annexed Texas and fought the Mexican-American War, the locus of disputes over slaves and slavery in the area shifted yet again, now to the border between Texas and Mexico.[101] At least one of the many American filibustering expeditions into Mexico was a slave-catching expedition. Slaveholders in the San Antonio area hired Texas Ranger Captain James Hughes Callahan to organize an expedition into Mexico in 1855 to capture fugitive slaves who had fled across the border. The Mexican army intercepted Callahan's forces soon after they crossed the border, compelling them to retreat to Texas. To cover their retreat, they set fire to a Mexican border village. The commanding officer at Fort Duncan, Captain Sidney Burbank (Massachusetts), ordered his troops to protect Callahan's forces as they recrossed the border but also to provide food and shelter to the villagers whose homes they had destroyed.[102] More than twenty years later, the federal government reimbursed the villagers approximately $50,000 for their losses.[103]

As chapter 2 shows, the international slave trade strongly affected U.S. relations with Spain as well as with Great Britain. Several of the suspected slave ships that U.S. navy and treasury vessels seized were Spanish ships, had Spanish financial backing, or were carrying the slaves of Spanish colonials. In addition to the numerous court cases these captures generated, the question of compensation for the slaves seized from the ships involved American officials in lengthy negotiations with Spanish officials. As chapter 2 also shows, the *Antelope* (1820) case affected U.S. relations with Portugal as well as with Spain.

The *Antelope* case offers a striking contrast to the more famous *Amistad* (1839) case because in the latter American officials refused to reimburse Spanish colonials for the losses they incurred as a result of the successful slave revolt aboard the ship.[104] John Quincy Adams also played dramatically different roles in the two cases. As Secretary of State, Adams had advised President James Monroe to surrender the slaves seized from the *Antelope* to their Spanish and Portuguese claimants. Twenty years later, when the U.S. Supreme Court heard the case of *United*

States v. Amistad (1841), Congressman Adams persuaded the court to affirm the freedom of the slave rebels.[105] The *Amistad* case offers, in turn, a striking contrast to the *Creole* (1841) case because in the latter, American officials insisted that the British government reimburse Southern slaveholders for the losses incurred as a result of the successful slave revolt aboard the ship.[106] The continuing presence of slavery produced a foreign policy that strangely alternated between antislavery and proslavery stances. But it was also a foreign policy in which the interests of Southern slaveholders seemed to trump any other interest or principle of action, even in cases that only indirectly affected their interests. Fehrenbacher is certainly correct to argue that the international posture of the United States prior to the Civil War was that of a slaveholding republic.[107]

International fugitive-slave and slave-loss cases involved the United States in disputes with a number of foreign nations during the 1791–1861 period. The cases that I discuss in this section are only a few of an indeterminate number of international fugitive-slave and slave-loss cases that affected U.S. relations with other countries, including countries other than Great Britain, Mexico, Portugal, and Spain, during this period.[108] Consequently, the federal expenditures that I report or estimate in this section provide only a glimpse of a much larger whole. They nonetheless demonstrate that federal activity in this policy area went well beyond domestic fugitive-slave cases.

In terms of early American state development, the primary result of this activity was to increase the legitimacy of the federal government in the Southern states and territories to the considerable extent that American foreign policy served the interests of Southern slaveholders. International fugitive-slave and slave-loss cases also reminded federal officials that they neglected those interests at their peril, encouraging them to develop decision-making repertoires that focused attention on how particular cases might affect those interests.

FUGITIVE-SLAVE RECOVERIES: NATIVE AMERICAN CASES

Federal officials were heavily involved in attempting to recover fugitive slaves from Native Americans on the Southern frontier. Federal treaties with Native American nations invariably contained fugitive-slave clauses. Disputes over fugitive slaves were most common in less settled Southern states and territories.[109] In Florida, Georgia, Alabama, and Mississippi, the Cherokees, Chickasaws, Choctaws, Creeks, and Seminoles not only practiced chattel slavery but they also remained relatively large, cohesive nations and retained relatively large, fertile lands well into the nineteenth century.[110]

In the case of the Creeks, the Treaty of Indian Springs (1821) stipulated that the federal government would establish a $250,000 annuity to pay the claims for property losses, including slave losses, which resulted from their pre-1802 "depredations" against Georgia citizens. In return, the Creeks would cede much of their Georgia lands to the state of Georgia; meaning that the state would gain both ways from the treaty. Eventually, Georgia citizens received a total of $108,944 from the annuity.[111] Applying the 20 percent rule, I would estimate $22,000 of that amount paid for slave claims.

The westward movement of Creeks into Alabama only relocated the site of their conflicts with European American settlers. The Creeks seized the opportunity of the War of 1812 to revolt against European American encroachments on their eastern Alabama lands. Yet they did not revolt uniformly. The Red Stick War (1813–1814) was as much a civil war between upper and lower Creeks as it was a war between Creeks and European Americans.[112] Upper Creeks laid waste to the settlements of lower Creeks as well as of European Americans along the Georgia-Alabama border. In turn, lower Creeks fought with Andrew Jackson's Tennessee volunteers at the decisive Battle of Horseshoe Bend. Jackson ignored the distinction between "friendly" and "unfriendly" Creeks when he forced the leaders of both factions to sign a peace treaty that ceded additional Creek lands to the United States. The federal government, though, did not ignore that distinction when it paid both "friendly" Creeks and European American settlers for their property losses, again including slave losses, during the war. The federal payments for those losses totaled $195,418. Of that amount, $38,106, or approximately 20 percent, paid for slave claims.[113]

Florida was the site of the most violent conflicts over slaves and slavery between Native Americans and European Americans. During the time of Spanish rule, slave runaways from Georgia and South Carolina to Florida were rampant, at least according to the complaints slaveholders from those two states registered with federal officials. Spanish colonial officials protected the runaways because they saw them, along with the Seminoles among whom many of them settled, as buffers against U.S. encroachments. In fact, Seminoles, not Creeks, had perpetrated most of the "depredations" that were covered by the Treaty of Indian Springs. The federal government did not, however, officially recognize the Seminoles as a separate nation from the Creeks until 1856, long after the U.S. army had removed both nations to Indian territory, despite the fact that relations between the nations were far from amicable. The Red Stick War increased the tensions between the two nations because many upper Creeks relocated to Florida after the war and became part of the Seminole nation. The federal policy of not recognizing the Seminoles as a separate nation further exacerbated those tensions, as when federal officials "raided" the Creek annuity to pay for Seminole "depredations."[114]

Georgia citizens responded to this perceived threat to their slaveholdings by taking the lead in a number of armed incursions into Spanish East Florida, culminating with the First Seminole War (1817–1818). To varying degrees, army regulars, volunteer and militia units from other states and territories, as well as "friendly" Native Americans, mostly Creeks, also participated in these incursions.[115] On the opposing side, Spanish colonials and African Americans fought with the Seminoles in attempting to repel them. The acquisition of Florida promised to stabilize the situation. It did not.

The acquisition of Florida made the federal government directly responsible for addressing an increasingly contentious set of problems revolving around the presence of slaves and slavery in the new territory. On the one hand, it faced the twin problems of Seminole slave raids on European American plantations in Florida and the surrounding states and of slave runaways from those plantations to Seminole maroon communities in the territory.[116] On the other, it faced the problem of protecting Seminole slaveholdings in the territory both from avaricious European American settlers who sought to acquire slaves by whatever means possible and from Creek "reverse" slave raids on Seminole lands. During his tenure as Secretary of War, Calhoun authorized payments of $1,000 to Captain Bell for the recovery of fifty-nine Seminole slaves seized by a Creek raiding party along the Georgia-Florida border as well as of $685 to an unnamed Seminole woman for the loss of a slave who was "stolen" from her by a European American settler in territorial Florida.[117] Whether inadvertently or not, federal officials actually encouraged "reverse" slave raids by offering Native Americans bounties for surrendering African Americans to local Indian agents and army officers on the presumption that they were the fugitive slaves of European American settlers. In 1827, six Creeks received a total of $400 in bounty money for surrendering eight African Americans to Major Alexander C. W. Fanning (Massachusetts) at Fort Gadsden in northwestern Florida.[118]

Slave disputes were a continuing source of conflict between and among European Americans and Native Americans in territorial Florida. In 1828, Indian Superintendent Thomas L. McKenney (Maryland) authorized Governor Du Val to pay territorial Justice Joseph L. Smith $5 per case for adjudicating slave disputes between Seminoles and European American settlers in Florida.[119] In 1832, Du Val himself received $1,285 in extra expenses for his role in arbitrating such disputes.[120] Seminole subagent and former Georgia Congressman Wiley Thompson received $7,000 in 1834 to settle the outstanding slave claims of European American settlers against the Seminoles in Florida in anticipation of their removal to Indian territory.[121] When Thompson became unavailable to discharge those duties, McKenney's successor, Elbert Herring (Connecticut), appointed Captain John B.

F. Russell (Massachusetts) to handle them, allocating $300 to cover his travel expenses to Florida.[122] Whatever Thompson and Russell accomplished, they did not remove many Seminoles or prevent a second Seminole war.

As in the case of the earlier conflicts in Spanish East Florida, slave disputes between Seminoles and European American settlers were one of the primary causes of the Second Seminole War. I discuss the war more fully in the next chapter because, as opposed to the earlier Florida incursions, it was an official U.S. military operation. Yet the war itself led to further disputes over the status of the African Americans who were living among the Seminoles. As we will see, army officials decided, as a calculated strategy to shorten the war, to promise these Black Seminoles their freedom if they agreed to emigrate to Indian territory. The army policy proved controversial because European American settlers claimed that many of the Black Seminoles were their slaves, who had either run away to Seminole lands or been seized from their plantations by Seminole raiding parties.[123] As many as 1,000 slaves in Florida, Georgia, and South Carolina had taken the opportunities the war offered to escape to Seminole lands.[124] The army policy also required unit commanders to determine the status of Black Seminoles whom their Native American allies had captured during the war.

In one infamous case, the commanding general in Florida, Thomas S. Jesup (Kentucky), offered to pay a group of Creek warriors $8,000 for ninety Black Seminoles whom they had captured in 1837. The Creeks rejected the offer as too low and, instead, sold them to James C. Watson, a Georgia slave dealer, for $14,600. In the meantime, the army had removed them to New Orleans. Watson dispatched his brother-in-law, Nathaniel F. Collins (Alabama), to gain possession of the sixty-seven Black Seminoles who remained in army custody.[125] Collins was able to obtain a favorable local court ruling, but the army removed them to Arkansas anyway on the rationale that they were prisoners of war. When Collins's efforts to reclaim the Black Seminoles proved futile, Watson petitioned Congress for compensation for his losses.

The Watson case became infamous because when he first petitioned Congress in 1838, his petition prompted Giddings to investigate the true causes and costs of the Second Seminole War. Giddings saw slave interests written all over a very expensive war effort.[126] As if to prove Giddings's point, Watson and, after his death in 1843, his family continued to petition Congress for compensation. Despite a series of favorable reports from House committees chaired by Southern congressmen, Congress failed to act on the matter until 1852. Following another favorable report from the Committee of Claims, now chaired by John R. J. Daniel (North Carolina Democrat), Congress finally agreed that Watson's heirs should be reimbursed the $14,600 he had paid for the Black Seminoles. It also ruled that they should be paid six percent interest on that sum, annually compounded from the date of purchase, which meant a total payment of approximately $33,000.[127]

Once the army had removed the Seminoles and the other four "civilized" nations to Indian territory, the problems of slave runaways to Native American lands and of Native American slave raids on European American plantations substantially decreased in the Southern states and territories. One of the primary purposes of Native American removal had been accomplished. But, again, the removal process only relocated those problems, though now they were primarily defined by the vulnerability of Native American slaveholdings in Indian territory to covetous European American settlers, corrupt Indian agents, and relatively safe escape routes to Mexico. In 1825, Arkansas territorial officials complained to Secretary of War James Barbour (Virginia National Republican) of the problem of European American settlers "stealing" Cherokee slaves. When Barbour failed to respond to their complaints, Indian subagent David Brearley took matters into his own hands and raised a volunteer force to attempt to recover the slaves.[128] The army also assisted Native Americans in recapturing fugitive slaves who had fled from Indian territory toward Mexico.[129] An 1854 Choctaw slave dispute in Indian territory received a federal court hearing, with the federal government eventually paying the trial costs to free the alleged fugitive slaves, who were, in fact, neither fugitives nor slaves.[130] Seminole subagent Marcellus M. Du Val and Creek agent James Logan were only the most conspicuous of the Indian agents who took advantage of the vulnerability of Native American slaveholdings in Indian territory to fraudulently acquire and sell slaves for personal profit.[131] The presence of slavery in both European American and Native American communities in the new southwestern territories continued to embroil the two groups in disputes between and among themselves until the Civil War, which was but one of the many ironies of the unofficial policy of "civilizing" Native Americans by encouraging them to become slaveholders.[132] Those disputes even continued into the war years because the conflict was also a civil war in Indian territory between hostile Confederate and Unionist factions within each of the five "civilized" nations.[133]

In this section, I have examined the other international dimension of fugitive-slave and slave-loss cases. I have discussed only a few of the indeterminate number of slave disputes between and among European Americans and Native Americans that required federal intervention and was able to provide actual or estimated costs in only a subset of those cases. Still, the cases that I discuss in this section provide further evidence that federal activity in this policy area went well beyond domestic fugitive-slave cases during the 1791–1861 period. Again, one major result of this activity was to increase the legitimacy of the federal government in the

Southern states and territories through a Native American policy that both directly and indirectly served the interests of Southern slaveholders.

CONCLUSION

The aggregate effects of federal involvement in fugitive-slave and slave-loss cases on early American state development were profound. Despite the relatively small sums of money that the federal government spent in this policy area, it affected relations between the Northern and Southern states, between the United States and major European colonial powers, and between the United States and powerful Native American nations. As a result, the federal government committed legal, diplomatic, and military resources in ways that it would otherwise not have. It developed executive, congressional, and judicial routines for solving problems that would otherwise not have been problems. In the case of fugitive-slave renditions, it created a separate legal apparatus that it might otherwise not have created, at least not within the same time frame. Finally, the continuing disputes over slaves and slavery between European Americans and Native Americans was one of the primary motives for Native American removals in the southeastern United States, which might not otherwise have occurred or, again, at least not within the same time frame. As we will discover in the next chapter, Native American removals had very significant effects on state development, especially in the case of the U.S. military's forcible removal of the Seminoles from Florida.

Partisan and sectional differences also emerged in this policy area. In 1787, convention delegates Butler (Georgia) and Sherman (Connecticut) sparred over adding a fugitive-slave clause to the proposed constitution. In 1817, Congressman Rich (Vermont Democratic Republican) contested Congressman Pindall's (Virginia Federalist) amendments to the Fugitive Slave Law of 1793. In 1842, Supreme Court Justices Story (Massachusetts National Republican) and Taney (Maryland Democrat) tangled over the *Prigg* case. In 1850, Senator Dayton (New Jersey Whig) opposed Senator Mason's (Virginia Democrat) far-reaching revisions to federal fugitive-slave law.

These partisan and sectional differences were, nevertheless, overshadowed by the general acceptance of the notion that the federal government should have authority over interstate fugitive-slave cases. Sherman's objection to the fugitive-slave clause was brief, and he later served on the Senate committee that drafted the Fugitive Slave Law of 1793.[134] Rich's due-process objections to the proposed 1817 amendments to that law presumed that a "fair" fugitive-slave law that protected Northern free blacks from being kidnapped by slave catchers was constitutionally mandated.[135] However their constitutional philosophies might have differed, Story and Taney concurred in the *Prigg* case that the fugitive-slave clause had been essential to Southern ratification of the Constitution and that federal enforcement of the clause was now essential to interstate comity.[136] Even on the eve of the Civil War, most Republicans joined Abraham Lincoln in accepting the constitutionality of a "fair" fugitive-slave law.[137]

The increasing authority of the federal government in this policy area did not involve only the fugitive-slave clause of the Constitution. It also involved the statutory powers Congress asserted under that clause, as well as the constitutional powers of the executive departments over military affairs and foreign relations, including relations with Native American nations. Despite the partisan and sectional differences that emerged in this policy area during the 1791–1861 period, federal officials consistently asserted those powers to protect slavery. This consistency was far from absolute. The Jay Treaty is prime evidence that it was not. Still, this consistency existed and, over time, it resulted in increasingly intrusive federal interventions into both interstate and international relations.[138] This upward trend suggests that federal officials had incurred legal, diplomatic, and political obligations and established a variety of administrative routines that cued them to act in ways that supported the continued existence of Southern slavery, regardless of their own personal feelings about the institution and, in many cases, without consciously intending any such effect. John Quincy Adams offers an excellent case for this argument. In his diplomatic and executive career, he supported slave interests not only in the *Antelope* case but also in negotiating the Treaty of Ghent with Great Britain and the Adams-Onís Treaty with Spain. He, however, viewed himself as promoting national interests, not slave interests. Even when he was a member of Congress and freed of executive and diplomatic constraints, Adams did not directly attack the institution of slavery but rather attacked it collaterally, as in his *Amistad* oral arguments or in his protracted campaign to repeal the gag rule on abolitionist petitions to Congress, both of which were framed more in terms of upholding national reputation than attacking racial slavery.[139] Of course, in some cases, such as in Butler's insistence on adding a fugitive-slave clause to the proposed constitution, the proslavery effect was consciously intended and motivated by a strong personal commitment to the institution.[140]

With respect to early American state development, this policy area had significant effects not only on the institutional development of the federal government but also on its authority, legitimacy, and the ways that it deployed its coercive powers and other state capacities. The most important institutional effect was the separate legal apparatus Congress created in order to enforce the Fugitive Slave Law of 1850. Federal officials would no longer have to depend on state and local officials to enforce federal fugitive-slave law. Nor would they have to depend on the private agency of Southern slaveholders and slave catchers. They would instead have to develop procedures that effectively utilized their own resources and capacities to capture and return fugitive slaves. The legal nationalization of fugitive-slave renditions signaled a durable shift in governing authority from the state to the federal level in this policy area. It also portended a post–Civil War federal government with steadily increasing capacities to enforce its own laws with its own agents.

Yet this process of legal nationalization was incomplete. Federal officials still relied on Southern slaveholders and slave catchers to start the rendition process. They also still relied on non-state actors to help enforce the law. Federal officials deputized private citizens to help capture fugitive slaves and prevent their rescues as well as hired private citizens to incarcerate and care for fugitive slaves and would-be slave rescuers. Though one of the congressional intentions behind the Fugitive Slave Law of 1850 was to bypass recalcitrant state and local officials, the *Booth* case demonstrates how federal officials still relied on their cooperation, or at least on their not actively interfering with the enforcement of the law. They also still relied on the cooperation of private citizens in their capacities as jurors and witnesses. In international slave disputes, federal officials relied on private citizens to serve on mixed commissions to negotiate settlements in disputes over slave losses and to serve in volunteer and militia units when disputes over fugitive slaves precipitated armed conflict, as they did with the Seminoles in Florida. This reliance on non-state actors to perform state functions was typical of the early American state. The practice increased its capacities without the need to invest in hiring more employees. It was, however, not a costless practice, either in terms of federal expenditures or the efficient performance of the assigned task. The Fugitive Slave Law of 1850 promised an increase in efficiency but also in costs.

The constitutional and statutory authority of Congress to enact fugitive-slave laws was widely accepted throughout the pre–Civil War period.[141] The specific nature of the fugitive-slave laws that Congress enacted, though, was skewed in such a way as to increase the legitimacy of the federal government in the Southern states and decrease it in the Northern states, especially because the enforcement of the laws was largely confined to the latter.[142] Even if slave rescues were relatively rare, they generally enjoyed local citizen support. Northern juries refused to convict alleged slave rescuers even when the evidence was overwhelmingly against them, much as Southern juries refused to convict alleged slave traders and smugglers. Among Northern state officials, this local support of slave rescuers was translated into a principled opposition to federal encroachments on state police powers. In this policy area, Northern state officials were the champions of states rights and Southern state officials, of federal powers.[143] Paradoxically or not, one of the bill of particulars in Southern secession documents was the resistance of Northern state officials to the enforcement of federal fugitive-slave law.[144] The federal government's handling of international slave disputes, with both European and Native American nations, also undoubtedly increased its legitimacy in the South as federal officials sought to resolve those disputes in ways favorable to the interests of Southern slaveholders.

The element of coercion involved in the enforcement of federal fugitive-slave law in the Northern states was certainly palpable, and not only to the fugitive slaves but also to those who attempted to assist them. The deployment of U.S. marshals, deputy marshals, citizen posses, militia units, and even army regulars to enforce the law in the North was another indicator of a lack of federal legitimacy in this policy area, obviously from the perspective of the fugitive slaves but also of those who attempted to assist them. In international slave disputes, foreign officials often denied the legitimacy of specific federal actions and the authority of particular federal officials to perform them. This attitude was conspicuous among Native Americans and also among British colonial officials who held very different notions of the extraterritoriality of slavery than most U.S. officials did. African Americans who rode the underground railroad to Canada or escaped to the British West Indies or Mexico tacitly rejected both federal authority and legitimacy through their actions. By the antebellum period, U.S. borders were probably much more porous for outgoing fugitive slaves than they were for incoming smuggled slaves.[145]

The federal enforcement of the constitutional rights of Southern slaveholders to the return of their fugitive slaves during the 1850s was the most important antebellum instance of the federal enforcement of the constitutional rights of individual citizens against the states. This federal effort established an ironic precedent for the federal enforcement of the new constitutional rights of the freed slaves against the states during Reconstruction. The principal sponsor of the Civil Rights Act of 1866, Senator Lyman Trumbull (Illinois Republican), modeled the enforcement provisions of the act on the Fugitive Slave Law of 1850 in superimposing federal law on state law, in mandating direct federal enforcement of federal law, and in subjecting to civil and criminal penalties state and private actors who interfered with federal enforcement efforts. The act even imposed the same $1,000 penalty on non-diligent U.S. marshals that the Fugitive Slave Law of 1850 had.[146] These similarities are astonishing when viewed from the perspective of the very different intentions of the two laws. But they are not astonishing in light of the fact that the Fugitive Slave Law of 1850 was the only standing precedent for the direct federal enforcement of a constitutional right. Trumbull's own gloss on this case of legal mimicry was that

[t]he act that was passed that time for the purpose of punishing persons who should aid negroes to escape to freedom is now to be applied by the provisions of

this bill to the punishment of those who shall undertake to keep them in slavery. Surely we have the authority to enact a law as efficient in the interests of freedom, now that freedom prevails throughout the country, as we had in the interest of slavery when it prevailed in a portion of the country.[147]

Unfortunately, the effectiveness of the antebellum efforts in "the interest of slavery" was greater than the Reconstruction efforts in "the interests of freedom." In the case of the Reconstruction efforts, they became much less effective after the Hayes administration withdrew army forces from the reconstituted Southern states to complete the Compromise of 1877.[148]

The deployment of army regulars to enforce the Fugitive Slave Law of 1850 represented another instance of how the presence of slavery influenced the ways that the federal government deployed its coercive powers and other state capacities during the 1791–1861 period.[149] Even though its enforcement efforts were not uniformly successful, the federal government proved itself capable of overcoming state and local resistance to the enforcement of its own laws. It thus demonstrated an effective law-enforcement capacity, and more resources flowed to its law-enforcement agencies. At the time those agencies were primarily military ones, but, largely because of interstate fugitive-slave cases, the federal government also developed a stronger civilian law-enforcement arm with more, and more empowered, U.S. marshals, commissioners, and justices.[150] That arm would grow much stronger after the Civil War, especially during the twentieth century, with the development of such new federal law-enforcement agencies as the Bureau of Alcohol, Tobacco, and Firearms (AFT), Federal Bureau of Investigation (FBI), and Secret Service.[151]

In comparison to the slave-trade and African colonization policy areas, the fugitive-slave policy area had a more domestic focus, in which the state governments have a more "natural" role. Even so, Southern politicians successfully pressed the case for legal nationalization, realizing that any concurrent-jurisdiction argument in this policy area was a double-edged sword.[152] Though the fugitive-slave policy area had more effect on the federal-state balance during the 1791–1861 period than the other two policy areas, it probably had less effect on the executive-legislative balance. The Fugitive Slave Law of 1850 was much more directive of executive action than any congressional legislation regarding the slave trade or African colonization had been. Still, all three policy areas showed how the presence of slavery affected long-term trends in American state development during the period. Those trends also grew much stronger after the Civil War, with new federal efforts to address, or, alternately, repress, the nation's troubled race relations as major contributing factors.

One distinctive feature of the fugitive-slave policy area was its impact on the balance of powers between the judiciary and the other two branches of the federal government during the 1791–1861 period, again probably because of its more domestic focus. In fugitive-slave cases, the judiciary intervened to resolve issues that had paralyzed congressional and, to a lesser extent, executive decision-making processes. The *Prigg* decision clearly demonstrated this effect. In his *Prigg* opinion, Taney, much more than Story, asserted a federal obligation to enforce the constitutional rights of Southern slaveholders against the Northern states, a challenge that Congress finally accepted in 1850.[153] One hundred years later, the nation witnessed a similar judicial-led dynamic on race relations, fortunately in a much more progressive direction, as the U.S. Supreme Court took the lead in brokering the end of Jim Crow.[154]

Historically, the military has been the primary engine of state development. As politics and history scholars are increasingly recognizing, the United States fit this European pattern during the 1791–1861 period. What they have failed to recognize is the extent to which the presence of slavery influenced the relationship between military development and state development during the period. Interstate fugitive-slave cases hardly exhausted the instances when federal officials deployed armed forces in "the interest of slavery."

5. The Slavery Garrisoned State

When the American state went to war before the Civil War, it often went to war to protect the Southern institution of slavery. The connection between war and the protection of slavery was strongest in the case of the Second Seminole War. It was also present in many skirmishes with Native Americans as well as with African Americans and Spanish colonials on the nation's borderlands. The story of the interrelationship between the presence of slavery, military deployments, and state development is a large part of the buried story of early American state development.

The relationship between war and state development has become a truism. Wars drive state development because wars require armies, and constant wars require standing armies. Armies, in turn, require state bureaucracies to finance and provision them and to coordinate their activities. Once those bureaucracies are in place, even state officials who desire to dismantle them face formidable obstacles. The ratchet effect means that post-war retrenchments never reach pre-war levels. Nations at war require strong states, and nations constantly at war acquire very strong states.

Charles Tilly pioneered the study of the relationship between wars and state development in Europe.[1] Tilly shows how the almost constant state of warfare in early-modern Europe first created strong states on the continent. Politics and history scholars have not studied the relationship between wars and state development in the United States as extensively. If they have studied the relationship, they have studied it largely as a twentieth-century phenomenon.[2] Prior to World War I, the relative isolation of the United States from major military powers spared it the major wars that European nations had experienced for centuries. This relative isolation is one aspect of the story of American exceptionalism. As the story goes, the United States had a weak state with a weak army before the twentieth century because it was involved in no major wars with other nations before the twentieth century, nor was it even threatened with such a war. Even politics and history scholars who have challenged this narrative, such as Max Edling, Sheldon Pollack, and Bruce Porter, have reaffirmed its general thrust, at least for the 1791–1861 period.[3]

American exceptionalism is, however, a relative matter. What is a major power and what is a major war are also relative matters. The United States may have been spared major wars with major powers during the 1791–1861 period, but it still was involved in one "less major" war with a "more major" power, the War of

1812.[4] It was also surrounded by the colonies of "more major" powers and involved in "less major" wars with "more minor" powers, the Mexican-American War and a long series of wars with various Native American nations.[5] It also experienced one devastating civil war during the nineteenth century, which, as Richard Bensel demonstrates, created two very strong states, one in the Unionist North and one in the Confederate South.[6] Though Bensel claims that the effects of the Civil War on state development were short-lived, Theda Skocpol counters that the war had lasting effects on state development because of the exponential growth of the Civil War pension programs.[7]

Even before the Civil War, the United States was involved in three "less major" wars. In addition to the War of 1812, the Second Seminole War and the Mexican-American War each had more than 1,000 U.S. combatant deaths.[8] David Mayhew details how the War of 1812 and Mexican-American War generated new policy regimes and administrative structures.[9] Extending Skocpol's research backward in time, Laura Jensen chronicles the expansion of veterans' benefit programs from disabled veterans to all veterans and their survivors during the pre–Civil War period.[10] John Mahon contends that the Second Seminole War had significant effects on the professionalization of the army and also served as a training ground for the Mexican-American War and Civil War officer corps. Braxton Bragg (North Carolina), Joseph E. Johnston (Virginia), George Meade (Pennsylvania), and George H. Thomas (Virginia) were among the prominent Civil War generals who saw action in all three wars.[11]

Politics and history scholars also have not sufficiently studied the relationship between the peacetime activities of the U.S. military and state development. At least in the American case, the army played a pivotal role in frontier settlement. Jackson Turner's frontier thesis turns out to be a myth. The American state not only walked by the side of the rugged American individualist as he conquered the West; it preceded him. In a frontal attack on the Turner thesis, Laurence Malone demonstrates how the army built the roads along which European American settlers moved westward and the fortifications that served as concentration points for their settlements.[12] The army also cleared Native Americans from the lands on which European Americans settled. This removal process frequently provoked armed conflicts, as it did in the case of the Creek and Seminole wars. Yet even when it did not, the army was involved in the process in a supervisory role. Army soldiers, engineers, and surveyors also preceded the construction of land and post offices, two other federal institutions that greatly promoted frontier settlement.[13] The relationship between frontier settlement and state development was reciprocal. In helping develop the American West, the army helped develop the American state.

The buried story of early American state development is the story of how the continuing presence of slavery in the Southern states was one cause of the wartime and peacetime activities of the U.S. military, which, in turn, contributed to state development. Even revisionist accounts of the relationship between military development and state development ignore this story.[14]

Before further exploring the role slavery played in that relationship, we should recall the many ways that the U.S. military was involved in the other slavery-related activities of the early American state. Lest we forget the U.S. navy as a major military institution, it engaged in efforts to suppress illegal slave trading and smuggling as well as assisted the American Colonization Society (ACS) in founding a colony of former American slaves on the west coast of Africa. We have also seen how the U.S. army engaged in efforts to suppress slave smuggling as well as assisted Indian agents, law-enforcement officials, and Southern slaveholders in recovering fugitive slaves. Finally, we have seen how the army's efforts to recover fugitive slaves sparked armed conflicts with Native Americans, African Americans, and European colonials as well as international disputes with Spanish, British, and Mexican officials. In this chapter, I reinvestigate several of these cases and introduce a number of others that show a similar interrelationship between the presence of slavery, military deployments, and state development.

However "small" the federal government was during the 1791–1861 period, it spent most of its resources on the military. Of the $1,797 million aggregate expenditures of the federal government during this period, $983 million (54.7 percent) were military expenditures.[15] The Second Seminole War (1835–1842) was not only the nation's longest war during the period but its largest slavery-related expenditure. At an estimated $30 million, the war would have accounted for 1.67 percent of total federal expenditures and 3.06 percent of total military expenditures from 1791 to the end of FY1861.[16] The U.S. military spent much more than $30 million on slavery-related activities over those years, though because of the lack of documentation, it is unclear exactly how much more.[17]

FLORIDA

Florida was the principal site of slavery-related military activities during the pre–Civil War period. As we have seen, the Second Seminole War was preceded not only by a first Seminole war but by several other American incursions into Spanish East Florida. These incursions had multiple motives and trajectories. They were, however, united by their irregular character and by their unannounced missions as slavery-protection and slavery-expansion expeditions.

The first incursion was clearly a filibuster. The "Patriot War" (1812–1814) began when a group of approximately 125 Georgia volunteers invaded Spanish East Florida on March 12, 1812.[18] The group had the official endorsement and assistance of Georgia officials, including Governor David B. Mitchell, and the unofficial encouragement and assistance of the Madison administration, which had been stymied in its efforts to acquire the territory by diplomatic means.[19] Whatever Madison's motives were for acquiring Florida, one of the primary motives of the filibusterers was to create a safe zone to prevent the slaves of Georgia slaveholders from running away to the protection of Spanish colonial officials and Seminole maroon communities in the territory or, alternatively, from being seized by Seminole raiding parties that crossed the Florida-Georgia border. They also sought to profit from capturing Black Seminoles whom, they alleged, were either the fugitive or "stolen" slaves of European American settlers.[20] The filibusterers' ultimate goal was to wrest the territory from Spanish rule.

The U.S. army played an ambiguous role in this incursion. As the filibusterers prepared to march into Florida, the acting commander at Point Peter battery, Major Jacint Laval (France), refused to assist them, despite the official approval they claimed that they had from the Madison administration. When Laval's superior officer, Colonel Thomas Adam Smith (Virginia), returned to the post a few days later, he decided to assist the filibusterers but still refused to take any offensive actions on their behalf.[21] The U.S. navy played a more active role in the incursion, though the local navy commander, Commodore Hugh Campbell (South Carolina), had also initially refused to assist the filibusterers and then, like Smith, ordered his gunboat captains to take only defensive actions on their behalf. When the filibusterers attacked Amelia Island, navy gunboats accompanied them, and at least one captain, Winslow Foster (Virginia), in apparent defiance of Campbell's orders, positioned his ship to bombard the island. This ostensible threat persuaded the Spanish colonials on the island to surrender it to the filibusterers without a shot being fired. The public controversy that ensued over the navy's involvement in the capture of Amelia Island was one of the factors that induced Madison to officially renounce a filibuster he had helped instigate.[22] In the end, the most active role army regulars played in the incursion was to cover the retreat of the main body of filibusterers back to Georgia after they had been repulsed by the combined Spanish, Seminole, and African American forces defending the colonial capital at Saint Augustine. A small core group remained in the territory for more than a year thereafter, unsuccessfully attempting to foment a general rebellion against Spanish rule.[23]

The second incursion (1814) was seemingly a legitimate War of 1812 operation against the British forces occupying northwestern Florida. Even then, General Andrew Jackson's invading force, which included a mixture of army regulars, militia,

Creek and Choctaw warriors, and his own Tennessee volunteers, skirmished with Seminoles who were allied with the British and seized Black Seminoles who were allegedly either the fugitive or "stolen" slaves of European American settlers.[24] This incursion was not only a prelude to the Battle of New Orleans but to a third incursion (1816) whose primary purpose was to destroy a Seminole maroon community that had occupied an old British fort on the Apalachicola River. Georgia and South Carolina officials demanded the destruction of this "Negro Fort" because they contended that it served as a magnet for slave runaways. Acting under Jackson's orders, Colonel Duncan L. Clinch (Georgia) laid siege to the fort with a force which, again, included a mixture of regulars, militia, Creeks, volunteers, and, this time, a Navy cruiser. During the siege of the fort, a cannonball from the cruiser struck the fort magazine. The resulting explosion destroyed the fort, killing most of the African Americans who remained inside. Creek warriors tracked down the survivors and kept or (re)sold them as slaves.[25]

The final American incursion into Florida was initially calculated to drive the Seminoles out of the northern part of the territory, but it turned into a filibuster nevertheless. During the First Seminole War (1817–1818), Jackson once again marched a mixture of forces into the territory in response to Georgia and South Carolina complaints of continuing problems with Seminole slave raids on their plantations and slave runaways to Seminole lands. Jackson himself described the war as "this savage and negro war."[26] After compelling the Seminoles and their African American allies to evacuate northern Florida for points further south, Jackson's forces marched on to occupy Pensacola. Jackson withdrew his forces from the town only when President James Monroe explicitly ordered him to do so. Congress nearly censured Jackson for his "unauthorized" actions during the war.[27]

Given that none of these incursions were regular military operations, the army did not document their costs. However, some of the federal expenses associated with the incursions were documented. The 1825 Treaty with the Choctaws, concluded with Secretary of War John C. Calhoun (South Carolina Democratic Republican) in Washington, granted the Choctaws $14,973 for their services during the 1814 incursion.[28] More than twenty years after the fact, Congress rewarded the navy personnel who blew up the "Negro Fort" with a $5,465 bounty.[29] During Calhoun's tenure, the Department of War also paid Jackson's Tennessee volunteers $50,000 for their services in the First Seminole War.[30] Soon after that war ended, Spanish officials, realizing that the next incursion might well be a full-scale invasion, decided to sell Florida to the United States. As the preceding chapter shows, Secretary of State John Quincy Adams (Massachusetts Democratic Republican) agreed during the treaty negotiations that the federal government would reimburse Florida residents for their property losses, including slave losses, from the war as well as from the earlier incursions into the territory.

As the last chapter also shows, the acquisition of Florida transformed the Seminole problem from an international problem into a domestic one. Even though the preacquisition incursions into the territory had driven the Seminoles onto lands further from European American settlements, European American clashes with Seminoles over land and slaves continued. In 1823, federal officials pressured the Seminoles into signing the Treaty of Moultrie Creek, which "obligated" the nation to remove west of the Mississippi River as soon as a mutually agreeable site for resettlement could be found.[31] This stipulation proved to be the window through which the Seminoles were able to delay removal for more than a decade. While many Seminoles resisted abandoning their Florida lands, the Black Seminoles were the most resistant because they believed that removal would mean (re)-enslavement to European American settlers.[32] Meanwhile, territorial officials and residents continued to petition their new federal government to remove the Seminoles from Florida in order to protect and possibly expand their land and slave holdings.[33]

Following the passage of the Indian Removal Act of 1830, federal officials negotiated new removal treaties with the Seminoles and the other four "civilized" nations. The Seminoles signed the Treaty of Payne's Landing in 1832, which again "obligated" the nation to move west of the Mississippi River.[34] This time, however, the treaty designated a resettlement site on western Creek lands, where the Seminoles were very reluctant to resettle because of their past conflicts with Creeks, again especially the Black Seminoles, who feared that Creeks would seize them as slaves or else (re)sell them as slaves to European American settlers.[35] The treaty also set aside $7,000 for settling slave disputes with European American settlers prior to removal. Both these factors continued to delay the removal process. The army deployed more troops to Florida during the summer of 1835 and prepared to use force to remove the Seminoles from the territory. But the Seminoles struck first.

The Second Seminole War began when the Seminoles ambushed an army detachment under the command of Major Francis L. Major Dade (Virginia) on December 28, 1835, near Bushnell, Florida. Seminole forces killed Dade and all but 4 of his 111 soldiers. During the initial years of the war, Black Seminoles formed the backbone of the resistance to the army efforts to remove them and the other Seminoles from Florida. Two years into the war, the new commanding general, Quartermaster General Thomas S. Jesup (Kentucky), adopted the strategy of promising Black Seminoles that they could emigrate to Indian territory along with the other Seminoles as free persons, notwithstanding any European American claims to them. Local officials protested Jesup's decision, and he was compelled to formally withdraw his offer. However, he unofficially pursued the strategy. By the end of 1838, most of the Black Seminoles had been removed from Florida.[36] Thereafter, the war slowly wound down to a rather indecisive conclusion. On August 14, 1842, then-commanding officer Colonel William J. Worth (New York), bowing to executive and congressional pressure to end an increasingly costly guerrilla war, simply declared it over, despite the fact that more than 300 "hostile" Seminoles remained in the southern part of the peninsula.[37] At seven years, the Second Seminole War was the nation's longest war until the Vietnam War. In pursuing the war effort, the federal government spent an estimated $30 million to remove approximately 3,000 Seminoles from Florida, roughly $10,000 per capita.[38]

Many factors caused the Seminoles to resist their removal from Florida and European American settlers to insist on it. Those factors include the understandable reluctance of the Seminoles to leave their lands, their equally understandable reluctance to settle on Creek lands in the new trans-Mississippian Indian territory, the general desire of European American settlers for Native American lands, and the general antipathy of European Americans toward Native Americans. But several special slavery-related factors explain why the Seminoles were the only Native American nation to violently resist removal for any length of time and also why European American settlers refused to accept anything less than a very costly campaign to remove them.[39] These factors include the continuing disputes over slaves between Seminoles and European American settlers in Florida and the surrounding states, the large number of African Americans living among the Seminoles whom European American settlers considered a powerful inducement to slave runaways, and the determination with which those Black Seminoles resisted removal because they equated removal with (re)enslavement to European Americans or, perhaps worse, Creeks. In the absence of these special slavery-related factors, the federal government would probably have eventually removed the Seminoles west of the Mississippi River anyway, just as it had already removed or was in the process of removing other Native American nations across the river. However, the federal government had to use such force in the case of the Seminoles because European American settlers in Florida and the surrounding states were so insistent on removal (but not before their alleged slaves were returned to them) and because the Black Seminoles were so resistant to removal (rightfully suspecting that they were the alleged slaves in question). Furthermore, the fact that the Seminoles had already been driven southward onto less desirable lands in Florida during the First Seminole War also meant that expropriating their lands was a less immediate concern in their case than in the case of the other four Native American nations targeted by the Indian Removal Act.[40] In the absence of slavery, Seminole removal may have been delayed for many years, possibly decades.[41]

Even before Jesup replaced territorial Governor Richard K. Call as the commanding officer in Florida, he wrote his superiors at the Department of War in December 1836 that the Second Seminole War was a "negro war," not an "Indian war," because he believed that the Black Seminoles formed the backbone of the

Seminole resistance to removal. He also warned his superiors that if the Seminole "insurgency" was "not speedily put down, the South will feel the effect of it on their slave population before the end of the next season."[42] A scholarly consensus concurs that the Second Seminole War was at least as much a "negro war" as it was an "Indian war" because of the unique role resistant Black Seminoles and insistent European American slaveholders played in the conflict.[43]

The Second Seminole War was distinct from other Indian wars and removals, even from the other southeast removals. It was also distinct from other cases of national expansion and filibustering. The annexation of Texas might have been a comparable case of slavery expansion. Yet "manifest destiny" would probably have engulfed Texas, within a similar time frame, even in the absence of slavery. Unlike in the case of the Second Seminole War, no scholarly consensus has emerged on the relationship between the presence of slavery and the annexation of Texas.[44] Even if Seminole removal would have occurred within a similar time frame in the absence of slavery, it would not have required seven years of warfare and an estimated $30 million to remove approximately 3,000 Seminoles from Florida. As we will see, the $10,000 per capita costs were much higher than in the case of the other southeast removals.

In the case of the Second Seminole War, the Department of War documented many of the costs of the war because it was a regular army (and navy) operation.[45] Documented army expenses from October 1, 1835, to September 30, 1840, were $18,948,183.[46] Documented navy expenses for 1838–1842 were $504,489.[47] Documented removal expenses as of June 6, 1842, were $144,226.[48] The army spent another $8,293 on a delegation of Seminoles that traveled, at its behest, from Arkansas to Florida in 1840 to attempt to convince the remaining Seminoles to emigrate.[49] The total for these four items is $19,603,121.

This total is, however, incomplete. Even assuming that the figures are complete for the times they cover, they do not cover the whole war period. Nor do they cover many of the nonmilitary costs of the war. During the war, the army salaried a large civilian workforce (including slaves) in Florida, paid one year's living expenses of territorial residents (and their slaves) who were dislocated by the war, and offered one year's living expenses to entice European Americans (with their slaves) to settle in Florida to act as a buffer against the Seminoles who remained in the southern part of the territory.[50] These policies benefited many (potential) Florida residents but they disproportionately benefited slaveholders. In his firsthand account of the war, Major John T. Sprague (Michigan) even intimated that Florida residents had sabotaged the war effort in order to keep federal money flowing into their pockets.[51] The estimates of the total costs of the Second Seminole War range from $20 to $40 million, with "at least $30 million" as the median.[52] Total federal expenditures also surged from $17.6 million in 1835 to $30.9 million in 1836 and total military expenditures from $9.6 million to $18 million. Both totals reached their pre–Mexican-American War peaks the next year, at $37.2 million and $20.3 million, respectively, when the Second Seminole War was at its height. At $30 million, the war would have absorbed 13.5 percent of total federal expenditures and 24 percent of total military expenditures from 1835 through 1842.[53]

The Second Seminole War was also costly in terms of lives. The U.S. military lost a total of 1,555 men in the war, though only 328 of the total were battle deaths.[54] Most of the deaths were from malarial diseases contracted while marching through the Florida swamps in futile pursuit of Seminoles. At the height of the war in 1837, more than three fifths of the authorized force of the army—4,552 of 7,130 men—was stationed in Florida, along with another 4,046 militia and volunteers. As a direct result of the war, Congress approved an increase in the authorized force of the army from 7,130 to 11,800 men in November 1837, which was the only such increase between the War of 1812 and the Mexican-American War.[55] The army did not record the number of deaths among its auxiliary forces, nor provide any reliable estimates of Seminole casualties.[56] Approximately 40,000 Americans saw service in the Second Seminole War, roughly one fourth of them regulars and three fourths militia and volunteers.[57]

The Second Seminole War was an important slavery-related policy episode not only because of the costs of the war but also because of the escalating level of coercion that the federal government applied against the Seminoles. Unlike the earlier military actions against the Seminoles in Florida, the Second Seminole War was a regular army operation and became more so over time. From 1836 to 1841, the proportion of regulars in the U.S. military force in the territory increased from 48 to 100 percent.[58] In his account of the war, Sprague has two "axes to grind." The first ax is directed at the civilian chain of command, which, he argues, had foisted an unnecessary guerrilla war on the army because it was too responsive to the demands of local slaveholders. The second ax is directed at the volunteer and militia units, which, he argues, were grossly overpaid and more of a handicap than an asset to the war effort.[59] An 1840 Treasury audit documents $1,827,536 in regular army pay and $3,070,024 in volunteer and militia pay during the first five years of the war.[60] Given that army regulars constituted 64 percent of the U.S. military force in the territory during those years, the per capita costs of the volunteer and militia units were nearly three times as high.[61] Sprague thus applauds the (belated) Department of War decision to use only regulars in the later stages of the war. He also recalls how local officials had protested that decision because it meant less money for constituents who served in the volunteer and militia units, just as they had protested Jesup's decision to offer Black Seminoles freedom in the West because it meant less slaves for constituents who claimed Black Seminoles as their fugitive or "stolen" slaves.[62]

Even though the Second Seminole War was not a success as a military operation, it was an organizational success for the regular army. By the end of the war,
the army had increased its authority relative to volunteer and militia units and its
autonomy relative to local constituency pressures.[63] It also exited the war a larger
force. While troop levels fell after the war, they remained higher than they had
been before the war. In 1834, 7,030 men served in the army, and in 1843, the figure
was 9,102, a roughly 30 percent increase.[64] Even this largely forgotten "Indian war"
had its ratchet effect.[65]

Post–Second Seminole War expenses also accumulated. In 1845, the federal
government reimbursed the Seminoles $13,000 for their abandoned improve-
ments in Florida.[66] In 1851, the new Department of Interior hired an agent, Luther
Blake (Alabama), to attempt to convince the remaining Florida Seminoles to emigrate to Indian territory. Though his mission failed miserably, his expenses totaled
$48,006.[67] The 1856 treaty that finally recognized the Seminoles as a separate nation
included a payment of $400 to the heirs of Foc-te-luc-te-harjoe ("Black Dirt") for
his services during the Second Seminole War.[68] In the meantime, a third, low-in-
tensity Seminole war (1855–1858) had flared up in Florida. The federal government
spent $70,352 to remove another group of 165 Seminoles to Indian territory at the
end of that war.[69] Yet even after the Third Seminole War, as many as 150 Seminoles
remained in southern Florida.[70]

This section has detailed a number of federal expenditures associated with U.S.
military operations in Florida from the 1814 incursion into Spanish East Florida to
the end of the Third Seminole War.[71] By far the largest of those expenditures were
associated with the Second Seminole War. The war was the federal government's
most expensive slavery-related policy episode and also one of its most important.
It significantly increased the capacities of both the U.S. military and the American
state.

THE SOUTHEAST REMOVALS

In the case of the other four "civilized" nations in the southeastern United States,
the removal process was less conflictual and costly, and the demands of local European American slaveholders were less central to the process. The Cherokees,
Chickasaws, Choctaws, and Creeks occupied lands more on the major axes of European American settlement. They faced more generalized European American
pressure for removal. Their African American slaves also fit the European American image of slaves more than the slaves of the Seminoles did.[72] Slave disputes
between them and local European American slaveholders were less common.
These differences do not mean, however, that their removals were not conflictual

or costly, or that the demands of local European American slaveholders were not an important factor in the process. Nor does it mean that the U.S. army played no role in their removals.

As was the case in territorial Florida, European American slaveholders in Georgia, Alabama, and Mississippi sought to expand their slaveholdings onto Native American lands. They also sought to better secure their slaveholdings against the possibility of slaves running away to Native American lands or, alternatively, of Native American raiding parties seizing their slaves. Native American removal solved multiple problems for European American slaveholders in many Southern localities. Local European American slaveholders were especially active in lobbying the federal government as well as their own state governments on the issue.[73] The House vote on the Indian Removal Act of 1830 strongly suggests that Southern congressmen were responsive to the demands of local European American slaveholders in supporting the act. Southwest expansion was slavery expansion, and Native American removal was necessary to both processes.[74]

The five "civilized" nations were slaveholding nations that existed amid a dominant European American slaveholding culture. This factor distinguished them from, in particular, the Native American nations in the Northern states and territories, as did the fact that they were still relatively large, cohesive nations and retained relatively large, fertile lands at the time of their removals.[75] Unlike the five "civilized" nations, the Native American nations in the Northern states and territories were not the targets of systematic removal campaigns. Their removals began earlier and also were more gradual, more piecemeal, and, generally, more peaceable. The Black Hawk War (1832), which might seem to have been an analogous case of a removal war to the Second Seminole War, was actually a testament to the piecemeal nature of the process in the North. Black Hawk's small band of approximately 500 Sauks was the only one that had not already moved west of the Mississippi River. The resulting "war" to remove them essentially consisted of one "battle," when American forces and their Sioux allies caught the band unawares as it encamped along the banks of the Mississippi River and killed as many as 165 of its members.[76] Furthermore, the presence of slavery within both European American and Native American communities in the southeastern United States greatly complicated the removal process even when it did not lead to war.

The extensive interaction between the five "civilized" nations and European American settlers and African American slaves during the late eighteenth and early nineteenth centuries had made those nations highly diverse population groups and transformed their own slaveholding patterns.[77] The preremoval censuses of the five "civilized" nations delineate these demographic changes. In the preremoval census of the Cherokee nation, which spread across the borders of Georgia, Alabama, Tennessee, and North Carolina, army census takers identify

16,542 individuals as Indian, 201 as white, and 1,592 as (presumably black) slaves.[78] In the preremoval census of the Choctaw nation in central Mississippi, they identify 17,963 individuals as Indian, 151 as white, and 512 as slaves. In the preremoval censuses of the Chickasaws in northern Mississippi and southwestern Tennessee and of the Creeks in Georgia and Alabama, the number of whites is not recorded, but the number of slaves is. The Chickasaw nation included 5,224 Indians and 1,156 slaves and the Creek nation, 21,762 Indians and 902 slaves. Finally, the preremoval census of the Seminole nation counts 4,883 Seminoles in Florida, but neither the number of whites nor of slaves living among the Seminoles is recorded. As one indication of their particularly contentious relations with the federal government, the Seminoles did not allow army census takers onto their lands, and in taking their own census, they refused to disaggregate their population by either race or status. According to contemporary estimates, approximately 800 Black Seminoles lived in Florida before the Second Seminole War.[79]

When the federal government removed these Native American nations west of the Mississippi River, it did not remove undifferentiated masses of Native Americans. It removed Native Americans divided into matrilineally related clans as well as into sometimes overlapping and sometimes cross-cutting factions organized along racial ("pure breed" or "mixed breed"), ideological ("traditionalist" or "modernist"), religious (anthropomorphic or Christian), occupational (hunting or agricultural), economic (subsistence-oriented or market-oriented), and labor-organization (nonslaveholding or slaveholding) lines.[80] It also removed several thousand African Americans and European Americans who were at least partially integrated into one or more Native American communities.[81] By the 1830s, few Native American communities were homogeneous, racially or otherwise, but still each community had somewhat different interests and somewhat different conflicts with neighboring European American communities. Local Indian agents and army officers attempted to arbitrate those conflicts short of violence, both before and during the removal process. Obviously, they were not always successful. While the Seminoles resisted removal most unitedly and violently, the other four "civilized" nations resisted to varying degrees and in varying ways. Even when they did not, the U.S. army was involved in the process in a supervisory capacity.

In the case of the Creek nation, a group of young "traditionalist" Creeks organized a series of armed forays directed at isolated European American settlements along the Georgia-Alabama border in a somewhat futile attempt to forestall their scheduled removal to Indian territory. As a result, the U.S. army had to temporarily divert soldiers from Florida to the Georgia-Alabama border in the short-lived Creek War of 1836 to begin the removal process. Even though the more "modernist" Creek leadership quickly moved to squelch the violence, the federal government still spent an estimated $250,000 on the war.[82] During the removal process, army detachments then accompanied the Creeks to their new lands to deter further resistance. Army officers also contracted with private suppliers to transport and provision the Creeks as they moved westward. In the peak Creek removal period (1836–1837), the federal government spent an estimated $930,000 to remove approximately 19,000 members of the Creek nation, roughly $49 per capita.[83]

The Cherokees organized no large-scale armed resistance to removal. Nonetheless, individual Cherokees fought removal and as many as 1,000 Cherokees fled removal to the inaccessible mountainous regions of North Carolina and Tennessee, where the federal government left them rather than bear the costs of attempting to remove them.[84] The nation as a whole also resisted removal for many years through the legal process, eventuating in two landmark Supreme Court decisions, *Cherokee Nation v. Georgia* (1831) and *Worcester v. Georgia* (1832).[85] Confronting no organized armed resistance to removal, the army played a less active role in the Cherokee removal process than it did in the case of either the Seminoles or Creeks. But army personnel still coordinated the process and hired private contractors to provision the Cherokees on their way westward. The Trail of Tears (1838–1839) exposed the ineptitude and, in many cases, venality of army contractors to a greater extent than in the case of the other southeast removals because the Cherokees traveled the furthest, and mostly on foot, to their new lands.[86] During the Trail of Tears, the federal government spent an estimated $1,260,000 to remove approximately 12,200 members of the Cherokee nation, roughly $103 per capita.[87]

From the European American perspective, the removal process went the smoothest in the case of the Chickasaws and Choctaws. Yet the process was anything but smooth from the perspectives of the Chickasaws and Choctaws, nor was it inexpensive. The Chickasaw nation was the only Native American nation that was to pay its own removal expenses through the sale of tribal lands. Federal officials adopted two controversial policies to effect that purpose in the removal treaty that they negotiated with the Chickasaws. First, the treaty preemptively allocated individual sections of tribal land to individual members of the Chickasaw nation so that they could sell the land to pay their own removal expenses and use any surfeit to defray their start-up costs in Indian territory. Second, in a policy that perfectly reflected the unofficial policy of encouraging plantation slavery among the five "civilized" nations, the treaty allocated Chickasaw slaveholders extra land, depending on how many slaves they owned.[88] Both policies clearly advantaged the Chickasaw slaveholding elites who had negotiated the treaty. They also created an explicitly two-tiered removal process, which further divided the nation into largely "mixed-breed," slaveholding and largely "pure-breed," nonslaveholding factions.[89] Notwithstanding these self-removal policies, the army ultimately arranged for transporting and provisioning many of the Chickasaws across the Mississippi River because European American settlers in Mississippi had swindled them out of their lands or else paid them fire-sale prices, knowing that they had to sell their lands quickly. During the peak Chickasaw removal period (1837–1838), the federal government spent an estimated $1,040,000 to remove approximately 5,900 members of the Chickasaw nation, roughly $178 per capita.[90]

The Choctaws also largely organized their own removals. During the winter of 1831–1832, they were the first of the five "civilized" nations to emigrate en masse across the Mississippi River, in part because the state of Mississippi had adopted the most draconian measures to pressure them to emigrate and in part because their traditional hunting grounds lay across the river in the newly designated Indian territory. The Choctaws were also the only one of the five "civilized" nations in which a sizable minority decided to live under state law rather than emigrate.[91] For the majority who emigrated, the army, once again, coordinated the process and hired private contractors to (inadequately) provision the removal parties. From 1831 to 1833, the federal government spent an estimated $850,000 to remove approximately 14,200 members of the Choctaw nation, roughly $60 per capita.[92]

Every Native American removal reflected the official binary relation between European Americans and Native Americans, which was the separation of the two races. Before the Civil War, the federal government had accomplished this racial separation in the eastern United States by forcing a number of Native American nations across the Mississippi River.[93] In the southeastern United States, the official binary relation between European Americans and Native Americans was, however, caught in the web of slavery, which was the official binary relation between African Americans and European Americans in those states and territories.[94] The Second Seminole War was exemplary in this respect. In fact, the war was a conflict in which the federal government triangulated the interests of many different parties. In pursuing its war efforts, the U.S. army pitted European Americans (soldiers and settlers) against both African Americans (Black Seminoles) and Native Americans ("Red" Seminoles). In removing Black Seminoles and recruiting them as guides, interpreters, negotiators, and even combatants in its war efforts, the army pitted African Americans (Black Seminoles) against Native Americans ("Red" Seminoles).[95] In employing Creeks and the members of several other Native American nations during the war as auxiliary soldiers, it pitted Native Americans (non-Seminoles) against both African Americans (Black Seminoles) and other Native Americans ("Red" Seminoles). If one adds the Creek War of 1836 to the equation, the army also pitted European Americans against Creeks as well as Creeks against each other because, like the earlier and much larger Red Stick War of 1813–1814, the conflict was as much a civil war as an Indian war.[96]

In the southeastern United States, the removal process was then not simply a process of moving an undifferentiated mass of Native Americans out of the way of the westward migration of an undifferentiated mass of European Americans. The process removed highly diverse Native American populations out of the way of, in particular, European American slaveholders and their African American slaves. The presence of slavery was not the sole cause of Native American removal in the southeastern United States, but the presence of slavery was crucial to its timing and, especially in the Seminole case, its heavy costs.

In the twelve years following the passage of the Indian Removal Act, the federal government spent an estimated $34.3 million to remove approximately 55,000 members of the five major Native American nations in the southeastern United States across the Mississippi River. This total would represent 11.5 percent of aggregate federal spending ($297 million) from the first effective year of the act (1831) through the final official year of the Second Seminole War (1842).[97] Again, most of the total was spent on that war, which was the removal process in the case of the Seminoles. The other removals, though, were not inexpensive, either in terms of their human or financial costs. Perhaps not surprisingly, the federal government kept no records of the costs to the Native Americans, in terms of lives lost and properties abandoned, stolen, or sold at bargain prices to European American settlers and speculators prior to their removal. It has been estimated that the Seminoles lost as much as one half of their population and the five "civilized" nations together as much as one third of their populations during the removal process and in their initial years in Indian territory.[98]

While Seminole removal was closely connected to conflicts over slaves and slavery in Florida and the surrounding states, the other four major removals in the southeastern United States might well have occurred within a similar time frame in the absence of slavery. The costs of removing their slaves were, however, slavery-related expenses. We can obtain a rough estimate of those expenses by multiplying the percentage of slaves in the preremoval censuses of each nation by its estimated removal costs. This method yields results of $113,400 ($1,260,000 × 9 percent) for the Cherokees, $187,200 ($1,040,000 × 18 percent) for the Chickasaws, $25,500 ($850,000 × 3 percent) for the Choctaws, and $37,200 ($930,000 × 4 percent) for the Creeks. The estimated total of the slavery-related removal expenses for these four nations would be $363,300.

In deploying the army to remove the five "civilized" nations across the Mississippi River, federal officials seemed unconcerned that the policy might overreach their authority to regulate "commerce" with "Indian tribes."[99] They were, rather, focused on satisfying the immediate demands of Southern whites, especially Southern white slaveholders, to remove Native Americans. By satisfying those demands, they could increase the legitimacy of federal institutions while, not coincidentally, also enhancing their own authority.

The southeast removals were also pivotal events in the early development of the U.S. army as it removed more than 50,000 Native Americans across the

Mississippi River. In the case of the Seminoles, it engaged in a seven year's war to accomplish the task, largely displacing the role that volunteer and militia units had played in prior Indian wars. In the case of each of the southeast removals, the army's efforts to organize, coordinate, and supply the removal parties represented a massive military intervention into Southern civil society as it developed an extensive network of contractors and subcontractors to accomplish the task. This network was then available to accomplish other tasks, such as meeting the basic supply needs of the U.S. military. The southeast removals also anticipated the military mobilizations that occurred, admittedly on a much more massive scale, during the Civil War, as well as the nation's four major twentieth-century wars.[100]

SLAVE REVOLTS

Without officially announcing any such policy, the U.S. army deployed troops in response to slave revolts, actual, rumored, or simply feared, in the Southern states and territories. Tommy Richard Young II documents the requests from Southern officials for more troops in response to local anxieties over slave control.[101] Within the limits of its manpower, the Department of War honored such requests. According to Young, the army had two primary duties on the Southern frontier, Indian pacification and slave control.[102] We have just seen how those two duties substantially overlapped in the case of the southeast Native American removals.

The army deployed troops in response to both of the two largest slave revolts on U.S. soil during the 1791–1861 period.[103] In response to the January 1811 slave revolt in Orleans territory, Brigadier General Wade Hampton (South Carolina) deployed an army regiment from the Baton Rouge garrison to the site of the revolt along the German Coast of the Mississippi River, north of New Orleans, at the request of territorial Governor William C. C. Claiborne. Though local plantation owners suppressed the revolt before the regiment arrived, it still marched through the area to deter further unrest.[104] Orleans territory and then the state of Louisiana was the site of seemingly constant troop movements and arms shipments because of rumored slave revolts, both before and after the German Coast revolt.[105]

After the August 1831 Southampton (Nat Turner) slave revolt in Virginia, Governor John B. Floyd decided not to request more federal troops because he felt that doing so would imply that his state could not control its own slave population. When the mayor of Norfolk, John E. Holt, requested and received assistance from nearby Fort Monroe, the commander of the state militia, General Richard Epps, sent the troops back to the fort. Such concerns did not, however, deter state and local officials elsewhere from requesting more troops; the Department of War was flooded with such requests. The department even generated a plan for a general redeployment of army forces from Northern to Southern garrisons. The Secretary of War, Lewis Cass (Michigan Democrat), ultimately decided against the plan as it became clear that the Southampton revolt was an isolated event. He also had to refuse most of the local requests for more troops because he lacked the manpower to fill them. The War Department, nonetheless, redeployed two army companies from Fort Johnston, North Carolina, to Wilmington and New Bern, near the Virginia border, as well as stationed another two companies in New Orleans.[106] Under the previous secretary of war, John H. Eaton (Tennessee Democrat), the army had already redeployed two companies from Fort Monroe to Wilmington in 1830 because of a rumored Christmas Day slave rebellion in that city.[107]

Although Charleston officials uncovered the Denmark Vesey conspiracy in July 1822 in its final planning stages, it still caused general unrest throughout South Carolina. In addition to overseeing the executions of Vesey and thirty-six of his alleged co-conspirators, South Carolina Governor Thomas Bennett secretly wrote the state's "own" secretary of war, John C. Calhoun, asking him to reinforce the army garrison in Charleston. Not surprisingly, Calhoun complied, ordering the redeployment of an army company from Saint Augustine to Charleston.[108]

Another case in which army officials deployed troops in response to an attempted slave insurrection was John Brown's October 1859 raid on Harpers Ferry, Virginia. Upon receiving word of the raid, Secretary of War Floyd, the former Virginia governor who had refused to request federal assistance following the Southampton revolt, now took a different view of such matters and dispatched a contingent of marines under the command of Colonel Robert E. Lee to Harpers Ferry. The marines staged the final assault on Brown's party and captured Brown himself. Lee returned to Harpers Ferry six weeks later with four army companies from Fort Monroe to ensure that Brown's execution was not disrupted by any rescue attempt, as had been widely rumored.[109]

In each of these four cases, the federal government fulfilled its constitutional commitment to suppress insurrections and domestic violence.[110] One of the charges in the Garrison indictment of the U.S. Constitution as a proslavery document claimed that the primary intention of the two "domestic violence" clauses was to obligate the federal government to suppress slave revolts.[111] At the Constitutional Convention, Rufus King (Massachusetts), Luther Martin (Maryland), and Gouverneur Morris (Pennsylvania) had each supported banning slave imports on the grounds that the federal government would be responsible for suppressing slave revolts.[112] In his typically acerbic fashion, Morris comments that the Northern states "are to bind themselves to march their militia for the defence of the Southern States . . . against those very slaves of whom they complain."[113] In his report on the convention to the Maryland legislature, Martin argues that the proposed constitution should have authorized Congress to immediately ban slave imports because "slaves weakened one part of the Union which the other parts are bound to protect."[114] Yet the possibility that the "domestic violence" clauses might require the federal government to suppress slave rebellions was not itself a subject of contention at the Constitutional Convention or in the state ratifying conventions.[115]

During the first seven decades of the existence of the federal government under the Constitution, federal officials deployed armed forces to suppress or deter slave rebellions in compliance with their constitutional duties. Unfortunately, we have no record of the costs of those deployments, but the deterrent effects were at least self-evident to the Southern officials who requested them. General Edmund P. Gaines (Virginia) even recommended to his superiors at the Department of War in 1832 that only army officers from the South should be stationed in the South because in the event of a slave revolt they would know "more intimately than Northern or Eastern men, the characters and peculiar habits of *the Southern people* of all colors."[116]

In an interesting recent study, Kathleen Sullivan analyzes the legislative response to the Vesey conspiracy in Charleston and Columbia.[117] The response at both the local and state levels was a strong assertion of police powers to control the state's large African American population, especially Charleston's large free African American population. Sullivan contends that this response demonstrates not only how local anxieties over slave control prompted Southern officials to assert state police powers but also how those same anxieties motivated them to defend those powers against possible federal encroachments. Accordingly, South Carolina officials staunchly defended the Negro Seamen Act, which was one of the state legislative responses to the Vesey conspiracy, from (determined) British and (much less determined) federal protests.[118] Virginia Governor Floyd's response to the Southampton revolt suggests that he shared similar concerns. Sullivan, though, does not mention South Carolina Governor Bennett's "secret" request for more federal troops in the aftermath of the Vesey conspiracy or how he was disappointed that the number of troops that "his" Secretary of War added to the Charleston garrison was not much greater.[119] In fact, the Vesey and Southampton cases both indicate that Southern officials were not reluctant, on ideological or any other grounds, to request federal assistance in cases in which they thought that it would help, rather than hinder, slave control; nor were Southern secretaries of war, including Floyd during John Brown's raid on Harpers Ferry, reluctant to provide it. Similarly, when Northern officials began to assert state police powers in ways that seemed to hinder slave control in fugitive-slave cases, Southern officials became the champions of federal police powers. In this instance, as in so many others, it was Southern, not Northern, elites who promoted early American state development.

FUGITIVE SLAVES

One powerful effect of the Fugitive Slave Law of 1850 was to nationalize the army's role in slave control. Federal officials now deployed army soldiers north of the Mason-Dixon line in order to keep African Americans in slavery.

Shortly after the passage of the new law, U.S. Marshal Charles Knox had requested and received army assistance in preventing a slave rescue in Detroit in October 1850.[120] Several months later, a group of free African Americans openly defied the law by rescuing a fugitive slave, Shadrach Minkins, from the Boston courthouse in February 1851.[121] In the wake of this highly publicized slave rescue, President Millard Fillmore authorized U.S. marshals to request the assistance of local army units to prevent future rescues.[122] During the Thomas Sims rendition in Boston in April 1851, Marshal Charles Devans did not request the assistance of army units to prevent his rescue, but municipal authorities did deploy the local militia, and the federal government paid the estimated $10,000 costs.[123] Following the slave-rescue "riot" outside Christiana, Pennsylvania, in September 1851, acting Secretary of State William S. Derrick (Pennsylvania) ordered the deployment of fifty soldiers and marines from Carlisle Barracks and the Philadelphia Navy Yard to the town to help restore order and (unsuccessfully) pursue the rescued slaves.[124]

The final fugitive-slave case in which federal officials deployed army regulars was the Anthony Burns rendition in Boston in June 1854. Initially, another antislavery "mob" attempted to rescue Burns, killing one deputy marshal, James Batchelder, in the attempt.[125] In order to prevent a recurrence, Marshal Watson Freeman deployed three companies of soldiers and marines from Fort Independence and the Charlestown Navy Yard on the streets surrounding the Boston courthouse.[126] After U.S. Commissioner Edward G. Loring remanded Burns to the custody of his owner, Charles F. Suttle, an armed force of approximately 1,600 soldiers, marines, militia, deputized marshals, and Boston police "escorted" the two men from the courthouse to the Treasury revenue cutter waiting to transport them back to Virginia.[127] The costs of this full-scale military deployment were not reported, but they undoubtedly exceeded the $10,000 estimate in the Sims case.[128] The whole episode proved so contentious that federal officials never again deployed army regulars in a fugitive-slave rendition.[129]

In enforcing a federal fugitive-slave law, federal officials were, once again, fulfilling one of their constitutional obligations. The use of the army to enforce such a law was, nevertheless, unprecedented, at least in the North. The convention delegates who agreed, through unanimous consent, to add a fugitive-slave clause to the proposed constitution certainly did not anticipate that the army would be used to enforce any enabling legislation. Not surprisingly, the deployment of army soldiers to enforce the Fugitive Slave Law of 1850 stoked the flames of sectional controversy over an already controversial law. Whatever the financial costs of those deployments were, the political significance of this policy area dwarfs those costs. While Southern secessionists complained of a lack of federal enforcement in fugitive-slave cases, Northern abolitionists complained of the opposite. On the first anniversary of the Sims rendition, Wendell Phillips decried the legal nationalization inherent in the Fugitive Slave Law of 1850, asserting that "not only is the slave statute held to be law, but . . . there is really no law beside it in the Free States,—to execute it, all other laws are set aside and disregarded."[130]

During the first seven decades of the existence of the federal government under the Constitution, federal officials also deployed armed forces to suppress domestic violence that was unrelated to slave control. The Whiskey Rebellion was the first of several such cases. Yet five of the fourteen pre–Civil War cases Robert Coakley discusses in his monograph on the topic are either (possible) slave revolts (Wilmington, Southampton, and Harpers Ferry) or fugitive-slave renditions (the Detroit and Anthony Burns cases).[131] Slave control was clearly one of the primary reasons that federal officials deployed armed forces to suppress domestic violence during the 1791–1861 period. As a result, the federal government acquired greater legitimacy in the South and greater authority in both the North and South.

SLAVERY IN THE TERRITORIES

The issue of slavery in the territories was the critical issue of the 1850s. The issue increased the supervisory costs of territories. It also required the intervention of the army in at least one territory during the decade.

Prior to the 1850s, the issue of slavery in the territories had a protracted history, dating back at least to the Northwest Ordinance of 1787. John Craig Hammond's recent work chronicles how the presence of slavery created controversy in every territory in the early republic, from Mississippi to Louisiana and from Ohio to Missouri.[132] Hammond also details how federal and territorial officials, even those with strong antislavery sympathies, were generally very solicitous of the interests of local slaveholders. For instance, Andrew Ellicott, who was a Quaker and the first provisional governor of Mississippi Territory, opposed congressional efforts to restrict slavery in the territory on the grounds that "slavery though disagreeable to us Northern people, it would certainly be expedient to let it continue in this district, where they [slaves] are numerous, upon the same footing it is at present in the southern States; otherwise emigrants possessed of that kind of property, would be induced to settle in the spanish territory."[133] Of course, many territorial officials had strong proslavery sympathies, such as Illinois territorial

Governor Ninian Edwards and Justice Alexander Stuart, both of whom sought transfers to Missouri so that they could more freely employ their slaves.[134] As late as 1839, President Martin Van Buren reappointed Henry Dodge territorial governor of Wisconsin despite the fact that he owned slaves.[135] Overall, the federal government did much less to keep slavery out of territories than it did to not keep the institution out of territories or, alternatively, to keep it in territories. Even with respect to the Northwest Ordinance, the first governor of Ohio Territory, Arthur St. Clair, interpreted its "article respecting slaves as a prohibition to any future introduction of them but not to extend to the liberation of those the people were already possessed of, and accquired [sic] under the sanction of law."[136]

The issue of slavery in the territories first became a major point of sectional controversy when Missouri applied for admission to the union as a slave state in 1819. The Missouri Compromise drew a line across the rest of the Louisiana Purchase, dividing free territory from slave territory. At the time, Missouri did not include the northwestern part of the present state. For the next sixteen years, this Platte region remained Indian territory, primarily Iowa and Sac-Fox lands, and presumably free territory, because it was north of the Missouri Compromise line. Over that time, the surrounding area became a major cotton-growing and slave-holding region. Local planters coveted the Native American lands and lobbied federal officials to acquire them. During the two years of 1836 and 1837, federal officials purchased the Platte region for a total of $18,320 in cash and gifts. The Native Americans who lived on those lands moved across the Missouri River to Kansas, and their former lands now became part of the slave state of Missouri. The Kansas-Nebraska Act was not the first violation of the Missouri Compromise.[137]

The Compromise of 1850 may have been the second. The compromise settled a number of lingering sectional disputes, but three of its provisions kept open the possibility of creating additional slave states. The first provision was to leave the Mexico cession open to slavery rather than extend the Missouri Compromise line to the Pacific or, worse from a Southern perspective, outlaw slavery in this huge new U.S. territory. (*Ex ante*, slavery was outlawed in the territory by Mexican law.) A second provision was important for its omission. In accepting the expedited admission of California as a free state, Congress deflected any attempt to also admit New Mexico as, presumably, a free state, which, in conjunction with the first provision, kept open the possibility of the territory's entering the union in the future as a slave state. The third provision was the $10 million side-payment to Texas to cede its claims to New Mexican lands, which, by settling a contentious border issue, not only kept open the possibility of New Mexico's future admission as a slave state but of Texas's future division into two or more slave states. While neither possibility came to fruition, both tantalized Southern sectionalists. It seems unlikely that they would have agreed to the compromise package in their absence.[138]

Four years later, the Kansas-Nebraska Act explicitly repealed the Missouri Compromise. The most immediate result of the repeal was "Bleeding Kansas," open warfare between antislavery and proslavery factions in the new Kansas Territory from 1855 to 1857. The Platte purchase meant that Kansas was bordered by a slave state. The "Border Ruffians" fully expected it to also become a slave state and were well positioned to force the issue over whatever opposition the "Jayhawkers" might mount.[139] The territorial militia was unable to keep the peace between the warring factions, in part because it was untrained and undisciplined and in part because it was aligned with one of the factions and thus not trusted by the other. The U.S. army had to intervene to restore the peace.

The pivotal event in restoring the peace in Kansas was Secretary of War Jefferson Davis's (Mississippi Democrat) September 1856 decision to authorize the local army commander, Brigadier General Persifor F. Smith (Pennsylvania), to place the territorial militia under his command.[140] From Davis's own perspective, he hoped the decision would stabilize conditions in Kansas and allow territorial residents to organize themselves as a proslavery territory and, eventually, state. The outgoing Pierce administration could also point to the decision as proof that it had pursued an even-handed policy in the territory, in hopes of minimizing the damage "Bleeding Kansas" was inflicting on the Democratic Party's electoral prospects in the Northern states.

Although the regular army expenses associated with the violence in Kansas were not documented, several other expenses associated with the violence were. At the end of 1856, the federal government paid the territorial militia $8,119 for its peace-keeping duties in Kansas.[141] Congress itself spent $2,400 on an 1856 investigation of the violence in Kansas, and a special 1858 territorial election required by its rejection of the Lecompton constitution cost another $10,000.[142]

Kansas was unique in generating such slavery-related federal expenses, but, as we have seen, it was not unique in witnessing slavery-related troop movements. Regardless of its human and financial costs, "Bleeding Kansas" was an important episode in the development of the army as it asserted its autonomy from constituency—both Border Ruffian and Jayhawker—demands in the territory in order to stanch the bleeding.[143]

The Constitution granted Congress plenary power over U.S. territories in another clause that did not precipitate any discussion at the Constitutional Convention.[144] The territories clause, however, became fodder for sectional controversy during the 1850s as the issue of slavery in the territories encouraged dueling expansive and cribbed readings of the clause. Republicans offered expansive readings to keep slavery "out," while Democrats offered cribbed readings to allow it "in." In his *Dred Scott* decision, Chief Justice Roger B. Taney, an old Southern Democrat, endorsed the latter view, but in ruling that not even territorial residents could keep slavery "out," he took a position that neither Northern Democrats nor Republicans could accept.[145] Yet even as the Supreme Court was considering the *Dred Scott* case, a territorial dispute over slavery had led to a strong assertion of federal power in one territory.

CONCLUSION

The U.S. military fought wars, removed Native Americans, suppressed domestic insurrections, returned fugitive slaves, and intervened in territorial disputes because of the continuing presence of slavery in the Southern states and territories. In each case, it performed one of the constitutional duties of the federal government and spent money, added personnel, and coerced people who resisted its policies. The presence of slavery was not the only reason that the U.S. military fought wars, removed Native Americans, suppressed domestic insurrections, and intervened in territorial disputes, but it was one reason, and it was of course the only reason that it returned fugitive slaves.

Substantial military expenditures sometimes occurred because of the presence of slavery during the 1791–1861 period. The Second Seminole War was conspicuous in this respect. Unfortunately, in other cases, such as the First Seminole War and "Bleeding Kansas," we lack documentation sufficient even to estimate the costs.

According to the person who demanded the documentation in the case of the Second Seminole War, it was an exemplary case of how the federal government deployed its military arm on behalf of slave interests. In his indictment of the war, Giddings accuses a nation, "which boasts of its justice, its honor, and love of liberty," of commencing a conflict "with a determination to re-enslave the Exiles [Black Seminoles]." After estimating the costs of the war at $40 million, Giddings pleads an inability to estimate "[t]he suffering of the Indians and Exiles amidst such prolonged persecution, such loss of lives and property."[146]

Partisan and sectional differences emerged in this policy area. In responding to Giddings's scathing critiques of the Second Seminole War, Southern Democrats, such as Edward Junius Black (Georgia), William O. Butler (Kentucky), and Mark Alexander Cooper (Georgia), were the most vocal defenders of the war effort.[147] The Indian Removal Act of 1830 exposed a sharp partisan and sectional division on the southeast Native American removals. While Native American removal had been the official policy of both the Monroe and John Quincy Adams administrations, Northern and, to a lesser extent, Southern Whigs held onto the vision of a voluntary, negotiated emigration of the five "civilized" nations westward.[148] Henry Clay (Kentucky) and Theodore Frelinghuysen (New Jersey) objected, in particular, to the coercive nature of the Jackson administration's removal policies.[149] The

Second Seminole War substantiated their fears. Though few Whigs framed the conflict as a war to protect slave interests in the same way that Giddings did, Horace Everett (Vermont) was another persistent Whig war critic.[150] The short-lived experiment in using bloodhounds to track Seminoles in southern Florida became an 1840 campaign issue and may have cost Van Buren some votes in the Northern states.[151] The congressional vote on the Fugitive Slave Law of 1850 was another highly sectional and, to a lesser extent, partisan vote. Many Northern Whigs and later Republicans, such as Charles Sumner (Massachusetts) and William Seward (New York), then opposed the use of the military to enforce the new law during the Pierce administration.[152] "Bleeding Kansas" saw further partisan and sectional divisions emerge over the issue of slavery in the territories, with Northern Democrats and Republicans temporarily coalescing to thwart the Southern-leaning policies of the Buchanan administration in the territory. The policy episode became a profile in courage physically for Sumner following his brutal caning at the hands of Preston Brooks (South Carolina) and politically for Stephen A. Douglas (Illinois) following his internecine opposition to the Lecompton constitution.[153] By the late 1850s, Northern Democrats (Douglas), Southern Democrats (Jefferson Davis), and Republicans (Abraham Lincoln) were presenting substantially different views of the extent of congressional power over slavery in the territories.[154]

Interregional differences also emerged in this policy area. The Southampton revolt prompted the Virginia legislature to debate the future of slavery in the state and pledge its support for African colonization.[155] Ten years earlier, the Vesey conspiracy had provoked a very different reaction from the South Carolina legislature, including passage of the Negro Seamen Act. Following British protests against the act, upper-South Attorney General William Wirt (Maryland National Republican) issued a written opinion in 1824 that declared it an unconstitutional intrusion on the exclusive powers of Congress to regulate foreign and interstate commerce. Seven years later, lower-South Attorney General John Berrien (Georgia Democrat) issued a written opinion claiming that it was a perfectly legitimate assertion of state police powers.[156] In the 1850s, fugitive-slave renditions encountered much less resistance in the lower than upper North.[157]

Even though the commitment of federal officials to the use of the military to protect slavery may have wavered depending on the partisan and sectional control of the federal government, federal officials remained committed to protecting the institution. After all, two Northern Whigs, President Fillmore and Secretary of State Webster, first decided to use the military to enforce federal fugitive-slave law in the wake of the Minkins rescue. Two Northern Democrats, President Pierce and Attorney General Cushing, continued that policy. Many federal officials were, of course, personally committed to the continued existence of slavery. Prime examples would be Southern Democrats Calhoun and Eaton, who as secretaries of war ordered troop deployments in response to slave conspiracies, actual or merely rumored. Yet Eaton's successor, Northern Democrat Cass, also ordered troop deployments in response to the Southampton revolt. Many federal officials, from Northern as well as Southern states, were committed to protecting slavery not because they were personally committed to the continued existence of the institution but because they considered it an integral part of Southern society, which, as long as it remained an integral part of Southern society, they were obligated to protect. Their political survival also depended on such a commitment. As exiting Southern politicians correctly perceived in the secession winter of 1860–1861, the Lincoln administration promised to be the first administration that was "soft" in its commitment to protecting slavery because its political survival did not depend on such a commitment. The fact that the incoming president pledged not to interfere with slavery in the states where it already existed did not belie the truth of this perception.[158]

The commitment of federal officials to the use of the U.S. military to protect slavery had important effects on state development. The coercive aspects of the slavery-related military actions described in this chapter are obvious. The army coerced European Americans, African Americans, Native Americans, Mexican Americans, Spanish colonials, fugitive slaves, would-be slave rescuers, slave rebels, alleged slave conspirators, abolitionist "mobs," and, in Kansas, Jayhawkers and Border Ruffians, all in order to protect slavery.[159] The army deployments in these cases suggest a significant degree of noncompliance with such federal policies as Native American removals, interstate fugitive-slave returns, and the efforts of the Pierce and Buchanan administrations to make Kansas a slave state. This lack of legitimacy was apparent among the victims of those policies but also among broader publics in the North.

On the other hand, slavery-related military actions probably increased the legitimacy of the federal government in the South. Andrew Cayton argues that the European American settlers of the trans-Appalachian Southern states and territories seriously questioned the legitimacy of a distant federal government that seemed unconcerned with their problems in the early republic.[160] The failure of federal officials to neutralize the Native American threat to their settlements was a major source of this unrest. If Cayton is right, then the slavery-related military actions against the Native American nations in those states and territories that commenced during the War of 1812 and continued in the following decades must have significantly increased federal legitimacy. Hammond adds that federal legitimacy in the trans-Appalachian Southern territories also depended on Congress's not attempting to restrict slavery in those territories.[161] Based on their Department of War decisions, Southern officials considered the use of the military to enforce fugitive-slave laws and to deter slave revolts perfectly legitimate uses of military power.[162] Southern Democrats in the Pierce and Buchanan administrations were not only the chief architects of the efforts to make Kansas a slave state; they viewed those efforts as a test of the willingness of Northern Democrats in Congress to vote to admit additional slave states and restore the sectional balance in the Senate, a test 40 percent of the Northern Democrats in the House failed when they voted against admitting Kansas into the union under the Lecompton constitution.[163] As a result, federal legitimacy suffered in the South.

Slavery-related military actions also expanded the authority of the regular army, both in general and relative to militia and volunteer units. Through such engagements as the Second Seminole War and "Bleeding Kansas," the army developed greater institutional autonomy from local constituency demands and became a more professional organization that was less dependent on auxiliary forces.[164] Correlatively, these military actions exposed the dangers of employing private agents to perform state functions. At least initially, the militia proved less than useful in the Second Seminole War and "Bleeding Kansas." The performance of army contractors and subcontractors in the southeast Native American removals was an even more conspicuous case of how private motives can sabotage public purposes, though in this case the nature of the public purpose was itself ambiguous. But whether the purpose was to remove Native Americans as cheaply as possible or as humanely as possible, army contractors and subcontractors failed on both counts.

At least with respect to the military, Bensel's claim that the Union and the Confederacy had to start from scratch in building strong states at the beginning of the Civil War is incorrect.[165] Both states benefited from the institutional development of the army in the pre–Civil War period.[166] Though slavery-related military actions were not the sole causes of that development, they were among the causes, especially in the case of the Second Seminole War, where both future Confederate (Bragg and Johnston) and Union (Meade and Thomas) generals saw action. The army's experience in "Bleeding Kansas" also prepared it for its role in the Reconstruction South. Many of the same middle-level officers, such as Thomas J. Wood (Kentucky) and William H. Emory (Maryland), served in both places, and the nature of their peacekeeping duties was similar in both places.[167] The U.S. military proved itself capable of fighting a seven year's war to expel the Seminoles from Florida while simultaneously coordinating the removal of another 50,000 Native Americans across the Mississippi River. These are not the actions of a weak state.[168]

The U.S. army also learned some valuable lessons from its early slave-related engagements. Persifor Smith, John Sprague, and other members of the army officer corps had been schooled in the need to decrease the military's dependence on auxiliary forces.[169] In the case of both slave revolts and Native American conflicts, army officers thought local militia unreliable because the first concern of militiamen would be protecting their own homes and families.[170] Army officers had also been schooled in the need to increase the military's independence from executive, congressional, and constituency pressures in order to fight wars on its own terms.

William Tecumseh Sherman (Pennsylvania), who certainly shared the officer corps' disdain of ill-trained militia, intermeddling politicians, and unappreciative citizens, learned yet another lesson from the Second Seminole War, which he executed with some efficiency during the Civil War. Soon after graduating from West Point and arriving at Fort Pierce, Florida, on his first military assignment, Lieutenant Sherman presented his plan to end the Second Seminole War in an October 24, 1840, letter to his brother-in-law. According to Sherman, "the most certain and economical method" to end the war was to "send a sufficient number of troops to literally fill the territory, declare martial law and then begin the war of extermination."[171]

In terms of early American state development, the army's slavery-related deployments were similar to the navy's efforts to suppress the slave trade in (obviously) increasing the power of the military in the military-civilian balance. But, as is generally true of military actions, they also increased the power of the federal government in the federal-state balance and the executive in the executive-legislative balance. Those dynamics were long-term dynamics in early American state development, and the presence of slavery contributed to all three during the 1791–1861 period. With respect to judicial policy-making, the *Dred Scott* decision was an even clearer case of a judicial response to congressional paralysis on the issue of slavery in the territories than *Prigg* was a judicial invitation to congressional action on the issue of interstate fugitive-slave returns.

The new prominent element in this policy area was the level of secrecy involved in many slavery-related military actions and the enhanced power that secrecy conferred on military officers on the periphery.[172] Except to those on the scene in a distant borderland area, the Patriot War was a covert action, publicly exposed only after navy gunboat captains helped the "Patriots" capture Amelia Island. Similarly, the Second Seminole War became a public event to those outside the immediate area only when Giddings seized hold of it. In both cases, the key policy decisions were made by military officers on the scene, General Jesup and Colonel Worth during the Second Seminole War and Colonel Smith and Commodore Campbell during the Patriot War, and only in Worth's case was his decision to "prematurely" end the war clearly in line with the intentions of his civilian superiors.[173] No matter how much the American state was committed to protecting slavery before the

Civil War, state actors knew that the path of least resistance was to keep specific actions directed toward that end "out of sight."[174]

In addition to the many other ways that the U.S. military supported the institution of slavery during the pre–Civil War period, the army and navy led the federal government in slave rentals. The effects of this practice on state development might seem trivial. Counterfactually, if federal officials had not rented slaves in any given instance, would they not have simply hired free white laborers instead? Probably, but slave labor never simply substituted for free labor.

6. Free Labor Not Preferred

The federal government employed slave labor in a variety of ways during the 1791–1861 period. Slave rentals formed part of the state capacities of both the military and civilian departments of the federal government. Slave rentals also influenced federal labor-management practices; overseers were employed to supervise both free laborers and slave laborers at major work sites. Finally, slave rentals effectively increased the autonomy of the middle- and low-level federal officials who made the actual hiring and management decisions at those sites.

These developmental effects were not as significant as the ones I discuss in previous chapters. By any estimate, slaves formed a much smaller part of the federal workforce than free white laborers did, even in the Southern states. Yet the number of slaves working at some Southern federal facilities was more than half the work force; the effects on their owners, supervisors, and co-workers could be very significant. Moreover, the federal government's use of slave labor shows how extensively the institution of slavery had worked its way into its normal operations, almost without notice or objection.

Not surprisingly, the U.S. military was the largest federal employer of slave labor because it was the largest federal employer of all types of labor for most of the 1791–1861 period. The military employed slave labor at its Southern army posts and navy yards, despite the fact that the navy had adopted regulations against the latter practice.[1] It also employed slave labor to build its Southern army posts and navy yards. Slaves even served in the military. They generally served as the personal servants of army and navy officers. They occasionally served as soldiers and sailors, despite the fact that both the army and navy had adopted regulations against slave enlistments.[2] Finally, the military employed slaves in a number of support roles in wartime as well as peacetime. During the Second Seminole War, army quartermasters employed more than 150 slaves in Florida to help supply the war effort, mostly as laborers but also as blacksmiths, carpenters, and even one engineer.[3]

The civilian departments of the federal government also employed slave labor. Slaves worked for the U.S. Post Office, which surpassed the military as the largest federal employer in the 1840s.[4] Again, slaves worked for the post office most often as the personal servants of postal officials, but sometimes they worked as clerks and even carriers, despite regulations forbidding African Americans, either free or enslaved, from carrying the mail.[5] Southern Indian agents were invariably slaveholders and frequently also slave traders, smugglers, dealers, and stealers.[6]

They employed their own slaves at their agencies as well as rented the slaves of other slaveholders to perform occasional work. The practice of employing slaves as personal servants was apparently quite common in both the military and civilian departments of the federal government. Many federal employers were slaveholders. They could supplement their incomes by employing their own slaves as personal servants instead of hiring free persons to perform similar custodial duties. The civilian departments of the federal government also employed slave labor to work on construction projects. The Commissioners of the City of Washington employed slaves to help build the nation's capital, again mostly as laborers but also as sawyers, carpenters, and even masons.[7]

Federal employment practices mirrored society. Given that slave labor was a prominent form of labor in the Southern states and territories, the federal government employed slave labor in the Southern states and territories, just as state and local governments did.[8] Since many federal employers were themselves slaveholders, they employed their slaves at their own workplaces and lobbied other federal employers to employ their slaves at other workplaces. None of these practices should be surprising. They suggest that federal employment practices were neutral in their effects on the continued existence of slavery in the South.

The presence of slavery was, however, not neutral in its effects on federal employment practices. In the absence of slavery, those practices would have been quite different, again especially in the Southern states and territories. Federal employment practices constituted an important but unappreciated public policy that had significant effects on early American state development. Though those practices were highly regulated from the top, they were largely shaped on the ground. This decentralization made federal hiring decisions highly sensitive to local milieus, such as, in the South, slave-rental markets. The presence of slavery also affected federal management practices. The use of overseers was a general management practice that affected both slaves and free white laborers at federal work sites. The latter were, of course, not pleased to be treated like slaves, but they were even less pleased when they lost employment opportunities because federal employers rented slaves.

The presence of slavery may even have affected the other side of the equation. Especially in frontier areas, federal employment practices encouraged slaveholders to purchase more slaves and motivated nonslaveholders to become slaveholders. The latter effect was most striking in the case of Northern army officers who bought slaves to serve as their personal servants.

Federal employment practices created several ironic tensions. On the one hand, the more internal improvements the federal government built in the Southern states and territories, the more slaves it leased from Southern slaveholders to build them. On the other hand, a number of prominent Southern politicians opposed a national system of internal improvements in the post–War of 1812 years on the grounds that it would generate a slippery slope of loose construction that might culminate in a federally mandated abolition of Southern slavery.

Yet Southern opposition to internal improvements was not universal, nor was it unidimensional or static over time. Some principled opposition to a national system of internal improvements undoubtedly existed in the Southern states and territories, but politics and history scholars have privileged the slavery-fearful strict constructionism of John Randolph (Virginia) and Nathaniel Macon (North Carolina) as speaking for the whole Southern Democratic-Republican caucus, when they were actually in the minority.[9] Furthermore, Southern opposition to internal improvements increased over time not simply as a result of single-minded conversions to Randolph's and Macon's strict constructionism. Some Southern politicians opposed a national system of internal improvements not on states-rights grounds but because they felt that it would disproportionately benefit other states at the expense of their own states.[10] By the time of the Missouri crisis, the expectation that the development of the trans-Appalachian and then trans-Mississippian West would naturally benefit the slave South more than the free North seemed increasingly counterfactual.[11] In the case of John C. Calhoun, his celebrated conversion from nationalist to states-rightist reflected a mixture of constitutional principles and regional interests as well as a strategic desire not to allow younger, less nationalistic South Carolina politicians, such as James Henry Hammond and Robert Barnwell Rhett, to outflank him.[12] Perhaps most significantly, Southern slaveholders were very eager for local contractors and subcontractors to rent their slaves whenever the federal government built internal improvements in their own states and territories, regardless of the larger principles or interests that might be at stake.

A further irony would be if the federal government could have built more internal improvements in the Southern states and territories with the same amount of money because slave labor was cheaper than free labor. Federal employers, contractors, and subcontractors who rented slave labor very often made that claim, but they rarely tried to prove it. In the most extensive source of federal employment practices I consulted, army quartermasters paid the same rate for slave labor as they paid for free labor in the same job category.[13] Other sources report that the pay rates for slave labor were substantially lower than for free labor, as much as one-half lower. In many of these cases, however, slave labor was not really cheaper than free labor because slaves were provided "free" food, clothing, shelter, and medical care at federal work sites; or, if it was cheaper, it was not because slaves were rented at lower pay rates but because of job shifting. Job shifting occurred when slaves were rented as laborers to perform skilled tasks or were later assigned to perform such tasks without any pay increase, tasks which free white laborers were specifically hired at higher pay rates to perform.[14] Job shifting problematizes the fact that federal employment records list slaves as disproportionately performing the least skilled types of labor, as "laborers" or "common laborers," and as not performing or only rarely performing the most skilled types of labor, such as masonry and carpentry. We will examine one case in which free white laborers unsuccessfully protested job shifting because of its adverse effects on their employment prospects. Obviously, slaves had both less capacity and less incentive to protest the practice than free white laborers did, while slaveholders may have been unaware of the practice or satisfied because they had received the market rate for their slave rentals. If either free white laborers or slaveholders protested the practice, this chapter also shows that federal employers could be just as obdurate as private employers were, though they were more likely to bend to the protests of slaveholders than to those of free white laborers, particularly if either their superiors or Congress began to investigate their employment practices.

In fact, slave labor could have been more expensive than free labor at certain work sites. The Washington commissioners paid people substantial sums of money to supervise, feed, clothe, house, and care for the slaves who worked on the construction of the nation's capital because they were typically working far from their places of residence. Overseers also supervised free white laborers at the work site, who, if they were similarly situated, received some of the same "benefits" as slaves. Without a precise analysis of exactly who received what benefits when and how much time the overseers devoted to supervising slaves as opposed to free white laborers, it would be very difficult to prove that slave labor was cheaper (or dearer) at this or any other federal work site.[15] In addition, federal employers did not employ slave labor solely in order to save money but sometimes also because it was the most available source of labor, because they thought it was the most competent type of labor for the assigned task, because local slaveholders lobbied them to employ slave labor, or because they simply wanted to earn extra income by employing their own slaves. Federal employers who rented slaves offered "cheaper" as a blanket justification for their slave rentals because it was the justification that was most likely to satisfy their cost-conscious superiors and an even more cost-conscious Congress.

A final irony is that federal employers who rented slaves assumed the authority of the slaveholders whose slaves they had rented. Unlike some Southern state and local governments, the federal government never owned slaves.[16] Yet federal employers frequently owned slaves who performed public work. They also frequently supervised other slaveholders' slaves whom they had rented to perform public work. If, for example, 137 slaves worked at the Pensacola navy yard in July 1855, which represented more than 50 percent of the workforce, then navy officers at the yard devoted a considerable amount of time to supervising slaves or to supervising the overseers whom they had hired to supervise slaves.[17] A federal employer who rented slaves acquired temporary authority, both supervisory and disciplinary, over those slaves. This temporary transfer of authority could, and did, generate conflicts between federal employers and the slaveholders whose slaves they had rented, as well as between them and the free white laborers whom they had hired to work at the same site.

The decisions federal officials made to use or to approve the use of slave labor at federal work sites were not framed as political decisions in support of the continued existence of slavery. Instead, they were framed as administrative decisions, based on the available labor supply and cost-efficiency calculations. For both these reasons, the federal government continued to employ slave labor during the Civil War, which, many believed, was a war to end slavery.

On June 16, 1862, the Senate failed by one vote to pass an amendment to a navy appropriations bill that would have prevented the U.S. military from employing slave labor "in any capacity whatever, in any navy yard, dock yard, arsenal, magazine, fort, or in the Naval Academy."[18] The amendment would have had some practical effect because the federal government still controlled a few fortifications within the seceding slave states at which it employed slave labor, such as at Forts Jefferson, Pickens, and Taylor in Florida. The amendment, though, was largely symbolic because the areas of the former United States where slave labor was most prevalent were not under federal control. Congress had also already begun to debate proposals to abolish slavery in the seceding slave states. The next month President Lincoln would circulate his draft Emancipation Proclamation. The Senate, nonetheless, rejected the amendment. Politically, the defeat of the amendment was consistent with the Lincoln administration's determination to accommodate the interests of the non-seceding slave states, which, however, did not prevent a majority of the Republican senators from supporting it.[19] Administratively, the defeat of the amendment was consistent with the federal government's long-standing dependence on slave labor at its Southern facilities as well as with well-entrenched hiring practices, according to which federal employers took advantage of local labor markets regardless of their own personal views about the propriety of employing any particular type of labor. The federal employment of slave labor would continue until at least June 1863.[20]

From 1791 to 1861, cabinet-level officials had established several policies that forbad employing slave labor for certain uses and at certain locations. Those policies had not been based on the professed superiority of free labor or the manifest immorality of slave labor but on more mundane economic anxieties and public-safety concerns. In any event, middle- and low-level federal officials routinely ignored such policies and continued to rent slave labor, without any official repercussions to themselves or others.

The presence of slavery was one factor that promoted the bureaucratic autonomy of middle- and low-level federal officials because cabinet-level officials were well aware of the symbolic impact of slave rentals. Either to actually forbid or to actively encourage them would have carried serious political costs. The presence of slavery thus helped shift the locus of policy-making in this policy area from the center to the periphery. Military officers assigned to distant army posts and navy yards especially enjoyed the benefits, and sometimes suffered the penalties, of this shift. Furthermore, they, in particular, had neither the time nor inclination to supervise a large number of employees, which left both their slave and free white employees subject to the uneven management of third-party supervisors.

Because of the lack of documentation, it is impossible to estimate the total number of slaves that the federal government rented during the 1791–1861 period and the total amount of money that it spent on slave labor. But it is clear that the federal government rented thousands of slaves during the period and spent hundreds of thousands of dollars on slave labor.[21] The federal government's use of slave labor also generated some fascinating cases of the more subterranean ways that the presence of slavery influenced its early practices.

MILITARY SLAVES

Two decades before the Senate rejected an amendment that would have barred the U.S. military from employing slave labor, the House of Representatives passed a resolution requesting that the army and navy report to Congress the number of African Americans, both free and enslaved, whom they employed.[22] This August 1, 1842, resolution was the congressional response to a scandal surrounding a number of questionable practices that a former army engineer, Francis L. Dancy (North Carolina), had employed in supervising the construction of a new seawall in Saint Augustine.[23] One of those questionable practices was how he had paid his slave employees themselves for their Sunday work. The Secretary of War, John C. Spencer (New York Whig), replied to the resolution with the most comprehensive report on the U.S. military's use of slave labor during the 1791–1861 period. His report includes correspondence from the heads of each of the five major divisions of the army as well as from its chief administrative officer.

In his reply, the adjutant general of the U.S. army, Roger Jones (Virginia), notes that only "free white male persons" could serve in the army at the time but that it had no regulations against employing "black or colored persons" in other capacities.[24] The correspondence from the heads of the five major divisions of the army reports that they employed a total of 687 slaves and 25 free blacks in various capacities, from common laborers to skilled masons. Only the chief of the Bureau of Topographical Engineers, John James Abert (Virginia), reported that his division did not currently employ any slaves or free blacks. He adds, however, that his engineers "do not hesitate to employ them on any appropriate duty, when they offer to hire."[25]

The Office of the Chief of Engineers, Joseph G. Totten (Connecticut), employed all the reported free blacks and a vast majority of the reported slaves (545) on the division's public-works projects across the nation.[26] Presumably, all the slaves were employed in the South, though Totten offers no geographic breakdown of where they were employed. The Office of the Quartermaster General, Thomas S. Jesup (Kentucky), employed 106 slaves, mostly in Florida, as the Second Seminole War wound down. Jesup comments that "in the unhealthy climates of the South, they are preferable to white men as laborers, deck hands, firemen, and cooks, and a regulation prohibiting their employment would be injurious to the service."[27] The Ordnance Office, acting head George Talcott (Connecticut), employed a total of seven slaves at three of its Southern arsenals and armories, in Baton Rouge, Little Rock, and Apalachicola (Florida), and twenty-one slaves at an arsenal under construction in Fayetteville, North Carolina. Finally, the Office of Commissary General of Subsistence, George Gibson (Pennsylvania), employed eight slaves, two in New Orleans and six in Florida.[28]

The congressional resolution did not request the costs associated with the military's use of slave labor, and none were supplied. If one assumes an average monthly cost of $15.25 per slave, the total costs for the month of August 1842 of the 687 slaves whom the army reportedly employed during that month would have been $10,476.75.[29] For the year, the costs would have been $125,721. Further extrapolations from this data seem unadvisable. Unfortunately, I was unable to find any other report of the total number of slaves whom the U.S. army employed at any other point in time during the 1791–1861 period. However, the 687 slaves that the army reportedly employed in August 1842 was not an insignificant number in light of the fact that the total size of the federal government's civilian workforce at the time was only about 18,000 employees. Army slave rentals would have represented approximately 3.8 percent of that total.[30]

The only division of the army for which I found longitudinal data on its employment practices was the Office of the Quartermaster General.[31] The National Archives holds the monthly reports that the quartermasters at army fortifications, temporary posts, and arsenals and armories filed with the central office on "persons and articles hired" from 1818 to 1905. I examined these reports at five-year intervals from 1818 to 1858. I tried to locate the August report for each of the selected years, and if I could not locate that report, I examined the report for the next closest month.[32] I rarely found all twelve monthly reports bundled together for any given army facility for any given year, whether because some monthly reports were never sent, because they were never received or filed, because they were misfiled, or because they were lost, destroyed, or stolen at some point in the intervening years.[33] In fact, the monthly reports were so incomplete for the first two selected years, 1818 and 1823, that I decided to exclude them from my analysis.[34] As reported in the following paragraphs, I found that the pattern of slave-labor employment at army facilities was stochastic. Not surprisingly, war was the primary reason for increases in such employment.

The monthly reports for August 1828 indicate that the quartermasters at six Southern army facilities employed a total of 28 slaves.[35] The majority of the slaves (16) were employed at Fort Jackson in Savannah.[36] The total monthly costs for those 28 slaves were $428.43. Extrapolated over the year, the total would be $5,141.

The monthly reports for August (or next closest month) 1833 indicate that the quartermasters at seven army facilities, all but one in the South, employed a total of 37 slaves.[37] Again, the majority of the slaves (22) were employed in Savannah. One of the slaves was employed in Pittsburgh, probably the personal slave of the quartermaster; they share the same last name. The total monthly costs for those 37 slaves were $685.38. Extrapolated over the year, the total would be $8,335.

The monthly reports for August (or next closest month) 1838 indicate that the quartermasters at 20 Southern army facilities employed a total of 176 slaves.[38] The vast majority of the slaves (155) were now employed at temporary posts in Florida as the Second Seminole War was at its peak. The total monthly costs for those 176 slaves were $4,380.15. Extrapolated over the year, the total would be $52,562.

The monthly reports for August (or next closest month) 1843 indicate that the quartermasters at 12 army facilities, all but two in the South, employed a total of 64 slaves.[39] With continued Seminole hostilities, the majority of the slaves (50) were still employed in Florida.[40] However, two new western posts employed two slaves each, Fort Scott in Kansas and Fort Washita in the Choctaw nation.[41] The total monthly costs for those 64 slaves were $975.89. Extrapolated over the year, the total would be $11,711.

The monthly reports for August (or next closest month) 1848 indicate that the quartermasters at eight Southern and western army facilities employed a total of 68 slaves.[42] With the recent conclusion of the Mexican-American War, the majority of the slaves (36) were now employed at temporary posts in Texas.[43] The total monthly costs for those 68 slaves were $1,588.73. Extrapolated over the year, the total would be $19,065.

The monthly reports for August (or next closet month) 1853 indicate that the quartermasters at six Southern and western facilities employed a total of only 16 slaves.[44] The majority of the slaves (13) were still employed in Texas. With army posts continuing to follow the westward movement of European American settlement, slave labor was much less prevalent in the local workforce and, not surprisingly, army officers rented fewer slaves. The total monthly costs for those 16 slaves were $299.49. Extrapolated over the year, the total would be $3,599.

Finally, the monthly reports for August 1858 indicate that the quartermasters at seven Southern and western facilities employed a total of 29 slaves.[45] The number had increased again because of the Third Seminole War. Thirteen of the slaves were employed in Florida. The total monthly costs for those 29 slaves were $603.82. Extrapolated over the year, the total would be $7,246.

If one averages the annual costs of slave labor at the reporting army facilities for the seven selected years from 1828 through 1858 over that whole period, then the quartermaster general's total slave-labor costs for the period would be $476,000. This estimate is obviously a rough estimate because of the stochastic nature of the data.

Outside the 1828–1858 time frame, Congress collected the employment data at army arsenals and armories from 1816 through 1821. In 1816, none of the facilities reported employing slave labor. That pattern changed in 1817, when the New Orleans armory began operations. From 1817 through 1821, army arsenals and armories reported that they had spent a total of $4,278 on slave labor. Almost all that money was spent to employ from three to four slaves to turn the waterwheel at the New Orleans armory. Army facilities in Augusta (Georgia), Charleston, Fort Hawkins (Georgia), Richmond, Washington, and Wilmington (North Carolina) also reported renting slaves on one or more occasion during those five years.[46]

A second data point on slave rentals also exists for the Office of the Chief of Engineers. The National Archives established a separate collection of the payroll records from October 1860 through March 1862 at Fort Jefferson, which was located on Dry Tortugas Island, west of the Florida Keys, to detail how the federal government continued to employ slave labor during the Civil War. Along with Forts Monroe (Hampton Roads), Pickens (Pensacola), and Taylor (Key West), Fort Jefferson was one of the only four Southern fortifications that remained under Union control at the commencement of the war. According to its slave rolls, the fort's slave-labor costs were $4,877 for the 16–36 slaves who worked as laborers, masons, and cooks at the fort during the nine months from October 1860 through June 1861.[47]

National Archives records indicate that the federal government also employed slaves at Forts Taylor and Pickens after Florida had seceded from the Union, though it did not establish separate collections for those forts. In fact, the records chronicle a case in which several Florida slaveholders, including Confederate Secretary of War and former U.S. Senator Stephen R. Mallory, had the chutzpah to complain to the Department of State in May 1861 that their slaves were transferred from Fort Jefferson to Fort Pickens without their consent, which, in their view, showed the determination of the new Lincoln administration to abolish slavery. The Department of War responded with a memorandum that denied any such determination, noting that the slaves in question were long-term rentals who had already been transferred from Fort Taylor to Fort Jefferson without protest.[48]

Captain Walter McFarland (New Jersey), who became the supervisory engineer at Fort Taylor in March 1862 and then also at Fort Jefferson three months later, continued to pay Florida residents for the labor of their former slaves after the Emancipation Proclamation, until he finally bowed to War Department pressure in June 1863 and began paying the latter themselves as free laborers.[49] McFarland did not identify the persons he employed by either race or status in his monthly reports on persons and articles hired.[50] His predecessor at Fort Taylor, Captain Edward Bissell Hunt (New York), had identified the persons he employed by race, but not status, in March 1858 and then again from July 1858 through October 1859. Given the fort's isolated location, all the employees he identified as blacks were probably slaves. If so, he spent a total of $17,933 for the labor of the 32–47 slaves who worked at the fort during those 17 months as laborers, stone cutters, blacksmiths, orderlies, and assistant carpenters.[51] Hunt also employed at least one overseer at a salary of $120 per month, sometimes supplemented by one or more assistant overseers at salaries ranging from $60 to $90 per month. Coincidentally or not, the last month that he recorded the number of his black workers he wrote his immediate superior to inquire about the propriety of employing the slaves of the overseer's wife.[52]

Based on the data from a number of sources, it is clear that the U.S. army employed many slaves, at many locations and in many capacities, before and even during the Civil War. It is also clear that the army hired overseers to supervise slaves as well as free white workers at work sites where large numbers of both types of laborers were employed. Interestingly, the army did not seem to distinguish sharply between its slave and free white employees, probably because it had adopted no regulations against slave rentals. Even if free white employees were disproportionately listed at the top end of the job ladder and slaves at the bottom, they often performed the same jobs at the same pay rates and worked side by side sawing timber, cutting stone, and hauling supplies.

Secretary of Navy Abel P. Upshur (Virginia Democrat) answered the same 1842 congressional resolution that Spencer did by reporting that his department currently did not employ any blacks at its navy yards, noting that departmental regulations prohibited such employment.[53] To prove Upshur wrong, at least prospectively, Ernest Dibble examined the employment records at the Pensacola navy yard. He found that as many as 200 slaves worked at the yard every year from 1847 through 1860. Dibble claims that local navy officers disguised the practice by listing slave laborers as "common laborers" in distinction to free white laborers, who were listed as "first-class laborers." He also found that the salary range for common laborers was $15–$30 per month as opposed to $32.50–$65 for first-class laborers.[54] If one takes the midpoint of the salary range for common laborers and assumes that the navy yard employed an average of 100 slaves per month from 1847 through 1860, the yard's slave-labor costs for those fourteen years would have been $378,000.[55] Ironically, navy yards were the federal work sites where the highest number and highest proportion of slaves appear to have been employed. At the Pensacola navy yard, slaves regularly represented more than 50 percent of the workforce.[56]

Other navy yards also employed slaves. Charles Ball wrote in his slave narrative that he had worked as a slave at the Washington navy yard.[57] The African American diarist Michael Shiner did, too, first as a slave and then, after his testamentary manumission, as a free person.[58] In 1829, Commandant Isaac Hull (Connecticut) reported that he employed thirteen slaves at the Washington navy yard, a figure which did not include the slaves navy personnel had themselves leased to the navy to work at the yard. In an earlier report, Hull had asserted that the slaves "were employed by special permission and that permission given because white men could not be found to work in the anchor shop." He added that "I consider them the hardest working men in the yard and it would require many weeks if not months to get a gang of hands for the anchor shop to do the work that is now done."[59] As we will see shortly, slaves also worked at the third major navy yard in the South, outside Norfolk, Virginia.

The Department of the Navy had adopted its regulations against employing African Americans at navy yards in 1818. The policy was a response to concerns that navy yard work would not only place black laborers in competition with white laborers but also provide slaves, particularly fugitive slaves masquerading as free persons, with too many opportunities to escape to freedom.[60] Dibble's study demonstrates how navy officers subverted departmental policy on the ground, and for multiple reasons. First, navy officers were often slaveholders themselves and desired to employ their own slaves at their workplaces. Second, local slaveholders lobbied navy officers to employ their slaves. As rational economic actors, they calculated that the probable gains offset the possible losses, especially because in frontier areas, such as Pensacola, the U.S. military was the largest employer, and few other opportunities for slave rentals existed. Third, free labor could be in short supply at the local level, as it was, again, especially in frontier areas. Fourth, slave labor could be more competent than free labor for the assigned task, as Commandant Hull suggests. Fifth, navy officers could save money by renting slave labor. At the Pensacola navy yard, they saved money in the process of masking their employment practices. By renting all slaves as common laborers, they could pay all masters of slaves the wage rates of common laborers even if their slaves performed more skilled tasks. For all these reasons, slaves formed a prominent part of the capacities of both the U.S. army and navy, though the navy's regulations against

slave rentals at navy yards did seem to prompt it to distinguish more sharply between its slave and free-white employees.

In his answer to the 1842 congressional resolution, Upshur admitted that a few
slaves might work for the U.S. navy as the personal servants of navy officers.[61] This
practice was quite common in the army. Dred Scott was the most famous case of
an army slave. Even Northern army officers bought slaves in order to employ them
as their personal servants.[62] Captain Martin Scott (Vermont) purchased a slave,
Jack, in 1826 for that purpose and Jack accompanied him to several Northern army
posts over the next few years.[63] Southern army officers frequently employed their
own slaves as personal servants. James Pemberton accompanied Jefferson Davis
(Mississippi) to West Point, and then on to assignments in Wisconsin, Illinois, and
Arkansas during his brief military career. Pemberton was also Davis's personal servant when he commanded the Mississippi militia during the Mexican-American
War.[64] While Dred Scott was unsuccessful in suing for his freedom based on his
Northern residences, Lieutenant Thomas B. W. Stockton's (New York) female
slave, Rachel, who had also spent time at Fort Snelling in Minnesota, successfully
sued for her freedom on that basis before the Missouri Supreme Court in 1836.[65]

General Zachary Taylor (Louisiana) went further in seeking employment for
his slaves. John Quincy Adams's secretary of war, James Barbour (Virginia National Republican), had ruled that army officers could not lease their own slaves to
the federal government because it was a clear conflict of interest. When Taylor was
reassigned from New Orleans to Fort Snelling in 1828, he left several of his slaves in
the charge of a third party in New Orleans with a request to find employment for
them. After this third party failed to find them employment, Taylor wrote to the
army surgeon in Pensacola, Thomas Lawson, to request his assistance in finding
them employment at the local navy yard. In fairness to Taylor, he told Lawson that
he expected Barbour's ruling to be rescinded by the next administration, clearly
anticipating that Andrew Jackson would win the upcoming presidential election
and that a Jackson administration would be more sympathetic to the concerns
of slaveholding army officers.[66] This case reveals the extent to which federal employees who owned slaves were implicated in soliciting the federal employment
of their own slaves. It also reveals the extent to which they were implicated in
adjudicating the propriety of such employment because Barbour was also a slaveholder, as had been his predecessor, John C. Calhoun (South Carolina Democratic
Republican), and as would be a majority of his successors.[67]

A related case involved the querulous Senator Mallory (Florida Democrat).
The paper trail in this case began when Lieutenant Horatio G. Wright (Connecticut) wrote Chief Engineer Totten in August 1851. Wright asked Totten whether
continuing to employ Mallory's slaves at Fort Jefferson violated an 1808 law that
prohibited elected federal officials from contracting with the federal government

now that Mallory had been elected to the U.S. Senate. Totten requested the opin-
ion of the Department of Treasury. In October, the second auditor, Edward Phelps
(Vermont), wrote Totten that employing Mallory's slaves was indeed improper.
After receiving word of this opinion, Mallory wrote Phelps a letter of protest on
December 23, 1851, contending that the slaves in question were actually being held
in trust for him and his wife by a third party. Four days later, Totten decided that
Mallory's slaves were employable.[68]

As Totten's reply to the 1842 congressional inquiry suggests, army engineers
extensively employed slave labor on military construction projects in the South. In
one particularly contentious case, the federal contractors responsible for building
new fortifications at Mobile Point, Alabama, eventually turned to slave labor as a
cost-saving measure. This case became a *cause célèbre* when the project ground to
an expensive halt in 1822, prompting a congressional inquiry and subsequent resolution authorizing Secretary of War Calhoun to investigate what, if any, failures
had occurred on the side of either the contractors or army engineers. In the course
of his investigation, Calhoun hired an independent assessor to determine the value
of the materials and labor employed on the project, including how much money
the contractors could have saved if they had employed slave labor throughout
the construction process. The assessor calculated that the contractors could have
saved $40,000, estimating the slave-labor costs at $40,000 and the comparable
free-labor costs at $80,000.[69]

According to Dibble, the use of slave labor on the Mobile Point project established the precedent for its use to build the Pensacola navy yard in the late 1820s.
The rationale was, again, to save money as well as a shortage of free labor. In this
case, the federal contractor was even able to rent slaves at $15 per month, instead
of the market rate of $17, by promising their owners that they would receive free
medical care with navy surgeons. Federal contractors also built the local army post,
Fort Pickens, with slave labor. As we have seen, army and navy officers thereafter
employed slaves at both the fort and navy yard until and even into the Civil War.
In total, Dibble estimated that the federal government spent $2 million in the Pen-
sacola area from 1826 to 1861 to spur its economic development. The profitability
of slave rentals to the U.S. military meant that the area developed, in particular, as
a slave society despite its unsuitability to plantation slavery. Dibble discovered that
even one of the navy surgeons, Isaac Hulse, who was from Long Island, New York,
bought slaves expressly in order to lease them to the military.[70]

In a fascinating case of the complicated position in which federal employers
placed themselves when they rented slave labor, Christopher Tomlins chronicles
how the use of slave labor at the Gosport (Norfolk) navy yard became the object
of a community-wide protest. The navy began the construction of new dry docks
at the yard in November 1827. The chief engineer, Loammi Baldwin, was from

Boston. He initially decided not to employ slave labor on the project because, in his own words, "I had strong prejudices against blacks as labourers."[71] But when local slaveholders protested, he reversed his decision. At that point, another group protested. Skilled white masons and stone cutters who worked, or had worked, at the navy yard complained to the secretary of navy, John Branch (North Carolina Democrat), about the use of "inferior" slave labor on the project.[72]

Baldwin defended his hiring practices on the grounds that slave labor was cheaper. He reported that he paid only $.72 per day for slave labor and $1 to $2 per day for free labor.[73] Navy officials seemed satisfied with Baldwin's explanation. The white workers were, however, not deterred. They filed another, more broadly based petition with the Department of Navy, adding the charge that supervisory personnel personally profited from the practice of employing slave labor at the navy yard by leasing their own slaves. Subsequently, the protesters wrote an anonymous letter of grievances to President Jackson, which was forwarded down the chain of command. Baldwin again defended his hiring practices to his superiors. Local slaveholders wrote letters of support attacking the character of the protesters. Baldwin's subordinates also wrote letters of support. One observed that slaves had long worked at the navy yard without protest.[74] The use of slave labor on the project continued unabated.

Then in August 1831 the Southampton slave revolt intervened.[75] The revolt turned the local community, including some of the slaveholders and supervisory personnel who had initially defended and profited from the practice, against the use of slave labor on the project as "unsafe." They helped organize a community-wide protest. Once again, Baldwin defended his hiring practices to his superiors. He insisted that "a few [blacks] have become excellent workmen and are equal to some of the whites who receive more than double their wages." Alluding to the extent to which the federal government depended on slave labor at its Southern facilities, he reminded navy officials that if they acceded to the petitioners' demands "that similar ones might be assigned for the dismissal of the blacks in all other Government works throughout the Southern states. What may be the consequences . . . it does not seem necessary for me to predict."[76] The use of slave labor on the project continued until it was completed in March 1834.

Based on his examination of Baldwin's employment records, Tomlins finds that, on average, 91 slaves worked on the project from May 1830 through October 1832, which would have represented approximately 30 percent of the workforce.[77] Linda Upham-Bornstein, who recently revisited this case to analyze the character of the protesters, quotes one of their petitions as claiming that approximately 300 of the 500 workers on the project were "[b]lacks, one half of whom do not belong to this place, but have been hired in the country around . . . thus adding to the pestiferous part of our population."[78]

To supervise the slaves working on the project, Baldwin hired not only an overseer but also a trainer to teach them how to cut stone. Unfortunately, neither Tomlins nor Upham-Bornstein reports the salary of the trainer, Samuel Johnson (Massachusetts). Upham-Bornstein does, however, report the salary of the overseer, Henry Singleton (Virginia), whose annual pay was initially $1,200 and subsequently increased to $1,620.[79] Singleton supervised both slaves and free white laborers who worked on the project. This practice was another ground of complaint. The free white laborers contended that the practice was "subversive to every principle of equality." As they explained in a later petition, slaves are "not our equals, because they are not white men, or free men."[80]

Tomlins finds the case fascinating because of the way that a Boston-bred civil engineer became such a vehement defender of the equal competence (if not equal worth) of slave labor.[81] The case is also fascinating because of the way that Baldwin's superiors so strongly supported him even though he was not a military officer. They undoubtedly appreciated the value of his employment policies both in terms of finishing the project and in saving costs.

In addition to army fortifications and navy yards, the U.S. military also built roads and other types of internal improvements. In the Southern states and territories, army officers (directly or indirectly) employed slaves to help construct these internal improvements. Mark Boyd collects the documentation in one case of a military road that was built with slave labor in territorial Florida in the mid-1820s.[82] In this case, Congress appropriated $20,000 to build the "first road" in Florida, from Pensacola to Saint Augustine.[83] The assistant quartermaster in Pensacola, Lieutenant Daniel E. Burch (Alabama), estimated that it would cost $51,000 for the army to build the road itself. He therefore decided to contract out work on the road to local planters, believing that they could build it for less money with slave labor. Burch accepted bids totaling $18,000 to construct various portions of the road, including an $8,000 bid from his future father-in-law, John Bellamy. The case was documented when cost overruns compelled Burch to request additional funds beyond the $20,000 originally appropriated for the project. Burch defended himself (and his future father-in-law) to Quartermaster General Jesup by arguing that bad weather and a relative shortage of slave labor had driven up costs and that, in any case, the road still cost half what it would have cost if it had been built by the army itself. Though he did not report the exact cost of building the road, his last comment suggests that it cost approximately $25,000.

Another documented case of the U.S. military's use of slave labor to build an internal improvement was the Dancy scandal, the scandal that prompted a congressional investigation of the military's use of slave labor. Dancy was a former army engineer who had been hired by the Office of the Chief of Engineers to supervise the construction of a new seawall in Saint Augustine. One of the charges against Dancy was that he had shortchanged Mrs. L. E. Whelden for the work her slave, Morgan, had performed on the project. In her deposition, Whelden testifies that she had "arranged" with one of Dancy's assistants to receive $15 per month for Morgan's labor as a teamster. She also testifies that after one month the assistant told her that henceforth she would only receive $12 per month because Morgan's subsistence cost $3 per month. Dancy himself offers two versions of why Whelden received only $12 per month. At first, he states that Morgan could not perform the same work as the other teamsters he had hired for $15 per month because he was a smaller "boy." Later, at his formal hearing, he states that Whelden received only $12 per month because Morgan himself received $3 per month working with Dancy's horses on Sundays.[84] The fact that Dancy had paid Morgan, instead of Whelden, for his Sunday work particularly upset army officials.[85] They decided not to press any charges against Dancy, despite the extensive record of his financial improprieties, because he had already resigned.[86] The case was but one instance in which a slaveholder had transferred her authority over her slave to a federal employer and was very dissatisfied with the result.

The Dancy scandal raised another issue that arose when federal employers rented slave labor. Would the parties fulfill their contract obligations? While the same issue arose in cases in which federal employers hired free labor, it was more complicated in cases in which they rented slave labor. In the latter cases, the actual laborers were usually not themselves parties to the contract, and slaveholders had to depend on the cooperation of their slaves to enforce it, especially if the work site was distant from their places of residence.[87] Slave rentals also often involved more informal arrangements between federal employers and slaveholders, in part because they so frequently skirted federal regulations, which, again, made it difficult to enforce the arrangement in a court of law or in a legislative or executive venue. Slaveholders confronted additional problems when they rented slaves to the federal government because it was typically not a personal arrangement between themselves and the specific people who supervised their slaves but rather mediated by a governing institution with its own independent authority. The federal personnel who supervised their slaves were not personally responsible to them in the same way that their own overseers were. In the eyes of slaveholders, all third-party slave managers were presumably suspect because they did not have personal investments in the slaves whom they supervised, but federal slave managers were probably the most suspect, even if they were from the South, as Dancy was. Still, on the other side of the equation, federal employers did not treat rented slaves much differently from free hires and developed similar micromanagement structures to supervise both types of labor, as at the Norfolk navy yard. These practices, of course, did not always sit well with either the free white laborers who worked at the site or the slaveholders whose slaves worked at the same site.

The cases that I have discussed in this section also demonstrate that when the U.S. military employed slave labor, the issue was never simply one of costs. Even in cases in which military officers saved money by renting slaves, they faced difficult issues of slave management, often complicated by the demands of the slaveholders whose slaves they had rented. Mallory's slave rentals to the military actually began creating problems three years before he became a U.S. senator. In 1848, Mallory wrote an angry letter of protest to Captain George W. Dutton (Pennsylvania), who was supervising the construction of Fort Jefferson. The letter alleged that navy personnel had assaulted one of his slaves who was working at the site and upbraided Dutton for allowing his slave to be assaulted.[88] The implication of Mallory's letter was that Dutton had proven himself to be not only a poor slave manager but a poor military officer. As in so many other cases, the use of slave labor had raised a special labor-management problem that would not have occurred if the federal government had employed only free labor during the 1791–1861 period.

SLAVES AT WAR

As we have already seen in the case of the Second Seminole War, the U.S. military frequently employed slaves in support capacities during times of war. Occasionally, slaves served in the armed forces during times of war, even when they were not supposed to.

During the first year of the Revolutionary War, both free blacks and slaves who had enlisted in the New England militias fought with George Washington's Continental Army in the North. After South Carolina delegate Edward Rutledge unsuccessfully attempted to persuade the Continental Congress to ban black enlistments in 1776, Washington and his staff decided to implement the policy anyway in deference to lower-South opposition to such enlistments.[89] Yet several Northern states (Connecticut, Massachusetts, New Hampshire, New York, and Rhode Island) and two upper-South states (Maryland and Virginia) continued to fill their troop quotas with blacks, including slaves, and Washington did not turn them away.[90] In 1778, he even encouraged Rhode Island to form a separate black militia unit, which included 88 slave enlistees, because of its chronic inability to meet its quotas.[91] Then in 1779, after the war had moved south, South Carolina delegate Henry Laurens convinced the Continental Congress to establish financial incentives to encourage state and local officials in his own state as well as in Georgia to enlist as many as 3,000 slaves. Laurens argued that the policy was necessary to raise sufficient manpower to wrest the British occupation of the two states. South Carolina Governor John Rutledge supported the policy, but both he and Laurens encountered stiff resistance in their own state. (By this time, John's brother, Edward, was a British prisoner of war.) In the end, neither South Carolina nor Georgia implemented the policy.[92] Slaves did, however, work for the military in other capacities in the lower South, such as in helping build Fort Moultrie and other Charleston fortifications.[93]

An unknown number of slaves enlisted in the army during the Revolutionary War. They or their heirs could have received military pensions or land bounties when the federal government later established and expanded those veterans' benefit programs.[94] The number of former slaves and heirs who received such benefits is also unknown. In 1930, the Department of War forwarded a request to the Bureau of Pensions to search its records for the disposition of the claims of African American Revolutionary War veterans. The subsequent search uncovered only one clearly identifiable case in which a slave enlistee or his heir received a pension or bounty, but those records are obviously an unreliable data source because of the strong incentives, on the part of both slave enlistees and enlisters, for incomplete disclosure.[95]

The one case was Cuff Wells (Connecticut), who served in the Continental Army as many as six years and gained his freedom for his service. After his death, his widow, Phillis Tatton, who had since remarried, petitioned Congress to receive a survivor's pension in 1831, which was eventually granted in 1842. Though the final House bill did not state the amount of the pension Tatton received, an earlier bill had stated $80 per year, retroactive to 1831, when she first petitioned Congress. She died in 1848 and therefore may have received as much as $1,440 in pension money.[96]

In the meantime, Congress had passed a "Black Militia" law in 1792 that prohibited black members of state and local militia from being mustered into the U.S. military. The army and navy treated the law as a precedent to prohibit black enlistments.[97] During the War of 1812, the navy in particular confronted a manpower shortage, and in 1813 Congress permitted free blacks to enlist in the navy. Free blacks served in the navy during the war, and reportedly sometimes slaves did, too. It has been estimated that the proportion of black sailors on navy ships during the war ranged from 10 to 20 percent.[98] At least one state (New York) permitted free blacks to enlist in its militia, again reportedly sometimes slaves, too.[99] While ostensibly free, Charles Ball saw duty with both the navy and army in the Chesapeake battle zone.[100] As they had during the Revolutionary War, slaves also contributed to the war effort by helping build military fortifications, such as in Baltimore harbor prior to the British bombardment of the harbor and in New Orleans prior to the anticlimactic battle outside that city.[101]

Retrospectively, two slaveholders petitioned Congress to award them land bounties based on their deceased slaves' military service in the War of 1812. During the second session of the 21st Congress (1831–1832), the House Committee on

Private Land Claims, chaired by John Benton Sterigere (Pennsylvania Democrat), reported favorably on Archibald Jackson's claim on the grounds that he was the legal heir of the slave, James Gammons, who, after all, had served in the army and consequently would have himself been entitled to a bounty.[102] The accompanying bill failed, however, to receive a third reading in the House. During the next Congress, the same committee, now chaired by Thomas Alexander Marshall (Kentucky Whig), again reported favorably on Jackson's claim. This time the bill passed the House only to die in the Senate.[103]

During the next two congresses, Benjamin Oden's (Maryland) claim received very different, and inconsistent, treatments. During the first session of the 23rd Congress (1833–1834), his claim received an initial unfavorable report from the Committee on Private Land Claims in December 1833. On behalf of the committee, John Carr (Indiana Democrat) wrote that Oden was not entitled to a land bounty for the military service of his slave, Frederick, because Frederick had illegally enlisted in the army and thus would not himself have been entitled to a bounty.[104] However, early the next year, Oden's claim received a favorable report from the same committee. The author of this new report, Cave Johnson (Tennessee Democrat), applied the same logic to Oden's claim that the previous congress had applied to Jackson's.[105] During the next Congress, Oden's claim was then tabled indefinitely after it received another unfavorable committee report. George Chambers (Pennsylvania Anti-Mason) returned to the argument that the federal government did not owe Oden a land bounty because Frederick had illegally enlisted in the army.[106] If nothing else, these committee reports betray the sectional biases of their authors. They also provide official confirmation that some slaves saw active duty with the army during the War of 1812, despite the existing regulations to the contrary.

A number of slaveholders also petitioned Congress for reimbursement for the losses they had incurred when their slaves were injured or killed while working for the army during the War of 1812. Congress uniformly denied these claims.[107] Most of the claims are for the deaths of slaves who were the personal servants of army officers, further evidence of how widespread the practice was. The committee reports argue that the officers must accept the liability for the risks in such cases.

After the War of 1812, the navy (1818) and army (1820) adopted new regulations against slave enlistments, though the navy continued to allow free-black enlistments.[108] In response to (unconfirmed) reports of navy crews that were majority African American, the navy adopted new regulations in 1839 that established a five percent quota on free-black enlistments.[109] In 1842, Senator Calhoun proposed something more drastic. He attempted to amend a bill to regulate navy enlistments to totally exclude African Americans from serving in the navy except as a "musician, steward, cook, or servant." His amendment passed the Senate, but it died in the House after Navy Secretary Upshur assured Congress that navy crews did not generally exceed the five percent benchmark for black sailors.[110]

Meanwhile, the Second Seminole War had begun. As the previous chapter shows, slaves performed a variety of roles for the military during the war. They acted as guides, interpreters, negotiators, and even soldiers. They also built fortifications and worked at army posts and navy yards in Florida. One slave guide, Louis Pacheco, allegedly led Major Dade's troops into the ambush that began the war. Pacheco survived the ambush and, depending on the truth of the allegations against him, either remained a Seminole collaborator or became a Seminole hostage.[111] When the army later removed him to Arkansas as part of a group of captured Seminoles, his owner, Antonio Pacheco, filed a claim for a slave loss. The House finally approved Pacheco's claim after protracted debate and several disputed votes, but because of the public controversy antislavery Congressman Joshua R. Giddings (again!) had created over the claim, it was never brought before the Senate.[112]

During the highly unusual floor debate on Pacheco's claim, Giddings insisted that the House had never approved such a claim in the past. He also cited the denial of James C. Watson's claim as a precedent for denying Pacheco's. His assertion was that "from the dawn of the Revolution to this day . . . this House has expressed but one opinion on this subject. They have at all times *refused to tax the people of the North to pay for the slaves of the South.*"[113] Upon being corrected by his colleagues, Giddings admitted that the House had approved one such claim in the past but only because it had been brought to the floor in a way that had escaped his notice.[114] The claim in question was that of Captain William De Peyster and Henry N. Cruger whose slave, Romeo, had helped negotiate the emigration of more than 1,000 Seminoles to Arkansas during the Second Seminole War. The army had allowed Romeo himself to emigrate along with his wife, a member of a highly influential Black Seminole family, to ensure their continued cooperation. Both houses of Congress eventually approved a maximum award of $1,300 to De Peyster and Cruger for the loss of Romeo's services.[115] Of course, as we saw in chapter four, both houses of Congress also eventually approved Watson's claim.

During the Mexican-American War, the U.S. military's use of slave labor shifted to staging posts in Texas. Apparently, slaves saw combat during the war only as the personal servants of army and navy officers. Jefferson Davis's slave, James Pemberton, was one such case. William O. Butler (Kentucky), Winfield Scott (Virginia), Zachary Taylor (Louisiana), William Worth (New York), and even Ulysses S. Grant (Illinois) also employed one or more slave as a personal servant during the war.[116] In his personal journal, Major Phillip Norbourne Barbour (Virginia) reported that three army officers stationed with him in Texas had lost slaves who escaped across the Rio Grande. He feared that "[i]f we are located on this border [much longer] we shall have to employ white servants."[117]

In both peace and war, slaves formed a prominent part of the capacities of both branches of the U.S. military, even if they were (mostly) excluded from active duty. The civilian departments of the federal government also employed slave labor, though the data points are fewer and the documented costs much less.

CIVILIAN DEPARTMENTS

According to the Constitution, the federal government is the supervisory government of the nation's (future) capital as well as of its own facilities and U.S. territories. The costs of developing, governing, and maintaining the areas under exclusive federal jurisdiction are federal costs. The federal government employed slaves to perform each of those functions.

In 1791, President Washington appointed three Commissioners of the City of Washington to supervise the construction of the nation's capital. This action followed a heated congressional debate over its location, which culminated in an alleged quid pro quo between Alexander Hamilton, on the one hand, and Thomas Jefferson and James Madison, on the other, to locate the capital south of the Mason-Dixon line in return for approving Hamilton's controversial plan to assume the Revolutionary War debts of the state governments.[118] Given the location of the capital on land Maryland and Virginia ceded to the federal government, it is hardly surprising that all three men whom Washington appointed to the commission were slaveholders.[119] The commissioners decided to use slave labor for the usual reasons, to attempt to save money, because of difficulties in recruiting free labor, to curb both the wage and non-wage demands of the free laborers whom they did recruit, because they hired slaveholders to oversee the project who wished to find employment for their own slaves, and because they themselves were slaveholders.[120]

My search of the accounts of the commissioners in the National Archives found a total of $17,671 in payment vouchers for slave labor from 1794 through 1802.[121] The commission undoubtedly spent much more than $17,671 on slave labor, but how much more is unclear because of the many gaps in its records.[122] I also found vouchers paying for the subsistence, clothing, medical care, and supervision of the men who worked on the construction of the capital but, in most cases, they did not separate the costs specifically for slaves from those for other laborers. For example, the commissioners paid Dr. John Crocker $166 to treat 72 black laborers and 43 white laborers from May 1, 1794, to May 1, 1795.[123] While most, if not all, of the black laborers were probably slaves, we cannot determine from the voucher exactly how many were slaves or how much was spent on their treatment or, for that matter, how much was spent on the treatment of black as opposed to white laborers.[124] Still, the voucher strongly suggests that slaves represented more than half the workforce in 1794–1795.

Slaves performed a wide array of jobs on the construction of the capital. Originally, they were rented to cut timber and quarry stone, but later they worked alongside white workers on all phases of the project and were paid at comparable rates.[125] They were employed as rafters, haulers, sawyers, roofers, brick and mortar makers, brick layers, plasterers, stone cutters, masons, and carpenters, though, again not surprisingly, they disproportionately performed unskilled labor.[126]

Although one cannot calculate the specific costs of the supervision of the slaves who worked on the construction of the capital from the commission records, the records indicate that the supervision costs were substantial. They also indicate that the commission established a relatively elaborate management structure to supervise the men who worked on the project. Some supervisors were general supervisors of both slave labor and free labor and were paid accordingly. James Hoban, who supervised the construction of the White House, was the highest paid employee of the commission. His quarterly salary was initially $366.66, later increased to $466.66. Hoban made another estimated $750 per year by employing his own slaves to help build the White House.[127] The commission hired other men as supervisors along with the slaves whom they themselves had rented to work on the construction of the capital. Samuel Smallwood, who later became the city's first elected mayor, fit this category. His salary was initially $20 per month, later increased to $400 per year.[128] Finally, several of the commissioners, such as Gustav Scott and William Thornton, owned slaves who worked on the project and supplemented their $400 quarterly salaries with slave earnings.[129]

Whatever the inadequacies of the data, this case demonstrates, yet again, that when federal officials rented slaves, they were not merely the employers of slave labor. They became the temporary masters of the slaves of other slaveholders. Like other slaveholders, they hired agents to manage "their" slaves or, as in this case, layers of agents.[130] It seems unlikely that the Washington commissioners would have established such an elaborate management structure for the project if slaves had not represented such a high percentage of the workforce. This case perfectly illustrates how the micromanagement structures for slave labor and free labor at federal work sites were often isomorphic, frequently overlapping, and sometimes multitiered.[131]

After the initial construction of the capital, the federal government employed slaves to help maintain it. Slaves worked on public-works projects, such as street cleaning and sewage disposal, around the city.[132] They also worked on finishing the capital during the Jefferson administration as well as on rebuilding it after British forces partially destroyed it during the War of 1812.[133] Much later, the federal government paid the city's "loyal" slaveholders approximately $900,000 to emancipate 2,989 of their slaves during the Civil War.[134]

We have already seen how the U.S. military employed slave labor in the territories. One documented case on the civilian side occurred in New Mexico. Territorial Governor William Carr Lane charged Grafton Baker with carrying a secret dispatch from Santa Fe to Washington in 1853 to inform the Pierce administration of developments along the Mexican border. Baker was the chief justice of New Mexico and owned one of the few African American slaves in the territory, who worked as his personal clerk and thus helped govern the territory. Congress reimbursed Baker $366.50 for the expenses of their thirty-day trip to the nation's capital.[135]

Other federal civilian officials also employed their own slaves as their personal clerks. This practice was reportedly common at Post Office headquarters in Washington.[136] Local postmasters also occasionally employed slaves as mail clerks.[137] These practices did not violate postal regulations. The Post Office had, however, adopted a regulation against employing either free blacks or slaves to carry the mail as early as 1802. This regulation was a "public safety" response to reports that at the time of the Gabriel conspiracy slaves were carrying the mail in several Virginia communities.[138] In a secret addendum that explained the new policy to staunchly proslavery Congressman James Jackson (Georgia Democratic Republican), Postmaster General Gideon Granger (Connecticut Democratic Republican) lectures Jackson that black mail carriers "will acquire information. They will learn that a man's rights do not depend on his color. They will, in time, become teachers to their brethren." Granger warns Jackson that they may even take the fateful step of assisting slave conspirators in communicating "from town to town, and produce a general and united operation against you."[139]

Thereafter there were many reports of blacks carrying the mail but no confirmed cases of slaves carrying the mail.[140] Beginning in 1838, Congress received a report from the postmaster general on the fines that his office had imposed on local postmasters and mail contractors for various infractions, including employing blacks to carry the mail. From 1838 through 1861, these reports listed ten such cases, all from slave states. Though in each case the report simply listed the carrier as "black," most, if not all, of the carriers were probably slaves.[141]

Southern Indian agents frequently employed slaves at their agencies, both their own and those of other slaveholders. For instance, Wiley Thompson, who was the subagent for the Florida Seminoles and a former Georgia congressman, employed an African American slave as a blacksmith at his agency in 1834 because he claimed to have been unable to find a reliable European American or Native American to do the work.[142] Indian agents also used black, sometimes slave, interpreters at their agencies for day-to-day dealings with individual Native Americans as well as to negotiate treaties with Native American delegations.[143] Joshua Pilchur (Tennessee), who was the regional Indian superintendent in Saint Louis, rented a slave, Charles, in 1839 for $3 per week to clean his office and run errands.[144] Pilchur's immediate predecessor, William Clark (Kentucky), was also a slaveholder. Much earlier, Clark's slave York had accompanied him on his famous voyage of discovery through the Louisiana Purchase.[145]

Whether or not slaves were still sailing on navy vessels in the 1850s, they were still sailing on Treasury revenue cutters. In 1851, Wilmington (North Carolina) customs collector Robert G. Rankin justified the practice, which had been continued through "*all administrations*" in his district, by explaining that "white labor cannot be obtained at the monthly rate of compensation allowed, and if it could, the service can be better performed as at present."[146] Rankin's explanation was intended to meet the objections Charles William Rockwell (Georgia), the commissioner of customs in the Department of Treasury, had raised against the practice to Treasury Secretary Thomas Corwin (Ohio Whig). In addition to referring to the several ways that the navy had proscribed the use of slave labor, Rockwell had written Corwin that all the slaves employed in the Wilmington district appeared to be the slaves of customs employees or their friends and that the practice was common only in one other (unnamed) district.[147] Rockwell subsequently wrote Rankin that an "adequate allowance" would be made to employ "competent [white] persons."[148] Rankin asserts his bureaucratic autonomy in his reply. He frankly acknowledges that he continued to employ slave sailors, though he now thinks that it might be possible to procure "competent" white sailors at $25 per month, which was apparently a higher rate than he had previously been allowed or than he paid the masters of his slave sailors.[149]

Compared to the military departments of the federal government, the civilian departments employed slaves at lower rates and in lower percentages. But the civilian departments were also, in general, smaller, less professionalized, and less habituated to data collection. Even the apparent exception, the Post Office, only sporadically filed employment reports with Congress. In any event, slave labor formed part of the capacities of both halves of the federal government. Slave rentals also contributed to the bureaucratic autonomy of federal officials in both halves. The use of slave labor was more heavily regulated from the center than the use of free labor was. As a result, slave rentals were more susceptible to rule avoidance by middle- and low-level officials on the periphery, rule avoidance that they were rarely required to justify and that then encouraged them to act with a similar independence in other transactions.

CONCLUSION

Especially on the civilian side, the cases discussed in this chapter are only sugges-
tive of the extent to which the federal government employed slave labor and the
aggregate costs that resulted from the practice. Even on the military side, the lack
of longitudinal data from the Office of the Chief of Engineers meant a loss of a
majority of the cases. It will require many more case-by-case investigations before
we will be able to offer a more accurate picture of the federal employment of slave
labor during the 1791–1861 period, the aggregate costs that resulted from the practice, and the peculiar management problems that were associated with it.

Obviously, sectional differences existed on where the federal government employed slave labor. The extent to which sectional, as well as partisan, differences
existed on when it employed slave labor is less obvious. Several disputes over the
U.S. military's use of slave labor and over particular slaves who had either worked
for or served in the military reached Congress, which exposed sectional and partisan differences over those practices. The Senate vote on Calhoun's amendment to
exclude African Americans from most categories of navy service was highly partisan and sectional. Democrats voted 16–2 in favor of the amendment and Whigs
14–8 in opposition, while the Southern vote was 17–0 in favor and the Northern
vote 16–7 in opposition.[150] The Senate did not, however, debate the amendment.
It then quietly died in the House, without being brought to the floor. The Jackson and Oden claims for their deceased slaves' land bounties were handled differently depending on the sectional and partisan affiliations of the congressmen
who handled them, but as private land claims they were, again, not debated on the
floor. The atypical case was Antonio Pacheco's claim for the loss of the services
of his slave during the Second Seminole War. The House debated and narrowly
approved his claim. This vote was also highly partisan and sectional. Democrats
voted 64–32 in favor of the bill and Whigs 63–36 in opposition, while the Southern
vote was 73–0 in favor and the Northern vote 95–28 in opposition.[151] Now, the
Senate avoided controversy by tabling the bill. Since both Calhoun's amendment
and Pacheco's claim generated unanimous Southern support, the partisan divisions were strictly within the Northern delegations, with Democrats much more
supportive than Whigs. The votes in the Northern delegations were 7–2 among
the Democrats in *support* of Calhoun's amendment and a unanimous 14–0 among
the Whigs in opposition, 32–22 among the Democrats in opposition to Pacheco's
claim and a nearly unanimous 63–3 among the Whigs.

As opposed to the strenuous Southern congressional objections raised to African Americans, whether free or enslaved, serving in the U.S. military, the supposition is that most members of Congress, from both the North and South, viewed

the federal employment of slave labor as an unobjectionable practice except in especially sensitive positions or at especially sensitive times. Presumably, they would continue to consider the practice unobjectionable as long as slave labor was such a prominent form of labor in one section of the country and the federal government (almost) exclusively employed it in that section of the country. Most members of Congress were probably unaware of the full extent of the practice anyway, given how much of it was undocumented and occurred on the Southern periphery. Indeed, federal officials appeared committed to keeping it "out of sight" on the periphery to avoid controversy.[152] The catalyst for the 1842 congressional inquiry into the extent of the practice within the U.S. military was, after all, not the diligence of an army division head or the outrage of an antislavery congressman but the complaint of a disgruntled slaveholder and even at that, the inquiry only exposed the army side of the practice.[153] It is therefore not surprising that the federal government continued to employ slave labor in the slave states even after most of them had seceded from the union and the Civil War had begun. Nor is it surprising that the Senate rejected a resolution that would have prohibited the military from continuing to employ slave labor as late as June 1862. Many years earlier, Baldwin and Jesup had both intimated that the federal government was highly dependent on slave labor at its Southern facilities.

The Norfolk navy yard case presents the paradox of a Boston-bred civil engineer defending the continued federal employment of slave labor at an especially sensitive time despite the protests of local slaveholders against the practice. Following the Southampton revolt, Norfolk-area slaveholders, of course, opposed the practice for reasons of slave control, not because of any antislavery or pro–free labor bias. The various regulations that cabinet-level officials adopted against the employment of slave labor in especially sensitive positions shared the same rationale. One might be tempted to interpret those regulations as solutions to a collective-action problem. If so, many slaveholders "free rode." Even in the Norfolk case, many local slaveholders continued to "permit" their own slaves to work on the project after a community-wide protest against the practice.

When federal employers rented slave labor, they sometimes incurred non-wage costs in addition to those that they incurred when they hired free labor. They also sometimes established additional management structures, as in the capital construction and Norfolk cases. This factor not only complicates the issue of whether slave labor was cheaper than free labor; it also placed the federal official who rented slave labor in the role of a master of slaves rather than simply an employer of their labor. In employing slave labor, the relationship between the federal government and particular slaveholders was usually contractual, at least implicitly, but the relationship between the federal government and particular slaves was rarely contractual, only possibly in cases in which masters had allowed slaves to rent out their own labor. However difficult it was for free laborers to enforce employment agreements during the pre–Civil War period, it was also difficult for slaveholders who had rented out their slaves and certainly more so for the slaves themselves, who were typically not even parties to such agreements. The Dancy scandal highlights these difficulties. This aspect of the federal employment of slave labor replicated the reality that the relationship between slaveholders and slaves was itself only contractual under special circumstances, as when slaveholders had allowed their slaves to rent out their own labor or when their slaves were in the process of buying their own freedom, and usually not even in those cases. The illiberal nature of the institution of slavery followed slaves into the federal workplace, just as it did into other workplaces.[154]

From the side of the federal government, the use of slave labor was another case in which federal officials employed private agents to perform public functions. The dangers of this practice were greater in the case of renting slave labor than hiring free labor because rented slaves were even less federal employees than free hires were. The rented slave had another master than his or her federal supervisor and the interests of the supervisor, slaveholder, slave, and broader public had somehow to be coordinated for the desired function to be performed. As the Dancy and Mallory cases demonstrate, this dual mastership impinged on job performance, though in both cases it was the supervisor, not the slaveholder or slave, who was allegedly culpable. The Dancy case also demonstrates the problems that could occur when the supervisor was himself a contract employee. Finally, the Norfolk case shows how the interests and prejudices of white workers at a federal work site could complicate the use of slave labor.

In terms of its effects on early American state development, the federal employment of slave labor had less significant effects than the policy areas discussed in previous chapters. The effects of the practice on the legitimacy, authority, and coercive capacities of the federal government were all microlevel effects, limited to the people who were immediately affected by the practice, though in the Norfolk case federal legitimacy probably suffered substantially in the local white labor force. Yet the practice still had some significant developmental effects on the early American state.

Especially on the military side, the federal employment of slave labor was a marker of its growing institutional autonomy. Many of the cases in which military officers rented slave labor were local decisions in violation of central policies. In the Norfolk case, Baldwin manifested a considerable degree of autonomy not only from local constituencies but from cabinet-level officials, despite the fact that he was a contract employee.

The federal employment of slave labor also affected how the federal government managed all its employees. The comparable pay scales and common overseers were indicative of this effect. Again, the capital construction case perfectly illustrates how slave management could become general labor management. In such cases, the Republican argument that slave labor demeaned free labor had a very concrete reference.[155]

While the effects of the federal employment of slave labor on the continued existence of slavery in the Southern states were limited by the number of slaves that the federal government actually employed, the impact appears to have been quite significant in some Southern communities.[156] The practice contributed to the development of both Norfolk and Pensacola as slave societies. Such distributive effects could have been very important at the local level, even if they were marginal nationally.

The federal employment of slave labor also had powerful symbolic effects. Future Republican leaders Salmon P. Chase (Ohio) and Owen Lovejoy (Illinois) were among the antislavery politicians who targeted those effects of the practice. When even the federal government used slave labor, regardless of how little or much it used, it showed just how much the institution of slavery had been "normalized."[157]

Counterfactually, one can imagine the symbolic effects of an "early" federal affirmative-action decision to never rent slave labor and, instead, to codify a preference for hiring free black labor over white labor. Federal officials sometimes codified a preference for employing white over black labor, whether free or enslaved, but that preference was not based on any overriding principle of action, either to affirm the superiority of free over slave labor or, less nobly, of white over black labor. Federal policy in this area was rather a response to a complicated vector of economic factors and political pressures. The result was a blanket endorsement of neither slave labor nor free labor. However, in practice, federal policy again leaned heavily southward. For the most part, Southern slaveholders had regulations in place against the use of slave labor when they wanted them in place (mail routes and navy yards) and not in place when they did not want them in place (military servants and construction projects). They were also generally able to rent their slaves to the federal government even when the regulations might work to their disadvantage.

This policy area was also significant because federal employment policies were so heavily executive-driven and, regarding the military, military-driven. The only congressional policy in this area during the whole 1791–1861 period was the 1792 "Black Militia" law, and even in that case, the law was applied to the U.S. military at the discretion of the U.S. military. General Washington's manpower decisions during the Revolutionary War established a long-term pattern. Congressional oversight was sporadic and clearly scandal-driven, as in the Mobile Point and Dancy cases, and even in those cases, Congress deferred to executive decision-makers. On the civilian side, Congress enacted a ban on black mail carriers at the behest of Postmaster General Granger, and his "secret" correspondence to the body explicitly associated the policy with the protection of slavery. Legislatures generally do not micromanage government employment policies, but in the early American state the presence of slavery reinforced a broader dynamic.

Federal employment policies on the use of slave labor also pushed decision-making to the periphery during the 1791–1861 period, in part because the policies at the center were so Janus-faced. The Rankin-Rockwell dispute over slave sailors highlights this policy ambiguity. Rockwell could only point to navy, not Treasury, regulations against the use of slave labor. Given the lack of policy clarity at the center, middle- and low-level federal officials sought to avoid responsibility both for refusing to employ slave labor and for not refusing to employ it. As one might predict, the result was many unreported slave rentals.

As long as the institution of slavery continued to exist in such a large section of the nation, most federal officials, regardless of their personal opinions about slavery or their partisan and sectional affiliations, felt an obligation to act dispassionately toward the institution, to treat slave labor equally to free labor. At least that generalization was true until the Republican victory in the 1860 presidential elections promised to throw the symbolic weight of the federal government on the other, antislavery side. It was also a victory that brought the nation to the brink of civil war.

7. The "House Divided" Revisited

In announcing his campaign to unseat Senator Stephen A. Douglas in Springfield, Illinois, on June 16, 1858, Abraham Lincoln claimed that the union was "a house divided against itself."[1] Lincoln could, however, have understood the metaphor in two different ways.

The first way is to think of the union as a townhouse with a temporary wall dividing a free side from a slave side. On this understanding, the union could not stand indefinitely as a house divided.[2] The temporary wall would eventually come down and the house become either all free or all slave. Originally, the expectation of the framers of the house had been that the two sides of the house would tear down the wall together, as the slave side gradually, and voluntarily, abolished slavery, just as the free side was in the process of gradually, and voluntarily, abolishing the institution. After all, the two sides had much in common. They had built the house together. They had fought two wars of independence together. Over time, though, the expectation of a gradual, voluntary abolition of slavery on the slave side seemed increasingly unrealistic, and the two sides of the house had become increasingly antagonistic toward each other. By the late 1850s, they were continually banging on the wall, not only rudely disturbing each other but threatening to unilaterally tear down the wall and occupy the other side of the house.[3] Yet it was not too late to prevent this worst-case scenario. It was still possible to reunite the two sides of the house in the belief that slavery was "in the course of ultimate extinction." It was still possible for the two sides to agree to tear down the wall together and make the house all free, while postponing the actual event to the indefinite future.[4]

This understanding of the metaphor was probably Lincoln's own understanding, at least at the time he delivered his "House Divided" speech. It is also the understanding held by most politics and history scholars writing about early American state development, at least until recently. According to this understanding, the proslavery principle was external to the American liberal experience. The institution of slavery was a temporary institution that might have negatively affected early American state development but still was not constitutive of it. In this sense, Louis Hartz's metanarrative of American state development as the unfolding of a liberal consensus remains dominant.[5]

The second way of understanding the "House Divided" metaphor is to think of the union as a temporary shelter, built of an unstable composite of free and slave materials, which could not long endure. On this understanding, the framers constructed this temporary shelter in order to meet more immediately pressing economic and security needs in 1787, until such time as a more permanent structure could be built of purer materials. Their preference was that it would be built of freer materials. Time had, however, belied their preferences and predictions. Their temporary shelter had developed into a more permanent structure. Worse, the slave materials had ossified and become more constitutive of its nature. It had thus become necessary to tear down the whole structure and build another one of freer materials, and to do so soon or else risk never being able to do so.[6]

Lincoln appeared to increasingly accept this latter understanding of the union as the Civil War progressed, as when he declared "a new birth of freedom" in his Gettysburg Address of November 19, 1863.[7] It is also an understanding that some politics and history scholars, such as Robin Einhorn and Don Fehrenbacher, have recently suggested in indicating how the continuing presence of slavery in the Southern states and territories was more constitutive of early American state development than had previously been thought.[8]

This study goes beyond other recent revisionist scholarship in explicating the multiple ways that the presence of slavery was constitutive of early American state development. In the preceding chapters, I show exactly how the presence of slavery was constitutive of state development and not merely an exogenous social force that occasionally affected public policy. I also demonstrate how the presence of slavery contributed to state development and did not merely act to depress it. Finally, I chronicle those effects on a number of different measures of state development, including state capacities (both human and fiscal resources), institutional autonomy, governing authority, state legitimacy, and the ability of government officials to coerce people (noncitizens as well as citizens). This concluding chapter summarizes these findings to press more strongly the argument that the presence of slavery was constitutive of early American state development.

STATE CAPACITIES

In terms of state capacities, my estimated total of major ($100,000+) slavery-related federal expenditures is $51 million.[9] This total represents 2.8 percent of total federal expenditures ($1,797 million) for the 1791–1861 period.[10] Most of the slavery-related total involves military expenditures, in particular on the Second Seminole War ($30 million), just as most of the federal total involves military expenditures ($983 million). For purposes of comparison, the federal government spent a total of approximately $55 million on internal improvements from 1800 to 1860.[11] Of course, many of those internal improvements were built with slave labor. My estimate of major slavery-related federal expenditures includes very few of those specific costs.

My estimate is conservative. Many slavery-related federal expenditures, including the slave-labor costs of any number of federal internal-improvement projects, were not documented; nor can they be reasonably estimated. Still, my slavery-related total is not insignificant, especially in light of the nondiscretionary nature of much government spending. Whether or not they are deployed, armies and navies require resources. Mail delivery, which was the largest civilian spending item of the federal government during the 1791–1861 period, also entails a considerable amount of sunk costs.[12] While the presence of slavery did not typically affect mail delivery, the abolitionist mailings controversy was one instance in which it did.[13]

The effects of the presence of slavery on federal employment are even harder to measure. For a long time, the enforcement of the nation's slave-trade laws was one of the incidental duties of U.S. navy crews, marshals, attorneys, justices, commissioners, customs collectors, and ship inspectors. Eventually, the navy established a separate African squadron but mostly through a reallocation of resources rather than an increase in resources. In 1859, both the African and Home squadrons received significant new resources for slave-trade suppression but, again, it is unclear how many of those resources were totally new or merely the result of a reallocation of resources from other squadrons. Still, slave-trade suppression was a major episode in the development of the U.S. navy. From FY1843 through FY1861, African Squadron manpower averaged 825 men, 8.1 percent of total navy manpower.[14]

Navy activity off the west coast of Africa, both before and after the creation of the African Squadron, was associated with Liberian colonization. The founding of Liberia also produced a new federal office. The colonial agent was a joint employee of the American Colonization Society (ACS) and federal government. Following Liberian independence, the federal government appointed its own commercial agent to the new nation in 1848. This agent informally served as a diplomatic counsel in Liberia until the United States formally recognized that nation's independence in 1862.

The enforcement of the nation's fugitive-slave laws was also an incidental duty of a number of federal employees, including U.S. marshals, attorneys, commissioners, justices, Indian agents, and military personnel. With the passage of the Fugitive Slave Law of 1850, Congress established a new legal apparatus to enforce the law. U.S. marshals now regularly appointed deputy marshals to capture fugitive slaves and prevent their rescues, U.S. commissioners now devoted more time and resources to fugitive-slave renditions, and military personnel now served as a coercive tool of last resort in such cases. Again, it is unclear how many of these resources were totally new and how many were simply reallocated. Nonetheless, the Anthony Burns rendition in Boston in 1854 involved the deployment of a federalized force of 1,600 men, this at a time when the total size of the U.S. army was only 10,894 men.[15]

In Florida, military personnel were involved in slave-catching expeditions long before 1850. Slave disputes were one of the causes of the Second Seminole War. Approximately 40,000 men saw military service during the war, prompting Congress to authorize a nearly two-thirds increase in the size of the army from 7,130 to 11,800 men.[16] While the actual increase in troop levels was temporary, postwar troop levels remained approximately 30 percent higher than pre-war levels, substantiating the ratchet effect typical of major military conflicts.[17] Otherwise, slavery-related military deployments were cases of the reallocation of existing resources rather than the creation of new ones.

The federal employment of slave labor is the clearest case of slavery-related federal employment. In August 1842, the U.S. army reported employing 687 slaves, which would have represented approximately 3.8 percent of the federal government's civilian workforce at the time.[18] The federal employment of slave labor is also the clearest case of a substitution effect. Even if slave labor was cheaper than free labor, the slave-labor supplement to federal employment would have been marginal. The federal employment of overseers to manage slave labor was a slave-labor supplement to federal employment but, in many cases, overseers managed free white laborers as well as slaves. Federal officials also hired overseers only when they employed a large number of people at a particular work site, so that the aggregate effects of the practice on federal employment levels were minimal. Federally employed slaves and overseers were, moreover, not federal employees. They were private agents whom federal officials employed to perform specific public functions. Yet the federal government's use of overseers was significant in showing how labor management practices spread from slave labor to free labor.

Federal officials employed private agents to perform public functions on a regular basis. Military officers employed temporary laborers, both free and enslaved, to work in army posts, at navy yards, and on public-works projects. They also deployed auxiliary soldiers to supplement army regulars during military engagements. To the degree that those engagements were slavery-related, the additional manpower was a slavery-related supplement to federal employment. During the Second Seminole War, the supplement was approximately 30,000 men.[19]

To enforce fugitive-slave law, U.S. marshals hired deputy marshals to help capture alleged fugitive slaves and slave rescuers, and U.S. attorneys hired private attorneys to help prosecute them. U.S. marshals also paid private citizens to care for alleged slave rescuers who were incarcerated as they awaited trial as well as to serve as jurors and testify as witnesses at their trials, and, again, to care for them if they were convicted and sentenced to prison. The federal government paid a private organization to transport Africans seized from suspected slave ships to Liberia and to care for them during their initial months in the colony or, later, nation. The federal government also paid as much as two thirds of the salary of an ACS official in Liberia to oversee the care of those recaptured Africans. As in fugitive-slave cases, U.S. attorneys hired private attorneys to help prosecute slave-trade cases; and U.S. marshals paid private citizens to care for alleged slave traders and smugglers who were incarcerated as they awaited trial, as well as to serve as jurors and testify as witnesses at their trials, and, again, to care for them if they were convicted and sentenced to prison.[20] The federal government also paid private citizens to care for recaptured Africans as they awaited their final disposition, whether it was transportation to Africa, the custody of a foreign national, or a state auction. If one could sum the total number of private agents whom federal officials employed in slavery-related cases, it would be a significant number. In the Margaret Garner rendition in Cincinnati in 1856, U.S. Marshal Hiram H. Robinson hired as many as fifty deputy marshals to prevent her rescue.[21]

The presence of slavery produced increases in the number of the people working for the federal government even if they did not appear on employment charts or in job statistics. We should recall how "small" the federal government was before the Civil War, not only in terms of spending but of manpower. From 1816 to 1851, federal military employment rose from 16,743 to 20,726 people, and civilian employment rose from 4,837 to 26,274 people, 21,391 of whom worked for the post office. The 1851 total of 47,000 federal employees is, again, minuscule by contemporary standards of a federal government with 4,443,000 employees, including 1,591,000 men and women in its armed forces.[22]

The federal government's extensive use of private agents to perform public functions was a sign of its lack of institutional development. The practice also probably decreased the effective performance of those functions. On the other hand, the practice may well have saved the federal government money because it was usually cheaper to employ a private citizen to perform a specific task than to add staff. During the Second Seminole War, army regulars were more effective than auxiliary soldiers; at least that was the presumption behind Congress's authorizing a wartime increase in the size of the army. It was also the presumption behind army commanders weaning the war effort from its reliance on militia and volunteer units. In this case, the Department of War probably saved money by adding staff, given the disparity in the pay and support costs between regular army units and militia and volunteer units. The army was, however, an early case of professionalization.[23] Relative to other public agencies at the time, it demonstrated a greater capacity to perform its assigned tasks, such as removing Native Americans and deterring slave rebellions, and hence saw substantial increases in its resources.

In other cases, it is more difficult to measure the relative effectiveness of regular and temporary employees. Private attorney Edward Ryan successfully prosecuted Sherman Booth for his role in the Joshua Glover slave rescue, but perhaps U.S. Attorney John Shaperstein would also have successfully prosecuted Booth.[24] Federal officials often treated their offices as private sinecures. U.S. Marshal William Morel certainly profited from his supervision of the Africans seized from the *Antelope*. Private organizations also could pursue controversial public purposes in ways that the federal government could not. With federal support, the ACS was able to pursue an African colonization project in a more effective way than either the society or federal government could have on its own.

Today, the federal government has developed institutionally to the point that its institutions are much more autonomous of exogenous social forces and local congressional and constituency demands. Less intermixing of private and public business occurs among federal officeholders. No attorney general would insist, as William Wirt did, that he should be able to retain a lucrative private practice and then subject his official duties to the dictates of that practice.[25] Contracts more tightly govern the performance of both regular and temporary federal employees. Nor are temporary employees governed in the same way that they were governed during the 1791–1861 period. Yet federal officials still hire temporary employees, including private attorneys to argue important court cases; private organizations still perform controversial public policies, as Halliburton did in occupied Iraq; federal officeholders still place personal profit above public service, as evidenced by the growing number of elected officials who are investigated for ethics violations; and temporary employees still are often treated like indentured servants, as any number of former congressional interns could attest.[26] The autonomy of state institutions is always a relative matter and certainly no guarantee against the foibles of human nature.

In sum, even if the presence of slavery did not translate into an increase in the number of federal employees, it translated into an increase in the number of people who worked for the federal government. It also influenced the ways that the federal government deployed its human and financial capacities. It, finally, affected how the federal government managed all its employees, black and white, free and enslaved.

INSTITUTIONAL AUTONOMY

Despite its continuing institutional weakness during the 1791–1861 period, the federal government added administrative structure. The presence of slavery was one reason why it became a "thicker" organization.

The fugitive-slave policy area is the clearest case of a slavery-related institutional development. The Fugitive Slave Law of 1850 mandated the establishment of an autonomous federal law-enforcement apparatus separate from and, in many ways, antagonistic to the Northern state apparatuses. In fugitive-slave cases, federal law-enforcement officials enforced the constitutional rights of slaveholders against the states in a way that anticipated the federal enforcement of the constitutional rights of freed slaves during Reconstruction and, much later and more successfully, those of their descendants during the Civil Rights revolution.[27]

As in other nations, the military paced the institutional development of the American state during the 1791–1861 period. The presence of slavery contributed, in turn, to the institutional development of the U.S. military. Both in Florida and Kansas, not only did the army assert its institutional autonomy from auxiliary forces and constituency demands in its conduct of the slavery-related military actions that occurred in those territories, but those actions themselves provided levers for future assertions of autonomy.[28] The enforcement of the nation's slave-trade laws eventually led to the formation of a separate African Squadron within the U.S. navy in 1843 and then, in 1859, to a substantial increase in its resources. Though the Civil War truncated this episode in the institutional development of the navy, it helped prepare the navy for its wartime blockade duties. In the case of African colonization, sympathetic federal officials subsidized a private organization rather than create a separate agency to colonize Africa. Yet this policy area was also an example of military development to the extent that the navy assisted the ACS's colonial enterprise and established a stronger international presence because of it.[29]

One of the most striking features about the federal employment of slave labor was the autonomy that middle- and low-level army and navy officers exercised in leasing it. According to Mark Wilson, the military was the one federal institution where this "mezzo-level" autonomy emerged before the Civil War, thus predating Daniel Carpenter's thesis about the importance of this factor to American state development after the war.[30] The division heads of the army enjoyed extraordinarily long tenures during the pre–Civil War period. Quartermaster General Thomas S. Jesup (Kentucky) served 42 years (1818–1860); Commissary General George Gibson (Pennsylvania), 35 years (1826–1861); Topographic Engineer John James Abert (Virginia), 32 years (1829–1861); Adjutant General Roger Jones (Virginia), 27 years (1825–1852); and Chief Engineer Joseph G. Totten (Connecticut), 26 years (1838–1864). Only the Ordnance Department witnessed significant turnover at the top, and even then George Bomford (New York) headed the department for 16 years (1832–1848).

By this measure of state development, the early American state remained, nevertheless, relatively weak, and the contribution of slavery was significant and enduring only in the area of law enforcement. On other measures of state development, the early American state grew much stronger, and the contribution of slavery was more significant and enduring.

GOVERNING AUTHORITY

Overall, the authority of the federal government increased substantially during the 1791–1861 period. The U.S. Constitution had authorized a number of shifts in governing authority from the state governments to the federal government. The subsequent practices of the federal government cemented these shifts. From a states-rights point of view, federal practice often exceeded constitutional authorization, and states-rights critiques of federal practices developed on the antislavery as well as the proslavery side of constitutional debate. The presence of slavery was integral both to federal expansion and continued opposition to it.

Again, the fugitive-slave policy area exemplifies these developments. The fugitive-slave clause of the Constitution had mandated interstate comity in the return of fugitive slaves. It did not explicitly grant the federal government any role in the process. In the Fugitive Slave Law of 1850, Congress carved out such a role, and, as implemented, the law further increased federal authority relative to the states. Proslavery forces had lobbied for the law. They now pressed for its maximum enforcement. Antislavery forces claimed that the law exceeded the constitutional authority of the federal government. They now sought its repeal.[31]

In the slave-trade policy area, the Constitution explicitly authorized a shift in governing authority over slave imports from the state governments to the federal government, though it delayed its effective date by twenty years. Even after Congress had passed the constitutionally authorized slave-import ban as well as a series of increasingly punitive slave-trade laws, it did not appropriate any money to fund interdiction activities until 1819, and most of that money was diverted to the ACS. Federal authority over slave-trade interdiction was not effectively asserted until 1859. This policy area was more ambiguous than the fugitive-slave policy area. Only the first delay, from 1789 to 1808, was clearly the result of a proslavery, states-rights critique of federal powers. On the other hand, the lax enforcement of the nation's slave-trade laws was not a major target of the abolitionist critiques of the proslavery practices of the federal government under the Constitution.[32]

Slavery-related military deployments substantiated the domestic violence and insurrection clauses. They also substantiated the constitutional powers of the legislative and executive branches of the federal government to raise armies (Second Seminole War), call forth the state (and territorial) militia (Second Seminole War, "Bleeding Kansas," and Burns rendition), govern territories (Florida, Kansas, and Louisiana), and oversee relations with other nations (Florida incursions and Native American removals). In total, these deployments strengthened federal authority relative to other governing authorities, both domestically and internationally. Only in the case of the domestic violence and insurrection clauses did a sustained antislavery critique emerge of the powers *per se,* as Rufus King (Massachusetts) and Gouverneur Morris (Pennsylvania) had anticipated at the Constitutional Convention. In the other cases, antislavery legislators, such as Joshua R. Giddings (Ohio Whig) and Charles Sumner (Massachusetts Whig), criticized instead the way that the executive departments had implemented their constitutional powers.

African colonization also fell under congressional and executive powers over foreign relations. In this policy area, any increase to federal authority was limited by the way that the executive departments "privatized" African colonization. Federal involvement in the enterprise also faced both antislavery (David Walker and William Lloyd Garrison) and proslavery (Littleton Tazewell and Thomas R. Dew) critiques. Similarly, the federal employment of slave labor tracked the constitutional authority of the federal government over its own facilities, the nation's (future) capital, and U.S. territories. Even though the federal employment of slave labor may not have increased the authority of the federal government, it increased the authority of the individual federal employees who rented and managed slave labor. In this policy area, antislavery politicians (Salmon P. Chase and Owen Lovejoy) sometimes targeted the general practice for its symbolic value, while proslavery politicians (John C. Calhoun and James Jackson) targeted particular instances of the use of slave labor that they thought unsafe.

The presence of slavery also affected the distribution of governing authority among various departments and levels of government during the 1791–1861 period. Given the coercive nature of the institution, it should not be surprising that the presence of slavery pushed early American state development even further in a military direction than otherwise would have been the case. The institution also pushed early American state development more in an executive direction. In conjunction with the latter dynamic, the slavery issue meant more covert policy-making and policy-making less at the center and more on the periphery, in part because of its tendency to create paralysis at the center, especially in Congress. The Second Seminole War brought together all four of these dynamics. On the civilian side, the Jackson and Van Buren administrations prosecuted the war largely out of public and congressional view, in the swamps of a distant territory, at least until Giddings intervened. On the military side, the major decisions of the war were made on the periphery, as in the case of Jesup's decision to offer the Black Seminoles freedom in the West and his implementation of that policy even after his civilian superiors in Washington had forced him to formally withdraw the offer. In renting slaves, army and navy officers also, more routinely, asserted their bureaucratic autonomy by making decisions on the periphery that violated cabinet-level policies. The slave-trade and African-colonization policy areas were other important examples of executive policy-making, as Presidents Monroe and Buchanan made the key decisions that drove public policy in both areas. Of the two, Congress played a larger role in the slave-trade than in the African-colonization policy area. This larger congressional role is also evident in the fugitive-slave policy area, which is another important example of a constitutionally authorized, though not constitutionally mandated, shift in the balance of powers between the federal and state governments. Finally, the Taney Court provides early examples of judicial policy-making that attempted to unravel policy deadlocks, both with respect to the issue of interstate fugitive-slave returns and the issue of slavery in the territories. In each of these policy areas, the presence of slavery contributed to long-term political dynamics that reshaped American governance during the pre–Civil War period.

The aggregate effects of slavery-related policy areas on federal authority during the pre–Civil War period were substantial. In part because of the presence of slavery, the federal government of 1861 was much stronger than the federal government of 1791 in the sense that it had much more governing authority as a matter of both constitutional law and practice. Southern secession and Civil War severely tested the authority of the federal government. It could not, however, have won the war without the prior growth of its authority, a process which, ironically, Southern slaveholding elites had done at least as much to advance as to retard. Nor could the federal government have won the war without a further expansion of its authority in the non-seceding states during the conflict.[33]

LEGITIMACY

State legitimacy depends on the public's opinion of the appropriateness of its state. It is very difficult to measure the legitimacy of a state in a pre-polling world. Presumably, a—if not the—major factor affecting state legitimacy is the public's opinion of the appropriateness of the specific actions that its state does or does not perform.[34] Without public-opinion polling data, we can make only informed judgments about how the specific slavery-related actions that the federal government did or did not perform during the 1791–1861 period affected its legitimacy.

On this measure of state development, slavery-related military deployments probably had the greatest impact. Southern politicians and citizens, especially slaveholders, demanded Native American removals, and they were undoubtedly satisfied with the result. The Carlson and Roberts study of the congressional vote on the Indian Removal Act of 1830 suggests this effect.[35] Similarly, Andrew Cayton's studies of how federal inaction against Native American "depredations" in the trans-Appalachian South decreased the legitimacy of the federal government in the region suggest that the southeast removals had a positive effect on its legitimacy.[36] While Alisse Portnoy shows how some determined opposition to those removals emerged in the Northern states, she also notes that the issue was somewhat peripheral to the concerns of most Northern politicians and citizens, except for those who were most embedded in the benevolent empire.[37] After all, the federal government had already removed most of "their" Native Americans. Cayton claims that the loyalties of the settlers of the trans-Appalachian North were stronger than those of the trans-Appalachian South in the early republic precisely because the federal government had been more solicitous of their concerns, including in "pacifying" the Native American nations in their region.[38] Carlson and Roberts, furthermore, find the typical second-party-system pattern; Northern congressmen were less united in opposing the Indian Removal Act than Southern congressmen were in supporting it.[39]

Military deployments to enforce the Fugitive Slave Law of 1850 were much more contentious, as was the whole policy area. Southern politicians and citizens, again especially slaveholders, demanded greater federal enforcement efforts in interstate fugitive-slave cases during the 1840s, made the promise of greater federal enforcement efforts one of their demands for continued union in the early 1850s, and declared continuing Northern resistance to greater federal enforcement efforts one of their primary justifications for secession in the winter of 1860–1861. Northern politicians and citizens, particularly abolitionists, viewed this policy area through a very different lens. For them, the greater federal enforcement efforts in their states were reasons *not* to grant the federal government legitimacy. Before Southern slaveholders argued for disunion on the basis of Northern resistance to greater federal enforcement efforts in this policy area, the Garrison abolitionists argued for disunion on the basis of those very efforts. At an 1857 disunion convention in Worcester, Wendell Phillips advocated disunion so that Massachusetts would no longer serve as "the bloodhound of South Carolina."[40]

The nation's slave-trade laws were much less contentious and more peripheral to the concerns of most Americans in both the North and South. The federal efforts to enforce (or not enforce) those laws probably had little effect on federal legitimacy, except among (potential) slave smugglers and traders. The federal efforts to support African colonization were somewhat more contentious but again peripheral to the concerns of most Americans to whom free African Americans were already an invisible part of the population. Those efforts probably also had little effect on federal legitimacy, especially since they were funded so circuitously. Despite antislavery criticisms of the general practice and several contested cases of the federal employment of slave labor, the effect on federal legitimacy was, once again, probably minimal. One suspects that this entire policy area was invisible to the vast majority of Americans, certainly in the Northern states and territories and also probably in the Southern states and territories because so much of the federal employment of slave labor occurred on the periphery.

As a whole, the various ways that the federal government reacted to the presence of slavery affected its legitimacy, in both the North and South, in terms of the specific actions it performed. But most dramatically, the various ways that the federal government reacted to the presence of slavery affected its legitimacy in the Northern states and territories in terms of the specific actions it did *not* perform and in the Southern states and territories, in terms of the specific actions many people feared it would perform. The lack of state legitimacy, which may provoke secession and civil war on the one hand, may necessitate state coercion on the other.

COERCION

During the 1791–1861 period, the presence of slavery prompted federal officials to coerce each of the three major population groups in the United States. State coercion often targeted two or more of the groups together.

The most coercive federal policy during this period was Native American removal. In the South, the army directed the removal of more than 50,000 Native Americans across the Mississippi River during the 1830s.[41] This total included an unrecorded number of African Americans who belonged to or were associated with one of the five "civilized" nations. At least in the case of the Seminoles, the connection between slavery and removal was extremely strong because of the presence of the Black Seminoles. Seminole removal joined Native Americans and African Americans as targets of state coercion. Seminole removal was also the most coercive Native American removal. It precipitated the nation's longest war of the nineteenth century.

The U.S. army also coerced individual African Americans, both free and enslaved, to protect the Southern institution of slavery. It deployed soldiers in response to slave rebellions, actual, rumored, or simply feared. It also deployed soldiers in response to slave rescues and attempted rescues, which involved the coercion of African American fugitive slaves as well as their would-be African American, European American, and Native American rescuers.[42] In fugitive-slave cases, civilian law-enforcement officers also played a coercive role. In Kansas, the army imposed an uneasy peace on warring factions of European American settlers. The navy coerced African, European, and American slave traders and smugglers as well as Africans seized from their custody, who, in turn, were subjected to coercive slave auctions, renditions to foreign powers, or resettlement in Liberia. U.S. marshals, attorneys, justices, commissioners, customs collectors, and ship inspectors also played a coercive role in slave-trading and slave-smuggling cases. In renting African American slaves, both federal military and civilian officials piggybacked on the coercive apparatuses that the Southern states had established to keep African Americans in slavery.[43] In each of these policy areas, the federal government became an auxiliary arm of those state apparatuses and, especially in fugitive-slave cases, an extraterritorial arm.

PARTY AND SECTION

Partisan and sectional differences emerged in many slavery-related policy episodes. Democratic Republican, Democratic, and Southern congressmen were generally more supportive of the proslavery side than Federalist, Whig, and Northern congressmen were. Section also had a stronger influence than party. Southern congressmen tended to vote together in slavery-related policy episodes, as did Northern congressmen. One of the critical factors in the politics of the 1791–1861 period was that Southern congressmen tended to vote together more than Northern congressmen did.[44]

Yet many slavery-related policy episodes expose internal fissures within these partisan and sectional alignments. In some of the episodes, which side was the proslavery side was also ambiguous. On the slave-trade issue, the upper and lower South divided. Moral opposition to slavery was not only more widespread in the upper South, but a proslavery position in the upper South could mean supporting a federal ban on slave imports in order to increase the demand for its surplus slaves. Upper-South delegates Luther Martin and George Mason spearheaded the battle for such a ban at the Constitutional Convention, where lower-South delegates Abraham Baldwin, the Pinckneys, and John Rutledge strongly opposed them. At least in the vote on the slave-trade clause, the Northern delegations also divided. The New England delegations voted with the lower-South delegations in favor of delaying any federal ban on slave imports, while the lower-North delegations aligned with the upper-South delegations in opposition to such a delay. The New England vote was allegedly part of a *quid pro quo*. The vote, however, also reflects the economic interests of New England slave traders. Mason, for one, "lamented that some of our Eastern brethren had from a lust of gain embarked on this nefarious trade."[45]

Federal support of African colonization similarly divided the upper and lower South. On this issue, the lower-North states aligned more with the upper-South states in supporting the enterprise and the New England states, with the lower-South states in opposing it. Of the eight state governments that financially supported African colonization—Maryland, Virginia, Connecticut, Pennsylvania, Indiana, New Jersey, Missouri, and Kentucky—seven were either upper-South or lower-North states. On this issue, which side was the proslavery side was also ambiguous. Both antislavery and proslavery extremes attacked African colonization.

The division on the fugitive-slave issue was more strictly sectional. Nevertheless, the issue frayed Southern unity because it more directly affected the upper-South than the lower-South states.[46] The issue also more directly affected the lower-North than the upper-North states as well as divided New England Whigs into "cotton" (Abbott Lawrence and Daniel Webster) and "conscience" (Sumner and Henry Wilson) camps.[47] Radical Northern Whigs (Horace Everett and Giddings) and Democrats (Chase and David Wilmot) also opposed particular military actions and employment practices that they thought buttressed the Southern institution of slavery.

In general, though, these policy areas did not produce sharp partisan and sectional divisions. Federal executive officials and most members of Congress seemed to accept the premise that one of the roles of the federal government was to protect slavery as long as the institution remained such an integral part of the Southern as well as national economies. Whether they were from the North or South, Federalist or Democratic Republican, Whig or Democrat, or antislavery or proslavery, federal officials routinely acted on that premise.

INTENTIONS AND EFFECTS

This generalization does not mean that federal officials never performed actions that had the opposite intention or effect. The slave-trade issue was also ambiguous because of its possible effects on the continued existence of Southern slavery. When the convention delegates added a slave-trade clause to the proposed constitution in 1787, at least one delegate (James Wilson) seemed to believe that they had dealt slavery a mortal blow and at least one member (Joseph P. Varnum) of the Congress that enacted a federal ban on slave imports in 1807 agreed because "I have so often heard gentlemen from the South express their dread of the final ruin of that country from slavery."[48] Some ACS officials (the Reverends Robert S. Finley and Ralph R. Gurley) saw African colonization as a means of gradual emancipation, and some supportive members of Congress (Henry Clay and Theodore Frelinghuysen) seemed to agree.[49] Some military (John James Abert) and Treasury (Charles Rockwell) officials may have interpreted the various rules and regulations that had been adopted to limit the federal employment of slave labor as fashioned to stigmatize slave labor.[50] Some territorial governors (John W. Geary) and army commanders (Persifor Smith) may have viewed military intervention in "Bleeding Kansas" as calculated to prevent the territory from "unfairly" becoming a slave state.[51] Even the Fugitive Slave Law of 1850 was part of a *quid pro quo* that admitted California into the union as a free state and abolished the domestic slave trade in the District of Columbia.

Yet, in each case, a counter-narrative emerged that portrayed these measures as proslavery in intention and effect. At least one lower-South convention delegate (Charles Cotesworth Pinckney) accused the upper-South delegates of supporting a federal slave-import ban on the grounds that it protected interstate slave markets.[52] Some upper-South ACS activists (the Reverend Philip Slaughter and Congressman Frederick P. Stanton) supported African colonization on the grounds that, in Stanton's words, "the free negro in this country is almost always a degraded being . . . both the whites and the slaves would be benefited by the removal of the free blacks."[53] At least one not entirely sympathetic executive official (Gideon Granger) justified as a necessary precaution against slave conspiracies one regulation that had been adopted to limit the federal employment of slave labor.[54] Some executive officials (Franklin Pierce and Jefferson Davis) may have viewed military intervention in "Bleeding Kansas" as designed to stabilize conditions in the territory so that it could "fairly" become a slave state.[55] Even the Compromise of 1850 seemed less a *quid pro quo* than a legislative package that had been specially crafted to quell the anxieties of Southern congressmen over their growing minority status by not restricting the spread of slavery into the Mexican cession.[56] The $10 million side-payment in the compromise package to Texas to cede its claims to New Mexican lands was also important in cultivating Southern hopes of adding new slave states.

If nothing else, these counter-narratives show the obvious. Not all federal officials were similarly motivated; they could support the same measures for very different, even inconsistent, reasons. Nonetheless, the preponderant effect, if not also intention, of the many federal policies, laws, rules, regulations, orders, actions, and inactions that impinged on the continued existence of Southern slavery during the 1791–1861 period was to protect the institution. The federal government protected domestic slave markets, helped open in Africa a safety valve for slavery, returned fugitive slaves, secured compensation for slave losses, removed obstacles to slavery expansion, deterred slave rebellions, and rented slave labor. If it had done none of the above, the institution of slavery would certainly have been much weaker.

Even if the effects of early American state development on the continuing presence of slavery were marginal, the effects of the continuing presence of slavery on early American state development were not. The latter effects also escalated over time. These findings are two key findings of this study.

During the 1791–1861 period, federal expenditures increased for interdictions of illegal slave-trading, support of the ACS's Liberian enterprise, renditions of fugitive slaves (at least until 1855), and employment of slave labor. They also increased for slavery-related military deployments until the Second Seminole War. After the war, they decreased but still remained at higher levels than they had been before the war. In the day-to-day performance of their other duties, federal personnel also had become more entangled with the effects of slavery. In the 1850s, they were more actively engaged in seizing slave ships, transporting recaptured Africans to Liberia, returning fugitive slaves, and monitoring slave rentals than they had been in previous decades. They also remained poised to deploy military forces in reaction to disputes over slavery in the western territories (Kansas) and attempted slave insurrections in the Southern states (Harpers Ferry). Only secession and civil war disentangled the activities of the federal government from the effects of slavery, and even then not immediately.

One counterfactual thought experiment is to think of all the things the federal government was doing in the 1850s and then think of how many of those things it would not have been doing or would have been doing differently if slavery had no longer existed in the United States. The antebellum federal government was building internal improvements, delivering the mail, protecting American commerce, interdicting illegal slave-trading on the high seas, guarding frontier settlements against Native American "depredations," conducting the nation's foreign affairs, governing its capital city and western territories, performing law-enforcement functions, and collecting customs duties. The presence of slavery affected each one of those activities. Slave labor built internal improvements, at least in the Southern states and territories, and controversies over slavery affected their number and location. Controversies over slavery also affected the delivery of the mail and the autonomy of the post office. The presence of slavery affected not only navy deployments to protect American commerce and interdict illegal slave-trading on the high seas but also army deployments to settle disputes over slavery in U.S. territories. Slavery expansion displaced Native American nations from the "old" southwestern frontier while ensuring continuing disputes over slaves on the "new" southwestern frontier. Slave interests had significant effects on how the federal government conducted the nation's foreign affairs as well as governed its capital city and western territories. Slave interests also influenced the law-enforcement functions of U.S. marshals, attorneys, and commissioners in interstate fugitive-slave cases, even, for the first time, transforming them into an effective federal police force. Finally, the presence of slavery influenced the rate and pace of the Treasury's collection of customs duties, and deterring slave smuggling remained one of the responsibilities of customs collectors and ship inspectors, as it did U.S. marshals, attorneys, justices, commissioners, and navy crews. In addition, the federal government engaged in a series of more targeted activities that it would not have in the absence of slavery, such as subsidizing the ACS's colonization project and deploying army units to deter slave revolts and rescues.

The findings of this study also suggest that time was an important political variable.[57] Early Southern protests against federal actions that Southern politicians perceived as not being sufficiently protective of the institution of slavery cued federal officials to anticipate such protests in the future and act accordingly, even if their personal preferences might have pulled them in the opposite direction. The greater solicitude of a Southern-dominated Democratic Republican administration for the War of 1812 slave claims than of a Northern-dominated Federalist administration for the Revolutionary War slave claims could have been a learned response as much as it was a sectional or party response. Gradually, as their antislavery constituencies and congressional majorities grew stronger, Northern congressmen became more vocal in protesting federal actions that seemed too protective of slavery. By the antebellum period, federal executive officials often found themselves calibrating and recalibrating their actions in order to steer the American state between the two extremes. The fact that Southern politicians had been the first "out of the box" in their demands on the American state and that they seemed more united and insistent than their opponents had, however, skewed the apparent median point.[58]

CONTINUITY AND CHANGE

As Richard Bensel chronicles, the Civil War created two American states, both stronger over their respective territories than the antebellum state had been. Somewhat paradoxically, the Confederate state was the stronger of the two Civil War states from his "state capacities" perspective.[59] Bensel exaggerates the extent to which the antebellum state was weak as well as the extent to which the Civil War states had to be built *de novo.* He also exaggerates the extent to which slavery was the cause of the weakness of the antebellum state and not also of its strength. His basic thesis is, however, correct. The Civil War states were new and stronger than the antebellum state had been. The linkages in institutions and personnel from the antebellum state to the post-Reconstruction state were few in number. Once again, war was a powerful engine of state development but, in the American case, a temporary one. Still, there are important counterexamples to Bensel's thesis.

The fugitive-slave policy area is the most important slavery-related counterexample to Bensel's thesis. The federal enforcement of the constitutional rights of slaveholders to the return of their fugitive slaves in the antebellum period anticipated the federal enforcement of the new constitutional rights of the freed slaves during Reconstruction. Both efforts required autonomous federal law-enforcement mechanisms and military interventions. Robert Kaczorowski cites the Fugitive Slave Law of 1850 as an ironic precedent for the early civil rights acts.[60]

Other scholars suggest other counterexamples. Tony Mullis details how the same army personnel saw action quelling civil disturbances in "Bleeding Kansas" and the Reconstruction South.[61] John Mahon traces the overlap between the officer corps in the Second Seminole War and in the Mexican-American and Civil Wars.[62] Mark Wilson shows how the institutional autonomy that the U.S. army had carved out for itself during the pre–Civil War period continued into the war and beyond.[63] In addition, the enforcement of the nation's slave-trade laws spurred the development of the U.S. navy, which also continued into the war and beyond.[64] African colonization anticipated the nation's late nineteenth- and early twentieth-century colonial adventures in the Pacific and Caribbean, which were also pursued by a combination of state and non-state actors.[65] This "mixed enterprise" model remains popular among state actors today.[66] Even the federal employment of slave labor continued during the Civil War and offered one long-lingering model of labor discipline that the abolition of slavery did not itself change, at least not immediately, for either former slaves or other laborers.[67] More generally, the idea of a federal government with its own governing authority, state legitimacy, and coercive powers carried over into the Civil War, in both the Unionist North and Confederate South. The Union victory in the war provided a powerful impetus to that idea.[68]

Yet these pre–Civil War policies were precedents for the post–Civil War policies only in an attenuated sense. American state actors did not typically refer to the former as precedents for the latter, perhaps not surprisingly because they were tainted by their associations with slavery. In modeling the enforcement provisions of the Civil Rights Act of 1866 on those of the Fugitive Slave Law of 1850, Lyman Trumbull (Illinois Republican) used one of the standard tools in any lawmaker's toolkit, but his admission of the precedent was still startling. The continuity in personnel between the antebellum and post-Reconstruction American states was also attenuated. The heavy Civil War casualties and the Reconstruction proscriptions against Confederate loyalists guaranteed as much. During the 1791–1861 period, the American state was distinctive as a "house divided" over racial slavery. Following the Compromise of 1877, the American state was distinctive as a "house united" on racial supremacy. Though a "house divided" was no more a guarantee of state weakness than a "house united" was a guarantee of state strength, the two states confronted quite different challenges. Race remained central to each challenge, but the division between free states and slave states no longer served as the main axis of state development in the United States.[69]

WHAT NEXT?

In closing, I would emphasize the exploratory nature of this study. Collectively, we need to do much more research on early American state development. We need to collect more evidence of how the continuing presence of slavery affected state development, both positively and negatively, during the 1791–1861 period. We need to collect more evidence of how other factors, both external and internal to the American state, affected state development. We need to collect more evidence of how those different factors affected each other as well as of their interactive effects on state development. I tell, in an exploratory way, one strand—I think a grossly underappreciated strand in the politics and history literature—of an interwoven story of early American state development. I also indicate, again in an exploratory way, how this one strand is interwoven with other strands, such as the market revolution, frontier settlement, and interstate wars. A full story would not only further investigate each of those strands but would investigate others, such as democratization, urbanization, changing gender roles, and shifting class loyalties.[70] It would also interweave all those strands more tightly together in demonstrating how they, individually and collectively, affected American state development during the 1791–1861 period. We have not yet reached the state of research where we can write such a grand narrative.

A grand narrative of American state development would also bring the story forward through the Civil War to the present. Race has remained central to state development, but so have such other factors as class, gender, and war.[71] How race has affected state development has become increasingly complicated over time. How Americans have understood race has also become increasingly complicated. Race was, however, not simply a bimodal category even during the 1791–1861 period. The relations between Native Americans and European Americans affected the relations between African Americans and European Americans as well as between Native Americans and African Americans, which, in turn, affected the relations between African Americans and European Americans along a cascading pattern of interactive effects. At least on the ground, federal officials triangulated the relations among Tocqueville's "three races in America."[72] Native American removals epitomize this triangulation, as it affected the relations among European Americans, Native Americans, African Americans, "mixed breeds," as well as intermarried whites, blacks, and reds. With Texas annexation and the Mexican-American War, Mexican Americans increasingly entered into the nation's racial politics. Whig opposition to the war had included opposition to incorporating a "mongrel" people which was, in Webster's words, "infinitely less elevated, in morals and condition, than the people of the Sandwich [Hawaii] Islands ... far less intelligent than the better class of our Indian neighbors."[73] Once incorporated, that people not only developed thicker relations with African Americans, European Americans, Native Americans, and their "mongrel" equivalents but more strongly influenced the relations among those groups. The Mexican Seminole colonies were typical of racially mixed, borderland communities.[74]

During the post–Civil War period, race continued to influence American state policy and development, though in different ways than it had during the pre–Civil War period. After the war, Congress began to enact immigration policies that targeted racial or ethnic groups other than African slaves.[75] In 1882, the Chinese became the first such group. Nine years later, the Immigration and Naturalization Service (INS) began as a small administrative agency—the Office of the Superintendent of Immigration—within the Department of Treasury to enforce the nation's new, more restrictive immigration policies.[76] In 1924, Congress enacted more general immigration policies that established national quotas on legal immigration to the United States. Since the quotas were based on prior rates of immigration to the United States, they were anything but race-neutral in severely limiting immigration from non-European countries. In fact, they initially excluded Latin American immigrants as well as Asian immigrants except for Filipinos, Hejazians (Saudis), Palestinians, Persians, Syrians, and Turks. The only areas of Africa within the quota system were British-ruled South Africa and the northern African nations of Abyssinia (Ethiopia), Egypt, Liberia, and Morocco at 100 immigrants each, which totally ignored the more than ten million descendants of African slaves living in the United States at the time.[77] In comparison, the quota for Great Britain alone was 85,131.[78] During World War II, Congress removed the exclusion on Chinese immigrants as well as permitted Latin American agricultural workers to enter the country under the Bracero Program. Then in 1965, it replaced the quota system with a more race-neutral policy that established an annual limit on the total number of immigrants to the United States on a "first come, first served" basis.[79] The primary focus of the INS shifted to physically controlling the national borders against the illegal immigration of unskilled workers from Latin America, especially from Mexico. As a result, the INS experienced an explosive growth in its budget and manpower, including the establishment of its own law-enforcement arm, until it was absorbed into the new Department of Homeland Security in 2003 and eventually renamed United States Citizenship and Immigration Services (USCIS).[80] These borderland initiatives are, again, hardly race-neutral.

The relations between European Americans and Native Americans also continued to influence American state policy and development during the post–Civil War period.[81] In the latter part of the nineteenth century, Native Americans remained the target of removal or, now, reservation policies in the western United States, and the U.S. army remained the primary agents of relocation. But then Congress passed the Dawes Act in 1887 and two years later essentially ceded Indian territory to encroaching European American settlers and speculators. The new Native American policy became one of assimilation. The role of the Bureau of Indian Affairs (BIA) shifted from a caretaker of treaty annuities to an active agent of social change.[82] In the 1930s, Congress oversaw another policy shift. It encouraged the BIA to abandon its coercive assimilation tactics, leaving both the agency and its Native American "clientele" uneasily balanced between an assimilation policy and a reservation policy.

The relations between African Americans and European Americans had the most powerful effects on American state policy and development during the post–Civil War period. With the end of Reconstruction, the federal government largely surrendered freed slaves to the exclusionary policies of the Southern states.[83] As Ira Katznelson demonstrates, the Southern veto did not so much prevent state development in the twentieth century as skew it in racially exclusionary directions. Congress enacted social-welfare programs, such as unemployment insurance and legislation protecting union-organizing activities, and established federal agencies, such as the Social Security Administration and National Labor Relations Board, to administer those programs. Under Southern direction, Congress, however, established those programs and agencies in such a way as to primarily benefit middle-class European Americans and to largely exclude potential African American beneficiaries by exempting the sectors of the economy in which they were most heavily concentrated.[84] The civil rights revolution broke the Southern veto, though at the cost of the "Solid South." Congress now pursued more racially inclusive policies toward African Americans.[85] This policy initiative required a significant expansion of the resources of the Department of Justice. It also required a substantial degree of departmental autonomy from local congressional and constituency demands. The Department of Justice called on U.S. attorneys, marshals, FBI agents, and National Guard units to implement these new, more inclusive policies in a way that mirrored the federal law-enforcement efforts in the Southern states during Reconstruction, when Congress had first created the department.[86]

This study has shown how the Southern veto operated during the pre–Civil War period. Again, the effect was not so much to prevent state development as to skew it in racially exclusionary directions. In this sense, the 1791–1861 period was similar to the 1877–1964 period. During both periods, Northern support, or at least acquiescence, was essential to Southern direction of American state development. At the end of each period, newly empowered congressional and executive officials attempted to boldly embark on a more inclusive course. The second "reconstruction" has been more successful than the first, but its ultimate goals remain elusive.[87] As the nation collectively strives to continue moving forward on issues of race, its history keeps dragging it backward. As much as ever, we need to get that history right. Race has been constitutive of the development of the American state from its very origins. A civil war was required to eradicate the house of slavery. Unfortunately, the "new birth of freedom" was only a partial birth. A Barack Hussein Obama presidency is certainly a sign of progress. Still, we are each left to ponder precisely how much progress, in light of the nation's deeply entrenched racial inequalities in income, education, and status, not to mention Southern governors who see nothing wrong with celebrating Confederate Month without any reference to slavery until the media calls attention to their political obtuseness or, worse, racial pandering. The American state is not and never has been color-blind. To envision color-blindness as the ultimate goal of public policy is to envision a public policy divorced from history.[88]

APPENDIX A

Federal Costs of Slave-Trade Suppression

Item by Years	Amount ($)
1819–1842:	
Navy slave-trade expenditures, 1819–1828;	
extrapolated for the period	480,000
Subtotal	480,000
FY1843–FY1859:	
African Squadron estimate; extrapolated for the period	6,536,000
Pons bounty estimate, 1845	22,500
Echo bounty estimate, 1858	7,500
Subtotal	6,566,500
FY1860–FY1861:	
African Squadron estimate; doubled for each fiscal year	1,538,000
Navy bounties, 1860–1861	125,700
Subtotal	1,663,700
1819–FY1861: Total	8,710,000

APPENDIX B

Federal Costs of African Colonization

Item	Date	Amount ($)
Kendall audit	1819–1830	264,710
Colonial agent*	1831–September 30, 1841	12,925
Fenix captives	1835	4,400
Two smuggled children	1836	200
In-kind subsidy	1843	1,500
Supplemental appropriation	1843	5,000
Pons captives	1845	37,800
Commercial agent †	1849–1861	13,000
Echo captives	1858	32,500
Multiple seizures	1860–1861	255,654
Total		627,689

*Assuming $1,600 per year, 1831–1833; $1,000 per year, 1834–1840; $1,125 for the first three quarters of 1841, at $1,500 per year.

† Assuming $1,000 per year for this whole time frame.

APPENDIX C

Major Slavery-Related Federal Expenditures*

Category	Totals †
Chapter 2:	
Slave-trade suppression, 1819–1861	8,710,000
Chapter 3:	
African colonization, 1819–1861	628,000
Chapter 4:	
Fugitive-slave renditions, 1850s	119,000
Treaty payments and commission costs in slave-claim cases, 1819–1853	382,000
Chapter 5:	
Second Seminole War, 1835–1842	30,000,000
Removing Native American slaves in the other southeast removals, 1831–1842	363,000
Texas debt relief, 1850	10,000,000
Chapter 6:	
Total army spending on slave labor, 1842	126,000
Quartermaster general spending on slave labor, 1828–1848	476,000
Pensacola navy yard spending on slave labor, 1847–1860	378,000
Total major slavery-related federal expenditures	51,000,000 ‡
Total federal expenditures for 1791–1861	1,797,000,000 ‡
Total major slavery-related federal expenditures as a percent of total 1791–1861 federal expenditures	2.8%

* $100,000 or more in (estimated) expenditures.
† Rounded to nearest thousand dollars.
‡ Rounded to nearest million dollars.

NOTES

1. For at least the early part of this period, slavery was still legal in many of the Northern states, either because they had not yet abolished slavery (New York and New Jersey) or because their emancipation acts were gradual (Pennsylvania and Connecticut). Still, as New York, New Jersey, and perhaps even Delaware were expected to abolish slavery in the near future, the union was effectively a "house divided," (almost) equally divided geographically between (prospective) free states and slave states by the time of the Constitutional Convention in 1787. See Patience Essah, *A House Divided: Slavery and Emancipation in Delaware, 1638–1865* (Charlottesville: University Press of Virginia, 1996); Joanne Pope Melish, *Disowning Slavery: Gradual Emancipation and "Race" in New England, 1780–1860* (Ithaca, NY: Cornell University Press, 1998); Gary B. Nash and Jean R. Soderlund, *Freedom by Degrees: Emancipation in Pennsylvania and Its Aftermath* (New York: New York University Press, 1991); and Arthur Zilversmit, *The First Emancipation: The Abolition of Slavery in the North* (Chicago: University of Chicago Press, 1967). No other society was so divided, as Anthony Marx suggests in his comparative study of postemancipation societies in Brazil, South Africa, and the United States. See Anthony W. Marx, *Making Race and Nation: A Comparison of the United States, South Africa, and Brazil* (Cambridge: Cambridge University Press, 1998), 41–42. At the Constitutional Convention, James Madison, in particular, emphasized this division. See Max Farrand, ed., *The Records of the Federal Convention of 1787* (1911; reprint, New Haven, CT: Yale University Press, 1937), 1:476, 486, 601; 2:10, 81.

2. Throughout this study, I use *negative* and *positive* in a developmental, not a normative, sense. By *politics and history literature*, I mean the work of economists, historians, political scientists, and sociologists who study American political development. The particular focus of this study is state development as a subcategory of political development and, more specifically, state development on the federal, rather than the state or local, level.

3. See Stephen Skowronek, *Building a New American State: The Expansion of National Administrative Capacities, 1877–1920* (Cambridge: Cambridge University Press, 1982).

4. See Karen Orren, *Belated Feudalism: Labor, the Law, and Liberal Development in the United States* (Cambridge: Cambridge University Press, 1991).

5. See Richard Franklin Bensel, *Yankee Leviathan: The Origins of Central State Authority in America, 1859–1877* (Cambridge: Cambridge University Press, 1990), 17.

6. Cross-national studies usually compare the United States to older Western states and rarely to newer or non-Western ones. The conclusions would clearly be different if the latter were the standards of comparison. See, for example, Louis B. Hartz, *The Founding of New Societies: Studies in the History of the United States, Latin America, South Africa, Canada, and Australia* (New York: Harcourt Brace, 1964).

7. See Daniel T. Rodgers, *Atlantic Crossings: Social Politics in a Progressive Age* (Cambridge, MA: Belknap Press of Harvard University Press, 1998).

8. See Edwin Amenta, *Bold Relief: Institutional Politics and the Origins of Modern American Social Policy* (Princeton, NJ: Princeton University Press, 1998); Kenneth Finegold and Theda Skocpol, *State and Party in America's New Deal* (Madison: University of Wisconsin Press, 1995);

Theda Skocpol, *Protecting Soldiers and Mothers: The Political Origins of Social Policy in the United States* (Cambridge, MA: Belknap Press of Harvard University Press, 1992); Margaret Weir, Ann Shola Orloff, and Theda Skocpol, ed., *The Politics of Social Policy in the United States* (Princeton, NJ: Princeton University Press, 1988).

9. See Ira Katznelson, "Flexible Capacity: The Military and Early American Statebuilding," in *Shaped by War and Trade: International Influences on American Political Development*, ed. Ira Katznelson and Martin Shefter (Princeton, NJ: Princeton University Press, 2002), 82–110.

10. See William J. Novak, *The People's Welfare: Law and Regulation in Nineteenth Century America* (Chapel Hill: University of North Carolina Press, 1996).

11. See, for example, Oscar Handlin and Mary Flug Handlin, *Commonwealth; A Study of the Role of Governance in the American Economy: Massachusetts, 1774–1861* (New York: New York University Press, 1947); Louis B. Hartz, *Economic Policy and Democratic Thought: Pennsylvania, 1776–1860* (Cambridge, MA: Harvard University Press, 1949); Nathan Miller, *The Enterprise of a Free People: Aspects of Economic Development in New York State during the Canal Period, 1792–1838* (Ithaca, NY: Cornell University Press, 1962); Harry N. Scheiber, *Ohio Canal Era: A Case Study of Government and the Economy, 1820–1861* (Athens: Ohio University Press, 1969).

12. Skocpol reached the same conclusion relative to social-welfare policy. See Skocpol, *Protecting Soldiers and Mothers*, chaps. 8–9. According to Suzanne Mettler and Andrew Millstein, in the early republic most Americans looked first to their state and local governments to address their common concerns. See Suzanne Mettler and Andrew Millstein, "American Political Development from Citizens' Perspective: Tracking Federal Government's Presence in Individual Lives over Time," *Studies in American Political Development* 21, no. 1 (Spring 2007): 115–118.

13. See Bensel, *Yankee Leviathan*, 114 (Table 3.1).

14. See Skowronek, *Building a New American State*, 19–20.

15. The "new institutionalists" also face definitional issues, such as in defining institutions, distinguishing private from public or governing institutions, and determining when private institutions that serve public purposes become governing institutions. See Karen Orren and Stephen Skowronek, *The Search for American Political Development* (Cambridge: Cambridge University Press, 2004), 81–84.

16. See Daniel R. Carpenter, *The Forging of Bureaucratic Autonomy: Reputation, Networks, and Policy Innovation in Executive Agencies, 1862–1920* (Princeton, NJ: Princeton University Press, 2001).

17. See Paul Pierson, *Politics in Time: History, Institutions, and Social Analysis* (Princeton, NJ: Princeton University Press, 2004).

18. See Sheldon D. Pollack, *War, Revenue, and State Building: Financing the Development of the American State* (Ithaca, NY: Cornell University Press, 2008), 39–40; Max Weber, *Politics as a Vocation* (1919; reprint, Philadelphia: Fortress Press, 1965), 2.

19. See Novak, *The People's Welfare*, 241–243. I offer some modifications to this view in chapter 4.

20. See Katznelson, "Flexible Capacity," 89, 98.

21. See Orren and Skowronek, *The Search for American Political Development*, 113–118, 123–131. By "intercurrences," they mean the layering of governing authorities on top of one another over time.

22. Obviously, this working definition assumes a number of threshold effects, such as how close to a monopoly on coercive power a political organization must possess for it to be a state and what percentage of citizens must think a political organization legitimate for it to be legitimate. I also assume that states can perform executive, legislative, and judicial functions in

multiple ways, from more to less formal, just as publics can authorize states to act on their behalf in multiple ways, from more to less direct.

23. See Orren and Skowronek, *The Search for American Political Development*, 174–178.

24. See Theda Skocpol, "Bringing the State Back In: Strategies of Analysis in Current Research," in *Bringing the State Back In*, ed. Peter B. Evans, Dietrich Rueschemeyer, and Theda Skocpol (Cambridge: Cambridge University Press, 1985), 4–6.

25. See Richard Franklin Bensel, *The Political Economy of American Industrialization, 1877–1900* (Cambridge: Cambridge University Press, 2000).

26. See Pierson, *Politics in Time*, 34–36, 42–44.

27. See Walter Dean Burnham, *Critical Elections and the Mainsprings of American Politics* (New York: Norton, 1970).

28. See Orren and Skowronek, *The Search for American Political Development*, 191–192.

29. See Skowronek, *Building a New American State*, chap. 2.

30. On this relative lack of bureaucratization, cf. Matthew A. Crenson, *The Federal Machine: Beginnings of Bureaucracy in Jacksonian America* (Baltimore: Johns Hopkins University Press, 1975); Richard R. John, "'Affairs of Office': The Executive Departments, the Election of 1828, and the Making of the Democratic Party," in *The Democratic Experiment: New Directions in American Political History*, ed. Meg Jacobs, William J. Novak, and Julian E. Zelizer (Princeton, NJ: Princeton University Press, 2003), 50–84; Lynn L. Marshall, "The Strange Stillbirth of the Whig Party," *American Historical Review* 72, no. 2 (January 1967): 445–468; William E. Nelson, *The Roots of American Bureaucracy, 1830–1900* (Cambridge, MA: Harvard University Press, 1982).

31. See John K. Mahon, *History of the Second Seminole War, 1835–1842* (Gainesville: University of Florida Press, 1967), 326–327.

32. See Robert Ralph Davis, Jr., "James Buchanan and the Suppression of the Slave Trade, 1858–1861," *Pennsylvania History* 33, no. 4 (October 1966): 446–459.

33. See Robert J. Kaczorowski, "The Inverted Constitution: Enforcing Constitutional Rights in the Nineteenth Century," in *Constitutionalism and American Culture: Writing the New Constitutional History*, ed. Sandra F. VanBurkleo, Kermit Hall, and Robert J. Kaczorowski (Lawrence: University Press of Kansas, 2002), 42–43.

34. See Tony R. Mullis, *Peacekeeping on the Plains: Army Operations in Bleeding Kansas* (Columbia: University of Missouri Press, 2004), 72, 221–223.

35. As we will see in chapter 6, this process was clearly evident during the construction of the nation's capital.

36. See Frederick Jackson Turner, *The Frontier in American History* (1920; reprint, New York: Holt, Rinehart & Winston, 1962).

37. See Andrew R. L. Cayton, "Radicals in the 'Western World': The Federalist Conquest of Trans-Appalachian North America," in *Federalists Reconsidered*, ed. Doron Ben-Atar and Barbara B. Oberg (Charlottesville: University Press of Virginia, 1998), 77–96; Andrew C. Isenberg, "The Market Revolution in the Borderlands: George Champlin Sibley in Missouri and New Mexico, 1808–1826," *Journal of the Early Republic* 21, no. 2 (Autumn 2001): 445–465; Richard R. John, "Governmental Institutions as Agents of Change: Rethinking American Political Development in the Early Republic, 1787–1835," *Studies in American Political Development* 11, no. 2 (Fall 1997): 347–380; Richard R. John, *Spreading the News: The American Postal System from Franklin to Morse* (Cambridge, MA: Harvard University Press, 1995); Katznelson, "Flexible Capacity," 90–91, 97, 99; Christopher McCrory Klyza, "The United States Army, Natural Resources, and Political Development in the Nineteenth Century," *Polity* 35, no. 1 (Fall 2002): 1–28; Laurence J. Malone, *Opening the West: Federal Internal Improvements before 1860* (Westport, CT: Greenwood, 1998);

Peter S. Onuf, "The Expanding Union," in *Devising Liberty: Preserving and Creating Freedom in the New American Republic,* ed. David Thomas Konig (Stanford, CA: Stanford University Press, 1995), 50–80; Malcolm J. Rohrbough, *The Land Office Business: The Settlement and Administration of American Public Lands, 1789–1837* (New York: Oxford University Press, 1968). In light of these and other federal activities during this period, several politics and history scholars have argued—over-argued, I think—that "laissez-faire" was also a myth on the federal level. See Brian Balogh, *A Government Out of Sight: The Mystery of National Authority in Nineteenth-Century America* (New York: Cambridge University Press, 2009); Frank Bourgin, *The Great Challenge: The Myth of Laissez-Faire in the Early Republic* (New York: George Braziller, 1989); William J. Novak, "The Myth of the 'Weak' American State," *American Historical Review* 113, no. 2 (June 2008): 752–772. Army engineers or former army engineers were usually involved in internal-improvement projects because West Point was the only engineering school in the United States from 1802 until 1824, when Rensselaer Polytechnic Institute was founded.

38. See Leonard A. Carlson and Mark A. Roberts, "Indian Lands, 'Squatterism' and Slavery: Economic Interests and the Passage of the Indian Removal Act of 1830," *Explorations in Economic History* 43, no. 3 (July 2006): 486–504; Adam Rothman, *Slave Country: American Expansion and the Origins of the Deep South* (Cambridge, MA: Harvard University Press, 2005).

39. I discuss counterfactual history below.

40. See Charles Grier Sellers, *The Market Revolution: Jacksonian America, 1815–1846* (New York: Oxford University Press, 1991), 44–47, 125–126. The institution of Southern slavery was also crucial to the market revolution in the Northern states to the extent that cotton exports were essential to the emergence of a national market in the United States as well as to its success in international markets. See Douglas C. North, *The Economic Growth of the United States, 1790–1860* (New York: Norton, 1966).

41. See Steven Deyle, *Carry Me Back: The Domestic Slave Trade in American Life* (New York: Oxford University Press, 2006), chap. 2; Robert William Fogel, *The Rise and Fall of American Slavery: Without Consent or Contract* (New York: Norton, 1989), chap. 4; James L. Huston, *Calculating the Value of the Union: Slavery, Property Rights and the Economic Origins of the Civil War* (Chapel Hill: University of North Carolina Press, 2002), chap. 2; Bonnie Martin, "'To Have and To Hold' . . . Human Collateral: Mortgaging Slaves to Build Virginia and South Carolina" (Ph.D. diss., Southern Methodist University, 2006); Seth Rockman, "The Unfree Origins of American Capitalism," in *The Economy of Early America: Historical Perspectives and New Directions,* ed. Cathy Matson (University Park: Pennsylvania State University Press, 2006), 335–361; Gavin Wright, *The Political Economy of the Cotton South: Households, Markets, and Wealth in the Nineteenth Century* (New York: Norton, 1978), chap. 2.

42. See Steven Deyle, "An 'Abominable' New Trade: The Closing of the African Slave Trade and the Changing Patterns of U.S. Political Power, 1808–60," *William and Mary Quarterly,* Third Series, 66, no. 4 (October 2009): 832–849; Deyle, *Carry Me Back,* chap. 2; Stanley L. Engerman, "Slavery and Its Consequences for the South in the Nineteenth Century," in *The Cambridge Economic History of the United States,* vol. 2, *The Long Nineteenth Century,* ed. Stanley L. Engerman and Robert E. Gallman (New York: Cambridge University Press, 2000), 350; Robert H. Gudmestad, *A Troublesome Commerce: The Transformation of the Interstate Slave Trade* (Baton Rouge: Louisiana State University Press, 2003), chaps. 3–4.

43. See Charles Tilly, *Coercion, Capital, and European States, A.D. 990–1990* (Cambridge, MA: Basil Blackwell, 1990), chap. 2, "Reflections on the History of European State-Making," in *The Formation of National States in Western Europe,* ed. Charles Tilly (Princeton, NJ: Princeton

University Press, 1975), 3–83, and "War Making and State Making as Organized Crime," in Evans, Rueschemeyer, and Skocpol, *Bringing the State Back In*, 169–186.

44. See Max M. Edling, *A Revolution in Favor of Government: Origins of the U.S. Constitution and the Making of the American State* (Oxford: Oxford University Press, 2003). The presence of the colonies of major European powers on or near American borders contributed to this Federalist view. Pollack and Bruce Porter also challenge this aspect of American exceptionalism but, in the end, reassert it, at least for the pre–Civil War period. See Pollack, *War, Revenue, and State Building*, chaps. 4–6; Bruce D. Porter, *War and the Rise of the State: The Military Foundations of Modern Politics* (New York: Free Press, 1984), chap. 7.

45. See David R. Mayhew, "Wars and American Politics," *Perspectives on Politics* 3, no. 5 (September 2005): 473–493. One institutional effect of the Mexican-American War was the creation of the Department of Interior in 1849 to govern the nation's greatly expanded western territories. At its creation, the department absorbed the General Land Office from the Department of Treasury and the Bureau of Indian Affairs from the Department of War. See Porter, *War and the Rise of the State*, 256–257, 292 (Table 7-2).

46. See Francis Paul Prucha, *The Sword of the Republic: The United States Army on the Frontier, 1783–1846* (New York: Macmillan, 1969).

47. See Bensel, *Yankee Leviathan*, chap. 3.

48. See Tommy Richard Young II, "The United States Army in the South, 1789–1835" (Ph.D. diss., Louisiana State University, 1973), 477–478. Several New England governors also refused to allow their militia to be deployed elsewhere because they opposed the war. See David S. Heidler and Jeanne T. Heidler, ed., *Encyclopedia of the War of 1812* (Annapolis, MD: Naval Institute Press, 2004), 181.

49. See Joel H. Silbey, *Storm over Texas: The Annexation Controversy and the Road to Civil War* (Oxford: Oxford University Press, 2005).

50. Black Seminoles were African Americans living in Florida who were loosely associated with the Seminole nation. Their statuses ranged from free persons to tenured farmers to chattel slaves. They, however, typically lived in their own communities so that even when they were slaves, they lived independently from their masters. The processes by which they became Black Seminoles also varied. Many were either the fugitive or "stolen" slaves of European American slaveholders, but others were freed slaves who had migrated to Seminole maroon communities or slaves whom Seminoles had "legitimately" acquired from European Americans or other Native Americans. The resistance of the Black Seminoles to removal receded significantly when the army promised them that they could emigrate to Indian territory as free persons. See John Missall and Mary Lou Missall, *The Seminole Wars: America's Longest Indian Conflict* (Gainesville: University Press of Florida, 2004), 10–12, 83, 128, 132–133.

51. Balogh's *Government Out of Sight* highlights several of these dynamics but ignores the presence of slavery as a contributing factor.

52. The author of such a narrative would still have to make judgments about which factors were the most important ones to address, in observance of the law of parsimony. On the need to place slavery more at the center of early American state development, see Katznelson, "Flexible Capacity," 105–106; Desmond S. King and Rogers M. Smith, "Racial Orders in American Political Development," *American Political Science Review* 99, no. 1 (February 2005): 75–92; Joseph Lowndes, Julie Novkov, and Dorian Warren, "Race and American Political Development," in *Race and American Political Development*, ed. Joseph Lowndes, Julie Novkov, and Dorian Warren (New York: Routledge, 2008), 1–30.

53. See Bensel, *Yankee Leviathan*, 13, 63; David Brion Davis, *Inhuman Bondage: The Rise and Fall of Slavery in the New World* (New York: Oxford University Press), 273; Robin L. Einhorn, *American Taxation, American Slavery* (Chicago: University of Chicago Press, 2006), 7–8; Ronald P. Formisano, "State Development in the Early Republic: Substance and Structure," in *Contesting Democracy: Substance and Structure in American Political History, 1775–2000*, ed. Bryon E. Shafer and Anthony J. Badger (Lawrence: University Press of Kansas, 2001), 21–22; Michael F. Holt, *The Rise and Fall of the American Whig Party: Jacksonian Politics and the Onset of the Civil War* (New York: Oxford, 1999), 5; Huston, *Calculating the Value*, 22; John, "Affairs of Office," 67; Orren and Skowronek, *The Search for American Political Development*, 88; Sellers, *Market Revolution*, 277.

54. See A. W. Marx, *Making Race*, 60, 120–122, 134–135, 155–156.

55. Cf. Forrest McDonald, *States' Rights and the Union: Imperium im Imperio, 1776–1876* (Lawrence: University Press of Kansas, 2000); Lewis O. Saum, "Schlesinger and 'The State Rights Fetish': A Note," *Civil War History* 24, no. 4 (December 1988): 351–359; Arthur M. Schlesinger, Sr., "The State Rights Fetish," in *New Viewpoints in American History* (New York: Macmillan, 1922), 220–244. From the other side of these debates, Marx overlooks that Northern elites were not necessarily opponents of slavery and also desired a weak state in certain instances, by, for example, opposing embargoes and other types of trade restrictions.

56. See Farrand, *Records of the Convention*, 2:364–365, 369–374, 415–416.

57. See Einhorn, *American Taxation*, chap. 5; Robin L. Einhorn, "Slavery and the Politics of Taxation in the Early United States," *Studies in American Political Development* 14, no. 2 (Fall 2000): 156–183. Einhorn's book is also a study of state-level tax policies. She argues that Southern slaveholders even saw state officials as unsafe formulators of tax policy and assessors of private property because they might be tempted to disproportionately tax slave property in order to curry the favor of nonslaveholding white majorities. See Einhorn, *American Taxation*, 232–233.

58. See Einhorn, *American Taxation*, 157; *Historical Statistics of the United States Millennial Edition Online*, Table Ea588–593, http://hsus.cambridge.org; Richard Sylla, "Experimental Federalism: The Economics of the American Government, 1789–1914," in Engerman and Gallman, *Cambridge Economic History of the United States*, 514–515. Sylla claims that federal land sales probably cost as much in administration as they generated in revenue. The federal government also levied a series of excise taxes during this period, but these taxes did not raise much revenue and tended to provoke popular resistance, as in the case of the Whiskey Rebellion.

59. The first direct tax was enacted during the quasi-war with France.

60. See Einhorn, *American Taxation*, 192–194, 199.

61. After all, both Federalists and Democratic Republicans seemed committed, whether on ideological or prudential grounds or both, to not levying direct taxes except when absolutely necessary. See Frederick Arthur Dalzell, "Taxation with Representation: Federal Revenue in the Early Republic" (Ph.D. diss., Harvard University, 1993); Edling, *Revolution in Favor of Government*, 212–216, 224–225; Dall Forsythe, *Taxation and Political Change in the Young Nation, 1781–1833* (New York: Columbia University Press, 1977), 38, 51–56, 58–61. But cf. Balogh, *Government Out of Sight*, 109–110.

62. See *Annals of Congress*, 18th Cong., 1st Sess., 1308.

63. See Pamela L. Baker, "The Washington National Road Bill and the Struggle to Adopt a Federal System of Internal Improvement," *Journal of the Early Republic* 22, no. 3 (Fall 2004): 437–464.

64. See John Lauritz Larson, *Internal Improvement: National Public Works and the Promise of Popular Government in the Early United States* (Chapel Hill: University of North Carolina Press, 2001), 125–126, 143–144. Calhoun was, of course, soon to veer sharply in a states-rights direction.

65. See Jeremy D. Bailey, *Thomas Jefferson and Executive Power* (New York: Cambridge University Press, 2007), 184–185.

66. See Baker, "The Washington National Road Bill," 447, 462; Carlton Jackson, "The Internal Improvement Vetoes of Andrew Jackson" *Tennessee Historical Quarterly* 25, no. 3 (Fall 1996): 261; Larson, *Internal Improvement*, 145, 190; Stephen Minicucci, "Internal Improvements and the Union, 1790–1860," *Studies in American Political Development*, 18, no. 2 (Fall 2004): 165–166. Admittedly, most of this spending occurred in the territories to circumvent Jackson's constitutional scruples, a point Baker stresses.

67. See Carter Goodrich, *Government Promotion of American Canals and Railroads, 1800–1890* (New York: Columbia University Press, 1960), 46, 288.

68. See Minicucci, "Internal Improvements," 181–182.

69. See Larson, *Internal Improvement*, 226–227. Several states and cities went bankrupt during the Panic of 1837 because of overspending on canals. Mixed public-private ventures also became more popular. See Goodrich, *Government Promotion*, 6–7, 11–12, 287, 289–290, 292, 294.

70. See Baker, "The Washington National Road Bill," 463–464; Goodrich, *Government Promotion*, 44; Larson, *Internal Improvement*, 105, 135–136; Minicucci, "Internal Improvements," 184.

71. See Don E. Fehrenbacher, *The Slaveholding Republic: An Account of the United States Government's Relations to Slavery* (New York: Oxford University Press, 2001), 11–13, 39–47, 150, 202, 233–236, 283–284.

72. The Southern proportion of the total white population of the United States was only 26 percent in the 1860 census. See *Historical Statistics of the United States*, Table Aa36–92.

73. See Philip H. Burch, Jr., *Elites in American History*, vol. 1, *The Federalist Years to the Civil War* (New York: Holmes & Meier, 1981), 236–237 (Table 1), 335–348 (Appendix B); Fehrenbacher, *Slaveholding Republic*, 132; Don E. Fehrenbacher, *The South and Three Sectional Crises* (Baton Rouge: Louisiana State University Press, 1980), 46.

74. Cf. Fehrenbacher, *Slaveholding Republic*, 91, 125, 132–133, 202, 251, 281–282; Leonard L. Richards, *The Slave Power: The Free North and Southern Domination, 1780–1860* (Baton Rouge: Louisiana University Press, 2001).

75. Fehrenbacher briefly discusses African colonization in the context of federal slave-trade policy. See Fehrenbacher, *Slaveholding Republic*, 153–154, 188–189. My own discussions of territorial policy, the governance of the nation's capital, and foreign relations appear in the context of one or more other policy areas.

76. The United States navy had adopted a policy against employing African Americans, both free and enslaved, at navy yards in 1818, but that policy did not explicitly cover construction projects at navy yards. See Morris J. MacGregor and Bernard C. Nalty, eds., *Blacks in the United States Armed Forces: Basic Documents*, vol. 1, *A Time of Slavery* (Wilmington, DE: Scholarly Resources, 1977), 218.

77. See Christopher L. Tomlins, "Nat Turner's Shadow: Reflections on the Norfolk Dry Dock Affair of 1830–1831," *Labor History* 33, no. 4 (Fall 1992): 494–518. I discuss this case further in chapter 6.

78. For a recent study emphasizing the bureaucratic autonomy of regional army officials, see Mark R. Wilson, "The Politics of Procurement: Military Origins of Bureaucratic Autonomy," in *Ruling Passions: Political Economy in Nineteenth-Century America*, ed. Richard R. John (University Park: Penn State University Press, 2006), 44–73.

79. See Donald E. Fehrenbacher, "Slavery, the Framers, and the Living Constitution," in *Slavery and Its Consequences: The Constitution, Equality, and Race*, ed. Robert A. Goldwin and Art Kaufman (Washington, DC: American Enterprise Institute, 1988), 1–22; Paul Finkelman, *Slavery*

and the Founders: Race and Liberty in the Age of Jefferson (Armonk, NY: M.E. Sharpe, 1996), chap. 1, and "The Proslavery Origins of the Electoral College," *Cardozo Law Review* 23 (2002): 1145–1157; William W. Freehling, "The Founding Fathers and Slavery," *American Historical Review* 77, no. 1 (February 1972): 81–93, and "The Founding Fathers, Conditional Antislavery, and the Nonradicalism of the American Revolution," in *The Reintegration of American History: Slavery and the Civil War* (New York: Oxford University Press, 1994), 12–33; Earl M. Maltz, "The Idea of a Proslavery Constitution," *Journal of the Early Republic* 17, no. 1 (Spring 1997): 37–59; Howard A. Ohline, "Republicanism and Slavery: Origins of the Three-Fifths Clause in the United States Constitution," *William and Mary Quarterly*, Third Series, 28, no. 4 (October 1971): 563–584; Robert M. Weir, "South Carolina: Slavery and the Structure of the Union," in *Ratifying the Constitution*, ed. Michael Allen Gillespie and Michael Lienesch (Lawrence: University Press of Kansas, 1989), 201–234; William M. Wiecek, "'The Witch at the Christening': Slavery and the Constitution's Origins," in *The Framing and Ratification of the Constitution*, ed. Leonard W. Levy and Dennis J. Mahoney (New York: Macmillan, 1987), 167–184, and "'The Blessings of Liberty': Slavery in the American Constitutional Order," in Goldwin and Kaufman, *Slavery and Its Consequences*, 23–44.

80. See Richard S. Newman, "Prelude to the Gag Rule: Southern Reaction to Antislavery Petitions in the First Federal Congress," *Journal of the Early Republic* 16, no. 4 (Winter 1996): 571–597.

81. See John, *Spreading the News:* 279–281. The controversy had, however, the opposite effect at the local level, in allowing postmasters the autonomy to decide when not to deliver "incendiary" mail.

82. See Barry R. Weingast, "Political Stability and Civil War: Institutions, Commitment, and American Democracy," in *Analytic Narratives*, ed. Robert Bates, Avner Greif, Margaret Levi, Jean-Laurent Rosenthal, and Barry R. Weingast (Princeton, NJ: Princeton University Press, 1998), 148–193.

83. See Mahon, *Second Seminole War*, 325–326; Missall and Missall, *Seminole Wars*, xv, 205, 224.

84. I present more expenditure than employment data because the former is less incomplete.

85. The process of filing, compiling, and preserving government records was poor during the pre–Civil War period, though it did improve over time. Data could have been lost at any point in the process. Records also could have been lost, destroyed, or stolen in the years since 1861. Or I was simply unable to find them because searching for materials at the National Archives is very much a hit or miss task.

86. Desmond King and Rogers Smith tread this danger. See King and Smith, "Racial Orders," 89.

87. On the uses and abuses of counterfactual history, see Martin Bunzl, "Counterfactual History: A User's Guide," *American Historical Review* 109, no. 3 (June 2004): 845–858; James D. Fearon, "Counterfactuals and Hypothesis Testing in Political Science," *World Politics* 43, no. 1 (January 1992): 169–195; David Hackett Fischer, *Historians' Fallacies: Toward a Logic of Historical Thought* (New York: Harper & Row, 1970), 15–21.

88. The pool of fugitive slaves to be extradited would certainly have been smaller than the pool to be returned.

89. The two cases would still have been somewhat different not only because of the different sequencing but also because in the British case the past was colonial, not member-state, slavery and it had a unitary, not a federal, form of government.

90. See Matthew E. Mason, "The Battle of the Slaveholding Liberators: Great Britain, the

United States, and Slavery in the Early Nineteenth Century," *William and Mary Quarterly,* Third Series, 59, no. 3 (July 2002): 665–696.

91. Gary Nash, for one, treated an "early" abolition of slavery in the United States as a real possibility. See Gary B. Nash, *Race and Revolution* (Madison: Madison House, 1990), chap. 1. In assessing alternative histories in this and other policy areas, a critical variable is why an "early" abolition occurred in the United States. An "early" abolition based on existing antislavery sentiments is, as Nash argued, a plausible (though, I think, unlikely) beginning to an alternative history, but an "early" abolition based on a radical transformation of European American racial attitudes is not. Yet absent such a transformation, we have no reason to believe that state action to gradually abolish slavery would have prompted more extensive efforts to attack the international slave trade or, for that matter, tackle racial inequality.

92. See Campbell Gibson and Kay Jung, "Historical Census Statistics on Population Totals by Race, 1790 to 1990, and by Hispanic Origin, 1970 to 1990, for the United States, Regions, Divisions, and States" (Washington, DC: U.S. Census Bureau, 2002), Table 1, http://www.census.gov/population/www/documentation/twps0056/twps0056.html.

93. See *Annual Reports of the American Colonization Society* (1818–1910; reprint, New York: Negro Universities Press, 1969), 50 (1867): 64. Prior to the Civil War, liberated slaves would have been slaves emancipated on the condition that they emigrate to Liberia, most often as testamentary bequests.

94. See ACS, *Annual Reports,* 1 (1818): 2.

95. See ACS, *Annual Reports,* 2 (1819): 9.

96. See ACS, *Annual Reports,* 1 (1818): 8. These widely shared beliefs discount the best-case scenario, that either the federal or state governments would have attempted to create a biracial society and undermined any colonization movement in that way.

97. See ACS, *Annual Reports,* 48 (1865): 18, 25, 33–34; 49 (1866): 14–15; 50 (1867): 12–13, 51.

98. On the changing variables issue, see Fearon, "Counterfactuals," 195. African colonization was implicitly coercive when slaveholders offered slaves the choice of manumission and emigration or else continued enslavement.

99. See ACS, *Annual Reports,* 10 (1827): 16–19. As it was, the ACS could claim that its goal was to colonize only a "critical mass" of the nation's free-black population, which would not have been a credible claim under this alternative scenario. The 1790 census enumerated 59,527 free blacks in the United States. See Gibson and Jung, "Historical Census Statistics," Table 1.

100. Though Secretary of State John Quincy Adams (Massachusetts Democratic Republican) had yielded the claim that Texas was part of the Louisiana Purchase in the Adams-Onís Treaty (1819), many Americans still considered it U.S. territory. After Mexico achieved independence in 1821, the efforts of Mexican officials to restrict the flow of slaves into Texas and to gradually emancipate those who were already in the province were half-hearted because of an overriding desire to populate the province. See Randolph B. Campbell, *An Empire for Slavery: The Peculiar Institution in Texas, 1821–1865* (Baton Rouge: Louisiana State University Press, 1989), 15–24; John R. Ficklen, "Was Texas Included in the Louisiana Purchase?" *Publications of the Southern History Association* 5, no. 5 (September 1901): 351–387.

101. After Mexico formally abolished slavery in 1829, the American slaveholders who had settled in Texas feared that Mexican officials would undertake more determined efforts to restrict or abolish slavery in the province, but such fears were probably secondary to the widespread separatist sentiments among the American settlers as a cause of the Texas revolution. See Campbell, *Empire for Slavery,* 25–49.

102. Some opposition still might have existed to national expansion *per se.* Both Calhoun

and Daniel Webster (Massachusetts Whig) adopted such positions, though they also opposed the Mexican-American War because of its potential to exacerbate sectional tensions, which, in fact, it did. See Frederick Merk, *Manifest Destiny and Mission in American History* (New York: Vintage, 1963), 152–153; Major L. Wilson, *Space, Time, and Freedom: The Quest for Nationality and the Irrepressible Conflict, 1815–1861* (Westport, CT: Greenwood Press, 1974), 115–116.

103. Cf. John Ashworth, *Slavery, Capitalism and Politics in the Antebellum Republic*, vol. 1, *Commerce and Compromise, 1820–1850* (New York: Cambridge University Press, 1995), 412–435; Fehrenbacher, *Slaveholding Republic*, 119–126; William W. Freehling, *The Road to Disunion*, vol. 1, *Secessionists at Bay, 1776–1854* (New York: Oxford University Press, 1990), chaps. 20–26; Stephen Hartnett, "Senator Robert Walker's 1844 Letter on Texas Annexation: The Rhetorical 'Logic' of Imperialism," *American Studies*, no. 38, 1 (Spring 1997): 27–54; Thomas R. Hietala, *Manifest Design: Anxious Aggrandizement in Late Jacksonian America* (Ithaca, NY: Cornell University Press, 1985), 10–54, 83–86, 152–166; Frederick Merk, *Slavery and the Annexation of Texas* (New York: Knopf, 1972); Michael A. Morrison, *Slavery and the American West: The Eclipse of Manifest Destiny and the Coming of the Civil War* (Chapel Hill: University of North Carolina Press, 1997), chaps. 1, 3; Richards, *Slave Power*, chaps. 5–6; Silbey, *Storm over Texas*, chaps. 1–5. For a counterfactual history of this case, see Gary J. Kornblith, "Rethinking the Coming of the Civil War: A Counterfactual Exercise," *Journal of American History* 90, no. 1 (June 2003): 76–105.

104. One group of Creeks violently resisted removal in the short-lived Creek War of 1836. See Kenneth L. Valliere, "The Creek War of 1836: A Military History," *Chronicles of Oklahoma* 57, no. 4 (Winter 1979–1980): 463–485.

105. See George Klos, "Blacks and the Seminole Removal Debates, 1821–1835," *Florida Historical Quarterly* 68, no. 1 (July 1989): 65.

106. See *American State Papers: Military Affairs* 7:760 (Jesup to B.[Benjamin] F. Butler, Acting Secretary of War, December 9, 1836), 821.

107. The war continued for four years after the army had removed almost all the Black Seminoles from Florida. See Missall and Missall, *Seminole Wars*, 133.

108. The time frame, though, would probably have been different. I discuss the Second Seminole War and other southeast Native American removals further in chapter 5.

109. This eventuality occurred after the Civil War when the army compelled four of these nations—Chickasaws, Choctaws, Creeks, and Seminoles—to emancipate their slaves. (The Cherokees had emancipated their slaves in 1863 as part of an effort to expel African Americans from their western settlements.) See Charles J. Kappler, *Indian Affairs: Laws and Treaties*, vol. 2, *Treaties* (Washington, DC: Government Printing Office, 1904), 911, 919, 932, 944; Claudio Saunt, "The Paradox of Freedom: Tribal Sovereignty and Emancipation during the Reconstruction of Indian Territory," *Journal of Southern History* 70, no. 1 (February 2004): 74. On the other hand, it is unlikely that these nations would have become slaveholding nations, to the extent that they did, without the encouragement of United States officials. See Renate Bertl, "Native American Tribes and Their African Slaves," in *Slave Cultures and the Cultures of Slavery*, ed. Stephan Palmié (Knoxville: University of Tennessee Press, 1995), 165; Kathryn E. Holland Braund, "The Creek Indians, Blacks, and Slavery," *Journal of Southern History* 57, no. 1 (November 1991): 626–630; Greg O'Brien, *Choctaws in a Revolutionary Age, 1750–1830* (Lincoln: University of Nebraska Press, 2002), 105; Rothman, *Slave Country*, 56–58.

110. For the consensus on the Second Seminole War, see Canter Brown, Jr., "Race Relations in Territorial Florida, 1821–1845," *Florida Historical Quarterly* 73, no. 3 (January 1995): 303–304; James W. Covington, *The Seminoles of Florida* (Gainesville: University of Florida Press, 1993), 91;

Klos, "Seminole Removal Debates," 77–78; Jane F. Lancaster, *Removal Aftershock: The Seminoles' Struggles to Survive in the West, 1836–1866* (Knoxville: University of Tennessee Press, 1994), 18; Mahon, *Second Seminole War,* 201, 326; Missall and Missall, *Seminole Wars,* 126; Kevin Mulroy, *Freedom on the Border: The Seminole Maroons in Florida, the Indian Territory, Coahuila, and Texas* (Lubbock: Texas Tech University Press, 1993), 29; Virginia Bergman Peters, *The Florida Wars* (Hamden, CT: Archon Books, 1979), 144–145; Kenneth W. Porter, *The Black Seminoles: History of a Freedom-Seeking People* (Gainesville: University of Florida Press, 1996), 67; Larry Eugene Rivers, *Slavery in Florida: Territorial Days to Emancipation* (Gainesville: University Press of Florida, 2000), 204; Bruce Edward Twyman, *The Black Seminole Legacy and North American Politics, 1693–1845* (Washington, DC: Howard University Press, 1999), 130.

111. See Fearon, "Counterfactuals," 193.

112. A quorum was not reached in both chambers of Congress until April 6, 1789.

113. The fiscal year was the calendar year until 1843, when it became July 1–June 30. In this study, I use calendar years except when it is necessary to be more precise in reporting my findings. The first Battle of Manassas occurred shortly after the end of FY1861, on July 21, 1861.

114. While not all the slave states seceded from the union, all the seceding states were slave states. The nonseceding slave states (Delaware, Maryland, Kentucky, and Missouri) were a small minority.

115. See Bensel, *Yankee Leviathan,* 13, 63.

116. See John Craig Hammond, *Slavery, Freedom, and Expansion in the Early American West* (Charlottesville: University of Virginia Press, 2007); Matthew E. Mason, *Slavery and Politics in the Early American Republic* (Chapel Hill: University of North Carolina Press, 2006); George William Van Cleve, *A Slaveholders' Union: Slavery, Politics, and the Constitution in the Early American Republic* (Chicago: University of Chicago Press, 2010).

117. In denying that these views capture the distinctive nature of the early American state, I am not denying that they describe important features of that state.

118. See Robert W. Johannsen, ed., *The Lincoln-Douglas Debates of 1858* (New York: Oxford University Press, 1965), 14–21.

119. See Alexis de Tocqueville, *Democracy in America,* ed. J. P. Mayer, trans. George Lawrence (Garden City, NY: Doubleday, 1969), vol. 1, chap. 18. Tocqueville famously connected the fate of African Americans and European Americans and of Native Americans and European Americans, but not of all three together.

120. See Michael K. Brown, *Race, Money, and the American Welfare State* (Ithaca, NY: Cornell University Press, 1999); Eric Foner, *Reconstruction: America's Unfinished Revolution, 1863–1877* (New York: Harper & Row, 1988); Carol A. Horton, *Race and the Making of American Liberalism* (New York: Oxford University Press, 2005); Ira Katznelson, *When Affirmative Action Was White: An Untold History of Racial Inequality in Twentieth-Century America* (New York: Norton, 2005); Desmond S. King, *Separate and Unequal: Black Americans and the U.S. Federal Government* (New York: Oxford University Press, 1995); King and Smith, *Racial Orders,* 81–84; Philip A. Klinkner, with Rogers M. Smith, *The Unsteady March: The Rise and Decline of Racial Equality in America* (Chicago: University of Chicago Press, 1999); Daniel Kryder, *Divided Arsenal: Race and the American State during World War II* (Cambridge: Cambridge University Press, 2000); Robert C. Lieberman, *Shifting the Color Line: Race and the American Welfare State* (Cambridge, MA: Harvard University Press, 1998); Rogers M. Smith, *Civic Ideals: Conflicting Visions of Citizenship in U.S. History* (New Haven, CT: Yale University Press, 1997); Richard M. Valelly, *The Two Reconstructions: The Struggle for Black Enfranchisement* (Chicago: University of Chicago Press, 2004).

121. See Marx, *Making Race,* 132–136.

122. To many European Americans, African "immigrants" were presumably undesirable for one reason (as blacks) but more desirable for another (as slaves).

123. See Fehrenbacher, *Slaveholding Republic,* 150, 201; Aaron S. Fogleman, "From Slaves, Convicts, and Servants to Free Passengers: The Transformation of Immigration in the Era of the American Revolution," *Journal of American History* 85, no. 1 (June 1998): 50.

124. See *Annual Reports of the American Colonization Society* 3 (1820): 32–33; Joseph L. Grabill, "The 'Invisible' Missionary: A Study in American Foreign Relations," *Journal of Church and State* 14, no. 1 (Winter 1972): 93–105.

125. See Balogh, *Government Out of Sight,* 146; H. R. Rep. No. 283, 27th Cong., 3rd Sess., 1843, 6–7.

126. See Kaczorowski, "Inverted Constitution," 46–50.

127. See Valelly, *Two Reconstructions,* 109–110, 200, 231.

128. See, for example, Charles P. Henry, *Long Overdue: The Politics of Racial Reparations* (New York: New York University Press, 2007).

129. In its 2009 Current Population Survey, the Census Bureau found a poverty rate of 24.9 percent among blacks, the highest among the population groups it surveyed. The rate was 11.2 percent among whites. See U.S. Census Bureau, "Statistical Abstract of the United States: 2011," Table 712, http://www.census.gov/compendia/statab/2011/tables/11s0712.pdf.

130. Cf. Fehrenbacher, *Slaveholding Republic,* 41–43; Smith, *Civic Ideals,* 169.

CHAPTER 2. SLAVERY AND CONTROLLING THE NATIONAL BORDERS

1. Don Fehrenbacher distinguishes between interdicting slave trading and interdicting slave smuggling, noting that the federal record was much better on the latter front than the former. He also criticizes W. E. B. Du Bois's classic study of the American suppression of the slave trade for not distinguishing those two activities in his claim that the federal government did little to enforce its own slave-trade laws. According to Fehrenbacher, the federal government did more than a little, with respect to slave smuggling, at least after the War of 1812. Cf. W. E. B. Du Bois, *The Suppression of the African Slave-Trade to the United States of America, 1638–1870* (1896; reprint, New York: Social Science Press, 1954), 109–110, 129–130, 154–158, 182–183; Don E. Fehrenbacher, *The Slaveholding Republic: An Account of the United States Government's Relations to Slavery* (New York: Oxford University Press, 2001), 148–150, 201–202, 385n67.

2. This was also true of state-level deterrence efforts. See Du Bois, *African Slave-Trade,* 85–86.

3. See David Eltis, *Economic Growth and the Ending of the Transatlantic Slave Trade* (New York: Oxford University Press, 1987), 92–93 (Table 2); Judd Scott Harmon, "Suppress and Protest: The United States Navy, the African Slave Trade, and Maritime Commerce, 1794–1862" (Ph.D. diss., College of William and Mary, 1977), 48–49, 206 (Table 2); Warren S. Howard, *American Slavers and the Federal Law, 1837–1862* (1963; reprint, Westport, CT: Greenwood, 1976), 239–240 (Appendix E); S. Ex. Doc. No. 49, 35th Cong., 1st Sess., 1858, 28–29. Christopher Lloyd documents the British West African Squadron's steamship total from 1843 through 1853, which showed an increase from two to nine steamships. See Christopher Lloyd, *The Navy and the Slave Trade: The Suppression of the African Slave Trade in the Nineteenth Century* (London: Longmans, 1949), 281–283 (Appendix C).

4. See Howard, *American Slavers,* 220–223 (Appendix A).

5. See Donald L. Canney, *Lincoln's Navy: The Ships, Men and Organization, 1861–65* (Annapolis, MD: Naval Institute Press, 1998), 1.

6. See Appendix A. My estimate is significantly lower than Du Bois's $12,355,500 estimate for 1819–1869. See Du Bois, *African Slave-Trade,* 122. In addition to covering a longer period of time, a number of other factors account for Du Bois's higher estimate, including his reliance on congressional appropriation figures. The latter factor is significant because not all the money Congress appropriated for slave-trade suppression was spent on that purpose; some was spent on other purposes, such as African colonization. One thing I attempt to accomplish in this and the next chapter that Du Bois did not, is to separate the money spent on African colonization from that spent on slave-trade suppression. In other respects, both our estimates are conservative because we did not attempt to estimate the pre-1819 costs of slave-trade suppression or the many indirect costs of the policy. Unfortunately, there is insufficient data to do either.

7. From May 29, 1819, to November 11, 1828, documented federal expenditures on slave-trade suppression were $200,153. See S. Doc. No. 3, 20th Cong., 1st Sess., 1827, 10–29; S. Doc. No. 1, 20th Cong., 2nd Sess., 1828, 139–140. Unless otherwise indicated, I rounded all expenditures to the nearest dollar.

8. See S. Ex. Doc. No. 40, 31st Cong., 1st Sess., 1850, 3.

9. During these two fiscal years, the African Squadron averaged 8.5 ships, much higher than its prior average of 4.7 ships. See Harmon, "Suppress and Protest," 232–237 (Appendix D).

10. See Letters Received; September 17, 1860 to June 22, 1861 [inclusive]; Box 1; Letters Received from the Navy Department, 1823–1909; Correspondence of the Office of the Secretary of the Treasury; General Records of the Department of the Treasury; Record Group 56; National Archives, College Park, MD. Navy crews received bounties for 5,028 recaptured Africans over those ten months, approximately 300 less than the total number they reportedly seized. The record-keeping on how many Africans were seized from suspected slave ships and what happened to them afterward was consistently poor, a perfect example of how federal officials tended to dehumanize black people at the time.

11. See *Historical Statistics of the United States Millennial Edition Online,* Table Ea636–643, http://hsus.cambridge.org.

12. See Matthew E. Mason, "'Keeping Up Appearances': The International Politics of Slave Trade Abolition in the Nineteenth-Century Atlantic World," *William and Mary Quarterly,* Third Series, 66, no. 4 (October 2009): 809–832.

13. See Eltis, *Economic Growth,* 90, 92–93 (Table 2), 94–95, 99 (Table 4); Harmon, "Suppress and Protest," 206 (Table 2), 238–243 (Appendix E). I converted Eltis's pound estimates into dollar estimates using his own exchange rate of $4.80 per pound in this and all subsequent Anglo-American comparisons in this chapter. See Eltis, *Economic Growth,* 290–291 (Appendix G). In this and several subsequent comparisons, the comparison years are slightly different because Eltis divides the British seizures into five-year intervals. The total number of Africans that U.S. navy crews seized from suspected slave ships is my own calculation based on multiple sources, as reported when I discuss each case below. The total includes only navy seizures.

14. Eltis claims that from 1815 to 1823 the British government spent almost $900,000 per year on such bribes. Various African leaders and the Portuguese crown were the primary beneficiaries. See Eltis, *Economic Growth,* 72–73, 88–89, 96, 328n37. On British state capacities, see Max M. Edling, *A Revolution in Favor of Government: Origins of the U.S. Constitution and the Making of the American State* (Oxford: Oxford University Press, 2003), 50–52.

15. See B. R. Mitchell, *Abstract of British Historical Statistics* (London: Cambridge University Press, 1988), 587–588 (Public Finance 4); Eltis, *Economic Growth,* 92–93 (Table 2), and

International Historical Statistics: Europe, 1750–1993 (New York: Palgrave Macmillan, 2007), 911–913 (Table G5); *Historical Statistics of the United States,* Tables Ea636–643, Ed26–47; Harmon, "Suppress and Protest," 206 (Table 2), 232–237 (Appendix D); Paul H. Silverstone, *The Sailing Navy, 1775–1854* (Annapolis, MD: Naval Institute Press, 2001), 26, 36, 38, 40, 42–44, 49–50, 53, 56, 62–63, 75, and *Civil War Navies, 1855–1883* (Annapolis, MD: Naval Institute Press, 2001), 15, 17, 22, 45–46. No comparison of the relative size of the two African squadrons is possible until 1843, when the U.S. navy finally established such a squadron. To estimate the squadron's manpower totals, I used the Harmon appendix for the names of its ships and the two Silverstone books for the ships' capacities.

16. See Eltis, *Economic Growth,* 99 (Table 4); Harmon, "Suppress and Protest," 238–244 (Appendix E); Howard, *American Slavers,* 214–223 (Appendix A).

17. See Du Bois, *African Slave-Trade,* 154–158.

18. As we will see, the federal slave-import ban also became a major issue to one group of lower-South activists during the 1850s.

19. This situation, however, changed over time with the lower-South states becoming slave-exporting states to the new Cotton Belt states and antislavery sentiment dissipating in the upper-South states. See Gordon E. Finnie, "The Antislavery Movement in the Upper South before 1840," *Journal of Southern History* 35, no. 3 (August 1969): 319–342; Matthew E. Mason, *Slavery and Politics in the Early American Republic* (Chapel Hill: University of North Carolina Press, 2006), 19–21; Donald L. Robinson, *Slavery in the Structure of American Politics, 1765–1820* (New York: Harcourt Brace Jovanovich, 1971), 211–212, 216–217, 295–298, 337–338; Kenneth M. Stampp, "The Fate of the Southern Antislavery Movement," *Journal of Negro History* 28, no. 1 (January 1943): 10–22.

20. See Stanley L. Engerman, "Slavery and Its Consequences for the South in the Nineteenth Century," in *The Cambridge Economic History of the United States,* vol. 2, *The Long Nineteenth Century,* ed. Stanley L. Engerman and Robert E. Gallman (New York: Cambridge University Press, 2000), 337, 350; Ronald T. Takaki, *A Pro-Slavery Crusade: The Agitation to Reopen the African Slave Trade* (New York: Free Press, 1971), 3–4.

21. See David L. Lightner, "The Door to the Slave Bastille: The Abolitionist Assault upon the Interstate Slave Trade, 1833–1839," *Civil War History* 34, no. 3 (September 1988): 235–252, and *Slavery and the Commerce Power: How the Struggle against the Interstate Slave Trade Led to the Civil War* (New Haven, CT: Yale University Press, 2006). Of course, in the absence of slavery I assume that American humanitarian groups would have targeted the international slave trade more, just as their British counterparts did.

22. See Bernard Bailyn, "The Central Themes of the American Revolution: An Interpretation," in *Essays on the American Revolution,* ed. Stephen G. Kurtz and James H. Hutson (Chapel Hill: University of North Carolina Press, 1973), 28; Donald E. Fehrenbacher, *Slaveholding Republic,* 11–12, 28, 39–40, and "Slavery, the Framers, and the Living Constitution," in *Slavery and Its Consequences: The Constitution, Equality, and Race,* ed. Robert A. Goldwin and Art Kaufman (Washington, DC: American Enterprise Institute, 1988), 6–7; William W. Freehling, "The Founding Fathers and Slavery," *American Historical Review* 77, no. 1 (February 1972): 86, and "The Founding Fathers, Conditional Antislavery, and the Nonradicalism of the American Revolution," in *The Reintegration of American History: Slavery and the Civil War* (New York: Oxford University Press, 1994), 16, 20; Earl M. Maltz, "The Idea of a Proslavery Constitution," *Journal of the Early Republic* 17, no. 1 (Spring 1997): 58, and "Slavery, Federalism, and the Structure of the Constitution," *American Journal of Legal History* 36, no. 4 (October 1992): 467–468; Jack N. Rakove, *Original Meanings: Politics and Ideas in the Making of the Constitution* (New York: Knopf, 1996), 93.

23. See Robin L. Einhorn, "The Early Impact of Slavery," in *The American Congress: The Building of Democracy,* ed. Julian E. Zelizer (Boston: Houghton Mifflin, 2004), 77–90. Another slavery-related clause—the three-fifths clause—was much more central to the structure of the new federal government.

24. See Max Farrand, ed., *The Records of the Federal Convention of 1787* (1911; reprint, New Haven, CT: Yale University Press, 1937), 2:183; Fehrenbacher, *Slaveholding Republic,* 33. Rutledge chaired the committee. The other members were Oliver Ellsworth (Connecticut), Nathaniel Ghorum (Massachusetts), Edmund Randolph (Virginia), and James Wilson (Pennsylvania).

25. John Langdon (New Hampshire) was the only Northern delegate to speak against compromise. Ibid., 373.

26. Ibid., 364. Martin also noted that the three-fifths clause would act as an incentive to slave imports.

27. Ibid.

28. Ibid., 364–365. Actually, the South Carolina legislature had banned slave imports earlier in the year, but on a session-to-session basis. Thus when Pinckney contended that his state would eventually ban slave imports on its own, he must have been referring to a more permanent ban. He later said that he personally would vote for one. His second cousin, Charles Cotesworth Pinckney, was more prescient in admitting that South Carolina might not enact such a ban for many years. See Du Bois, *African Slave-Trade,* 11, 86–87; Farrand, *Records of the Convention,* 2:371, 373.

29. See Farrand, *Records of the Convention,* 2:370; Thomas Jefferson, *Notes on the State of Virginia* (Chapel Hill: University of North Carolina Press, 1955), 162. Mason, however, seemed much more opposed to the slave trade than to slavery. See Peter Wallenstein, "Flawed Keepers of the Flame: The Interpreters of George Mason," *Virginia Magazine of History and Biography* 102, no. 2 (April 1994): 229–260.

30. See Farrand, *Records of the Convention,* 2:371.

31. Ibid. Charles Cotesworth Pinckney stated that he would accept some restrictions on slave imports but threatened disunion if such imports were absolutely prohibited. See ibid., 371–372.

32. Ibid., 2:372. Georgia was the only state that had not acted to restrict slave imports by the time of the convention. It eventually prohibited them in 1798. See Du Bois, *African Slave-Trade,* 71.

33. North Carolina had taxed slave imports but not prohibited them. It took the latter action in 1794. See Du Bois, *African Slave-Trade,* 12, 72.

34. See Paul Finkelman, *Slavery and the Founders: Race and Liberty in the Age of Jefferson* (Armonk, NY: M.E. Sharpe, 1996), 19–29; Robinson, *Slavery in American Politics,* 226–227, 230–231. But cf. Fehrenbacher, *Slaveholding Republic,* 35, 352n88. In the votes on the two clauses, the South Carolina and the three represented New England delegations (Connecticut, Massachusetts, and New Hampshire) were the only delegations to vote for both clauses. See Farrand, *Records of the Convention,* 2:416, 449n, 453. The slave-trade clause did permit Congress to impose a $10 per capita duty on slave imports prior to 1808.

35. See Fehrenbacher, *Slaveholding Republic,* 42–43.

36. See Finkelman, *Slavery and the Founders,* 28–29. The fugitive-slave clause, in contrast, brought slavery within the powers of Congress but in a way that did not entail any positive congressional action.

37. See Farrand, *Records of the Convention,* 3:161.

38. Ibid., 254.

39. Ibid., 325; Clinton Rossiter, ed., *The Federalist Papers* (New York: New American Library, 1999), 243 (paper 42).

40. See Fehrenbacher, *Slaveholding Republic,* 37–38; Robinson, *Slavery in American Politics,* 235–239.

41. See Fehrenbacher, *Slaveholding Republic,* 137–138; Robinson, *Slavery in American Politics,* 299–302.

42. On this policy episode, see William C. diGiacomantonio, "'For the Gratification of a Volunteering Society': Antislavery and Pressure Group Politics in the First Federal Congress," *Journal of the Early Republic* 15, no. 2 (Summer 1995): 169–197; Fehrenbacher, *Slaveholding Republic,* 138–139; Richard S. Newman, "Prelude to the Gag Rule: Southern Reaction to Antislavery Petitions in the First Federal Congress," *Journal of the Early Republic* 16, no. 4 (Winter 1996): 571–597, and *The Transformation of American Abolitionism: Fighting Slavery in the Early Republic* (Chapel Hill: University of North Carolina Press, 2002), 48–49; Howard A. Ohline, "Slavery, Economics, and Congressional Politics, 1790," *Journal of Southern History* 46, no. 3 (August 1980): 335–360; Robinson, *Slavery in American Politics,* 302–311. The full name of the Pennsylvania antislavery society was the Pennsylvania Society for Promoting the Abolition of Slavery, for the Relief of Free Negroes unlawfully Held in Bondage, and for Improving the Condition of the African Race. The society's membership was predominantly Quaker. The two Quaker yearly meetings were the New York and western New England meeting and the Pennsylvania, New Jersey, Delaware, and western Maryland and Virginia meeting.

43. See *Annals of Congress,* 1st Cong., 2nd Sess., 1510, 1513–1514. Smith's not-so-subtle allusion was to the Quakers. Baldwin had made a similar allusion at the Constitutional Convention and now as a member of Congress he joined in a general attack on Quaker "intermeddling." Benjamin Franklin, who was the titular president of the Pennsylvania antislavery society and had decided not to introduce its antislavery memorial to the convention, was sharply criticized for signing its petition to Congress. See diGiacomantonio, "For the Gratification," 176–177, 187; Farrand, *Records of the Convention,* 2:372.

44. See diGiacomantonio, "For the Gratification," 177.

45. See *American State Papers: Miscellaneous* 1:13 ("Abolition of Slavery," March 5, 1790), 12. Foster was a pastor and Harvard Divinity School graduate.

46. See *Annals,* 1st Cong., 2nd Sess., 1524; diGiacomantonio, "For the Gratification," 192–193. Richard Newman argues that Southern congressional unity was first forged during this policy episode. See Newman, "Prelude to the Gag Rule," 596–597. In analyzing the vote, I considered Delaware, Maryland, Virginia, and North Carolina upper-South states and South Carolina and Georgia lower-South states. The later gag rule immediately tabled antislavery petitions.

47. For these early slave-trade laws, see H. R. Ex. Doc. No. 7, 36th Cong., 3rd Sess., 1860, 633–634.

48. See Du Bois, *African Slave-Trade,* 93, 108–109; Fehrenbacher, *Slaveholding Republic,* 140–141; Gene A. Smith, "U.S. Navy Gunboats and the Slave Trade in Louisiana Waters, 1808–1811," *Military History of the West* 23, no. 2 (Fall 1993): 147; Frances J. Stafford, "Illegal Importations: Enforcement of the Slave Trade Laws along the Florida Coast, 1810–1828," *Florida Historical Quarterly* 46, no. 2 (October 1967): 124–125.

49. See Carl E. Prince and Mollie Keller, *The U.S. Customs Service: A Bicentennial History* (Washington, DC: Department of Treasury, 1989), 85.

50. See Harmon, "Suppress and Protest," 238 (Appendix E). Congress created the Department of Navy in 1798.

51. See H. R. Rep. No. 184, 20th Cong., 1st Sess., 1828; *Senate Journal,* 22nd Cong., 1st Sess., December 5, 1831, 538.

52. See John Craig Hammond, *Slavery, Freedom, and Expansion in the Early American West*

(Charlottesville: University of Virginia Press, 2007), 27. Mississippi territory initially included the future states of Mississippi and Alabama.

53. Ibid., 30–31; John Craig Hammond, "'They Are Very Much Interested in Obtaining an Unlimited Slavery':'Rethinking the Expansion of Slavery in the Louisiana Purchase Territories, 1803–1805," *Journal of the Early Republic* 23, no. 3 (Fall 2003): 353. Louisiana territory initially included the entire Louisiana Purchase. Congress had rejected a domestic slave-trade ban in Mississippi. See Hammond, *Slavery, Freedom, and Expansion*, 23–27.

54. See Jed Handelsman Shugerman, "The Louisiana Purchase and South Carolina's Reopening of the Slave Trade in 1803," *Journal of the Early Republic* 22, no. 2 (Summer 2002): 263–290. South Carolina's action, in turn, prompted another failed attempt to impose a $10 per capita duty on slave imports. See Fehrenbacher, *Slaveholding Republic*, 142–143.

55. See Fehrenbacher, *Slaveholding Republic*, 148; Hammond, *Slavery, Freedom, and Expansion*, 47, 191n39. In response to local protests, Congress had allowed the Louisiana territorial ban on the domestic slave trade to lapse in 1805 when it reorganized the territory into Orleans (Louisiana) and Upper Louisiana (Missouri) territories. See Hammond, "Very Much Interested," 354, 374, and *Slavery, Freedom, and Expansion*, 31, 47, 50, 187n22. The correspondence of territorial officials registers the protests. See Clarence Edwin Carter, ed., *The Territorial Papers of the United States* (Washington, DC: Government Printing Office, 1934–1969), 9:222 ([Governor William C. C.] Claiborne to the President [Thomas Jefferson], April 15, 1804), 9:246 (Claiborne to the President, July 1, 1804), 9:261 (Claiborne to the Secretary of State [James Madison], July 13, 1804), 9:263 (John Gurley [territorial attorney general] to the Postmaster General [Gideon Granger], July 14, 1804), 9:265–266 (Hatch Dent [territorial court clerk] to James McCulloch [Baltimore city elector], July 14, 1804), 9:285 (Claiborne to the President, August 30, 1804), 9:305 (Claiborne to the Secretary of State, October 3, 1804), 9:312 (Claiborne to the Secretary of State, October 22, 1804), 9:314 (Claiborne to the President, October 27, 1804), 9:320 (Claiborne to the Secretary of State, November 5, 1804), and 9:340 (Claiborne to the President, November 25, 1804).

56. See *American State Papers: Foreign Relations* 1:25 ("Message to Congress," December 2, 1806), 68–69. As in Mason's case, Jefferson's anti–slave-trade credentials were much stronger than his antislavery credentials. See Finkelman, *Slavery and the Founders*, chaps. 5–6.

57. See *Annals*, 9th Cong., 2nd Sess., 231–232, 266–267, 626, quote at 626; Du Bois, *African Slave-Trade*, 97–111; Fehrenbacher, *Slaveholding Republic*, 144–147; Matthew E. Mason, "Slavery Overshadowed: Congress Debates Prohibiting the Atlantic Slave Trade to the United States, 1806–1807," *Journal of the Early Republic* 20, no. 1 (Spring 2000): 64–68; Robinson, *Slavery in American Politics*, 324–338. As we have seen, Randolph later used the same language to oppose federally funded internal improvements.

58. See Lloyd, *Slave Trade*, 61. Great Britain banned slave imports into its colonies ten days after Congress banned slave imports into the United States. This "race to be first" was clearly part of the "liberator nation" competition, though Denmark was actually first in 1793. See Fehrenbacher, *Slaveholding Republic*, 91, 136; Mason, "Keeping Up Appearances," 1–2.

59. See *American State Papers: Foreign Relations* 3:271 ("Great Britain," February 15, 16, and 20, 1815), 748; Lloyd, *Slave Trade*, 67–68.

60. See Heidler and Heidler, *Encyclopedia of the War of 1812*, 286; John S. Kendall, "Shadow over the City," *Louisiana Historical Quarterly* 22, no. 1 (January 1939): 146. Holmes was the brother of Mississippi territorial Governor David Holmes. His mission could have been a response to the growing number of slaves smuggled into Louisiana following the passage of the federal slave-import ban in 1807, which ended South Carolina's "legal" slave imports, many of whom had been transshipped to New Orleans. Based on ship manifests, James McMillin calculates that

1,733 slaves were smuggled into Louisiana from 1805 through 1807 and 5,596 from 1808 through 1810, more than a 300 percent increase. See James A. McMillin, *The Final Victims: Foreign Slave Trade to North America, 1783–1810: The Carolina Lowcountry and the Atlantic World* (Columbia: University of South Carolina Press, 2004), 32 (Table 7), 98. The Holmes mission may also have been a response to the 1811 German Coast slave revolt, which was widely rumored to have been instigated by the slaves of a group of French Haitian refugees who had been granted special permission to emigrate from Cuba to Louisiana with their slaves in 1809. See Kendall, "Shadow over the City," 144; Adam Rothman, *Slave Country: American Expansion and the Origins of the Deep South* (Cambridge, MA: Harvard University Press, 2005), 94–95. But cf. Robert L. Paquette, "Revolutionary Saint Domingue in the Making of Territorial Louisiana," in *A Turbulent Time; The French Revolution and the Greater Caribbean,* ed. David Barry Gaspar and David Patrick Geggus (Bloomington: Indiana University Press, 1997), 219. I discuss the German Coast revolt in chapter 5.

61. See Box 622; SG–Illegal Service, including blockade running, piracy, smuggling, and filibustering; Subject File, U.S. Navy, 1775–1901; O–1910; Office of Naval Records and Library, Record Group 45; National Archives, Washington, DC. The first folder in this box is full of correspondence discussing Lafitte's slave-trade activities.

62. See Eugene C. Barker, "The African Slave Trade in Texas," *Quarterly of the Texas State Historical Association* 6, no. 1 (July 1902): 145–149; Randolph B. Campbell, *An Empire for Slavery: The Peculiar Institution in Texas, 1821–1865* (Baton Rouge: Louisiana State University Press, 1989), 11–12; Fehrenbacher, *Slaveholding Republic,* 149; Harmon, "Suppress and Protest," 123–124. Slave smuggling, though, continued on a smaller scale in the border area between Louisiana and Texas, which remained part of a newly independent Mexico. One incident involving four slaves in Natchitoches in 1833 generated $538 in costs. See Barker, "Slave Trade in Texas," 151–152; Campbell, *Empire for Slavery,* 53; Du Bois, *African Slave-Trade,* 291 (Appendix C); J. Villasana Haggard, "The Neutral Ground between Louisiana and Texas, 1806–1821," *Louisiana Historical Quarterly* 28, no. 4 (October 1945): 1081–1082; H. R. Rep. No. 574, 4th Cong., 1st Sess., 1836; H. R. No. 43, 25th Cong., 2nd Sess., 1837.

63. See Du Bois, *African Slave-Trade,* 113–114; Fehrenbacher, *Slaveholding Republic,* 149; Harmon, "Suppress and Protest," 118–121; Stafford, "Illegal Importations," 126–127.

64. See Clyde N. Wilson, et. al., ed., *The Papers of John C. Calhoun* (Columbia: University of South Carolina Press, 1959–2003), 5:632 (Calhoun to David B. Mitchell, February 16, 1821); Royce Gordon Shingleton, "David Brydie Mitchell and the African Importation Case of 1820," *Journal of Negro History* 58, no. 3 (July 1973): 327–340; Stafford, "Illegal Importations," 129–130.

65. See *American State Papers: Foreign Relations* 5:343 ("Foreign Vessels Engaged in Smuggling through Florida," January 13, 1821); Du Bois, *African Slave-Trade,* 114, 166; H. R. Doc. No. 107, 15th Cong., 2nd Sess., 1819, 8–9; H. R. Doc. No. 36, 16th Cong., 1st Sess., 1820, 5–6; H. R. Doc. No. 42, 16th Cong., 1st Sess., 1820, 6–12; Stafford, "Illegal Importations," 129–132. The Adams-Onís Treaty was negotiated in 1819, but it took another two years for the Spanish government to sign and the U.S. Senate to ratify the treaty. One of Andrew Jackson's missions as the first provisional governor of Florida was to shut down slave-smuggling operations in the territory. See Carter, *Territorial Papers,* 12:34 (Andrew Jackson to [Colonel] Robert Butler, April 12, 1821), 12:38–39 (Jackson to the Secretary of State [John Quincy Adams], May 1, 1821), and 12:57 (The President [James Monroe] to Jackson, May 23, 1821). However, slave smuggling did not end completely on this frontier in 1821, any more than it did on the southwestern frontier. One incident involving (probably) eight slaves occurred in 1837 in Saint Joseph, on the Florida Panhandle. See Carter, *Territorial Papers,* 25:537 (Solicitor of the Treasury [Matthew Birchard] to the Secretary of State

[John Forsyth], June 6, 1838); Dorothy Dodd, "The Schooner *Emperor:* An Incident of the Illegal Slave Trade in Florida," *Florida Historical Society Quarterly* 13, no. 3 (January 1935): 117–128.

66. See *The Merino* 22 U.S. 391 (1824), at 407–408. American soldiers occupied Pensacola during the First Seminole War. Bushrod was George's nephew and also the first ACS president.

67. Of the 109 slaves, 84 were from the *Constitution,* 19 from the *Merino,* and six from the *Louisa.*

68. See Du Bois, *African Slave-Trade,* 117–118; Rothman, *Slave Country,* 195–196. The logic was that they had been seized before 1819. As we will see below, "outside the territorial limits of the United States" quickly came to mean Liberia.

69. See S. Doc. 3, 20th Cong., 1st Sess., 1827, 24–27; S. Doc. No. 1, 20th Cong., 2nd Sess., 1828, 139. U.S. marshals had to rent jail cells as well as courtrooms from state and local officials because the federal government had neither during this period. Marshals also paid deputies, witnesses, jurors, as well as jailers and doctors for their services and were themselves unsalaried employees who were paid by retaining the fees they collected. See Frederick S. Calhoun, *The Lawmen: United States Marshals and Their Deputies, 1789–1989* (Washington, DC: Smithsonian Institution Press, 1990), 56–57.

70. See H. R. Doc. No. 168, 19th Cong., 1st Sess., 1826, 87. The local court ordered (further) restitution for the *Constitution, Louisa,* and *Merino* claimants under the terms of the Adams-Onís Treaty, which required the federal government to redress the outstanding claims of Spanish colonials against the United States or its citizens. Under this decision, the *Louisa* claimants received a total of $9,981. The *Merino* claimants, however, received only $6,175, which was half their court-ordered restitution, and Treasury officials refused to pay any further restitution to the *Constitution* claimants. See H. R. Rep. No. 281, 19th Cong., 1st Sess., 1826; H. R. Rep. No. 49, 20th Cong., 1st Sess., 1828.

71. See Smith, "Navy Gunboats," 140–141.

72. See *American State Papers: Foreign Relations* 5:343 (Foreign Vessels Engaged in Smuggling through Florida, January 13, 1821), 77; Carter, *Territorial Papers,* 23:404 ([Colonel] George M. Brooke to the Quartermaster General [Thomas S. Jesup], January 1, 1826).

73. See *Annual Reports of the American Colonization Society* (1818–1910; reprint, New York: Negro Universities Press, 1969), 4 (1821): 25–28.

74. For the provisions of the law, see *Statutes at Large* 3 (1819): 532–534.

75. See H. R. Doc. No. 11, 16th Cong., 1st Sess., 1819. As we will see in the next chapter, Congress supported or at least acquiesced in Monroe's diversion until 1828.

76. See ACS, *Annual Reports,* 4 (1821): 27–28.

77. See Harmon, "Suppress and Protest," 239 (Appendix E).

78. The other three ships escaped shortly after they were seized. See Du Bois, *African Slave-Trade,* 291 (Appendix C).

79. See 26 F. Cas. 832 (C.C.D. Mass. 1822; No. 15551); John T. Noonan, Jr., *The* Antelope: *The Ordeal of the Recaptured Africans in the Administrations of James Monroe and John Quincy Adams* (Berkeley: University of California Press, 1977), 69–74. Both President Monroe and Secretary of State Adams pressed Story to rule in favor of the French claimants. See Noonan, *The* Antelope, 70–71.

80. See Noonan, *The* Antelope, 76–77; S. Doc. No. 3, 20th Cong., 1st Sess., 1827, 16–17.

81. See *Statutes at Large* 3 (1820): 600–601. Congress had already increased the criminal penalties for slave-trade violations in 1818. See *Statutes at Large* 3 (1818): 450–453.

82. If there were no Africans aboard the ship when it was captured, district attorneys found it difficult to prosecute the case because federal justices generally required physical evidence for

cases to continue. Sometimes ship owners kept crews and even captains in the dark about the nature of their missions until they reached Africa, which made criminal prosecutions difficult. Libeling suspected slave ships proved to be the easiest part of the process, yet even this step was not without its pitfalls because ship owners registered their ships with other countries, flew other flags, and otherwise took measures that made even civil prosecutions difficult. Warren Howard's *American Slavers* covers the legal aspects of slave-trade seizures in great detail.

83. The Spanish governor of Cuba had licensed the *Antelope* to transport "new negroes" to the New World. After he had captured the *Antelope*, Smith's own ship, the *Columbia*, was shipwrecked off the northeast coast of Brazil, where he had procured more slaves, which explains not only why he was sailing the *Antelope* when it was captured but also why there were Portuguese claimants in the case. See Noonan, *The* Antelope, 14, 28–31.

84. See *The Antelope*, 23 U.S. 66 (1825); Noonan, *The* Antelope, 111–114, 125–128, 131–132. U.S. District Attorney Richard Wylly Habersham refused to prosecute Smith for piracy. He was acquitted of the lesser charges that were brought against him. See Noonan, *The* Antelope, 51–53.

85. See Noonan, *The* Antelope, 135–137. The exact number is unknown.

86. A bill that would have appropriated $11,700 to buy the recaptured Africans from Wilde in order to also resettle them in Liberia failed to pass the House, on a 99–39 vote. See ibid., 147–150.

87. See Noonan, *The* Antelope, 46, 80; S. Doc. No. 3, 20th Cong., 1st Sess., 1827, 10–11. Thompson paid Habersham $432 to uncover Morel's scheme. Morel received another $335 for transporting the recaptured Africans who had been awarded to the U.S. government to Norfolk for passage to Liberia. See Noonan, *The* Antelope, 80, 134; S. Doc. No. 3, 20th Cong., 1st Sess., 1827, 16–17, 28–29.

88. See Noonan, *The* Antelope, 141–142; S. Doc. No. 3, 20th Cong., 1st Sess., 1827, 12–13, 28–29; S. Doc. No. 1, 20th Cong., 2nd Sess., 1828, 139.

89. As already noted, slave-smuggling incidents continued on a smaller scale. One New Orleans case involving 15 slaves in 1826 generated $5,112 in costs. See S. Doc. No. 3, 20th Cong., 1st Sess., 1827, 28–29. For the relative lack of slave smuggling into the United States during this period, see Engerman, "Slavery and Its Consequences," 337; Fehrenbacher, *Slaveholding Republic*, 149–150, 386nn66–68; Howard, *American Slavers*, 154, 302–303n22; Kenneth Kiple, "The Case against a Nineteenth-Century Cuba-Florida Slave Trade," *Florida Historical Quarterly* 49, no. 4 (April 1971): 345–355.

90. Spanish officials on Cuba enacted slave-import restrictions in 1830, but the only determined effort to enforce them occurred in the mid-1840s. Beginning in 1850, Brazilian officials launched a more determined and successful effort to restrict slave imports, but one consequence was a surge of slave imports to Cuba. In both cases, British diplomatic pressure spurred the restriction efforts. See Harmon, "Suppress and Protest," 130–131, 145–146; H. R. Doc. No. 148, 28th Cong., 2nd Sess., 1845; H. R. Ex. Doc. No. 7, 36th Cong., 3rd Sess., 1860; S. Ex. Doc. No. 73, 32nd Cong., 1st Sess., 1852; Hugh Thomas, *The Slave Trade: The Story of the Atlantic Slave Trade, 1440–1870* (New York: Simon & Schuster, 1997), chaps. 34–36.

91. See ACS, *Annual Reports*, 13 (1830): 13.

92. See Harmon, "Suppress and Protest," 254–256 (Appendix H).

93. See Douglas R. Egerton, *Charles Fenton Mercer and the Trial of National Conservatism* (Jackson: University Press of Mississippi, 1989), chaps. 11–12. Mercer was also a vocal supporter of the ACS and one of its vice presidents. As the next chapter shows, this new political climate also negatively affected the society's fortunes.

94. See Harmon, "Suppress and Protest," 239 (Appendix E).

95. See H. R. Doc. No. 54, 21st Cong., 2nd Sess., 1831, 3–4. When the *Grampus* arrived to aid the *Kremlin*, the *Fenix* was on the far side of the ship, shielded from view.

96. See "Letter from Treasury Department, 4th Auditor's Office, in response to Senate Resolution of February 25, 1843," December 1, 1843; Record Group 45; National Archives. The ACS resettled only 36 of the 82 *Fenix* Africans in Liberia. See ACS, *Annual Reports*, 19 (1835): 16, 28.

97. The other *Guerero* Africans presumably either died in the shipwreck or became Cuban slaves after the Spanish crew of the *Guerero* seized control of the wrecker that had rescued them, along with approximately 250 Africans, and sailed it to Havana. See H. R. Rep. No. 4, 25th Cong., 2nd Sess., 1836, 2–3.

98. See *Statutes at Large* 4 (1829): 354.

99. See H. R. Rep. No. 4, 25th Cong., 2nd Sess., 1836, 2–3; *Senate Journal*, 25th Cong., 2nd Sess., December 4, 1837, 755.

100. See Stafford, "Illegal Importations," 132.

101. See Eltis, *Economic Growth*, 92 (Table 2), 99 (Table 4). The U.S. total includes the 220 *La Penseé* and 82 *Fenix* Africans but not the 281 *Antelope* Africans because the last was not a navy seizure.

102. See Matthew E. Mason, "The Battle of the Slaveholding Liberators: Great Britain, the United States, and Slavery in the Early Nineteenth Century," *William and Mary Quarterly*, Third Series, 59, no. 3 (July 2002): 671.

103. See Harmon, "Suppress and Protest," 107–108; ACS, *Annual Reports*, 24 (1840): 7.

104. See *Statutes at Large* 8 (1842): 576.

105. Northern Whigs were generally more antislavery than Northern Democrats, though this generalization was not necessarily true of the Southern wings of the two parties. See Daniel Walker Howe, *The Political Culture of the American Whigs* (Chicago: University of Chicago Press, 1979), 37–38.

106. See Fehrenbacher, *Slaveholding Republic*, 157–165; H. R. Rep. No. 283, 27th Cong., 3rd Sess., 1843, 478–729; Harmon, "Suppress and Protest," 71–75; Howard, *American Slavers*, 8–12; Mason, "Keeping Up Appearances," 820–828. John Quincy Adams opposed taking this step as secretary of state notwithstanding his future career as an antislavery Whig congressman.

107. See S. Ex. Doc. No. 20, 27th Cong., 3rd Sess., 1843. Tyler had brought Upshur into the cabinet following the mass resignation of his Whig cabinet members in September 1841, after he had vetoed several major party initiatives.

108. Webster remained Tyler's Secretary of State when all his other cabinet members resigned in order to complete the treaty negotiations with Great Britain. After those negotiations concluded, Webster resigned. Upshur then moved from Navy Secretary to Secretary of State, though he soon died, along with new Navy Secretary Thomas W. Gilmer (Virginia Whig), in an explosion during a ceremonial cannonade aboard the USS *Princeton*.

109. After all, neither Upshur nor Tyler was necessarily an opponent of slave-trade suppression. Tyler strongly supported the slave-trade article of the Webster-Ashburton Treaty when it came under Southern attack in the mid-1850s. See Manisha Sinha, *The Counterrevolution of Slavery: Politics and Ideology in Antebellum South Carolina* (Chapel Hill: University of North Carolina Press, 2000), 137; Takaki, *Pro-Slavery Crusade*, 71–72.

110. See Harmon, "Suppress and Protest," 233 (Appendix D); Howard, *American Slavers*, 239 (Appendix E).

111. See Harmon, "Suppress and Protest," 232–237 (Appendix D); S. Ex. Doc. No. 39, 35th Cong., 1st Sess., 1858, 16. In 1842, the U.S. navy had twenty-nine ships. In 1859, it had forty-eight. See Harmon, "Suppress and Protest," 232, 237 (Appendix D).

112. See *Historical Statistics of the United States*, Table Ea636–643; S. Ex. Doc. No. 40, 31st Cong., 1st Sess., 1850, 3. The squadron's size remained relatively stable, at approximately four ships, until 1858. See Harmon, "Suppress and Protest," 232–237 (Appendix D).

113. See Eltis, *Economic Growth*, 99 (Table 4); Howard, *American Slavers*, 214–223 (Appendix A). The Home Squadron captured a slave-laden ship with 318 Africans aboard near the end of this period, which would increase the U.S. total to two slave-laden ships with approximately 1,200 Africans abroad. Judd Harmon did not distinguish ship seizures in terms of those with and those without Africans aboard, but his figures for the 1843–1859 seizure totals of the respective African squadrons were 24 (US) and 574 (GB). See Harmon, "Suppress and Protest," 206 (Table 2).

114. See Du Bois, *African Slave-Trade*, 185–186; Fehrenbacher, *Slaveholding Republic*, 173. See also George E. Brooke, "The Role of the US Navy in the Suppression of the African Slave Trade," *American Neptune* 21, no. 2 (January 1961): 33; Donald L. Canney, *Africa Squadron: The U.S. Navy and the Slave Trade, 1842–1861* (Washington, DC: Potomac Books, 2006), 57–58, 226–227; Howard, *American Slavers*, 13, 41, 67–68; David F. Long, *Gold Braid and Foreign Relations: Diplomatic Activities of U.S. Naval Officers, 1798–1883* (Annapolis, MD: Naval Institute Press, 1988), 320.

115. See H. R. Ex. Doc. No. 104, 35th Cong., 2nd Sess., 1859, 3.

116. Ibid., 7–8, 11.

117. See Harmon, "Suppress and Protest," 2–3.

118. See *House Journal*, 33rd Cong., 1st Sess., April 13, 1854, 634; *House Journal*, 33rd Cong., 1st Sess., July 31, 1854, 1241.

119. Before the Buchanan administration, seven of the African Squadron's nine navy secretaries were from the South. The two exceptions were both Massachusetts Democrats—David Henshaw and George Bancroft—who served brief tenures. Indeed, Henshaw was a Tyler recess appointment whom the Senate refused to confirm. On the Southern dominance of the navy during this period, see Canney, *Africa Squadron*, 226; Harold D. Langley, *Social Reform in the United States Navy, 1798–1862* (Urbana: University of Illinois Press, 1967), 30; Long, *Gold Braid*, 314; John H. Schroeder, *Shaping a Maritime Empire: The Commercial and Diplomatic Role of the American Navy, 1828–1861* (Westport, CT: Greenwood, 1985), 58–59, 187–188. For official confirmation that slave-trade suppression was also not a Treasury Department priority at this time, see Carter, *Territorial Papers*, 26:740 (Secretary of the Treasury [John C. Spencer] to the Mayor and Council of St. Augustine, September 18, 1843).

120. See Howard, *American Slavers*, 218, 223 (Appendix A).

121. The exact number of *Echo* Africans who died is unknown.

122. See Log of Letters Sent; letters dated December 14, 1858, April 13, 1859, and July 21, 1860 (National Archives Microfilm Publication M160, roll 2); Letters Sent, September 8, 1858–February 1, 1872; Records of the Office of the Secretary of the Interior Relating to the Suppression of the African Slave Trade and Negro Colonization, 1854–1872; Record Group 48; National Archives, College Park, MD. Hamilton claimed that the deaths of the Africans in his custody caused him to lose any sympathy he might have had for the slave-trade revival movement in South Carolina. The "philosopher" of that movement, Leonidas Spratt, served as the *Echo* defense attorney. See Takaki, *Pro-Slavery Crusade*, 215–216, 225–226.

123. A navy vessel had originally taken Townsend to Boston, where a conviction would have been more likely, but U.S. Commissioner Edward G. Loring ruled that he should be tried in the judicial district closest to the location of his alleged offense. See Sinha, *Counterrevolution*, 161. As we will see in chapter 5, Loring also played a key role in the Anthony Burns fugitive-slave rendition.

124. See Tom Henderson Wells, *The Slave Ship Wanderer* (Athens: University of Georgia Press, 1967), 1, 86–87.

125. See H. R. Ex. Doc. No. 7, 36th Cong., 3rd Sess., 1860, 632–36; Wells, *The Wanderer*, 6–7, 47. Lamar was active in the slave-trade revival movement, but he was also a shrewd businessman who was entranced by the potential profits of slave smuggling. See Wells, *The Wanderer*, 4–5.

126. See Wells, *The Wanderer*, 54–56. At least in this case the jurors had the excuse that the prosecution had been unable to present any of the *Wanderer* Africans in court. Lamar and several accomplices were able to cajole the county jailer to release into their custody the only two *Wanderer* Africans whom U.S. Marshal James Spullock had been able to recapture. The ultimate fate of the *Wanderer* Africans is unknown. As the multiple indictments suggest, Spullock was able to track their initial movements, but Lamar effectively arranged for them to be transported to more distant locations for resale. Ibid., 29, 42–45, 86.

127. See Log of Letters Sent; letters dated February 14, 1859, and December 31, 1859; M160, roll 2; National Archives; Wells, *The Wanderer*, 57. Interior records list a payment of $3,500 to Jackson himself for "services in Savannah" and another payment of $2,500 to his firm for the *Wanderer* and *Angelita* cases. The latter was a libel case that was dismissed. See Howard, *American Slavers*, 219 (Appendix A).

128. See Wells, *The Wanderer*, 58.

129. See Log of Letters Sent; letter dated November 6, 1861; National Archives, M160, roll 2; Wells, *The Wanderer*, 65–67. Farnum was a well-known filibuster but his exact role on the *Wanderer* is unclear. See Wells, *The Wanderer*, 63–64.

130. See Wells, *The Wanderer*, 59. Lamar and three accomplices did plead guilty to one crime. While Farnum was awaiting trial, they broke him out of jail so that they could attend a party together. (Ever the gentlemen, they returned Farnum to the jailhouse the next morning.) For this crime, they were fined $250 and received thirty-day prison sentences. They served their sentences in Lamar's downtown business office. Ibid., 69–70.

131. Ibid., 59–61. Corrie was tried in Charleston because it was his place of residence. Marshal Hamilton refused to assist in the prosecution because he claimed that he still had not been fully reimbursed for his costs in the *Echo* case. See Sinha, *Counterrevolution*, 168.

132. See Harmon, "Suppress and Protest," 140, 192, 236–237 (Appendix D); Howard, *American Slavers*, 59, 240 (Appendix E). Among the reassigned ships were five steamships that the navy had chartered and then purchased, at a cost of $1,350,000, for a bout of gunboat diplomacy against Paraguay. See Robert Ralph Davis, Jr., "James Buchanan and the Suppression of the Slave Trade, 1858–1861," *Pennsylvania History* 33, no. 4 (October 1966): 452; Howard, *American Slavers*, 59.

133. See [James Buchanan], *Mr. Buchanan's Administration on the Eve of the Rebellion* (New York: D. Appleton, 1866), 261–263; S. Ex. Doc. No. 39, 35th Cong., 1st Sess., 1858. For the multiple motives behind Buchanan's decision, see Davis, "Buchanan and the Slave Trade," 457–459; Karen Fisher Younger, "Liberia and the Last Slave Ships," *Civil War History* 54, no. 4 (December 2008): 431–432.

134. The Senate Committee on Foreign Relations voted to circulate Slidell's resolution confidentially among the other members of the Senate. Two years later, the Senate, in executive session, voted to make it public. See S. Rep. No. 195, 34th Cong., 1st Sess., 1856.

135. See *House Journal*, 34th Cong., 3rd Sess., December 15, 1856, 105–106. In analyzing this vote, I consider all fifteen slave states, including Delaware and Missouri, Southern states.

136. See Sinha, *Counterrevolution*, 174–175; Takaki, *Pro-Slavery Crusade*, 224.

137. See Takaki, *Pro-Slavery Crusade*, 104–105, 107–111.

138. See *House Journal*, 34th Cong., 3rd Sess., December 15, 1856, 109–110. In analyzing this vote, I consider Delaware, Maryland, Virginia, North Carolina, Tennessee, Kentucky, and Missouri upper-South states and South Carolina, Georgia, Florida, Alabama, Mississippi, Louisiana,

Arkansas, and Texas lower-South states. All eighteen of the Southern congressmen who voted for the resolution were either Know Nothings or Whigs, while only twelve Southern Know Nothings and Whigs voted against it. Among the Southern delegations, the vote then was also a partisan vote.

139. See *House Journal*, 34th Cong., 3rd Sess., December 15, 1856, 112–113.

140. Even Manisha Sinha, who criticizes Takaki for discounting the political significance of the slave-trade revival movement, stresses that no state ever took official action to nullify a federal slave-trade law. The only "nullification" that occurred was at the hands of a federal justice. Although South Carolina Governor James Adams's 1856 recommendation to the legislature to investigate the advisability of state action to reopen the slave trade received a favorable committee report, it also spurred an oppositional movement in the state, with Orr at its head, and no final action was taken on the recommendation. Two years later, the South Carolina senate voted to abrogate the slave-trade article of the Webster-Ashburton Treaty, but no other state legislative body took similar action. See Sinha, *Counterrevolution*, 131–134, 147–148.

141. Ibid., 183–184; Takaki, *Pro-Slavery Crusade*, 231–238. South Carolina and, to a lesser extent, Florida opposed the decision, which was also intended to attract British support for the Confederacy. See Mason, "Keeping Up Appearances," 829.

142. See Frederick Moore Binder, *James Buchanan and the American Empire* (Selingsgrove, PA: Susquehanna University Press, 1994), 261, 274; Davis, "Buchanan and the Slave Trade," 450, 459.

143. See Howard, *American Slavers*, 220–223 (Appendix A). The crew members of one of these ships, the *W. R. Kibby*, had managed to unload the Africans on the ship just prior to capture, except for three children whom they had apparently overlooked in the hold. The total is at least 5,346 recaptured Africans because in the case of one of the ships Howard provides the number landed in Liberia, not the number seized from the ship, presumably because he could find no record of the latter.

144. See Harmon, "Suppression and Protest," 206, Table 2. Because of the way that Eltis divides the British seizures into five-year intervals, I could not compare the British and American totals for seizures of slave-laden ships during this two-year period. Another reason for the improved performance of the U.S. African Squadron was the relocation of its base of operations from the Cape Verde Islands to the west coast of Africa. See Howard, *American Slavers*, 59.

145. See *Statutes at Large* 12 (1860–1861): 21, 40–41, 132, 219.

146. See *Historical Statistics of the United States*, Table Ea636–643. Obviously, FY1862 showed a sharp increase in both total navy and federal expenditures because of the Civil War.

147. See Ron Soodalter, *Hanging Captain Gordon: The Life and Trial of an American Slave Trader* (New York: Atria, 2006), 222–225.

148. In fact, Gordon bankrupted himself paying his legal fees and buying special meals and privileges for himself and his two indigent fellow officers. The latter were convicted of lesser charges. See ibid., 92–93, 118, 239–240.

149. Ibid., 119. The crew members were also convicted of lesser charges; see ibid., 88–89.

150. Ibid., 124. At the official *per diem* rate of $1.50, the witness expenses could have been as much as $540. See *Statutes at Large* 10 (1853): 167. In addition to witness, jail, and juror fees, the federal government also paid for Gordon's medical care, including the fees of the three doctors who "saved" his life after he attempted to commit suicide the night before his execution. See Soodalter, *Hanging Captain*, 210–211.

151. See Soodalter, *Hanging Captain*, 103–105.

152. See Fehrenbacher, *Slaveholding Republic*, 198; Howard, *American Slavers*, 224–235

(Appendix B); Soodalter, *Hanging Captain*, 9. Based on Howard's data, Soodalter found 125 slave-trade cases from New York in 1837–1861, with a conviction rate of 16 percent.

153. See Soodalter, *Hanging Captain*, 235–236. Another important difference between the two trials was the fact that the jury was also sequestered during the second trial. Ibid., 133.

154. See Wells, *The Wanderer*, 66.

155. See Davis, "Buchanan and the Slave Trade," 450; Robert Ralph Davis, Jr., "Buchanan Espionage: A Report on Illegal Slave Trading in the South in 1859," *Journal of Southern History* 37, no. 2 (May 1971): 271–278; Howard, *American Slavers*, 147–154. Based on Sylviane Diouf's recent research, the rumor that the *Clotilda* landed more than a hundred African slaves near Mobile in July 1860 was more than a rumor, but that incident occurred after Slocumb's report. See Sylviane A. Diouf, *Dreams of Africa in Alabama: The Slave Ship Clotilda and the Story of the Last Africans Brought to America* (Oxford: Oxford University Press, 2007). But cf. Howard, *American Slavers*, 301–302n21; Wells, *The Wanderer*, 86–87.

156. See U.S. Marshal Charles Clark (Maine) to Secretary of Interior Smith, June 30, 1861 [July 10, 1861, notation to send him $400]; Robert Murray (U.S. Marshal, southern district of New York) to [George C.] Whiting (chief clerk, Department of Interior), May 11, 1861 [May 14, 1861, notation to send him $300]; James Aiken (U.S. Marshal for Delaware) to Whiting, September 3, 1861 [attached May 2, 1865, note from Aiken stating that he has $272 left in his account]; M160, roll 6; National Archives.

157. Lincoln formalized this arrangement in a May 2, 1861, executive order. See Davis, "Buchanan and the Slave Trade," 449–450; Howard, *American Slavers*, 69, 258–260 (Appendix L). As the next chapter shows, the department's new responsibilities included African colonization.

158. See H. R. Ex. Doc. No. 7, 36th Cong., 3rd Sess., 1860, 135, 245. The initial payments for the *C. Perkins* witnesses were dated July 3, 1858, and they were dismissed April 8, 1859. See H. R. Ex. Doc. No. 7, 135, 307. Though it is unlikely that they were paid all that time, if they had been, the total would have been $837. The document does not indicate if the same two witnesses received the travel payments and the room and board payments in the *Haidee* case, nor why there was such a disparity in the latter. The federal government also paid from $700 to $800 to salvage the *C. Perkins* from Havana harbor. See H. R. Ex. Doc. No. 7, 374.

159. See Log of Letters Sent; letter dated February 27, 1861; M160, roll 2; National Archives.

160. See Harmon, "Suppress and Protest," 84, 142, 199; Howard, *American Slavers*, 59.

161. See H. R. Ex. Doc. No. 57, 37th Cong., 2nd Sess., 1862. The Lincoln administration finally agreed to such a treaty the same year that it formally recognized Liberian and Haitian independence, issued the draft Emancipation Proclamation, abolished slavery in the District of Columbia, offered a similar compensated emancipation plan to the border states (which they rejected), and abandoned its colonization efforts.

162. See David G. Surdam, *Northern Naval Superiority and the Economics of the American Civil War* (Columbia: University of South Carolina Press, 2001), 3–8.

163. The adjustment of the northeastern boundary with Canada was probably the most pressing issue settled by the Webster-Ashburton Treaty. See Howard Jones, *To the Webster-Ashburton Treaty: A Study in Anglo-American Relations, 1783–1843* (Chapel Hill: University of North Carolina Press, 1977), 85–86.

164. See Mason, "Keeping Up Appearances," 810–811, 822, 832.

165. See Aaron S. Fogleman, "From Slaves, Convicts, and Servants to Free Passengers: The Transformation of Immigration in the Era of the American Revolution," *Journal of American History* 85, no. 1 (June 1998): 50. The next federal immigration law, which targeted criminals and prostitutes, was not enacted until 1875. Seven years later, Congress passed legislation to exclude

Chinese immigrants, which was probably a more comparable case to the slave-import ban in targeting a specific ethnic or racial group. Prior to the slave-import ban, Congress passed legislation to help enforce the restrictions that every Southern state had enacted during the initial years of the Haitian Revolution against the immigration of Caribbean blacks, both free and (with their masters) enslaved, but this legislation was auxiliary to the state restrictions and did not constitute a federal ban on such immigration. (When South Carolina did not renew its slave-import ban in 1803, it maintained its Caribbean restrictions.) Similarly, the Alien Act of 1798 sought to bar "seditious" immigrants, but the act was only in force for two years, and no immigrant was denied entry into the country or deported under it. See Du Bois, *African Slave-Trade,* 84–87; Fehrenbacher, *Slaveholding Republic,* 141–142; Alan Frank January, "The First Nullification: The Negro Seamen Acts Controversy in South Carolina, 1822–1860" (Ph.D. diss., University of Iowa, 1978), 88, 92–93; Tim Matthewson, *A Proslavery Foreign Policy: Haitian-American Relations during the Early Republic* (Westport, CT: Praeger, 2003), 129–130; Robinson, *Slavery in American Politics,* 316–318; *Statutes at Large* 2 (1803): 205–206; Alan Taylor, "The Alien and Sedition Acts," in *American Congress,* 70; Daniel J. Tichenor, *Dividing Lines: The Politics of Immigration Control in America* (Princeton, NJ: Princeton University Press, 2002), 54, 99, 106–107.

166. Some of these costs were included in navy audits and estimates. Other costs were African colonization expenditures, which I document in the next chapter.

167. See Hammond, *Slavery, Freedom, and Expansion,* 14, 24–25, 31, 40, 45–46, 48–50, 53, 57; Hammond, "Very Much Interested," 356–358, 363–365, 374–375, 378–379.

168. Arguably, there was also a lack of cooperation in the North, at least in New York, but at lower levels and not as evidence of widespread disaffection with the federal government.

169. See Harmon, "Suppress and Protest," 237 (Appendix D); *Historical Statistics of the United States,* Tables Ea636–643, Ed26–47; Silverstone, *Sailing Navy,* 40, 42–44, 63, 75; Silverstone, *Civil War Navies,* 15, 22, 45–46.

170. See Howard, *American Slavers,* 258 (Appendix L). This policy area is a perfect example of what Karen Orren and Stephen Skowronek mean by intercurrences.

171. See Fehrenbacher, *Slaveholding Republic,* 191–192.

172. Unfortunately, this consensus did not carry over to the venality of slavery.

CHAPTER 3. THE FIRST AMERICAN COLONY

1. The society's official name was the American Society for Colonizing the Free People of Colour of the United States. The society was not formally dissolved until 1964, though it had been inactive since 1912.

2. These trajectories partially overlapped. The 1819–1861 time frame spans the years from when the ACS first received federal support to the Civil War. Given that the society reported its budgets in calendar years, I will report the federal support it received in calendar, not fiscal, years (which differed after 1842).

3. See Henry Noble Sherwood, "The Formation of the American Colonization Society," *Journal of Negro History* 2, no. 3 (July 1917): 227.

4. See ibid., 227–228. Key became one of the Board of Managers.

5. The ACS counted its annual meetings from its first anniversary meeting in 1818, not from its initial annual meeting in 1817.

6. See P. J. Staudenraus, *The African Colonization Movement, 1816–1865* (New York: Columbia University Press, 1961), 169–178.

7. See *Annual Reports of the American Colonization Society* (1818–1910; reprint, New York: Negro Universities Press, 1969), 17 (1834): 28 [Appendix].

8. Ibid., 32 (1849): 15; 39 (1856): 7; 40 (1857): 19; and 46 (1863): 12.

9. Ibid.; 42 (1859): 18–19.

10. Ibid., 44 (1861): 19. For children, the Senate reduced the rate to $50 per capita.

11. Ibid., 2 (1819): 10–11; 4 (1821): 29; 5 (1822): 47–48; 7 (1824): 7; 10 (1827): 13, 77–79; 14 (1831): 24–25; 26 (1843): 11–12; 32 (1849): 34; 36 (1853): 47–48; and 41 (1858): 31–37.

12. Ibid., 6 (1823): 23; 7 (1824): 70–71; 10 (1827): 30; 14 (1831): 24; 15 (1832): 16–21; 17 (1834): 27; 31 (1848): 26–27; 32 (1849): 18; and 41 (1858): 31–37.

13. For example, Key was one Southern ACS official who took a strong emancipationist stance, while prominent Massachusetts orator, educator, and statesman Edward Everett was one Northern ACS official who took a strong "noninterference with slavery" stance. See ibid., 11 (1828): 20–21, and 15 (1832): xii–xiii.

14. In the course of one speech, Clay defined the society's goal as removing the annual increase of free blacks, removing all free blacks, removing the annual increase of all blacks, incrementally removing all blacks coincident to a very gradual abolition of slavery in the United States, or, at least, removing enough blacks to preserve the essential "whiteness" of American society. See ibid., 10 (1827): 16–20.

15. See Eric Burin, *Slavery and the Peculiar Solution: A History of the American Colonization Society* (Gainesville: University Press of Florida, 2005), 33; Alisse Portnoy, *Their Right to Speak: Women's Activism in the Indian and Slave Debates* (Cambridge, MA: Harvard University Press, 2005), 175; Staudenraus, *African Colonization*, 205–206; Marie Tyler-McGraw, *An African Republic: Black & White Virginians in the Making of Liberia* (Chapel Hill: University of North Carolina Press, 2007), 2.

16. See *Annual Reports of the American Colonization Society* 21 (1837): 21–23; 30 (1847): 22; 31 (1848): 8–9, 21; and 34 (1851): 40–41.

17. For an interesting discussion of the feasibility issue, see William W. Freehling, "'Absurd' Issues and the Cause of the Civil War: Colonization as a Test Case," in *The Reintegration of American History: Slavery and the Civil War* (New York: Oxford University Press, 1994), 138–157. But cf. Burin, *Peculiar Solution*, 20–21; Douglas R. Egerton, "Averting a Crisis: The Proslavery Critique of the American Colonization Society," *Civil War History* 43, no. 2 (June 1997): 151–152; Donald L. Robinson, *Slavery in the Structure of American Politics, 1765–1820* (New York: Harcourt Brace Jovanovich, 1971), 439–440.

18. See *Annual Reports of the American Colonization Society* 1 (1818): 10; 4 (1821): 24; 14 (1831): xxi; 15 (1832): 17–18; 19 (1835): 7–8; 26 (1843): 6 [Appendix]; 33 (1850): 16; 34 (1851): 39; 35 (1852): 14; and 43 (1860): 39.

19. Ibid., 24 (1841): 15; 26 (1843): 7, 10–11 [Appendix]; 27 (1844): 41–43; 30 (1847): 18–19; and 34 (1851): 39–43.

20. Ibid., 21 (1837): 22; 31 (1848): 21; and 34 (1851): 40–41.

21. Ibid., 14 (1831): 18; 21 (1837): 24; and 50 (1867): 28.

22. Mercer had retired from Congress in 1839.

23. I discuss the Kendall audit further below. At the time, Kendall was a member of Jackson's "Kitchen Cabinet." He later became postmaster general.

24. See *Annual Reports of the American Colonization Society* 36 (1853): 47–48. Mercer noted that the society had only $746 in cash at the time of its first expedition to Africa.

25. See Appendix B. I calculated the 1819–1861 receipts by subtracting the 1862–1866 receipts from the 1867 fiftieth anniversary total. See *Annual Reports of the American Colonization Society* 46 (1863): 52; 47 (1864): 18; 48 (1865): 27; 49 (1866): 25; and 50 (1867) 21, 24.

26. See Walter I. Trattner, "The Federal Government and Social Welfare in Early Nineteenth-Century America," in *Compassion and Responsibility: Readings in the History of Social Welfare Policy in the United States*, ed. Frank R. Breul and Steven J. Diner (Chicago: University of Chicago Press, 1980), 160. Congress supported a number of private organizations with land grants during this period. Trattner shows how sectionalism affected even this distributive process, with a land grant to the Kentucky Institution for the Tuition of the Deaf and Dumb in 1826 balancing the earlier Connecticut grant. See ibid., 163–164.

27. Yet it is important to distinguish the federal money spent on each purpose because the policies had very different consequences for state development. However imperfectly, I attempt that task in this and the preceding chapter.

28. See Brian Balogh, *A Government Out of Sight: The Mystery of National Authority in Nineteenth-Century America* (New York: Cambridge University Press, 2009), 146; Goodrich, *Government Promotion*, 6–7, 11–12, 287, 289–290, 292, 294.

29. Within the last seven years, five major studies of the African colonization movement have appeared: Burin, *Peculiar Solution;* Claude Andrew Gregg, *The Price of Liberty: African Americans and the Making of Liberia* (Chapel Hill: University of North Carolina Press, 2004); Portnoy, *Right to Speak;* Tyler-McGraw, *African Republic;* Allen Yarema, *The American Colonization Society: An Avenue to Freedom?* (Lanham, MD: University Press of America, 2006).

30. See Sherwood, "Formation," 227–228.

31. See *Annual Reports of the American Colonization Society* 2 (1819): 3; 6 (1823): 5; and 8 (1825): 5. Webster and the Marquis de Lafayette also became honorary vice presidents during the 1820s. Ibid., 6 (1823): 5; 8 (1825): 5.

32. Jackson resigned in 1822. It is not clear why Smith's name disappears from the list in 1819.

33. The others were scattered among the lower South (one from Georgia), the lower North (two from Pennsylvania and one from New York), and New England (one each from Connecticut and Massachusetts). Mercer's valedictory address chronicled the ACS's upper-South bias in contesting the Kennedy Report claim that the society was Northern in origin, largely based on the critical, intermediary role New Jersey Reverend Robert Finley had played in its founding. (I also discuss the Kennedy Report further below.) Mercer details the alternate role Virginia statesmen played in inspiring the colonization movement. In addition to his own role, he especially applauds the advocacy of two former Virginia governors and presidents, Thomas Jefferson and James Monroe. See *Annual Reports of the American Colonization Society* 36 (1853): 38–48. For further discussion of Mercer's role in founding the ACS and its upper-South bias, see Douglas R. Egerton, "'Its Origin Is Not a Little Curious': A New Look at the American Colonization Society," *Journal of the American Republic* 5, no. 4 (Winter 1985): 463–480; Egerton, "Averting a Crisis," 142–156.

34. In the 15th Congress (1817–1819), Democratic Republicans controlled 76 percent of the House seats. The second-party division was four Democrats and three Whigs.

35. See Burin, *Peculiar Solution*, 1, 33; Portnoy, *Right to Speak*, 4–6, 91–93, 97–98, 172–173; Staudenraus, *African Colonization*, vii–viii; Tyler-McGraw, *African Republic*, 1–2. Initially, the society's founders left open the colonial site, but they quickly agreed on a site on the west coast of Africa, near, but not too near, the British free-black colony of Sierra Leone.

36. See *Annual Reports of the American Colonization Society* 6 (1823): 23; 7 (1824): 70–71; and 10 (1827): 30.

37. Ibid., 1 (1818): 9; 10 (1827): 22, 78; 11 (1828): 20–21; 14 (1831): 22, 24 [Appendix]; 15 (1832): xii–xiii; 17 (1834): xxi; 18 (1835): 5; 21 (1837): 23; 31 (1848): 20; 34 (1851): 35, 37; and 36 (1853): 50–51.

38. Despite the spectrum of opinion on slavery within the society, a moderate "necessary evil" position seems to have been the dominant position, at least in its early years. See ibid., 14 (1831): 26–27; Burin, *Peculiar Solution*, 14, 22; Portnoy, *Right to Speak*, 102, 174–175; Staudenraus, *African Colonization*, vii; Tyler-McGraw, *African Republic*, 4. But cf. Egerton, "A Little Curious," 479–480.

39. See *Annual Reports of the American Colonization Society* 34 (1851): 38. This address was Clay's last presidential address. He died later that same year.

40. See Sherwood, "Formation," 223. For the controversy over Randolph's speech, see *Annual Reports of the American Colonization Society* 3 (1820): 21; and 14 (1831): 22.

41. See Sherwood, "Formation," 223.

42. Not all emancipators were European Americans. The society's fiftieth anniversary total included nine emigrants from Indian territory. See *Annual Reports of the American Colonization Society* 50 (1867): 64. The Cherokees even had their own auxiliary. See Theda Perdue, *Slavery and the Evolution of Cherokee Society, 1540–1866* (Knoxville: University of Tennessee Press, 1979), 92–94. In the case of liberated slaves and recaptured Africans, one might question the voluntariness of the choice. At the society's first anniversary meeting, Clay speculated that liberated slaves would be a prolific source of emigration precisely because they did not have much choice in the matter. See *Annual Reports of the American Colonization Society* 1 (1818): 10. Southern laws requiring liberated slaves to move out of state within a certain period of time after they had been liberated as well as barring them from moving into state if they had been liberated elsewhere narrowed their options. By the 1850s, all but three slave states (Arkansas, Delaware, and Missouri) had enacted such laws. Their options were further narrowed when many of the northwestern states, including Illinois, Indiana, Iowa, Michigan, and Oregon, also began enacting black exclusion laws. See ibid., 30 (1847): 10; 31 (1848): 9–10; 34 (1851): 11–16; 35 (1852): 13; 36 (1853): 49, 51–52; 43 (1860): 39; and 44 (1861): 30, 40–41; Ira Berlin, *Slaves without Masters: The Free Negro in the Antebellum South* (New York: New Press, 1992), 138, 138–139n2; Eugene H. Berwanger, *The Frontier against Slavery: Western Anti-Negro Prejudice and the Slavery Extension Controversy* (Urbana: University of Illinois Press, 1967), 43–51; Leon F. Litwack, *North of Slavery: The Negro in the Free States, 1790–1860* (Chicago: University of Chicago Press, 1961), 66–74. On the other hand, these laws were rarely enforced, slaves could, and did, choose to remain in slavery rather than emigrate, and even recaptured Africans had some choice in the matter, at least about whether to remain in Liberia or not.

43. See *Annual Reports of the American Colonization Society* 15 (1832): 17–18; 19 (1835): 7–8; 26 (1843): 14; 31 (1848): 9; 36 (1853): 21; and 41 (1858): 30; George M. Fredrickson, *The Black Image in the White Mind: The Debate on Afro-American Character and Destiny, 1817–1914* (1971; reprint, Middletown, CT: Wesleyan University Press, 1987), chap. 1.

44. See *Annals of Congress*, 14th Cong., 2nd Sess., 1817, 481–483; *Annual Reports of the American Colonization Society* 4 (1821): 23–30; 5 (1822): 41–48; and 10 (1827): 77–79; H. Doc. No. 277, 21st Cong., 1st Sess., 1830.

45. See *Statutes at Large* 3 (1819): 532–534. While the federal government continued to subsidize the ACS's African colonization project, Haiti and other colonization sites in the Western Hemisphere remained under both public and private consideration until at least the Emancipation Proclamation. Eric Burin claims that President Lincoln's recognition of Haiti and Liberia was associated with his search for alternative colonization sites. After the Emancipation Proclamation, he abandoned those efforts, though the Department of Interior continued to subsidize one Haitian colonization project into 1863. This project imploded in 1864, and the approximately 400 African American colonists returned to the United States. In the end, the Interior Department

spent only $37,391 of the $600,000 Congress had appropriated in 1862 for colonization purposes. See *Annual Reports of the American Colonization Society* 46 (1863): 15; Burin, *Peculiar Solution,* 162–163; S. Ex. Doc. No. 55, 39th Cong., 1st Sess., 1866, 2–3; Michael Vorenberg, "Abraham Lincoln and the Politics of Black Colonization," *Journal of the Abraham Lincoln Association* 14, no. 2 (Winter 1993): 23–46.

46. See *Annual Reports of the American Colonization Society* 2 (1819): 15; 3 (1820): 10–11, 15–16; 5 (1822): 103–109; 6 (1823): 12, 17; 11 (1828): 32–33; and 36 (1853): 45. According to the ACS, Alabama, Louisiana, and South Carolina had also sold recaptured Africans into slavery. Ibid., 3 (1820): 16; 36 (1853): 45.

47. See H. Rep. No. 101, 19th Cong., 2nd Sess., 1827, 4.

48. See *Annual Reports of the American Colonization Society* 36 (1853): 38; Caleb Perry Patterson, *The Negro in Tennessee, 1790–1865* (Austin: University of Texas Press, 1922), 95. Only a few ACS vice presidents ever took the step of formally resigning from what was, in most cases, a strictly honorary post. Thomas S. Grimké, a South Carolina state senator and brother of the soon-to-be-famous antislavery sisters, Sarah and Angelina, was apparently the only person to refuse the honor. See *Annual Reports of the American Colonization Society* 13 (1830): xv.

49. See *Annual Reports of the American Colonization Society* 11 (1828): 32; Burin, *Peculiar Solution,* 17.

50. See S. Rep. No. 178, 20th Cong., 1st Sess., 1828, 11, 14–15; quote at 11.

51. See H. Rep. No. 283, 27th Cong., 3rd Sess., 1843, 457, 462–463; quotes at 457. All emphases in these and subsequent quotes are in the original.

52. See *Annual Reports of the American Colonization Society* 16 (1833): 37; John R. Van Atta, "Western Lands and the Political Economy of Henry Clay's American System, 1819–1832," *Journal of the Early Republic* 21, no. 4 (Winter 2001): 633–665. Clay's bill listed African colonization as one of the three purposes for which states could use the money, along with education and internal improvements. In 1827, Maryland had become the first state to appropriate funds for African colonization. It later established its own separate colony at Cape Palmas. See *Annual Reports of the American Colonization Society* 11 (1828): 48, 78–79; and 17 (1834): 16–17; Penelope Campbell, *Maryland in Africa: The Maryland State Colonization Society, 1831–1857* (Urbana: University of Illinois Press, 1971), 11, 35–36, 53, 55.

53. See *Annual Reports of the American Colonization Society* 19 (1835): 7, 12–13; 20 (1836): 48; and 21 (1837): 35–36, 42. The society had last petitioned Congress in 1830. See H. Doc. No. 277, 21st Cong., 1st Sess., 1830.

54. See *Annual Reports of the American Colonization Society* 21 (1837): 19; Staudenraus, *African Colonization,* 187. The society had first asked for a federal charter in one of its early memorials to Congress. Ibid., 4 (1821): 29–30. Congress, however, had not acted on the request and the society was eventually chartered by the state of Maryland in 1831. Ibid., 16 (1833): 19. Two founders had succeeded Washington and preceded Clay as society presidents, Charles Carroll, the last living signer of the Declaration of Independence (1830–1832), and James Madison, the last living signer of the Constitution (1833–1836).

55. See *Register of Debates,* 24th Cong., 2nd Sess., 1837, 564–568, 636; quotes at 565, 567. A group of society members who lived in the nation's capital submitted the memorial.

56. See *Annual Reports of the American Colonization Society* 13 (1830): xvi; 17 (1834): xxvi; and 22 (1838): 32. Southard had also served as John Quincy Adams's Navy Secretary. On the Whig dominance of the society at this time, see Portnoy, *Right to Speak,* 18.

57. See *Annual Reports of the American Colonization Society* 15 (1832): xx. Webster was the exception. He remained a vice president, but he did not become active in the society until the last

two years of his life, following his famous "Seventh of March" speech in support of the Compromise of 1850, which included an endorsement of colonization. Ibid., 34 (1851): 19–20; 35 (1852): 26–27; Charles M. Wiltse, ed., *The Papers of Daniel Webster: Speeches and Formal Writings* (Hanover, NH: University Press of New England, 1988), 2:550 ("The Constitution and the Union," March 7, 1850).

58. See Portnoy, *Right to Speak*, 100, 165–186. Benjamin Lundy would be included in this group except for the fact that he remained a colonizationist until his death in 1837.

59. See William Lloyd Garrison, *Thoughts on African Colonization* (1832; reprint, New York: Arno Press, 1968).

60. See William Jay, *An Inquiry into the Character and Tendency of the American Colonization and American Anti-Slavery Societies* (1835; reprint, New York: Negro Universities Press, 1969); *Debate at the Lane Seminary, Cincinnati, Speech of James A. Thome, of Kentucky, delivered at the Annual Meeting of the American Anti-Slavery Society, May 6, 1834, Letter of the Rev. Dr. Samuel H. Cox against the American Colonization Society* (Boston: Garrison & Knapp, 1834).

61. See Portnoy, *Right to Speak*, 100, 169–170, 173–178, 183–186.

62. See *Annual Reports of the American Colonization Society* 11 (1828): 47; 12 (1829): xii, 23–24, 69; 14 (1831): iii; 15 (1832): xxx; 17 (1834): iii, vi–x; and 19 (1835): 10; Portnoy, *Right to Speak*, 170–172, 174, 184.

63. The state legislature funded this commitment during its next session but, to punctuate the lack of antislavery intent, restricted the use of the money to colonizing Virginia blacks who were already free. As a result, most of the money went unspent. In 1850, the state legislature placed a $1 tax on free blacks to fund a new colonization initiative; again with relatively meager results. See *Annual Reports of the American Colonization Society* 21 (1837): 15; 22 (1838): 6–7; and 34 (1851): 9–10; Tyler-McGraw, *African Republic*, 47, 57.

64. See Thomas R. Dew, *Review of the Debate in the Virginia Legislature of 1831 and 1832* (1832; reprint, Westport, CT: Negro Universities Press, 1970). For further discussion of this policy episode, see David F. Ericson, *The Debate over Slavery: Antislavery and Proslavery Liberalism in Antebellum America* (New York: New York University Press, 2001), chap. 5; Alison Goodyear Freehling, *Drift toward Dissolution: The Virginia Slavery Debate of 1831–1832* (Baton Rouge: Louisiana State University Press, 1982).

65. See *Annual Reports of the American Colonization Society* 12 (1830): x; 19 (1836): 10; 21 (1837): 23; 31 (1848): 21; and 33 (1850): 16. See also ibid., 10 (1827): 14 [Key]; 11 (1828): 19 [Key]; 12 (1829): v–vi [Mercer]; 13 (1830): xii [Frelinghuysen]; 26 (1853): 38 [Mercer].

66. See *Annual Reports of the American Colonization Society* 21 (1837): 17. On this dilemma, see Burin, *Peculiar Solution*, 33; Portnoy, *Right to Speak*, 100–101; Staudenraus, *African Colonization*, 205–206; Tyler-McGraw, *African Republic*, 27, 53.

67. See Portnoy, *Right to Speak*, 100, 174.

68. See David Walker, *David Walker's Appeal, in four articles, together with a preamble, to the coloured citizens of the world, but in particular, and very expressly, to those of the United States of America* (1829; reprint, New York: Hill and Wang, 1995).

69. Marie Tyler-McGraw stresses the importance of eyewitness accounts in dissuading Virginia blacks from emigrating to Liberia. See Tyler-McGraw, *African Republic*, 65–66. The ACS attempted to counter the negative eyewitness reports with its own positive ones. It responded to the high mortality rates among the colonists by insisting that all colonial enterprises, including Jamestown and Plymouth, experienced high mortality rates in their initial stages. It also blamed many of the colonists' deaths on their own improvidence rather than their lack of immunity to tropical diseases. See *Annual Reports of the American Colonization Society* 7 (1824): 22; 9: (1826):

23; 13 (1830): 7; 15 (1832): 3; 17 (1834): 4–5; 31 (1848): 23–24; and 34 (1851): 42. For a critical assessment of the latter claim, see Tom W. Shick, "A Quantitative Analysis of Liberian Colonization from 1820 to 1843 with Special Reference to Mortality," *Journal of African History* 12, no. 1 (1971): 45–59.

70. Crummell was the only one of the three who supported the ACS's colonization efforts; the others preferred to establish independent African American colonies. See Burin, *Peculiar Solution*, 30, 160; Tyler-McGraw, *African Republic*, 20, 24, 26–27, 166–167; Staudenraus, *African Colonization*, 9–11, 19, 34, 244. Cuffee had died in 1817, soon after the formation of the ACS.

71. See *Annual Reports of the American Colonization Society* 17 (1834): viii–ix; 30 (1847): 6, 8–10, 12–13; Burin, *Peculiar Solution*, 83–84; Staudenraus, *African Colonization*, 188–189; Tyler-McGraw, *African Republic*, 73, 81.

72. One of the reasons that the Lincoln administration's colonization efforts foundered was the stiff resistance of many African American leaders. See Burin, *Peculiar Solution*, 165; Staudenraus, *African Colonization*, 247–248; Tyler-McGraw, *African Republic*, 172; Vorenberg, "Abraham Lincoln and Colonization," 43.

73. See *Annual Reports of the American Colonization Society* 20 (1836): 8; Burin, *Peculiar Solution*, 61–62. Burin also details how jurists in several Southern states, including Alabama, Georgia, and Virginia, attempted to foreclose even this option by refusing to accept testamentary emigration bequests. Ibid., 137–138.

74. See Burin, *Peculiar Solution*, 24; Portnoy, *Right to Speak*, 102; Staudenraus, *African Colonization*, 187, 224–227, 236–237; Tyler-McGraw, *African Republic*, 53–54.

75. See *Annual Reports of the American Colonization Society* 17 (1834): xvi–xvii, xxiii, 12, 17, 36, 26–47; 18 (1835): 11, 21; and 22 (1838): 4–5. The society felt that it had to colonize slaves who had been promised emancipation on condition of emigration or else they risked remaining in slavery. Almost all of its colonists during the late 1830s and early 1840s were liberated slaves. The society also attempted to enforce a policy of colonizing only free African Americans who could pay their own emigration expenses, but few potential emigrants fit this category. Ibid., 25 (1842): 9, 16; Burin, *Peculiar Solution*, 25–26; Tyler-McGraw, *African Republic*, 73, 128.

76. The ACS was part of the "benevolent empire." Clergy represented a substantial portion of its membership, which overlapped with that of other "benevolent empire" organizations, such as the American Bible Society, American Education Society, American Board of Commissioners for Foreign Missions, and the American Temperance Society. See Burin, *Peculiar Solution*, 16; Peter Duignan and Clarence Clendenen, *The United States and the African Slave Trade, 1619–1862* (1963; reprint, Westport, CT: Greenwood Press, 1978), 58; Joseph L. Grabill, "The 'Invisible' Missionary: A Study in American Foreign Relations," *Journal of Church and State* 14, no. 1 (Winter 1972): 99–100; Portnoy, *Right to Speak*, 18, 22–24; Staudenraus, *African Colonization*, 15–22; Tyler-McGraw, *African Republic*, 3.

77. See Staudenraus, *African Colonization*, 178, 186.

78. In defense of the [Dorthea] Dix Bill (1854), which would have granted ten million acres of public lands to the states to aid the mentally ill, Senator Solomon Foot (Vermont Whig) reviewed the social assistance that the federal government had provided during the first sixty years of its existence. See *Congressional Globe*, 33rd Cong., 1st Sess., 1854, 456, 550–551. Foot's review shows a clear break with the Jackson administration. For example, both federal land grants to eleemosynary institutions occurred during the Monroe and Adams administrations. Characteristically, the Dix bill passed Congress only to be vetoed by a Democratic president, Franklin Pierce. For a somewhat different perspective on this policy episode, see Michele Landis Dauber, "The Sympathetic State," *Law and History Review* 23, no. 2 (Summer 2005): 387–442.

79. Actually, as we will see shortly, these two roles were initially held by different people. The ACS established a local assembly in 1825 in response to a strike among the colonists against its colonial agent. See *Annual Reports of the American Colonization Society* 9 (1826): 15–16; Staudenraus, *African Colonization*, 91–92, 95–96.

80. See "Letter from Treasury Department," December 1, 1843; Box 622; SG–Illegal Service, including blockade running, piracy, smuggling, and filibustering; Subject File, U.S. Navy, 1775–1901; 0–1910; Office of Naval Records and Library, Record Group 45; National Archives, Washington, DC. In 1834, the federal government reduced its contribution to $1,000, and the ACS raised its contribution to $1,400. See *Annual Reports of the American Colonization Society* 17 (1834): 23; Staudenraus, *African Colonization*, 186. The Treasury Department letter, however, states that Thomas Buchanan's annual (federal) salary was $1,500 at the time of his death in September 1841.

81. See *Annual Reports of the American Colonization Society* 26 (1843): 10. Buchanan had added the formal title of governor in 1839 so that Roberts also became the first black governor of Liberia. In 1847, he then became the first president of an independent Liberia. Ibid., 23 (1840): 3; and 31 (1848): 46. Several other colonists had temporarily been appointed agents following the deaths of colonial agents.

82. Ibid., 26 (1843): 9–12 [Appendix]. This memorial also urges the federal government to reappoint a colonial agent.

83. Hence, the ACS retained a colonial agent in Liberia and a building to temporarily house "its" emigrants. Ibid., 29 (1846): 39; 31 (1848): 19; and 32 (1849): 12.

84. Ibid., 4 (1821): 7–13; Staudenraus, *African Colonization*, 59–62. The death of colonial agents was a perennial problem for the ACS and federal government. For the society, the problem was evidence for the argument that Africa was the natural home of African Americans but fatal to European Americans. (As already noted, it somewhat callously discounted the deaths of colonists as, in many cases, the results of their own improvidence.) The society thus concluded that European Americans could not displace either Africans or African Americans in Africa in the same way that they were displacing Native Americans in North America. See ibid., 34 (1851): 42–43; 36 (1853): 26–27; 45 (1862): 24; and 48 (1865): 30–31.

85. Ibid., 5 (1822): 15; Staudenraus, *African Colonization*, 62. Four colonists died on this second expedition.

86. By the time Ayres arrived in Sierra Leone, two of the four colonial agents who were already in the colony had died and illness had forced a third to sail back to the United States. See *Annual Reports of the American Colonization Society* 5 (1822): 13–14; Staudenraus, *African Colonization*, 62. An older Matthew Perry was the first African Squadron commander.

87. See *Annual Reports of the American Colonization Society* 5 (1822): 8–17, 64–66; Staudenraus, *African Colonization*, 63–65.

88. See *Annual Reports of the American Colonization Society* 6 (1823): 25; 7 (1824): 12, 26–27; 8 (1825): 32; 9 (1826): 50; 10 (1827): 53; and 11 (1828): 38; S. Doc. 3, 20th Cong., 1st Sess., 1827, 10–29; S. Doc. No. 1, 20th Cong., 2nd Sess., 1828, 139–40; "Letter from Treasury Department," December 1, 1843; Record Group 45; National Archives. As the preceding chapter shows, this presence also enabled navy vessels to capture a number of suspected slave ships.

89. See *Annual Reports of the American Colonization Society* 13 (1830): 13.

90. Ashmun was the first joint colonial agent. He was also the target of the 1823–1824 strike.

91. Ibid., 7 (1824): 19–20; Staudenraus, *African Colonization*, 89–90.

92. See *Annual Reports of the American Colonization Society* 7 (1824): 26–27; H. Doc. No. 193, 20th Cong., 1st Sess. (1828), 7, 11.

93. See *Annual Reports of the American Colonization Society* 26 (1843): 7, 28; and 45 (1862): 6.

94. On the squadron's multiple missions, see ibid., 26 (1843): 28–30.

95. Ibid., 23 (1840): 3–4; and 24 (1841): 7.

96. Ibid., 27 (1844): 34.

97. Ibid., 22 (1838): 3.

98. Ibid., 50 (1867): 6.

99. Ibid., 23 (1843): 6–12 [Appendix].

100. See H. R. Doc. No. 162, 28th Cong., 1st Sess. (1844); "Letter from Treasury Department," December 1, 1843; Record Group 45; National Archives.

101. The Kennedy report was also a response to a memorial from a colonization convention held the previous May in Washington. See *Annual Reports of the American Colonization Society* 26 (1843): 18–20.

102. By 1843, two state governments had funded colonization endeavors—Maryland and Virginia—and four state auxiliaries had established their own separate settlements or colonies—Maryland, Mississippi, New York, and Pennsylvania. Ibid., 34 (1851): 82. The New York and Pennsylvania societies had organized a joint settlement at Bassa Cove. The Mississippi society had founded a settlement at Sinoe. The Louisiana auxiliary later collaborated on the Sinoe venture.

103. See H. Rep. No. 283, 27th Cong., 3rd Sess., 1843, 4–7; quotes at 5, 6. The Tazewell report also analogizes Native American removal and African colonization but distinguishes them on the grounds that the latter involves foreign territory. See S. Rep. No. 178, 20th Cong., 1st Sess., 1828, 6.

104. See *Annual Reports of the American Colonization Society* 34 (1851): 27, 31, 69–71; 35 (1852): 31; 36 (1853): 17; 37 (1854): 11–12, 19; 38 (1855): 43, 49; 42 (1859): 51; 43 (1860): 12, 50; 44 (1861): 21, 44; and 45 (1862): 7, 15, 26. Great Britain recognized Liberian independence in 1848, though it contested the new nation's ability to establish its own tariff rates on the grounds that the United States still treated it as a colony. This dispute had actually preceded Liberia's declaration of independence. It was finally resolved in 1852. Ibid., 29 (1846): 25–33; and 36 (1853): 8.

105. Ibid., 23 (1840): 9–10; 31 (1848): 17–18; 32 (1849): 21.

106. Ibid., 34 (1851): 8, 34, 84; Burin, *Peculiar Solution,* 29–30; Staudenraus, *African Colonization,* 243–245; Tyler-McGraw, *African Republic,* 79, 128.

107. See *Annual Reports of the American Colonization Society* 35 (1852): 6; and 37 (1854): 4; Burin, *Peculiar Solution,* 29; Staudenraus, *African Colonization,* 242–243.

108. See Staudenraus, *African Colonization,* 245. These distinguished attendees all were or were to become ACS vice presidents, except for Fillmore, who became a life director in 1853. See *Annual Reports of the American Colonization Society* 32 (1849): 20; 36 (1853): 15; 35 (1852): 30; and 37 (1854): 15–16. Fillmore inserted an endorsement of African colonization in his 1852 annual message to Congress but at the last minute deleted the passage on the advice of his cabinet. See Burin, *Peculiar Solution,* 28.

109. Corwin had been an ACS vice president since 1848; Crittenden became one in 1854. See *Annual Reports of the American Colonization Society* 31 (1848): 28; and 37 (1854): 15.

110. Ibid., 36 (1853): 12–13.

111. Ibid., 20 (1836): 60; and 38 (1855): 39.

112. Ibid., 34 (1851): 84; 35 (1852): 52; 36 (1853): 5; 37 (1854): 8. Revenues did not, however, rise as quickly as emigrant applications, and the society soon had to again begin refusing emigrants. Ibid., 38 (1855): 4; and 39 (1856): 5.

113. Ibid., 36 (1853): 9–10, 18; 39 (1856): 6; and 40 (1857): 8, 32. Maryland and Virginia were the early exceptions.

114. Wayne does not refer to the "general welfare" language of the preamble because he claims to be a strict constructionist. Ibid., 37 (1854): 40–41. This claim seems somewhat incongruous with the general tenor of a speech that advocates federal support for a private organization pursuing an overseas colonization project.

115. Ibid., 37 (1854): 38–41; quote at 40. Interestingly, at the 1851 annual meeting, Congressman and ACS Vice President Frederick P. Stanton (Tennessee Democrat) had delivered a constitutional defense of African colonization in which he referred to two other constitutional warrants for the enterprise. He invoked the fugitive-slave clause under the logic that removing free blacks made enforcement of fugitive-slave laws easier and the domestic-violence clause under the logic that free blacks were the most likely source of such violence. Ibid., 34 (1851): 65.

116. Ibid., 26 (1843): 15–17; H. Rep. No. 469, 28th Cong., 1st Sess., 1844.

117. See *Annual Reports of the American Colonization Society* 45 (1862): 15–18.

118. Ibid., 32 (1849): 15; and 46 (1863): 7, 12.

119. On U.S. relations with Haiti, see Gordon S. Brown, *Toussaint's Clause: The Founding Fathers and the Haitian Revolution* (Jackson: University Press of Mississippi, 2005); Don E. Fehrenbacher, *The Slaveholding Republic: An Account of the United States Government's Relations to Slavery* (New York: Oxford University Press, 2001), 111–118; Tim Matthewson, *A Proslavery Foreign Policy: Haitian-American Relations during the Early Republic* (Westport, CT: Praeger, 2003); Robinson, *Slavery in American Politics,* 361–376.

120. See *Annual Reports of the American Colonization Society* 36 (1853): 8. Eventually, the society ceased appealing for U.S. recognition of Liberia and instead appealed to President Buchanan to at least grant it special trading privileges. Buchanan's "Catch-22" reply was that he could not grant the latter without the former. Ibid., 38 (1855): 16; 40 (1857): 27; 42 (1859): 51; 43 (1860): 12, 50; and 44 (1861): 21, 44.

121. Ibid., 35 (1852): 35.

122. Ibid., 38 (1855): 42. The resolution established a process by which a vote of the membership could overrule the board's decision.

123. Ibid., 38 (1855): 26–27; Burin, *Peculiar Solution,* 31.

124. The chronology in this section overlaps the chronology of the last chapter, but here the focus is African colonization rather than slave-trade suppression.

125. See Willis D. Boyd, "The American Colonization Society and the Slave Recaptives of 1860–1861: An Early Example of United States-African Relations," *Journal of Negro History* 47, no. 2 (April 1962): 125.

126. See H. Rep. No. 283, 27th Cong., 3rd Sess., 1843, 463. In his report on the audit, Kendall mentions only a few examples of federal expenditures on African colonization.

127. See Judd Scott Harmon, "Suppress and Protest: The United States Navy, the African Slave Trade, and Maritime Commerce, 1794–1862" (Ph.D. diss., College of William and Mary, 1977), 239 (Appendix E).

128. See *Annual Reports of the American Colonization Society* 19 (1835): 16, 28.

129. Ibid., 20 (1836): 5, 33.

130. Ibid., 30 (1847): 35, 38; 31 (1848): 13–14; 32 (1849): 11; and 35 (1852): 6–7, 36. The ACS received one in-kind shipment of supplies for the *Pons* captives. Ibid., 30 (1847): 6.

131. Ibid., 41 (1858): 19.

132. Ibid., 41 (1858): 47. The last year that there was a broad-based geographic representation of state auxiliaries at the society's annual meeting was 1855, when thirteen states were represented, including Virginia, Georgia, Mississippi, Missouri, and Louisiana. Ibid., 38 (1855): 13–15. By 1860, only four Northern states were represented, a situation which, not surprisingly,

continued through the Civil War and into Reconstruction. Ibid., 43 (1860): 36; 44 (1861): 36; 45 (1862): 37; 46 (1863): 40; 47 (1864): 47–48; 48 (1865): 43; 49 (1866): 49; and 50 (1867): 45–46. Burin argues that the Northern membership seized control of the society when it was reorganized in 1838 to provide the predominantly Northern auxiliaries with more power, but that timing seems premature. See Burin, *Peculiar Solution*, 24.

133. See *Annual Reports of the American Colonization Society* 40 (1857): 8.

134. See Tyler-McGraw, *African Republic*, 128–129.

135. See *Annual Reports of the American Colonization Society* 43 (1860): 45.

136. Ibid., 42 (1859): 18–20, 46. Seys's appointment resurrected the colonial agent's dual role.

137. The ACS had urged Buchanan to take this step. Ibid., 41 (1858): 27; 42 (1859): 39.

138. Ibid., 42 (1859): 42.

139. Ibid., 44 (1861): 16; and 45 (1862): 9; Warren S. Howard, *American Slavers and the Federal Law, 1837–1862* (1963; reprint, Westport, CT: Greenwood, 1976), 220–223 (Appendix A). Again, the exact number is unknown.

140. The Liberian government also justified the contract transfer on grounds of national sovereignty. See Karen Fisher Younger, "Liberia and the Last Slave Ships," *Civil War History* 54, no. 4 (December 2008): 436. The ACS denied the profitability of the contracts, claiming that its costs were higher than even the $150 per capita in the initial agreement with Buchanan. See *Annual Reports of the American Colonization Society* 42 (1861): 18. But cf. Burin, *Peculiar Solution*, 32.

141. See *Annual Reports of the American Colonization Society* 44 (1861): 12–15, 47–48; and 45 (1862): 46. This new arrangement substantially delayed the reimbursement process. The last federal payment to the ACS was in 1865, and the last ACS payment to the Liberian government was in 1868. Ibid., 49 (1866): 6, 25; 52 (1869): 20.

142. See W. D. Boyd, "Slave Recaptives," 119.

143. The numbers were so large that the Liberian government worried about its ability to absorb all its new residents. See *Annual Reports of the American Colonization Society* 44 (1861): 12, 15–16.

144. The federal government paid for the temporary shelters that were built on Key West to house these recaptured Africans; for their food, clothing, and medical care in their temporary quarters; and for chartering ships to transport them to Liberia. Ibid., 44 (1861): 11; S. Ex. Doc. No. 1, 36th Cong., 2nd Sess., 1860, 42. U.S. Marshal Fernando Moreno received at least $27,651 for their care, including $5,499 in doctor fees, and claimed that he was owed much more. See H. R. Ex. Doc. No. 7, 36th Cong., 2nd Sess., 1860, 647; S. Ex. Doc. No. 1, 36th Cong., 2nd Sess., 1860, 42; "US Marshal Fernando Moreno (southern district of Florida) to Secretary of Interior [Jacob] Thompson," May 5, 1860, to December 16, 1860 [inclusive], (National Archives Microfilm Publication M160, roll 6); Letters Received, September 8, 1858–February 1, 1872; Records of the Office of the Secretary of the Interior Relating to the Suppression of the African Slave Trade and Negro Colonization, 1854–1872; Record Group 48; National Archives, College Park, MD; Younger, "Last Slave Ships," 433. Willis Boyd contends that the problems associated with the Key West Africans motivated the Lincoln administration's search for alternative colonization sites in the Western Hemisphere. See *Annual Reports of the American Colonization Society* 44 (1861): 41; and 45 (1862): 16, 18, 23–24; W. D. Boyd, "Slave Recaptives," 126.

145. See *Statutes at Large* 11 (1859): 404. This appropriation included another $45,000 for the African Squadron.

146. Ibid., 12 (1860): 40–41.

147. See H. Rep. No. 602, 36th Cong., 1st Sess., 1860.

148. See *Statutes at Large* 12 (1861): 132, 219.

149. In addition, a "large balance" was returned to the treasury. See Secretary of Interior [John Palmer] Usher to Thaddeus Stevens, chair House Ways and Means Committee," February 9, 1863; M160, roll 1, 201; Record Group 48; National Archives.

150. The deaths of the recaptured Africans were at least in part due to the gross negligence of ACS and federal officials. Many of the *Echo* and Key West Africans died before they were even transported to Liberia because of their weakened state at the time of capture and the less-than-ideal conditions in Charleston and on Key West. The conditions on the first of two ships that the ACS chartered to transport the Key West Africans to Liberia were not much better than on a slave ship. In the case of the *Echo* Africans, the federal government chartered the ship and bears at least partial responsibility for their deaths. See *Annual Reports of the American Colonization Society* 42 (1859): 19; and 44 (1861): 11; W. D. Boyd, "Slave Recaptives," 114–116.

151. See *Annual Reports of the American Colonization Society* 44 (1861): 16; Howard, *American Slavers*, 220–223.

152. See *The Records of the American Colonization Society*, ser. 4, *Financial Papers, 1818–1963* (Washington, DC: Library of Congress), Ledger G (1859–1876), roll 276, 74, 77. The society received more than $30,000 for the *Echo* Africans probably because of the uncertainty over how many actually survived. For some unknown reason, it only received $15.50 for the transportation and care of the three *W. R. Kibby* children. See ACS, *Records*, Ledger G, roll 276, 77. (This figure may have been a transcription error.) My calculations ignore the complication that the federal contract provided for the ACS to receive $50, not $100, for children. It is not clear that navy personnel or any other party kept such a tally except in the case of the *W. R. Kibby*. The deaths or disappearances of recaptured Africans during their first year in Liberia may also account for the apparent shortfall. At $380,000, the ACS would have received $9,500 in transfer fees.

153. See *The Records of the American Colonization Society*, Ledger G, roll 276, 74, 77. As noted above, I could not track the amount of federal money that the ACS received in FY1859–FY1861 because the society reported its receipts in calendar years.

154. I calculated the 1859–1861 total by adding the receipts for those years from the ACS's annual budget reports. See *Annual Reports of the American Colonization Society* 43 (1860): 51; 44 (1861): 50; and 45 (1862): 59.

155. See *Annual Reports of the American Colonization Society* 50 (1867): 64. The society reported three other categories of emigrants, 68 status unknown, 346 from Barbados (who emigrated as a group during the Civil War), and 753 freedmen (who had been, in one way or another, freed during the war and thereafter immigrated to Liberia). As already mentioned, ACS officials were extremely disappointed with the low number in the latter category because they had expected the abolition of slavery to spark a dramatic increase in emigrants. See *Annual Reports of the American Colonization Society* 48 (1865): 18, 25, 33–34; 49 (1866): 14–15; and 50 (1867): 12–13, 51.

156. Another factor that delayed the reimbursement process was the great caution Seys exercised in certifying the adequacy of the care of the recaptured Africans in Liberia. See *Annual Reports of the American Colonization Society* 46 (1863): 49; Boyd, "Slave Recaptives," 117, 120.

157. The 1820 census reports 233,634 free blacks and 1,538,022 slaves out of a total population of 9,638,453. See Campbell Gibson and Kay Jung, "Historical Census Statistics on Population Totals by Race, 1790 to 1990, and by Hispanic Origin, 1970 to 1990, for the United States, Regions, Divisions, and States" (Washington, DC: U.S. Census Bureau, 2002), Table 1, http://www.census .gov/population/www/documentation/twps0056/twps0056.html. On the relatively low proportion of freed slaves in the American case, see Orlando Patterson, *Slavery and Social Death: A Comparative Study* (Cambridge, MA: Harvard University Press, 1982), 257–261.

158. See *Annual Reports of the American Colonization Society* 11 (1828): 54–58.

159. Ibid., 20 (1836): 54–59; 23 (1840): 35.

160. Ibid., 31 (1848): 45–53. The society, of course, celebrated this similarity. Ibid., 31 (1848): 7. It was under the colony's federal structure that the separate settlements had been incorporated into Liberia. Eventually, in 1857, the independent Maryland colony at Cape Palmas was incorporated into Liberia under the nation's federal structure. Ibid., 21 (1837): 16; 41 (1858): 18.

161. Ibid., 7 (1825): 16.

162. On this paternal model and the evolution of territorial governance in the United States, see Jack E. Eblen, *The First and Second United States Empires: Governors and Territorial Government, 1784–1912* (Pittsburgh: University of Pittsburgh Press, 1968).

163. Tom Shick compares Liberia to the Dutch colonization of South Africa in these terms, though he discounts the extent to which Liberian colonization was also a mixed enterprise. See Tom W. Shick, *Behold the Promised Land: A History of Afro-American Settler Society in Nineteenth Century Liberia* (Baltimore: Johns Hopkins University Press, 1977), 136. Cf. Balogh, *Government Out of Sight*, 146; Fehrenbacher, *Slaveholding Republic*, 154; Staudenraus, *African Colonization*, 57; Younger, "Last Slave Ships," 441.

164. See Younger, "Last Slave Ships," 427–428, 441.

165. See *Annual Reports of the American Colonization Society* 34 (1851): 41–42.

166. On the Liberia-Hawaii comparison, see Grabill, "Invisible Missionary," 100–103.

167. See S. Rep. No. 178, 20th Cong., 1st Sess., 1828, 11.

168. See Fredrickson, *Black Image*, 3, 20; Rogers M. Smith, *Civic Ideals: Conflicting Visions of Citizenship in U.S. History* (New Haven, CT: Yale University Press, 1997), 169.

169. See Younger, "Last Slave Ships," 439. According to Younger, the recaptured Africans had been apprenticed to host families in Liberia to help acculturate them to their new environment, but many families treated them more like slaves than apprentices. In one early case involving a Colombian privateer, the federal government had allowed the recaptured Africans to decide their own fates. One of them chose to remain in the United States, three disappeared, and ten others agreed to be transported to Liberia with the understanding that they would be able to return to their native land. See *Annual Reports of the American Colonization Society* 7 (1824): 117–118; Bruce L. Mouser, "Baltimore's African Experiment, 1822–1827," *Journal of Negro History* 80, no. 3 (Summer 1995): 120; Younger, "Last Slave Ships," 429n11. (Younger reports the number transported to Liberia as 1,110; I assume this is a typographical error.) African American émigrés also could and did return to the United States. See Tyler-McGraw, *African Republic*, 140–141.

CHAPTER 4. THE SLAVE-CATCHING REPUBLIC

1. See Stanley W. Campbell, *The Slave Catchers: Enforcement of the Fugitive Slave Law, 1850–1860* (Chapel Hill: University of North Carolina Press, 1968); Thomas D. Morris, *Free Men All: The Personal Liberty Laws of the North, 1780–1861* (Baltimore: Johns Hopkins University Press, 1974); Karen Orren, "'A War between Officers': The Enforcement of Slavery in the Northern United States, and of the Republic for Which It Stands, before the Civil War," *Studies in American Political Development* 12, no. 2 (Fall 1998): 343–382. This is not to say that each of these works is not very successful in doing what it attempts to do.

2. See Clarence Edwin Carter, ed., *The Territorial Papers of the United States* (Washington, DC: Government Printing Office, 1934–1969), 22:465 (John Bell, acting Indian agent, to Thomas Metcalfe, Kentucky congressman, n.d. [1822]). Like other Native American nations, the five

"civilized" nations had long been slaveholding nations, but over time they, in particular, became more like European American slaveholding nations. Their slave populations became more African American and less Native American, and the nations developed more plantation-style slavery. While significant differences remained between their slaveholding practices and European American slaveholding practices, the gap between them narrowed over time. See Donna L. Akers, *Living in the Land of Death: The Choctaw Nation, 1830–1860* (East Lansing: Michigan State University Press, 2004), 118, 127, 140–142; James R. Atkinson, *Splendid Land, Splendid People: The Chickasaw Indians to Removal* (Tuscaloosa: University of Alabama Press, 2004), 23–24; Renate Bertl, "Native American Tribes and Their African Slaves," in *Slave Cultures and the Cultures of Slavery*, ed. Stephan Palmié (Knoxville: University of Tennessee Press, 1995), 164–165; Kathryn E. Holland Braund, "The Creek Indians, Blacks, and Slavery," *Journal of Southern History* 57, no. 1 (November 1991): 624, 626–630; James Taylor Carson, *Searching for the Bright Path: The Mississippi Choctaws from Prehistory to Removal* (Lincoln: University of Nebraska Press, 1999), 81; Wyatt F. Jeltz, "The Relations of Negroes and Choctaw and Chickasaw Indians," *Journal of Negro History* 33, no. 1 (January 1948): 30–31; William G. McLoughlin, *Cherokee Renascence in the New Republic* (Princeton, NJ: Princeton University Press, 1986), xix, 337, 342–343; William G. McLoughlin, "Red Indians, Black Slavery and White Racism: America's Slaveholding Indians," *American Quarterly* 26, no. 4 (December 1974): 370; Kevin Mulroy, *Freedom on the Border: The Seminole Maroons in Florida, the Indian Territory, Coahuila, and Texas* (Lubbock: Texas Tech University Press, 1993), 1–2, 7–8, 17–18; Greg O'Brien, *Choctaws in a Revolutionary Age, 1750–1830* (Lincoln: University of Nebraska Press, 2002), 105; Theda Perdue, *Slavery and the Evolution of Cherokee Society, 1540–1866* (Knoxville: University of Tennessee Press, 1979), 50, 56–60, 68–72; Larry Eugene Rivers, *Slavery in Florida: Territorial Days to Emancipation* (Gainesville: University Press of Florida, 2000), 190, 193–195; Claudio Saunt, *A New Order of Things: Property, Power, and the Transformation of the Creek Indians, 1733–1816* (Cambridge: Cambridge University Press, 1999), 120–121, 124, 134; Fay A. Yarbrough, *Race and the Cherokee Nation: Sovereignty in the Nineteenth Century* (Philadelphia: University of Pennsylvania Press, 2008), 4, 116, 118.

3. See Frederick S. Calhoun, *The Lawmen: United States Marshals and Their Deputies, 1789–1989* (Washington, DC: Smithsonian Institution Press, 1990), 55. This policy area is another good example of an intercurrence because some authority over U.S. marshals not only continued to reside with the Department of State but also with the Departments of Interior and Treasury.

4. See Robert H. Baker, *The Rescue of Joshua Glover: A Fugitive Slave, the Constitution, and the Coming of the Civil War* (Athens: Ohio University Press, 2006), 234n15; Don E. Fehrenbacher, *The Slaveholding Republic: An Account of the United States Government's Relations to Slavery* (New York: Oxford University Press, 2001), 226; Paul Finkelman, "The Treason Trial of Castner Hanway," in *American Political Trials*, ed. Michael R. Belknap (Westport, CT: Greenwood, 1981), 81; Robert J. Kaczorowski, "The Inverted Constitution: Enforcing Constitutional Rights in the Nineteenth Century," in *Constitutionalism and American Culture: Writing the New Constitutional History*, ed. Sandra F. VanBurkleo, Kermit Hall, and Robert J. Kaczorowski (Lawrence: University Press of Kansas, 2002), 35; Karen Orren, "War between Officers," 348; Karen Orren and Stephen Skowronek, *The Search for American Political Development* (Cambridge: Cambridge University Press, 2004), 135.

5. Indian affairs were foreign relations in the early republic.

6. Quantitative analyses of the secession votes in the three Southern states—Tennessee, Texas, and Virginia—that held popular referenda on secession found the strongest support for secession in the counties with the highest percentage of slaveholders. See Dale Baum, *The Shattering of Texas Unionism: Politics in the Lone Star State during the Civil War Era* (Baton Rouge:

Louisiana State University Press, 1998), 50 (Table 11), 52; Daniel W. Crofts, *Reluctant Confederates: Upper South Unionists in the Secession Crisis* (Chapel Hill: University of North Carolina Press, 1989), 361–366 (Appendix I). This generalization was also true of the delegates to the Southern secession conventions. See Ralph A. Wooster, *The Secession Conventions of the South* (Princeton, NJ: Princeton University Press, 1962), 261 (Table 67), 262 (Table 68), 265 (Tables 69–70).

7. For obvious reasons, fugitive slaves disproportionately escaped from upper-South as opposed to lower-South states. This difference was an important dimension in the Senate debate over the proposed fugitive-slave law of 1850 but, in the end, Southern senators united behind the bill. See *Congressional Globe*, 31st Cong., 1st Sess., 1850, 1583–1584, 1591–1592, 1598, 1600–1604, 1613–1614. Jeffrey Hummel and Barry Weingast speculate that over time this difference could have created a divided South, where the hold of slavery had become very tenuous in the upper South. See Jeffrey Rogers Hummel and Barry R. Weingast, "The Fugitive Slave Act of 1850: An Instrumental Interpretation," in *Party, Process, and Political Change in Congress*, vol. 2, *Further New Perspectives on the History of Congress*, ed. David W. Brady and Matthew D. McCubbins (Stanford, CA: Stanford University Press, 2007), 385–386. William Freehling suggests that over time the federal slave-import ban could have had the same effect to the extent that, in conjunction with the interstate slave trade, the ban was gradually draining the upper South of slaves. See William W. Freehling, "The Divided South, Democracy's Limitations, and the Causes of the Peculiarly North American Civil War," in *The Reintegration of American History: Slavery and the Civil War* (New York: Oxford University Press, 1994), 176–219.

8. Cf. Arthur Bestor, "State Sovereignty and Slavery: A Reinterpretation of Proslavery Constitutional Doctrine, 1846–1860," *Journal of the Illinois State Historical Society* 54, no. 2 (Summer 1961): 117–180; Mark E. Brandon, *Free in the World: American Slavery and Constitutional Failure* (Princeton, NJ: Princeton University Press, 1998), 106, 114–116, 176; Fehrenbacher, *Slaveholding Republic*, 241; William W. Freehling, *The Road to Disunion*, vol. 2, *Secessionists Triumphant* (New York: Oxford University Press, 2007), 349–351; James L. Huston, *Calculating the Value of the Union: Slavery, Property Rights and the Economic Origins of the Civil War* (Chapel Hill: University of North Carolina Press, 2002), 105, 119–120, 129, 227; Michael A. Morrison, *Slavery and the American West: The Eclipse of Manifest Destiny and the Coming of the Civil War* (Chapel Hill: University of North Carolina Press, 1997), 168, 192, 211–213.

9. Abraham Lincoln, among other Republican leaders, expressed fears of a "Dred Scott II" decision affirming the extraterritoriality of slavery. See Fehrenbacher, *Slaveholding Republic*, 281–282; Robert W. Johannsen, ed., *The Lincoln-Douglas Debates of 1858* (New York: Oxford University Press, 1965), 19, 65, 67, 79, 230–233, 250–251, 279.

10. I list two major ($100,000+) expenditures in this policy area in Appendix C. They total approximately $500,000.

11. See Fehrenbacher, *Slaveholding Republic*, 36; Paul Finkelman, *Slavery and the Founders: Race and Liberty in the Age of Jefferson* (Armonk, NY: M.E. Sharpe, 1996), 179n5; Howard A. Ohline, "Republicanism and Slavery: Origins of the Three-Fifths Clause in the United States Constitution," *William and Mary Quarterly*, Third Series, 28, no. 4 (October 1971): 566–567; William M. Wiecek, "'The Blessings of Liberty': Slavery in the American Constitutional Order," in *Slavery and Its Consequences: The Constitution, Equality, and Race*, ed. Robert A. Goldwin and Art Kaufman (Washington, DC: American Enterprise Institute, 1988), 33. Several scholars argue that the fugitive-slave clause was part of the "dirty compromise" or an even grander scheme of intersectional compromises over slavery, but Fehrenbacher strongly, and, I think, rightly, disagrees. Cf. Fehrenbacher, *Slaveholding Republic*, 36, 353n91; Finkelman, *Slavery and the Founders*, 27; Staughton Lynd, "The Compromise of 1787," in *Class Conflict, Slavery, and the United States*

Constitution: Ten Essays (Indianapolis: Bobbs-Merrill, 1967), 188–189, 207; Gary B. Nash, *Race and Revolution* (Madison: Madison House, 1990), 42; George William Van Cleve, *A Slaveholders' Union: Slavery, Politics, and the Constitution in the Early American Republic* (Chicago: University of Chicago Press, 2010), 163–164.

12. See Max Farrand, ed., *The Records of the Federal Convention of 1787* (1911; reprint, New Haven, CT: Yale University Press, 1937), 2:443.

13. Ibid. Charles Pinckney (South Carolina) co-sponsored Butler's original motion.

14. Ibid., 453–454.

15. Ibid., 454.

16. See Fehrenbacher, *Slaveholding Republic*, 44; Finkelman, *Slavery and the Founders*, 100–102; Earl M. Maltz, "The Idea of a Proslavery Constitution," *Journal of the Early Republic* 17, no. 1 (Spring 1997): 57; Morris, *Free Men All*, 17–18.

17. See Farrand, *Records of the Convention*, 3:254, 325; quote at 254.

18. See Fehrenbacher, *Slaveholding Republic*, 212; Finkelman, *Slavery and the Founders*, 100–102; Kaczorowski, "Inverted Constitution," 32–34; Morris, *Free Men All*, 21–22.

19. Davis's legal status was also in dispute because his master had moved from Maryland to a border area that he thought was in Virginia but was actually in Pennsylvania. He therefore failed to register Davis as a slave pursuant to Pennsylvania's gradual emancipation act, a failure that made Davis legally a free person. See Finkelman, *Slavery and the Founders*, 83–85.

20. Paul Finkelman speculated that, in the end, even Southern congressmen thought the bill was too draconian. See ibid., 91.

21. See *Annals of Congress*, 15th Cong., 1st Sess., 446, 513. Pindall chaired the committee.

22. Ibid., 825–827, 829–830, 837–838.

23. Ibid., 827–828, 830, 838–839.

24. Ibid., 840. The partisan difference was not nearly as significant. Democratic Republicans voted 70–52 for the bill and Federalists, 14–17 against it. John Holmes (Massachusetts Democratic Republican), Jonathan Mason (Massachusetts Federalist), and Henry Storrs (New York Federalist) were among the Northern congressmen who spoke of the importance of intersectional compromise in supporting the bill. Ibid., 828, 838–839.

25. Ibid., 231–239; quote at 236. The two Smiths were unrelated.

26. Ibid., 242–255.

27. The Senate bill would have required more evidence for a certificate of removal than merely the testimony or disposition of the claimant. Ibid., 258–259.

28. Ibid., 259.

29. Ibid., 1393.

30. See Carter, *Territorial Papers*, 22:744–745 (Governor Du Val to the Secretary of War, September 23, 1823).

31. See H. R. Rep. No. 60, 20th Cong., 2nd Sess., 1829. Ringgold also reports that 251 slaves had been temporarily housed in the prison for safekeeping at the request of either private parties or law-enforcement officials who were traveling through the district. On the prevalence of this practice, see Matthew E. Mason, *Slavery and Politics in the Early American Republic* (Chapel Hill: University of North Carolina Press, 2006), 135; Josephine F. Pacheco, *The Pearl: A Failed Slave Escape on the Potomac* (Chapel Hill: University of North Carolina Press, 2005), 34–36. Ringgold used Washington County prison for such purposes because, again, there were no federal prisons at the time.

32. See Fehrenbacher, *Slaveholding Republic*, 214.

33. The Pennsylvania legislature had enacted a new "personal liberty" law in 1826 that

explicitly extended some due-process protections to African Americans claimed as fugitive slaves. See Morris, *Free Men All*, 51–52.

34. See Orren, "War between Officers," 359; *Prigg v. Pennsylvania* 41 U.S. 539 (1842), at 615–616.

35. See *Prigg*, 627–630, 632–633.

36. Ibid., 665–666. Prigg had made one unsuccessful attempt to obtain a certificate of removal from a state judge. McLean argues that he should have made another attempt or, alternatively, attempted to obtain the certificate from a federal justice. His overriding concern was to ensure at least some due process for alleged fugitive slaves. Ibid., 667–673.

37. See Morris, *Free Men All*, 219–222 (Appendix).

38. Ibid., 132–133.

39. See Alvin F. Oickle, *Jonathan Walker, the Man with the Branded Hand: An Historical Biography* (Everett, MA: Lorelli Slater, 1998), 45–46. Florida did not become a state until the next year.

40. The blacks were (poorly) sailing the ship because Walker had become incapacitated with a high fever. Ibid., 56–57.

41. Ibid., 60–66.

42. Ibid., 98. Walker was also tried six months later for civil trespass and damages, found guilty, and fined another $15. See Ibid., 149.

43. Ibid., 150–152. Walker's branding had made him a cause célèbre to the abolitionists.

44. Ibid., 124.

45. The group eventually swelled to seventy-six African Americans. Some members of the group were free and fleeing with enslaved spouses or children. With respect to the Bells, Daniel had purchased his freedom, but the widow of the person who had freed Mary and their eight children in his will was challenging the will in probate court. Chaplain was acting as their attorney in that case. See Pacheco, *The Pearl*, 57–58, 66–67.

46. Ibid., 53–54. Another Smith associate, Charles Cleveland, who was president of the Philadelphia Anti-Slavery Society, was ready to assist the African Americans once they reached Philadelphia. Both Smith and Cleveland probably contributed money to help pay for the escape attempt. Ibid., 68–69.

47. Someone probably tipped off local authorities about the escape attempt, which would explain why the posse was in pursuit so soon after the *Pearl* embarked. An ill wind also stalled the *Pearl* on the Potomac. Ibid., 58–60.

48. Ibid., 148. Key was the son of Francis Scott. It is not clear what happened to all the recaptured slaves, but many were eventually sold south. With respect to the Bells, Daniel was able to raise enough money to purchase the freedom of his wife and their youngest son, but the other members of their family were sold south. Ibid., 113–124.

49. Ibid., 158. Drayton may have told Sayres that only one family was fleeing; Drayton himself was apparently surprised by the size of the final group. Ibid., 67–68.

50. Ibid., 163–164. They were fined $140 and $100, respectively, on each of the seventy-four counts upon which they were convicted.

51. Ibid., 229–232. Two of the recaptured slaves were from Virginia. Ibid., 64.

52. Ibid., 148. At the trial, Congressman Horace Mann (Massachusetts Whig), who was helping defend Drayton and Sayres, suggested that Key stood to make as much as $4,500 on the case, but it is unclear how he arrived at that figure. Ibid., 152–153.

53. During the lengthy court proceedings, Key retained two leading members of the Washington bar, Joseph H. Bradley and Walter Jones, to help him prosecute the case. See Pacheco, *The*

Pearl, 159, 161. Both Bradley and Jones had served on the Board of Managers of the American Colonization Society.

54. Ibid., 63–64, 74–87.

55. Ibid., 77–79, 167–188.

56. See Clyde N. Wilson et al., ed., *The Papers of John C. Calhoun* (Columbia: University of South Carolina Press, 1959–2003), 26:228, 230 ("The Address of Southern Delegates in Congress, to their Constituents," January 22, 1849). The other indictment was the way that Northern lawmakers were allegedly denying the Southern states their equal rights to the territories. Of the 124 Southern members of Congress at the time, 48 signed the address, only 2 of whom were Whigs. See Michael Perman, *Pursuit of Southern Unity: A Political History of the American South* (Chapel Hill: University of North Carolina Press, 2009), 65.

57. See *Jones v. Van Zandt* 46 U.S. 215 (1847); Morris, *Free Men All,* 73–74, 188–192.

58. See *Congressional Globe,* 31st Cong., 1st Sess., 1850, 1604. Another upper-South senator, Thomas G. Pratt (Maryland Whig), engaged in a very determined, but ultimately unsuccessful, effort to make the bill even stronger by requiring the federal government to indemnify slaveholders in cases of slave rescues. Ibid., 1850, 1590–1610.

59. Ibid., 1850, 1587.

60. See Holman Hamilton, *Prologue to Conflict: The Crisis and Compromise of 1850* (New York: Norton, 1964), 161–164.

61. Other features of the law were (1) claimant paid U.S. commissioner $10 if alleged fugitive slave was remanded to his or her custody and only $5 otherwise; (2) court-approved deposition from state of origin attesting to the identity of alleged fugitive slave was considered sufficient evidence for reclamation; (3) alleged fugitive slave could not testify in court; and (4) civil and criminal penalties for obstructing the process were established. See Morris, *Free Men All,* 145–146. The last three features were similar to the 1793 law.

62. See Herman V. Ames, *State Documents on Federal Relations,* vol. 6, *Slavery and Union, 1845–1861* (Philadelphia: University of Pennsylvania Press, 1906), 29–32; Fehrenbacher, *Slaveholding Republic,* 233.

63. In fact, even the new Republican administration in 1861 was determined to enforce the law as a union-saving measure. See Roy B. Basler, ed., *The Collected Works of Abraham Lincoln* (New Brunswick, NJ: Rutgers University Press, 1953), 4:263–264 ("First Inaugural Address–Final Text," March 4, 1861); Fehrenbacher, *Slaveholding Republic,* 248–249.

64. All these figures are from Campbell, *Slave Catchers,* 207 (Table 12).

65. See Campbell, *Slave Catchers,* 130. This sum includes court costs of $6,872 and a $7,294 reimbursement to the city of Boston to cover its expenses. Campbell notes that contemporary estimates in the Burns case ranged as high as $100,000, though it is not clear what costs those estimates included. As we will see in the next chapter, regular army soldiers as well as local militia units were deployed to prevent his rescue; presumably the contemporary estimates attempt to gauge those costs.

66. See Treasury Ledgers, 15:346 (July 1, 1849–June 1, 1854), 16:561 (July 1, 1854–June 30, 1859), 17:802 (July 1, 1859–June 30, 1864); Appropriation Ledgers for the Treasury and Other Departments; Department of the Treasury; Record Group 39; National Archives, College Park, MD. Campbell obtained his Burns total from these ledgers, but he cites them in only two other cases.

67. See Leonard W. Levy, "Sims' Case: The Fugitive Slave Law in Boston in 1851," *Journal of Negro History* 35, no. 1 (January 1950): 72; Julius Yanuck, "The Garner Fugitive Slave Case," *Mississippi Valley Historical Review* 40, no. 1 (June 1953): 63n74. Again, it is unclear what costs these estimates included. The abolitionist Samuel J. May estimated the local militia expenses (which the

federal government paid) in the Sims case at $10,000 and the pay of the "as many as 50" deputy marshals in the Garner case at $22,000. See Samuel J. May, *The Fugitive Slave Law and Its Victims* (New York: American Anti-Slavery Society, 1861), 17, 54. Toni Morrison immortalized the Garner case in her Pulitzer Prize–winning novel, *Beloved*.

68. Campbell acknowledges that his population of fugitive-slave cases is probably only a fraction of the whole. See Campbell, *Slave Catchers*, 112–113. His population certainly did not include cases in which slaveholders did not even attempt to recover their fugitive slaves because of the expected futility of the attempt. On the significance of this factor, see Gary Collison, "'This Flagitious Offense': Daniel Webster and the Shadrach Rescue Cases, 1851–1852," *New England Quarterly* 48, no. 4 (December 1995): 624n42; Gerald G. Eggert, "The Impact of the Fugitive Slave Law on Harrisburg: A Case Study," *Pennsylvania Magazine of History and Biography* 109, no. 4 (October 1985): 537; John Hope Franklin and Loren Schweninger, *Runaway Slaves: Rebels on the Plantation* (New York: Oxford, 1999), 159–160; Hummel and Weingast, "Fugitive Slave Act," 390–391.

69. See Jonathan Katz, *Resistance at Christiana: The Fugitive Slave Rebellion, Christiana, Pennsylvania, September 11, 1851* (New York: Thomas Y. Crowell, 1974), 238. President Fillmore not only authorized U.S. District Attorney John W. Ashmead to charge Hanway with treason but to spare no necessary expenses in prosecuting the case. Those necessary expenses included paying Francis Wharton, who was an expert in treason law, a $150 consulting fee. They also included paying one African American witness $12.50 for ten days of service as well as reimbursing him for the costs of a new suit of clothes for his court appearance. In addition, U.S. Marshal Henry H. Kline paid two men $5 apiece to recover the body of Edward Gorsuch, the Maryland slaveholder who had been killed in the "riot" that occurred when he, his son, Kline, and several deputy marshals attempted to recover his fugitive slaves from a Christiana farmhouse. See Thomas P. Slaughter, *Bloody Dawn: The Christiana Riot and Racial Violence in the Antebellum North* (New York: Oxford University Press, 1991), 73, 107, 117, 132.

70. See H. R. Doc. No. 510, 70th Cong., 2nd Sess., 1929, 21; Luther A. Huston, *The Department of Justice* (New York: Praeger, 1967), 9–10.

71. See Baker, *Joshua Glover*; Nat Brandt, *The Town That Started the Civil War* (Syracuse, NY: Syracuse University Press, 1990); Nat Brandt, with Yanna Kroyt Brandt, *In the Shadow of the Civil War: Passmore Williamson and the Rescue of Jane Johnson* (Columbia: University of South Carolina Press, 2007); Gary Collison, *Shadrach Minkins: From Fugitive Slave to Citizen* (Cambridge, MA: Harvard University Press, 1997); David R. Maginnes, "The Case of the Court House Rioters in the Rendition of the Fugitive Slave Anthony Burns, 1854," *Journal of Negro History* 56, no. 1 (January 1971): 31–42; Monique Patenaude Roach, "The Rescue of William 'Jerry' McHenry: Antislavery and Racism in the Burned-Over District," *New York History* 82, no. 2 (Spring 2001): 135–154; Jayme A. Sokolow, "The Jerry McHenry Rescue and the Growth of Northern Antislavery Sentiment during the 1850s," *Journal of American Studies* 16, no. 3 (December 1982): 427–443. For still other cases, see Gerald G. Eggert, "Impact of Fugitive Slave Law," 537–569; Jean Richardson, "Buffalo's Antebellum African American Community and the Fugitive Slave Law of 1850," *Afro-Americans in New York Life and History* 27, no. 2 (July 2003): 29–46; Carol Wilson, "Active Vigilance Is the Price of Liberty: Black Self-Defense against Fugitive Slave Recapture and Kidnaping of Free Blacks," in *Antislavery Violence: Sectional, Racial, and Cultural Conflict in Antebellum America*, ed. John R. McKivigan and Stanley Harrold (Knoxville: University of Tennessee Press, 1999), 108–127. Samuel May's *Fugitive Slave Law* provides a summary of the cases.

72. In the Johnson rescue, Passmore Williamson spent 100 days in jail for contempt of court because he (truthfully) denied that he knew the whereabouts of Johnson and her two children. Williamson had also participated in the Christiana rescue. See Brandt, *In the Shadow*, 68, 142. In

the Oberlin case, U.S. District Attorney George W. Belden indicted thirty-seven men for their role in Price's rescue but, in the end, only brought two of them to trial. After spending twenty-eight days in jail awaiting and during their trials, Simeon Bushnell and Charles H. Lanston were convicted and sentenced to spend, respectively, sixty and twenty additional days in jail. Nat Brandt claims that the federal government spent "thousands" on the case. See Brandt, *Town That Started*, 116, 183, 189, 250.

73. See Baker, *Joshua Glover*, 101, 109, 119–120. In 1855, the Wisconsin Supreme Court ruled that state habeas corpus proceedings could block federal prosecutions. See Baker, *Joshua Glover*, 130–132.

74. See *Ableman v. Booth* 62 U.S. 506 (1859); Baker, *Joshua Glover*, 128. Taney also ruled that state habeas corpus decrees could not block federal prosecutions. See *Booth*, 524. Even in *Kentucky v. Dennison* (1860), Taney's ruling that governors could not be legally compelled to return fugitive slaves was more an officeholders rights than a states rights decision. See *Kentucky v. Dennison* 65 U.S. 66 (1860); Orren, "War between Officers," 362–364. On Taney's jurisprudence and slavery, cf. Don E. Fehrenbacher, *The Dred Scott Case: Its Significance in American Law and Politics* (New York: Oxford University Press, 1978), 234; Mark A. Graber, *Dred Scott and the Problem of Constitutional Evil* (New York: Cambridge University Press, 2006), 28–30, 48, 54–55, 59–60, 64; Earl Maltz, *Slavery and the Supreme Court, 1825–1861* (Lawrence: University Press of Kansas, 2009), 33–34, 281–282, and "Slavery, Federalism, and the Structure of the Constitution," *American Journal of Legal History* 36, no. 4 (October 1992): 478–480, 494, 496–497.

75. The Wisconsin legislature rescinded its personal-liberty law in 1861. Booth also received a midnight pardon from President James Buchanan. See Baker, *Joshua Glover*, 168, 172.

76. Ibid., 101, 111; *Caleb Cushing Papers, General Correspondence* (Washington, DC: Library of Congress), Box 71 (Ryan to Cushing, December 11, 1854).

77. See Morris, *Free Men All*, chap. 10.

78. See Campbell, *Slave Catchers*, 132, 168. Hummel and Weingast measure the success of the law in terms of the per capita decrease in the number of fugitive slaves reported in the 1860 as compared to 1850 census. See Hummel and Weingast, "Fugitive Slave Act," 388, 390–391, 394. Franklin and Schweninger claim, however, that both censuses greatly underreport the number of fugitive slaves, suggesting that any reported decrease might have been the result of data unreliability. See Franklin and Schweninger, *Runaway Slaves*, 279. Other scholars cite a decline in the number of fugitive-slave cases in the second half of the decade, most notably in the upper North, but such a decline could be explained equally by a decrease in the number of cases as in the determination of federal officials to enforce an unpopular law. See Baker, *Joshua Glover*, 56; Fehrenbacher, *Slaveholding Republic*, 238; Morris, *Free Men All*, 166; Jane H. Pease and William H. Pease, *The Fugitive Slave Law and Anthony Burns: A Problem in Law Enforcement* (Philadelphia: J. B. Lippincott, 1975), 50. Campbell's figures show a slight decrease in fugitive-slave cases from 1850–1854 to 1855–1860, from 33.20 per year to 27.67 per year, as well as in the upper North, from an already low 2 per year to 0.8 per year. See Campbell, *Slave Catchers*, 199–207 (Tables 1–12).

79. The Fugitive Slave Law of 1850 was not repealed until 1864. See Campbell, *Slave Catchers*, 194–195.

80. See Cassandra Pybus, "Jefferson's Faulty Math: The Question of Slave Defections in the American Revolution," *William and Mary Quarterly*, Third Series, 62, no. 2 (April 2005): 243–264. Pybus's estimate was a conservative correction to Thomas Jefferson's widely repeated claim that as many as 100,000 American slaves fled to freedom during the war.

81. Fehrenbacher, *Slaveholding Republic*, 91–92; *Statutes at Large* 8 (1783): 83.

82. See *Annals of Congress*, 4th Cong., Special Sess., 860–861. Senate approval of the treaty

included a reservation on its West Indian trade article. The House also voted on the treaty on the logic that it had to fund the mixed commissions established under various treaty articles. It approved the treaty by a narrow 51–48 margin. See Jerald A. Combs, *The Jay Treaty: Political Battleground of the Founding Fathers* (Berkeley: University of California Press, 1970), 187. The Jay Treaty controversy lends support to the view that the Federalists were more antislavery than the Democratic Republicans, even in the South. See Paul Finkelman, "The Problem of Slavery in the Age of Federalism," in *Federalists Reconsidered,* ed. Doron Ben-Atar and Barbara B. Oberg (Charlottesville: University of Virginia Press, 1998), 142–143; Matthew Mason, "'Nothing Is Better Calculated to Excite Divisions': Federalist Agitation against Slave Representation during the War of 1812," *New England Quarterly* 75, no. 4 (December 2002): 540. In 1785, Jay had founded the New York Society for Promoting the Manumission of Slaves, and Protecting Such of Them as Have Been, or May Be Liberated.

83. See *Statutes at Large* 10 (1853): 768; 11 (1859): 571.

84. See *American State Papers: Foreign Relations* 3:271 ("Great Britain," February 15, 16, and 20, 1815), 746.

85. See John Bassett Moore, *History and Digest of the International Arbitrations to which the United States Has Been a Party* (Washington, DC: Government Printing Office, 1898), 1:367n1. On this policy episode, see Fehrenbacher, *Slaveholding Republic,* 91–98. Matthew Mason notes how Adams was a "bulldog" in pursuing these claims. See Matthew E. Mason, "The Battle of the Slaveholding Liberators: Great Britain, the United States, and Slavery in the Early Nineteenth Century," *William and Mary Quarterly,* Third Series, 59, no. 3 (July 2002): 675–676. The other four American treaty negotiators were former Senator James A. Bayard (Delaware), House Speaker Henry Clay (Kentucky), former Secretary of Treasury Albert Gallatin (Pennsylvania), and Minister to Sweden Jonathan Russell (Rhode Island).

86. See Moore, *History and Digest,* 1:416–419. The unsuccessful slavery-related American claim involved the slave of a Florida resident who had escaped to British Cumberland Island, which was dismissed because at the time Florida was still Spanish territory. In addition to the *Creole,* the other two successful claims where British colonial officials had liberated slaves on ships that had sought shelter in Caribbean ports were the *Enterprise* ($49,000) and *Hermosa* ($16,000). The British government had already paid a total of $116,180 in the *Comet* and *Encomium* cases on the grounds that slavery was still legal in its colonies at the time of those seizures. Ibid., 411.

87. Ibid., 415n1. (I correct Moore's math in this note; he divides instead of multiplies the American expenses by the exchange rate for pounds.)

88. Ibid., 425.

89. See Donald V. Macdougall, "Habeas Corpus, Extradition, and a Fugitive Slave in Canada," *Slavery & Abolition* 7, no. 3 (December 1986): 119.

90. See Roman J. Zorn, "An Arkansas Fugitive Slave Incident and Its International Repercussions," *Arkansas Historical Quarterly* 16, no. 2 (Summer 1957): 139–149.

91. See *Statutes at Large* 8 (1842): 576.

92. See Zorn, "Arkansas Fugitive," 148–149; S. Doc. No. 135, 28th Cong., 1st Sess., 1844; H. R. Doc. No. 160, 28th Cong., 1st Sess., 1844; H. R. Doc. No. 114, 28th Cong., 2nd Sess., 1845.

93. See James W. Covington, "The Negro Fort," *Gulf Coast Historical Review* 5, no. 2 (June 1990): 79–91; James G. Cusick, *The Other War of 1812: The Patriot War and the American Invasion of Spanish East Florida* (Gainesville: University Press of Florida, 2003); John Missall and Mary Lou Missall, *The Seminole Wars: America's Longest Indian Conflict* (Gainesville: University Press of Florida, 2004), chaps. 2–3; Saunt, *New Order of Things,* chaps. 10, 12. I discuss these incursions

in their aspects as fugitive-slave conflicts with the Seminoles in the next section and as military conflicts with the Seminoles in the next chapter.

94. See S. Ex. Doc. No. 82, 33rd Cong., 1st Sess., 1854; S. Ex. Doc. 158, 48th Cong., 1st Sess., 1884. The federal government did not pay the claims from the 1814 incursion because Congress decided that it was a legitimate wartime operation against the British forces who were occupying northwestern Florida at the time. See Moore, *History and Digest*, 5:4528.

95. I base my 20 percent estimate on the distribution of the Red Stick War awards. (I discuss this case shortly.) To the extent that the expansion of slavery was one of the motives for the acquisition of Florida, one could argue that the whole amount was slavery related. See Fehrenbacher, *Slaveholding Republic*, 118; Mason, *Slavery and Politics*, 185–186; Kenneth W. Porter, *The Negro on the American Frontier* (New York: Arno, 1971), 210; Donald L. Robinson, *Slavery in the Structure of American Politics, 1765–1820* (New York: Harcourt Brace Jovanovich, 1971), 406–407; Adam Rothman, *Slave Country: American Expansion and the Origins of the Deep South* (Cambridge, MA: Harvard University Press, 2005), 168; Bruce Edward Twyman, *The Black Seminole Legacy and North American Politics, 1693–1845* (Washington, DC: Howard University Press, 1999), 45, 83–85, 106.

96. See Cusick, *Other War*, 305–307.

97. See Carter, *Territorial Papers*, 9:323–24 (Marquis of Casa Calvo to Claiborne, November 6, 1804), 9:331–332 (Marquis of Casa Calvo to Claiborne, November 10, 1804), 9:683 (Antonio Cordero to Claiborne, October 2, 1806), 9:764 (Claiborne to Governor [Manuel María de] Salcedo, October 1, 1807), 9:765 (Claiborne to the Secretary of State [James Madison], October 5, 1807); Villasana Haggard, "The Neutral Ground between Louisiana and Texas, 1806–1821," *Louisiana Historical Quarterly* 28, no. 4 (October 1945): 1069–1073. Again, the Louisiana-Mexico border was disputed because U.S. officials claimed Texas was part of the Louisiana Purchase.

98. See S. Ex. Doc. No. 25, 19th Cong., 2nd Sess., 1826.

99. See Randolph B. Campbell, *An Empire for Slavery: The Peculiar Institution in Texas, 1821–1865* (Baton Rouge: Louisiana State University Press, 1989), 48–49.

100. See Michael A. Morrison, "Martin Van Buren, the Democracy, and the Partisan Politics of Texas Annexation," *Journal of Southern History* 61, no. 4 (November 1995): 695–724.

101. This border had of course also been disputed and was the ostensible cause of the Mexican-American War.

102. On the Callahan expedition as a slave-catching expedition, see Campbell, *Empire for Slavery*, 63; William Dean Carrigan, "Slavery on the Frontier: The Peculiar Institution in Central Texas," *Slavery & Abolition* 20, no. 2 (August 1999): 78–79; Robert E. May, "Young American Males and Filibustering in the Age of Manifest Destiny: The United States Army as a Cultural Mirror," *Journal of American History* 78, no. 3 (December 1991): 878–879; Robert E. May, "Manifest Destiny's Filibusters," in *Manifest Destiny and Empire: American Antebellum Expansionism*, ed. Sam W. Haynes and Christopher Morris (College Station: Texas A & M Press, 1997), 158; Mulroy, *Freedom on the Border*, 78–80; Ernest C. Shearer, "The Callahan Expedition, 1855," *Southwestern Historical Quarterly* 64, no. 4 (April 1951): 430–451; Ronnie C. Tyler, "The Callahan Expedition of 1855: Indians or Negroes?" *Southwestern Historical Quarterly* 70, no. 4 (April 1967): 574–585; Ronnie C. Tyler, "Fugitive Slaves in Mexico," *Journal of Negro History* 57, no. 1 (January 1972): 8. In the case of the other filibusters into Mexico as well as elsewhere in Spanish America, no comparable consensus exists that slave interests were the driving forces. Cf. Tom Chaffin, "'Sons of Washington': Narciso López, Filibustering, and U.S. Nationalism, 1848–1851," *Journal of the Early Republic* 15, no. 1 (Spring 1995): 79–108; Tom Chaffin, *Fatal Glory: Narciso López and the First Clandestine U. S. War against Cuba* (Charlottesville: University Press of Virginia, 1996); Earl W.

Fornell, "Texans and Filibusters in the 1850's," *Southwestern Historical Quarterly* 59, no. 4 (April 1956): 411–428; May, "Young American Males," 864, 873–874, 886, "Manifest Destiny's Filibusters," 148, 158–162, 165; William O. Scroggs, *Filibusters and Financiers: The Story of William Walker and His Associates* (1916; reprint, New York: Russell & Russell, 1969); Ernest C. Shearer, "The Carvajal Disturbances," *Southwestern Historical Quarterly* 65, no. 2 (October 1951): 201–229; Joseph Allen Stout, Jr., *The Liberators: Filibustering Expeditions into Mexico, 1848–1862* (Los Angeles: Westernlore Press, 1973); Joseph Allen Stout, Jr., "Post-War Filibustering, 1850–1865," in *The Mexican War: Changing Interpretations*, ed. Odie Faulk and Joseph Allen Stout, Jr. (Chicago: Swallow Press, 1973), 192–202.

103. See S. Ex Doc No. 31, 44th Cong., 2nd Sess., 1868; Tyler, "Callahan Expedition," 582. Postannexation, the federal government continued to seek a slave-extradition treaty with Mexico, now on behalf of Texas slaveholders. Ironically, it was finally successful in 1862, after Texas had seceded from the union. See Sean Kelley, "'Mexico in His Head': Slavery and the Texas-Mexico Border, 1810–1860," *Journal of Social History* 37, no. 3 (Spring 2004): 718; Tyler, "Fugitive Slaves in Mexico," 4, 9–11.

104. See Fehrenbacher, *Slaveholding Republic*, 194–195.

105. See Fehrenbacher, *Slaveholding Republic*, 194; John T. Noonan, Jr., *The Antelope: The Ordeal of the Recaptured Africans in the Administrations of James Monroe and John Quincy Adams* (Berkeley: University of California Press, 1977), 159; *United States v. Amistad* 40 U.S. 518 (1841).

106. See Robert M. Cover, *Justice Accused: Antislavery and the Judicial Process* (New Haven, CT: Yale University Press, 1975), 109–115; William Lee Miller, *Arguing about Slavery: The Great Battle in the United States Congress* (New York: Alfred A. Knopf, 1996), 444–454. The House censured Giddings for a series of resolutions he presented in support of the *Creole* rebels. He then resigned and was overwhelmingly re-elected in the ensuing special election.

107. See Fehrenbacher, *Slaveholding Republic,* chap. 4.

108. For example, U.S. relations with France were strained when American naval vessels seized three French ships as suspected slave ships off the west coast of Africa in 1821. See Noonan, *The* Antelope, 69–74.

109. See Charles J. Kappler, *Indian Affairs: Laws and Treaties*, vol. 2, *Treaties* (Washington, DC: Government Printing Office, 1904), 48, 204; Twyman, *Black Seminole Legacy,* 15.

110. See McLoughlin, *Cherokee Renascence,* 430.

111. See H. R. Rep. No. 826, 30th Cong., 1st Sess., 1848, 21. The reason for the 1802 cutoff was that in that year Congress enacted new legislation that directed the federal government to acquire Native American lands in Georgia on behalf of the state of Georgia. See Tim Allen Garrison, "United States Indian Policy in Sectional Crisis: Georgia's Exploitation of the Compact of 1802," in *Congress and the Emergence of Sectionalism: From the Missouri Compromise to the Age of Jackson*, ed. Paul Finkelman and Donald R. Kennon (Akron: Ohio University Press, 2008), 101–103.

112. See Missall and Missall, *Seminole Wars*, 21.

113. I calculated these figures from the list of documented payments in Richard S. Lackey, *Frontier Claims in the Lower Mississippi* (New Orleans: Polyanthos, 1977), 31–67.

114. On these events, see Missall and Missall, *Seminole Wars,* chap. 2. As Missall and Missall note, the U.S. policy of not recognizing the Seminoles as a separate nation from the Creeks had some basis in fact. Many Creeks and Seminoles shared a common ancestry, and many upper Creeks had moved to Florida even before the Red Stick War as the lower Creeks consolidated their power over the Creek nation in western Georgia and eastern Alabama. Ibid., 9, 22.

115. I discuss the U.S. military's role in these incursions in the next chapter.

116. On these problems, see Carter, *Territorial Papers*, 22:762–764 (Petition to the President by Inhabitants of the Territory, October 4, 1823), 22:857–858 (Petition to Congress by the Inhabitants of East Florida, March 8, 1824), 23:434 (Delegate Joseph M. White to the Secretary of War [James Barbour], January 31, 1826), 23:462–463 (Memorial to the President [John Quincy Adams] by the Inhabitants of St. Johns County, March 26, 1826), 23:717 (White to Thomas L. McKenney, General Superintendent of Indian Affairs, January 7, 1827), 23:1003 (Report of the Legislative Council of Indian Affairs, January 17, 1828), 24:6 (White to the Secretary of War, May 1, 1828), 24:667–668 (Memorial to Congress by the Legislative Council, February 1832), 24:679 (Memorial to Congress by Inhabitants of the Territory, March 26, 1832), 25:100 (General Duncan L. Clinch to the Adjunct General [Roger Jones], January 22, 1835).

117. See Wilson, *Papers of Calhoun*, 6:398 (Calhoun to Captain John R. Bell, acting Indian agent in Florida, September 28, 1821), 9:591 (Thomas L. McKenney, Bureau of Indian Affairs, to William Ward, Choctaw Agency, February 23, 1825).

118. See H. R. Doc. No. 6, 20th Cong., 1st Sess., 1827, 8–11.

119. See Carter, *Territorial Papers*, 24:8n21 (McKenney to Du Val, May 5, 1828).

120. Ibid., 24:408–409 (Secretary of War [John H. Eaton] to Du Val, May 17, 1830), 24:718 (Secretary of War [Lewis Cass] to William B. Lewis, second auditor in Treasury Department, June 25, 1832).

121. Ibid., 25:34 (Elbert Herring, Bureau of Indian Affairs, to Wiley Thompson, July 10, 1834). This money was allocated under the Treaty of Payne's Landing (1832), which "obligated" the Seminoles to emigrate to Indian territory. See Kappler, *Indian Affairs*, 345.

122. Ibid., 25:41 (Herring to John B. F. Russell, July 21, 1834).

123. As already noted, Black Seminoles were African Americans living in Florida who were, willingly or not, associated with the Seminole nation.

124. See Canter Brown, Jr., "Race Relations in Territorial Florida, 1821–1845," *Florida Historical Quarterly* 73, no. 3 (January 1995): 304.

125. In the interim, twenty-three of the Black Seminoles had died. Watson was familiar to the Creeks because he had worked as an army contractor on earlier Creek removals. See James E. Sefton, "Black Slaves, Red Masters, White Middlemen: A Congressional Debate of 1852," *Florida Historical Quarterly* 51, no. 2 (October 1972): 115–116.

126. Giddings later wrote a scathing monograph on U.S. Seminole policy. See Joshua R. Giddings, *The Exiles of Florida: The Crimes Committed By Our Government against the Maroons Who Fled from South Carolina and Other Slave States* (1858; reprint, Baltimore: Swallow, 1997).

127. See *Statutes at Large* 10 (1852): 734. The favorable committee reports were first from the Committee on Indian Affairs in 1842, chaired by Robert Looney Carruthers (Tennessee Whig), and then from the Committee of Claims in 1844, 1846, 1848, 1850, and 1852. Alexander Stephens (Georgia Whig) chaired the latter committee in 1844; Daniel thereafter. In 1848, David Wilmot (Pennsylvania Democrat) wrote a highly critical minority report. See H. R. Rep. No. 558, 27th Cong., 2nd Sess., 1842; H. R. Rep. No. 132, 28th Cong., 1st Sess., 1844; H. R. Rep. No. 535, 29th Cong., 1st Sess., 1846; H. R. Rep. No. 724, 30th Cong., 1st Sess., 1848; H. R. Rep. No. 102, 31st Cong., 1st Sess., 1850; H. R. Rep. No. 45, 32nd Cong., 1st Sess., 1852. On this whole policy episode, see Sefton, "Black Slaves, Red Masters," 113–128.

128. See Carter, *Territorial Papers*, 20:154–155 ([Indian agent] George Gray to the Secretary of War, November 30, 1825), 20:743 (George Gray to the Secretary of War, August 30, 1828), 20:821 (Acting Governor Robert Crittenden to the Secretary of War, December 29, 1828). A major migration of Cherokees to Arkansas had occurred in 1817–1819. See Perdue, *Cherokee Society*, 61. For further discussion of the conflicts between western Cherokees and European American settlers

in Arkansas, see Kathleen Du Val, "Debating Identity, Sovereignty, and Civilization: The Arkansas Valley after the Louisiana Purchase," *Journal of the Early Republic* 26, no. 1 (Spring 2006): 25–59.

129. See Brad Agnew, *Fort Gibson: Terminal on the Trail of Tears* (Norman: University of Oklahoma Press, 1980), 143; Porter, *Negro on the Frontier*, 428. Maroon communities existed in northern Mexico, allied with nearby Native American communities and Mexican provincial officials, who saw them as buffers against U.S. encroachments. See Mulroy, *Freedom on the Border*, 52–60, 71–72; Porter, *Negro on the Frontier*, 457–458.

130. See Daniel F. Littlefield, Jr., *Africans and Creeks: From the Colonial Period to the Civil War* (Westport, CT: Greenwood Press, 1979), 217, 226. In 1854, Attorney General Cushing ruled that federal fugitive-slave law applied in Indian territory. See H. R. Doc. No. 510, 70th Cong., 2nd Sess., 1929, 21; Littlefield, *Africans and Creeks*, 213.

131. See Littlefield, *Africans and Creeks*, 191–193, 194–197; Jane F. Lancaster, *Removal After-shock: The Seminoles' Struggles to Survive in the West, 1836–1866* (Knoxville: University of Tennessee Press, 1994), 63, 70, 75, 78–79, 87, 100–102; Mulroy, *Freedom on the Border*, 48, 50–51, 65–66, 75. Marcellus was former Florida territorial Governor William's brother; apparently, both were now involved in slave dealings in Indian territory. Marcellus Du Val and Logan eventually lost their positions because of such allegations. Pre-removal, subagent Gad Humphreys lost his position on similar grounds after Superintendent McKenney had explicitly ordered Indian agents not to engage in slave transactions with Native Americans. See Carter, *Territorial Papers*, 23:536 (McKenney to [Governor William] Du Val, May 8, 1826), 24:381 (Thomas L. McKenney to Governor Du Val, March 18, 1830); Missall and Missall, *Seminole Wars*, 78–80. As chapter two shows, at least one Indian agent, David B. Mitchell, lost his position because of allegations that he was involved in slave smuggling.

132. Creeks and Seminoles were, in particular, embroiled in such disputes until the United States finally recognized the Seminoles as a separate nation in 1856 and allotted them their own lands in Indian territory. See H. R. Ex. Doc. No. 15, 33rd Cong., 2nd Sess., 1854; Littlefield, *Africans and Creeks*, 159–161, 168–169, 179; Lancaster, *Removal Aftershock*, 68; Missall and Missall, *Seminole Wars*, 207, 221.

133. See Akers, *Land of Death*, 130, 142; Bertl, "Native American Tribes," 169; Arrell M. Gibson, *The Chickasaws* (Norman: University of Oklahoma Press, 1971), 227–237; Janet Halliburton, "Black Slavery in the Creek Nation," *Chronicles of Oklahoma* 56, 3 (Fall 1978): 312–313; Lancaster, *Removal Aftershock*, 132–134; Littlefield, *Africans and Creeks*, 233–240; McLoughlin, "Red Indians, Black Slavery," 380; McLoughlin, *Cherokee Renascence*, 451; Perdue, *Cherokee Society*, 126–139; Yarbrough, *Cherokee Nation*, 23.

134. See *Annals of Congress*, 2nd Cong., 2nd Sess., 623; Finkelman, *Slavery and the Founders*, 93.

135. See *Annals of Congress*, 15th Cong., 1st Sess., 825.

136. See *Prigg*, 611–612 (Story), 626 (Taney).

137. See Morris, *Free Men All*, 204–206.

138. Even if a downturn occurred in the mid-1850s, it occurred from a substantially higher base than at any prior point in time.

139. See Maltz, *Slavery and Supreme Court*, 64–65; Mason, *Slavery and Politics*, 217–218. Mason stresses that Secretary of State Adams also adopted a hard-line stance against conceding any mutual search and seizure rights to Great Britain on nationalist grounds. Mason, *Slavery and Politics*, 90, 93, 221–222.

140. See Malcolm Bell, Jr., *Major Butler's Legacy: Five Generations of a Slaveholding Family* (Athens: University of Georgia Press, 1987), 84–85, 128.

141. The abolitionists were the major exceptions. See, for example, Lysander Spooner, *The Unconstitutionality of Slavery*, 3rd ed. (Boston: Bela Marsh, 1860), 279–289 (Appendix A).

142. Of the 332 fugitive-slave cases in Campbell's population, only 6 were from slave states (3 each from Delaware and Missouri), with another 2 from the District of Columbia. All of them were from the upper South. See Campbell, *Slave Catchers*, 199–206 (Tables 1–11).

143. See Cover, *Justice Accused*, 161–162; Fehrenbacher, *Slaveholding Republic*, 241; Freehling, *Secessionists Triumphant*, 349–351; Maltz, "Slavery, Federalism, and the Constitution," 494.

144. See David Stephen Heidler and Jeanne T. Heidler, ed., *Encyclopedia of the American Civil War: A Political, Social, and Military History* (New York: Norton, 2002), 2242 (South Carolina), 2244 (Mississippi), 2248 (Georgia), 2251 (Texas). Campbell stresses how his research proved these Southern claims to be exaggerated. See Campbell, *Slave Catchers*, 169.

145. On Mexico and the British West Indies as alternate "underground railroads," see Kelley, "Mexico in His Head," 718; Mulroy, *Freedom on the Border*, 3. Kelley estimates that 4,000 slaves escaped from Texas to Mexico from the time of its independence to the Civil War. Franklin and Schweninger estimate that from 1,000 to 2,000 slaves annually rode the underground railroad to Canada in the three decades prior to the war. See Franklin and Schweninger, *Runaway Slaves*, 367n49. Fehrenbacher assesses various estimates of the number of slaves smuggled into the United States after 1807 and concludes that it was probably much lower than the number of slaves who fled to the Northern states and Canada. See Fehrenbacher, *Slaveholding Republic*, 149.

146. See *Statutes At Large* 14 (1866): 27–30.

147. See *Congressional Globe*, 39th Cong., 1st Sess., 1866, 475.

148. See Valelly, *Two Reconstructions*, 109–110.

149. The Civil Rights Act of 1866 also followed this precedent. See *Statutes At Large* 14 (1866): 29.

150. See F. S. Calhoun, *The Lawmen*, 82–93.

151. See Jeffrey B. Bumgarner, *Federal Agents: The Growth of Federal Law Enforcement in America* (Westport, CT: Greenwood, 2006).

152. Senator Andrew Pickens Butler (South Carolina Democrat) apotheosized Taney's concurrent-jurisdiction argument during the 1850 Senate debate over Mason's fugitive-slave bill, but none of his Southern colleagues responded in kind. See *Congressional Globe*, 31st Cong., 1st Sess., 1850, 1588, 1595, 1598.

153. See *Prigg*, 617–618 (Story), 628–29 (Taney).

154. See James T. Patterson, *Brown v. Board of Education: A Civil Rights Milestone and Its Troubled Legacy* (New York: Oxford University Press, 2002).

CHAPTER 5. THE SLAVERY GARRISONED STATE

1. See Charles Tilly, *Coercion, Capital, and European States, A.D. 990–1990* (Cambridge, MA: Basil Blackwell, 1990), chap. 2, "Reflections on the History of European State-Making," in *The Formation of National States in Western Europe*, ed. Charles Tilly (Princeton, NJ: Princeton University Press, 1975), 3–83, "War Making and State Making as Organized Crime," in *Bringing the State Back In*, ed. Peter B. Evans, Dietrich Rueschemeyer, and Theda Skocpol (Cambridge: Cambridge University Press, 1985), 169–186. See also Brian M. Downing, *The Military Revolution and Political Change* (Princeton, NJ: Princeton University Press, 1993); Thomas Ertman, *Birth of the Leviathan: Building States and Regimes in Medieval and Early Modern Europe* (Cambridge: Cambridge University Press, 1997); Samuel E. Finer, "State- and Nation-Building in Europe: The Role

of the Military," in Tilly, *Formation of National States*, 84–163; Geoffrey Parker, *The Military Revolution: Military Innovation and the Rise of the West*, 2nd ed. (Cambridge: Cambridge University Press, 1996).

2. See, for example, Marc Allen Eisner, *From Warfare State to Welfare State: World War I, Compensatory State Building and the Limits of the Modern Order* (University Park: Pennsylvania State University Press, 2000); Suzanne Mettler, *Soldiers to Citizens: The G. I. Bill and the Making of the Greatest Generation* (New York: Oxford University Press, 2005).

3. See Max M. Edling, *A Revolution in Favor of Government: Origins of the U.S. Constitution and the Making of the American State* (Oxford: Oxford University Press, 2003); Sheldon D. Pollack, *War, Revenue, and State Building: Financing the Development of the American State* (Ithaca, NY: Cornell University Press, 2008); Bruce D. Porter, *War and the Rise of the State: The Military Foundations of Modern Politics* (New York: Free Press, 1984).

4. In the eighteenth century, the Revolutionary War was also a "less major" war with a "more major" power.

5. At the end of the nineteenth century, the United States fought one of those colonial powers in the Spanish-American War and, as I discuss further in this chapter, American forces also battled Spanish colonials in Florida before it was acquired by the United States.

6. See Richard Franklin Bensel, *Yankee Leviathan: The Origins of Central State Authority in America, 1859–1877* (Cambridge: Cambridge University Press, 1990), chap. 3.

7. Cf. ibid., 2, 367; Theda Skocpol, *Protecting Soldiers and Mothers: The Political Origins of Social Policy in the United States* (Cambridge, MA: Belknap Press of Harvard University Press, 1992), 59–60. The dismantling of state structures after wars is another part of the story of American exceptionalism.

8. The Mexican-American War had 13,283 U.S. combatant deaths and the Second Seminole War, 1,555. See Congressional Research Service (CRS), "American War and Military Operations Casualties: Lists and Statistics," 2 (Table 1), http://www.fas.orga/sgp.crs.natsec/RL32492http://www.fas.orga/sgp.crs.natsec/RL32492; John T. Sprague, *The Origin, Progress, and Conclusion of the Florida War* (1848; reprint, Gainesville: University of Florida Press, 1964), 548–550 (Appendix). The Correlates of War project uses 1,000 combatant deaths among all parties as its threshold for interstate wars. See http://www.coreelatesofwar.org; J. David Singer and Melvin Small, *The Wages of War, 1816–1965: A Statistical Handbook* (New York: Wiley, 1972), 35. Perhaps not surprisingly, the U.S. army did not provide any reliable estimates of the number of combatant deaths among the Seminoles during the Second Seminole War. See John Missall and Mary Lou Missall, *The Seminole Wars: America's Longest Indian Conflict* (Gainesville: University Press of Florida, 2004), 206. Perhaps also not surprisingly, neither the CRS nor Singer and Small include the Second Seminole War on their lists of wars. See CRS, "American War," 2 (Table 1); Singer and Small, *Wages of War*, 38 (Table 2.3).

9. See David R. Mayhew, "Wars and American Politics," *Perspectives on Politics* 3, no. 5 (September 2005): 475–476.

10. See Laura Jensen, *Patriots, Settlers, and the Origins of American Social Policy* (Cambridge: Cambridge University Press, 2003).

11. See John K. Mahon, *History of the Second Seminole War, 1835–1842* (Gainesville: University of Florida Press, 1967), 321–322, 326–327.

12. See Laurence J. Malone, *Opening the West: Federal Internal Improvements before 1860* (Westport, CT: Greenwood, 1998), 3–4, 10, 25, 52–72, 117–118. See also Brian Balogh, *A Government Out of Sight: The Mystery of National Authority in Nineteenth-Century America* (New York: Cambridge University Press, 2009), 212–213; Andrew R. L. Cayton, "'Separate Interests' and the

Nation-State: The Washington Administration and the Origins of Regionalism in the Trans-Appalachian West," *Journal of American History* 79, no. 1 (June 1992): 40–41; Richard R. John, "Governmental Institutions as Agents of Change: Rethinking American Political Development in the Early Republic, 1787–1835," *Studies in American Political Development* 11, no. 2 (Fall 1997): 370–371; Ira Katznelson, "Flexible Capacity: The Military and Early American Statebuilding," in *Shaped by War and Trade: International Influences on American Political Development*, ed. Ira Katznelson and Martin Shefter (Princeton, NJ: Princeton University Press, 2002), 90–91, 97, 99; Christopher McCrory Klyza, "The United States Army, Natural Resources, and Political Development in the Nineteenth Century," *Polity* 35, no. 1 (Fall 2002): 5, 26n5; Richard White, '*It's Your Misfortune and None of My Own': A New History of the American West* (Norman: University of Oklahoma Press, 1991), 57–59; Mark R. Wilson, "The Politics of Procurement: Military Origins of Bureaucratic Autonomy," in *Ruling Passions: Political Economy in Nineteenth-Century America*, ed. Richard R. John (University Park, PA: Penn State University Press, 2006), 57.

13. See Jensen, *Patriots, Settlers, and the Origins of American Social Policy*, 228; Richard R. John, *Spreading the News: The American Postal System from Franklin to Morse* (Cambridge, MA: Harvard University Press, 1995), and "Governmental Institutions," 371–372; Katznelson, "Flexible Capacity," 90; Peter S. Onuf, "The Expanding Union," in *Devising Liberty: Preserving and Creating Freedom in the New American Republic*, ed. David Thomas Konig (Stanford, CA: Stanford University Press, 1995), 75; Malcolm J. Rohrbough, *The Land Office Business: The Settlement and Administration of American Public Lands, 1789–1837* (New York: Oxford University Press, 1968).

14. For example, Pollack's *War, Revenue, and State Building* barely mentions slavery.

15. See *Historical Statistics of the United States Millennial Edition Online*, Table Ea636–643, http://hsus.cambridge.org. This total includes army and navy expenditures but not military pensions and other benefits, which would increase the total to $1,071 million (59.1 percent).

16. See *Historical Statistics of the United States*, Table Ea636–643; Missall and Missall, *Seminole Wars*, xv.

17. A large percentage of the federal spending on slave-trade suppression, African colonization, and fugitive-slave recoveries was also military spending. As we will see in the next chapter, federal spending on slave labor followed the same pattern. In Appendix C, I list the three major ($100,000+) expenditure items that I discuss in this chapter.

18. See James G. Cusick, *The Other War of 1812: The Patriot War and the American Invasion of Spanish East Florida* (Gainesville: University Press of Florida, 2003), 83, 89–90.

19. Madison had already authorized the illegal occupation of Spanish West Florida, from Pensacola to Baton Rouge. He had an active agent on the scene, former Georgia Governor, Congressman, and Brigadier General George Mathews, who personally recruited and initially commanded the filibusterers. Mitchell later took command of the filibusterers when their campaign ground to an ignominious halt. See ibid., 3–4, 32, 138–139. As we have seen, Mitchell subsequently became an Indian agent who was relieved of his position after he was accused of slave smuggling.

20. Throughout the five decades of Seminole-American conflicts in Florida, American settlers generally made the claim that Black Seminoles were their fugitive or "stolen" slaves, but they were rarely able to prove the claim in specific cases.

21. Smith also relieved Laval of his duties because Laval's refusal to assist the filibusterers had precipitated a mutiny at the post, which, to Smith, indicated a failure of command. Ibid., 91–92.

22. Ibid., 120–125, 138. As discussed in chapter two, Amelia Island was a slave-smuggling haven that was again invaded by American forces in 1817 for that reason.

23. Ibid., 287–291.

24. See Missall and Missall, *Seminole Wars*, 24. As noted in the last chapter, Congress decided that this incursion was a legitimate War of 1812 operation and refused to fund claims for property losses from the incursion.

25. On this incursion, see James W. Covington, "The Negro Fort," *Gulf Coast Historical Review* 5, no. 2 (June 1990): 79–91. At least 200 black people were killed in the explosion. Ibid., 86; Missall and Missall, *Seminole Wars*, 30.

26. See H. R. Doc. No. 14, 15th Cong., 2nd Sess., 1818, 58. On the First Seminole War, see Missall and Missall, *Seminole Wars*, chap. 2.

27. See Missall and Missall, *Seminole Wars*, 48–50. The authorization issue was hotly contested in Monroe's own cabinet meetings. Matthew Mason claims that Jackson's actions transformed the acquisition of Florida from a national into a sectional issue, but he seems to overlook how a number of national (Madison) and local (Mitchell) actors had already accomplished that task. See Matthew E. Mason, *Slavery and Politics in the Early American Republic* (Chapel Hill: University of North Carolina Press, 2006), 185–186.

28. See Charles J. Kappler, *Indian Affairs: Laws and Treaties*, vol. 2, *Treaties* (Washington, DC: Government Printing Office, 1904), 213.

29. See *Statutes at Large* 6 (1839): 778. In some cases, the sailors had died and their heirs received the money. The amount was half the assessed value of the maroons whom the Creeks had captured after the destruction of the fort.

30. See Clyde N. Wilson et al., ed., *The Papers of John C. Calhoun* (Columbia: University of South Carolina Press, 1959–2003), 2:422 (Calhoun to Robert Brent, Army Paymaster General, July 24, 1818).

31. See Kappler, *Indian Affairs*, 204.

32. See George Klos, "Blacks and the Seminole Removal Debates, 1821–1835," *Florida Historical Quarterly* 68, no. 1 (July 1989): 66, 77.

33. See Clarence Edwin Carter, ed., *The Territorial Papers of the United States* (Washington, DC: Government Printing Office, 1934–1969), 22:762–64 (Petition to the President by Inhabitants of the Territory, October 4, 1823), 22:857–858 (Petition to Congress by the Inhabitants of East Florida, March 8, 1824), 23:434 (Delegate Joseph M. White to the Secretary of War [James Barbour], January 31, 1826), 23:462–463 (Memorial to the President [John Quincy Adams] by the Inhabitants of St. Johns County, March 26, 1826), 23:717 (White to Thomas L. McKenney, General Superintendent of Indian Affairs, January 7, 1827), 23:1003 (Report of the Legislative Council of Indian Affairs, January 17, 1828), 24:6 (White to the Secretary of War, May 1, 1828).

34. See Kappler, *Indian Affairs*, 344–345.

35. Federal officials insisted on settling the Seminoles on western Creek lands, again, because they considered the Seminoles part of the Creek nation. See Missall and Missall, *Seminole Wars*, 84–85.

36. Ibid., 128–130, 132–133.

37. Ibid., 200–202.

38. Ibid., xv, 205, 224.

39. As I discuss further below, a group of Creeks violently resisted removal for a brief time.

40. See Klos, "Removal Debates," 55.

41. In fact, local army officers had urged delaying any attempt to forcibly remove the Seminoles from Florida. Later, Jesup recommended ending the war "early," in 1838, and establishing a Seminole "reservation" in southern Florida, but again territorial protests prevailed. Shortly thereafter, Jesup asked to be relieved of his command. See Carter, *Territorial Papers*, 25:495 (Thomas S.

Jesup to the Secretary of War [Joel Poinsett], March 14, 1838); Missall and Missall, *Seminole Wars,* 146–152; Samuel J. Watson, "The Uncertain Road to Manifest Destiny: Army Officers and the Course of American Territorial Expansionism, 1815–1846," in *Manifest Destiny and Empire: American Antebellum Expansionism,* ed. Sam W. Haynes and Christopher Morris (College Station: Texas A&M University Press, 1997), 72.

42. See *American State Papers: Military Affairs* 7:760 (Jesup to B[enjamin] F. Butler, Acting Secretary of War, December 9, 1836), 821.

43. See Canter Brown, Jr., "Race Relations in Territorial Florida, 1821–1845," *Florida Historical Quarterly* 73, no. 3 (January 1995): 303–304; James W. Covington, *The Seminoles of Florida* (Gainesville: University of Florida Press, 1993), 91; Klos, "Seminole Removal Debates," 77–78; Jane F. Lancaster, *Removal Aftershock: The Seminoles' Struggles to Survive in the West, 1836–1866* (Knoxville: University of Tennessee Press, 1994), 18; Mahon, *Second Seminole War,* 201, 326; Missall and Missall, *Seminole Wars,* 126; Kevin Mulroy, *Freedom on the Border: The Seminole Maroons in Florida, the Indian Territory, Coahuila, and Texas* (Lubbock: Texas Tech University Press, 1993), 29; Virginia Bergman Peters, *The Florida Wars* (Hamden, CT: Archon Books, 1979), 144–145; Kenneth W. Porter, *The Black Seminoles: History of a Freedom-Seeking People* (Gainesville: University of Florida Press, 1996), 67; Larry Eugene Rivers, *Slavery in Florida: Territorial Days to Emancipation* (Gainesville: University Press of Florida, 2000), 204; Bruce Edward Twyman, *The Black Seminole Legacy and North American Politics, 1693–1845* (Washington, DC: Howard University Press, 1999), 130.

44. For the lack of consensus in the Texas case, see Don E. Fehrenbacher, *The Slaveholding Republic: An Account of the United States Government's Relations to Slavery* (New York: Oxford University Press, 2001), 118–126.

45. Even so, the Second Seminole War costs might not have been documented if Giddings had not inquired into the costs of the war when he began to suspect its true origins. The navy was involved in the war effort in a support role and, later, in attempting to flush Seminoles out of the Everglades. See Missall and Missall, *Seminole Wars,* 125–126, 177, 187–188.

46. See H. R. Doc. No. 8, 26th Cong., 2nd Sess., 1840, 7, 10, 12–13, 15.

47. See H. R. Rep. No. 582, 28th Cong., 1st Sess., 1844, 86.

48. See H. R. Doc. No. 247, 27th Cong., 2nd Sess., 1842, 11–12.

49. See H. R. Doc. No. 247, 27th Cong., 2nd Sess., 1842, 3.

50. See Missall and Missall, *Seminole Wars,* 190–191, 208–209.

51. See Sprague, *Florida War,* 268–269.

52. See James W. Covington, *The Seminoles of Florida* (Gainesville: University of Florida Press, 1993), 72; Lancaster, *Removal Aftershock,* 18; Mahon, *Second Seminole War,* 226, 326; Missall and Missall, *Seminole Wars,* xv; Mulroy, *Freedom on the Border,* 29; Peters, *Florida Wars,* 262; Porter, *Black Seminoles,* 106; Twyman, *Black Seminole Legacy,* 140. In comparison, Mexican-American War costs were $63.5 million. See Paul Studenski and Herman E. Kroos, *Financial History of the United States,* 2nd ed. (New York: McGraw-Hill, 1963), 123–124.

53. See *Historical Statistics of the United States,* Table Ea636–643.

54. See Sprague, *Florida War,* 548–550 (Appendix). Nearly one third of the battle deaths occurred during Dade's Massacre. A low ratio of battle deaths was, of course, typical of "old-style" warfare (and medicine). Only 1,733 of the 13,283 Mexican-American War casualties were battle deaths. See CRS, "American War," 2 (Table 1).

55. See Mahon, *Second Seminole War,* 226; Sprague, *Florida War,* 104.

56. See Missall and Missall, *Seminole Wars,* 205–206. The auxiliary forces included Native

Americans, mostly Creeks but also Choctaws, Delawares, and Shawnees, as well as local militia and volunteer units. See Sprague, *Florida War,* 102. Mahon estimates 55 battle deaths among the militia and volunteers. See Mahon, *Second Seminole War,* 325.

57. See Mahon, *Second Seminole War,* 325. Again in comparison, approximately 80,000 Americans saw service in the Mexican-American War. See CRS, "American War," 2 (Table 1).

58. See Sprague, *Florida War,* 103–106.

59. Ibid., 93–95, 101–103.

60. See H. R. Doc. No. 8, 26th Cong., 2nd Sess., 1840, 12.

61. See Sprague, *Florida War,* 103–106. Though army regulars constituted an increasingly higher percentage of the military force in Florida, a greater number of militia and volunteers saw service during the war because of their relatively short terms of service, typically six months or less. Basic army pay was $7 per month plus provisions, while militia could earn as much as $20 per month plus provisions. See Jane F. Lancaster, "William Tecumseh Sherman's Introduction to War, 1840–1842: Lesson for Action," *Florida Historical Quarterly* 72, no. 1 (July 1993): 65.

62. See Sprague, *Florida War,* chap. 10. Local officials also protested Colonel Worth's decision to reduce the nonmilitary costs of the war. Sprague was Worth's son-in-law.

63. See Mahon, *Second Seminole War,* 326–327; Watson, "Uncertain Road," 72.

64. See *Historical Statistics of the United States,* Table Ed26–47.

65. On the ratchet effect and American wars, see Pollack, *War, Revenue, and State Building,* 96, 233, 296. Pollack, however, does not mention the Second Seminole War.

66. See H. R. Ex. Doc. No. 2, 29th Cong., 1st Sess., 1845, 529.

67. See S. Ex. Doc. No. 71, 33rd Cong., 1st Sess., 1854, 25. The army also had liberally funded an emigration mission from Indian territory to the Florida Seminoles in 1849, but it did not record the costs. See Lancaster, *Removal Aftershock,* 76–77.

68. See Kappler, *Indian Affairs,* 761. Foc-te-luc-te-harjoe was the leader of a group of Seminoles who decided to emigrate rather than resist removal at the beginning of the war. See Missall and Missall, *Seminole Wars,* 206–207. The treaty statement that he was the "chief of a friendly band of Seminole warriors who fought for the United States during the Seminole War" suggests that some members of the group returned to Florida to assist the army's war efforts.

69. See S. Ex. Doc. No. 1, 35th Cong., 2nd Sess., 1858, 478; Lancaster, *Removal Aftershock,* 123–124.

70. See Missall and Missall, *Seminole Wars,* 221.

71. The number is of course incomplete. Except for the Second Seminole War, most of the costs associated with these military operations were not documented or even estimated.

72. While scholars disagree over how well Native American slavery fit the European American model, they agree that Seminole slavery least fit the model. See Renate Bertl, "Native American Tribes and Their African Slaves," in *Slave Cultures and the Cultures of Slavery,* ed. Stephan Palmié (Knoxville: University of Tennessee Press, 1995), 168; Missall and Missall, *Seminole Wars,* 10; Mulroy, *Freedom on the Border,* 1–2, 7–8, 17–18; Rivers, *Slavery in Florida,* 190, 193–194; Claudio Saunt, *A New Order of Things: Property, Power, and the Transformation of the Creek Indians, 1733–1816* (Cambridge: Cambridge University Press, 1999), 124, 134; Fay A. Yarbrough, *Race and the Cherokee Nation: Sovereignty in the Nineteenth Century* (Philadelphia: University of Pennsylvania Press, 2008), 116, 118.

73. To a significant degree, Native American removal in the southeastern United States was a state-driven process until the federal government seized the initiative in 1830 with the Indian Removal Act. See Tim Allen Garrison, "United States Indian Policy in Sectional Crisis: Georgia's Exploitation of the Compact of 1802," in *Congress and the Emergence of Sectionalism: From the*

Missouri Compromise to the Age of Jackson, ed. Paul Finkelman and Donald R. Kennon (Akron: Ohio University Press, 2008), 117–118; Ronald N. Satz, *American Indian Policy in the Jacksonian Era* (Lincoln: University of Nebraska Press, 1974), 3–4, 11–12.

74. See Leonard A. Carlson and Mark A. Roberts, "Indian Lands, 'Squatterism' and Slavery: Economic Interests and the Passage of the Indian Removal Act of 1830," *Explorations in Economic History* 43, no. 3 (July 2006): 500–501; Adam Rothman, *Slave Country: American Expansion and the Origins of the Deep South* (Cambridge, MA: Harvard University Press, 2005), 11–13, 39–42, 166, 219. This generalization is also true of the trans-Mississippian territories. See H. Jason Combs, "The Platte Purchase and Native American Removal," *Plains Anthropologist* 47, no. 182 (August 2002): 265–274; Kathleen Du Val, "Debating Identity, Sovereignty, and Civilization: The Arkansas Valley after the Louisiana Purchase," *Journal of the Early Republic* 26, no. 1 (Spring 2006): 25–59; Daniel H. Usner, Jr., *American Indians in the Lower Mississippi Valley: Social and Economic Histories* (Lincoln: University of Nebraska Press, 1998), chaps. 5–7.

75. See R. Douglas Hurt, *The Indian Frontier, 1763–1846* (Albuquerque, NM: University of New Mexico Press, 2002), 165; William G. McLoughlin, *Cherokee Renascence in the New Republic* (Princeton, NJ: Princeton University Press, 1986), 430.

76. On the Black Hawk War, see Hurt, *Indian Frontier,* chap. 7.

77. Several provocative studies have argued that their interactions with African Americans and European Americans had not only made Native American population groups more diverse but, as a countervailing trend, induced them to think of themselves as "red" in order to distinguish themselves from "black." The imputed rationale was that they did not want whites to lump them together with blacks as inferior peoples. On a practical level, this trend meant that they attempted to segregate themselves from blacks by adopting the same discriminatory practices whites had adopted toward blacks, such as antimiscegenation laws, denial of membership privileges, and, especially after the Civil War, forced eviction from the community. See James M. Merrell, "The Racial Education of the Catawba Indians," *Journal of Southern History* 50, no. 3 (August 1984): 363–384; James P. Ronda, "'We Have a Country': Race, Geography, and the Invention of Indian Territory," *Journal of the Early Republic* 19, no. 4 (Winter 1999): 739–755; Nancy Shoemaker, "How Indians Got to Be Red," *American Historical Review* 102, no. 3 (June 1997): 625–644; Yarbrough, *Cherokee Nation,* chaps. 2–3.

78. For these census figures, see Michael F. Doran, "Negro Slaves of the Five Civilized Tribes," *Annals of the Association of American Geographers* 68, no. 3 (September 1978): 346 (Table 2). The army conducted these censuses in order to estimate removal costs. The results suggest that the census takers treated slaves and blacks as coterminous categories.

79. See Porter, *Black Seminoles,* 28. Again, the status of these Black Seminoles varied.

80. See Donna L. Akers, *Living in the Land of Death: The Choctaw Nation, 1830–1860* (East Lansing: Michigan State University Press, 2004), 133; Arrell M. Gibson, *The Chickasaws* (Norman: University of Oklahoma Press, 1971), 126, 134; McLoughlin, *Cherokee Renascence,* 451; Greg O'Brien, *Choctaws in a Revolutionary Age, 1750–1830* (Lincoln: University of Nebraska Press, 2002), 112–114; Saunt, *New Order of Things,* 54–55, 99–100; Yarbrough, *Cherokee Nation,* 19.

81. With a specific focus on the Cherokees, Yarbrough's *Cherokee Nation* explores how this racial intermixing affected the internal structure of Native American nations, both before and after removal.

82. See H. R. Doc. No. 291, 24th Cong., 1st Sess., 1836, 5. Kenneth Valliere claims that it was unlikely that these Creeks would have resisted removal if the Seminoles had not first. See Kenneth L. Valliere, "The Creek War of 1836: A Military History," *Chronicles of Oklahoma* 57, no. 4 (Winter 1979–1980): 466.

83. See S. Doc. No. 59, 23rd Cong., 1st Sess., 1834, 2. Unlike in the case of the other southeast removals, the army did not record or estimate the Creek removal costs. The army's preestimate was $1,080,545 to remove every member of the Creek nation who remained east of the Mississippi River in 1834, which, by its count, was 22,264. The army generated this preestimate by multiplying that number of Creeks by its estimate of the per capita removal and one year's subsistence costs. I, in turn, prorate the preestimate based on Grant Foreman's estimate of how many Creeks were actually removed in 1836–1837, which is 19,000. See Grant Foreman, *Indian Removal: The Emigration of the Five Civilized Tribes of Indians* (1932; reprint, Norman: University of Oklahoma Press, 1972), 179n4, 183, 187. (Foreman's work remains the best single source on the southeast removals.) In the case of each of the five "civilized" nations, many groups self-removed, at various times and to various locations, or else for various reasons and in various ways never removed. In fact, the army based its preestimate of the Creek removal costs on the per capita removal costs of several groups of Creeks that had self-removed in 1827–1829 (and it therefore was probably a significant underestimate). By April 1830, the federal government had spent $166,382 on the removal and subsistence costs of these early groups. See H. R. Doc. No. 74, 20th Cong., 1st Sess., 1828; H. R. Doc. No. 91, 21st Cong., 1st Sess., 1830, 5.

84. See McLoughlin, *Cherokee Renascence*, 450.

85. See *Cherokee Nation v. Georgia* 30 U.S. 1 (1831); *Worcester v. Georgia* 31 U.S. 515 (1832).

86. The Seminoles enjoyed the "luxury" of navy transportation from Florida to New Orleans. See Missall and Missall, *Seminole Wars*, 206–207.

87. See H. R. Rep. No. 288, 27th Cong., 3rd Sess., 1843, 2. Prior to the Trail of Tears, the federal government spent $79,882 on Cherokee bands that had self-removed in the late 1820s. See H. R. Doc. No. 91, 21st Cong., 1st Sess., 1830. The leaders of the main body of Cherokees who self-removed in early 1836, also prior to the Trail of Tears, violated a pact among the Cherokee leaders not to cede tribal lands to the United States, on pain of death, when they signed the Treaty of New Echota (1835). Three of these men, Major Ridge, his son John, and Elias Boudinot, were assassinated in Indian territory in 1839. See Theda Perdue, *Slavery and the Evolution of Cherokee Society, 1540–1866* (Knoxville: University of Tennessee Press, 1979), 66–67, 73.

88. See Kappler, *Indian Affairs*, 419. Chickasaw slaveholders received one extra half section of land if they owned less than ten slaves and one whole extra section if they owned ten or more slaves. Of the five "civilized" nations, the Chickasaws had the highest proportion of slaves, who made up 18 percent of the population. See Doran, "Negro Slaves," 346 (Table 2).

89. Each removal was multitiered in the sense that individual Native Americans could always secure their own means of transportation or purchase their own provisions if they had the means to do so, instead of relying on profit-seeking army contractors.

90. See H. R. Doc. No. 65, 27th Cong., 3rd Sess., 1843, 2. The army estimate was relatively high in the case of the Chickasaws because it included more than their first year's subsistence costs in their new lands, not only underscoring the degree to which the army estimates were not strictly comparable across nations but also its unrealistic assumption that one year would be sufficient to normalize conditions in Indian territory.

91. An estimated 6,000 Choctaws decided not to emigrate, a decision that meant divesting themselves of tribal lands and sovereignty. The Mississippi Choctaws generally did not prosper, and as many as 3,500 of them emigrated to Indian territory in the mid-1840s. See Ronald N. Satz, "The Mississippi Choctaw: From the Removal Treaty to the Federal Agency," in *After Removal: The Choctaw in Mississippi*, ed. Samuel J. Wells and Roseanna Tubby (Jackson: University Press of Mississippi, 1986), 7, 13–15.

92. See H. R. Doc. No. 107, 28th Cong., 2nd Sess., 1845, 19.

93. This racial separation was more complete on a symbolic level than it was on a physical level.

94. As we saw in chapter three, there also existed an unofficial policy of separating free African Americans from European Americans, prompting ACS officials, among others, to frequently analogize African colonization to Native American removal. Alisse Portnoy's *Right to Speak* explores the irony involved in the tendency of the proponents of African colonization to oppose Native American removal and of the proponents of Native American removal to oppose African colonization.

95. As the "Black Dirt" treaty payment suggests, the army even recruited Black Seminoles whom it had removed to Arkansas to return to Florida to serve in these roles. Kevin Mulroy argues that the war drove a permanent wedge between them and the other Seminoles. See Mulroy, *Freedom on the Border*, 32–34. On the army's widespread use of Black Seminole interpreters during the war, see H. R. Doc. No. 225, 25th Cong., 3rd Sess., 1839; Missall and Missall, *Seminole Wars*, 169; Sprague, *Florida Wars*, 268–269.

96. See Valliere, "Creek War," 474.

97. See *Historical Statistics of the United States*, Table Ea636–643.

98. See Michael F. Doran, "Population Statistics of Nineteenth Century Indian Territory," *Chronicles of Oklahoma* 53, no. 4 (Winter 1975–1976): 498 (Table II).

99. This clause was one of the clauses that Madison urged the Committee of Detail to insert into its draft constitution. See Max Farrand, ed., *The Records of the Federal Convention of 1787* (1911; reprint, New Haven, CT: Yale University Press, 1937), 2:324. It was not debated thereafter.

100. On the Civil War, see Mark R. Wilson, *The Business of Civil War: Military Mobilization and the State, 1861–1865* (Baltimore: Johns Hopkins University Press, 2006).

101. See Tommy Richard Young II, "The United States Army in the South, 1789–1835" (Ph.D. diss., Louisiana State University, 1973), chaps. 9–10.

102. Ibid., 4–6, 520–521.

103. Stanley Engerman counts four major slave revolts on U.S. soil during the 1791–1861 period, but he includes two slave conspiracies (Gabriel and Vesey) that were suppressed in their final planning stages. See Stanley L. Engerman, "Slavery and Its Consequences for the South in the Nineteenth Century," in *The Cambridge Economic History of the United States*, vol. 2, *The Long Nineteenth Century*, ed. Stanley L. Engerman and Robert E. Gallman (New York: Cambridge University Press, 2000), 347. Several scholars also consider the Second Seminole War a major slave revolt. See Brown, "Race Relations in Florida," 304; Rivers, *Slavery in Florida*, 13, 203, 219, 228; William B. Skelton, *An American Profession of Arms: The Army Officer Corps, 1784–1861* (Lawrence: University Press of Kansas, 1992), 351; Twyman, *Black Seminole Legacy*, 18, 115–116, 121, 146. The Black Seminoles also allegedly instigated at least one slave revolt in Indian territory. See Daniel F. Littlefield, Jr., and Lonnie E. Underhill, "Slave 'Revolt' in the Cherokee Nation, 1842," *American Indian Quarterly* 3, no. 3 (Summer 1977): 121–131.

104. See Young, "Army in the South," 469–474. In his study of the German Coast revolt, James Dormon claims that it cost at least two European American and eighty-seven African American lives, twenty-one through state executions. See James H. Dormon, "The Persistent Specter: Slave Rebellion in Territorial Louisiana," *Louisiana History* 18, no. 4 (Fall 1977): 397–398.

105. See Tommy Young II, "The United States Army and the Institution of Slavery in Louisiana, 1803–1835," *Louisiana Studies* 13, no. 3 (Fall 1974): 201–222. Another major Louisiana slave revolt occurred at Pointe Coupée in 1795 before it became U.S. territory, though the unrest apparently spread to several plantations on the Mississippi side of the river. The army executed twenty-three slaves for allegedly participating in the rebellion. See Adalberto Aguirre, Jr., and

David V. Baker, "Slave Executions in the United States: A Descriptive Analysis of Social and Historical Factors," *Social Science Journal* 36, no. 1 (January 1999): 20; David J. Libby, *Slavery and Frontier Mississippi, 1720–1835* (Jackson: University Press of Mississippi), 37. Adam Rothman estimates that one third of the U.S. army was stationed in and around New Orleans during the early decades of the nineteenth century, in part to control its large black population. See Rothman, *Slave Country*, 116.

106. See Kenneth S. Greenberg, ed., *The Confessions of Nat Turner and Related Documents* (Boston: Bedford Books of St. Martins' Press, 1996), 18; Young, "Army in the South," 507–513. Thomas Parramore claims that the Southampton revolt cost 55 European American lives and "no more than 50" African American lives in the mayhem that followed, as well as another 19 through state executions. See Thomas C. Parramore, *Southampton County, Virginia* (Charlottesville: University Press of Virginia, 1978), 103–104, 116.

107. See Young, "Army in the South," 501.

108. See Herbert Aptheker, *American Negro Slave Revolts* (1943; reprint, New York: International Publishers, 1968), 268–273; Wilson, *Papers of Calhoun*, 7:210 (Bennett to Calhoun, July 15, 1822), 219 (Calhoun to Major James Bankhead, commanding officer in Charleston, July 22, 1822), and 220 (Calhoun to Bennett, July 22, 1822). The Gabriel (Prosser) conspiracy in Virginia in 1800 was similar to the Vesey conspiracy in that it was discovered before the event and to the Southampton revolt in that then-Governor James Monroe mobilized the state militia in response. He also mobilized the state militia in response to another, apparently much smaller slave conspiracy near Richmond in 1802. See Douglas R. Egerton, *The Virginia Slave Conspiracies, 1800 and 1802* (Chapel Hill: University of North Carolina Press, 1993), 74–76, 133–134.

109. See Robert W. Coakley, *The Role of Federal Military Forces in Domestic Disorders, 1789–1878* (Washington, DC: Government Printing Office, 1998), 190–193.

110. The two relevant clauses are Article I, section 8, which refers to a congressional power to suppress insurrections, and Article IV, section 4, which refers to a federal guarantee of assistance to the states in cases of domestic violence. At the convention, these two clauses evolved out of the republican guarantee clause. See Farrand, *Records of the Convention*, 2:47–49.

111. See Wendell Phillips, *The Constitution, A Proslavery Compact* (1844; reprint, New York: Negro Universities Press, 1969), 4. Both George William Van Cleve and David Waldstreicher have recently summarized the case for a proslavery constitution. See George William Van Cleve, *A Slaveholders' Union: Slavery, Politics, and the Constitution in the Early American Republic* (Chicago: University of Chicago Press, 2010), chaps. 3–4; David Waldstreicher, *Slavery's Constitution: From Revolution to Ratification* (New York: Hill and Wang, 2009), chap. 5.

112. See Farrand, *Records of the Convention*, 2:220, 222, 364.

113. Ibid., 2:222.

114. Ibid., 2:364.

115. At the convention, the delegates debated whether the state legislature or executive could invoke the domestic violence clause. They compromised on allowing the executive to invoke the clause when the legislature was not in session. See ibid., 2:317–318, 466–467, 628–629.

116. Quoted in Young, "Army in the South," 521.

117. See Kathleen Sullivan, "Charleston, the Vesey Conspiracy, and the Development of the State Police Power," in *Race and American Political Development*, ed. Joseph Lowndes, Julie Novkov, and Dorian Warren (New York: Routledge, 2008), 59–79.

118. See Sullivan, "Charleston, the Vesey Conspiracy," 70–74. See also Philip M. Hamer, "Great Britain, the United States, and the Negro Seamen Acts, 1822–1848," *Journal of Southern History* 1, no. 1 (February 1935): 3–28, "British Counsels and the Negro Seamen Acts, 1850–1860," *Journal*

of Southern History 1, no. 2 (May 1935): 130–168; Alan Frank January, "The First Nullification: The Negro Seamen Acts Controversy in South Carolina, 1822–1860" (Ph.D. diss., University of Iowa, 1978). The act required black sailors to be imprisoned while their ships were docked in Charleston.

119. See Wilson, *Papers of Calhoun,* 7:227 (Bennett to Calhoun, July 30, 1822).

120. See Coakley, *Role of the Military,* 132–133; Floyd Benjamin Streeter, *Political Parties in Michigan, 1837–1860: An Historical Study of Political Issues and Parties in Michigan from the Admission of the State to the Civil War* (Lansing: Michigan Historical Commission, 1918), 130–131.

121. See Gary Collison, *Shadrach Minkins: From Fugitive Slave to Citizen* (Cambridge, MA: Harvard University Press, 1997), 124–133. Deputy Marshal Patrick Riley had confined Minkins in the courthouse because the state of Massachusetts had closed its jails to fugitive-slave renditions. Ibid., 121.

122. Ibid., 139–141. Secretary of State Daniel Webster (Massachusetts Whig) had urged Fillmore to grant this authority to prevent another embarrassing slave rescue in his adopted state. The Detroit case was probably unknown to Fillmore and Webster.

123. See Samuel J. May, *The Fugitive Slave Law and Its Victims* (New York: American Anti-Slavery Society, 1861), 17. Much later, when Devans became Attorney General of the United States in 1877, he hired Sims as a Department of Justice messenger. See Frederick S. Calhoun, *The Lawmen: United States Marshals and Their Deputies, 1789–1989* (Washington, DC: Smithsonian Institution Press, 1990), 77.

124. See Calhoun, *The Lawmen,* 85–86; Coakley, *Role of the Military,* 133; W. U. Hensel, *The Christiana Riot and the Treason Trials of 1851: An Historical Sketch* (1911; reprint, New York: Negro Universities Press, 1969), 40–41; Jonathan Katz, *Resistance at Christiana: The Fugitive Slave Rebellion, Christiana, Pennsylvania, September 11, 1851* (New York: Thomas Y. Crowell, 1974), 123. The slaves escaped to Canada. See Thomas P. Slaughter, *Bloody Dawn: The Christiana Riot and Racial Violence in the Antebellum North* (New York: Oxford University Press, 1991), 77–79.

125. Congress later refused to compensate Batchelder's widow for his death. Senators William Seward (New York Whig) and Charles Sumner (Massachusetts Whig) led the opposition to her private bill, though the bill did pass the Senate only to die in the House. See S. Rep. No. 356, 33rd Cong., 1st Sess., 1854; *House Journal,* 33rd Cong., 1st Sess., May 29, 1854, 947–948; *Senate Journal,* 33rd Cong., 1st Sess., July 31, 1854, 605. A federal grand jury also indicted eight men, including Theodore Parker and Wendell Phillips, for their role in the rescue attempt, but a series of adverse court rulings and acts of popular resistance to the legal process ultimately persuaded U.S. District Attorney Benjamin Franklin Hallett to drop the case. See David R. Maginnes, "The Case of the Court House Rioters in the Rendition of the Fugitive Slave Anthony Burns, 1854," *Journal of Negro History* 56, no. 1 (January 1971): 31–42; Earl M. Maltz, *Fugitive Slave on Trial: The Anthony Burns Case and Abolitionist Outrage* (Lawrence: University Press of Kansas, 2010), 100–106; Albert J. von Frank, *The Trials of Anthony Burns: Freedom and Slavery in Emerson's Boston* (Cambridge, MA: Harvard University Press, 1998).

126. See Coakley, *Role of the Military,* 134–135.

127. Ibid., 136–137. Franklin Pierce's Attorney General, Caleb Cushing (Massachusetts Democrat), had issued a formal opinion authorizing the deployment of army soldiers for this purpose following the rescue attempt. Ibid., 134. Fortunately, Burns's minister, Leonard Grimes, eventually raised sufficient funds to purchase his freedom. See Maltz, *Fugitive Slave on Trial,* 95–99.

128. As noted in the last chapter, the contemporary estimates in the Burns case range as high as $100,000, though those estimates include costs other than military costs.

129. Another result of the controversy was that the Massachusetts legislature removed Loring

from his state judicial post in 1858. To reward his party loyalty, President James Buchanan appointed him to the Court of Claims in Washington. Ibid., 153, 156.

130. See Wendell Phillips, *Speeches, Lectures, and Letters* (Boston: Lee and Shepard, 1891), 1:94 ("Sims Anniversary," April 12, 1852).

131. See Coakley, *Role of the Military*, chaps. 2–10. Obviously, other cases could be added—the German Coast slave revolt seems a clear omission—but five of fourteen is an approximate proportion.

132. See John Craig Hammond, *Slavery, Freedom, and Expansion in the Early American West* (Charlottesville: University of Virginia Press, 2007), chaps. 2–7.

133. See Carter, *Territorial Papers*, 10:5 (Andrew Ellicott to the Secretary of State, Timothy Pickering, September 24, 1797); Hammond, *Slavery, Freedom, and Expansion*, 21–22. Pickering was also antislavery and yet opposed to territorial restrictions on slavery in Mississippi. See Hammond, *Slavery, Freedom, and Expansion*, 23.

134. See Carter, *Territorial Papers*, 14:365 ([Congressman] Matthew Lyon to the President [James Madison], January 26, 1810); 16:299 (Judge Stuart to the Secretary of State [James Monroe], February 13, 1813); Hammond, *Slavery, Freedom, and Expansion*, 61, 122. Later as a U.S. senator, Edwards, however, did not support the unsuccessful campaign to reopen the ban on slavery in the Illinois state constitution. See Suzanne Cooper Guasco, "'The Deadly Influence of Negro Capitalists': Southern Yeomen and Resistance to the Expansion of Slavery in Illinois," *Civil War History* 47, no. 1 (March 2001): 7–29; Hammond, *Slavery, Freedom, and Expansion*, 123; N. Dwight Harris, *The History of Negro Servitude in Illinois* (1904; reprint, New York: Haskell House, 1969), chap. 4; James Simeone, *Democracy and Slavery in Frontier Illinois: The Bottomland Republic* (De Kalb: Northern Illinois University Press, 2000).

135. See Carter, *Territorial Papers*, 27:1165 (Delegate [James Duane] Doty to the President [Van Buren], February 1, 1839); 27:1209n68 (Secretary of State [John Forsyth] to Delegate Doty, March 2, 1839). On the general proslavery bias of territorial officials, see Fehrenbacher, *Slaveholding Republic*, 258, 261.

136. See Carter, *Territorial Papers*, 2:248 (Governor Arthur St. Clair to President George Washington, May 1, 1790). St. Clair's dispensation included the children of those slaves. See Fehrenbacher, *Slaveholding Republic*, 256–257. Fehrenbacher and several other scholars argue that the Northwest Ordinance did not keep slavery out of the northwest territories and that local antislavery movements were necessary to accomplish the task, as in Illinois. See Fehrenbacher, *Slaveholding Republic*, 56–58; Paul Finkelman, *Slavery and the Founders: Race and Liberty in the Age of Jefferson* (Armonk, NY: M.E. Sharpe, 1996), chaps. 2–3; William W. Freehling, "The Founding Fathers, Conditional Antislavery, and the Nonradicalism of the American Revolution," in *The Reintegration of American History: Slavery and the Civil War* (New York: Oxford University Press, 1994), 22–23; Hammond, *Slavery, Freedom, and Expansion*, chaps. 5–7; Mason, *Slavery and Politics*, 149–150; Leonard L. Richards, *The Slave Power: The Free North and Southern Domination, 1780–1860* (Baton Rouge: Louisiana University Press, 2001), 73–74. On the other hand, the ordinance had considerable value as a legal, political, and moral precedent for those movements. The status of slavery also had some independent force in skewing the settlement patterns of territories, as Ellicott suggests. See also Carter, *Territorial Papers*, 2:332–333 (Report of St. Clair to the Secretary of State [Thomas Jefferson], February 10, 1791); 19:67 (William Rector [surveyor general for Illinois, Missouri, and Arkansas] to Josiah Mays [commissioner of the General Land Office], April 14, 1819).

137. See Combs, "Platte Purchase," 265–274; H. Jason Combs, "The South's Slave Culture Transplanted to the Western Frontier," *Professional Geographer* 56, no. 3 (November 2004):

361–371. Federal officials negotiated treaties with a total of eight Native American nations or bands to acquire the region. The aggregate costs were $13,670 in cash and $4,650 in the value of gifts. See Combs, "Platte Purchase," 272–273.

138. See Holman Hamilton, *Prologue to Conflict: The Crisis and Compromise of 1850* (New York: Norton, 1964), 17–18, 47–48, 50, 57–58, 97–98, 103–106, 155, 159. The Taylor administration had originally paired the early admissions of both California and New Mexico in an effort to bypass the controversy over slavery in the Mexican cession. Given the admission of California, the division of Texas or the later admission of New Mexico as a slave state would have restored the sectional balance in the Senate, which remained a Southern priority throughout the decade. See Barry R. Weingast, "Political Stability and Civil War: Institutions, Commitment, and American Democracy," in *Analytic Narratives*, ed. Robert Bates, Avner Greif, Margaret Levi, Jean-Laurent Rosenthal, and Barry R. Weingast (Princeton, NJ: Princeton University Press, 1998), 186–188.

139. See Christopher Phillips, "'The Crime against Missouri': Slavery, Kansas, and the Cant of Southernness in the Border West," *Civil War History* 48, no. 1 (March 2002): 60–81. The events in Kansas dislocated, yet again, the Native American nations and bands that had vacated the Platte region.

140. See Tony R. Mullis, *Peacekeeping on the Plains: Army Operations in Bleeding Kansas* (Columbia: University of Missouri Press, 2004), 221–223. The violence in Kansas did not end completely. John Brown, for example, simply moved his antislavery vigilantism out of the army's reach to southeastern Kansas, before moving on to New York and Harpers Ferry. See Coakley, *Role of the Military*, 185–187. The violence did, however, fall to more politically acceptable levels.

141. See H. Ex. Doc. No. 34, 34th Cong., 3rd Sess., 1857, 2.

142. See Treasury Ledgers, 16:43, 464 (July 1, 1854–June 30, 1859); Appropriation Ledgers for the Treasury and Other Departments; Department of the Treasury; Record Group 39; National Archives, College Park, MD. Congress later reimbursed former territorial Governor Wilson Shannon $165 for the extraordinary expenses he incurred during the violence in the territory and the widow of former territorial Governor Robert J. Walker $13,004. See *Statutes at Large* 12 (1861): 142; 16 (1871): 503. Other territorial governors as well as Kansas residents also sought compensation for their losses from the violence in the territory, but Congress never funded their claims. See H. R. Ex. Doc. No. 111, 35th Cong., 1st Sess., 1858; H. R. Misc. Doc. No. 43, 35th Cong., 2nd Sess., 1859; H. R. Ex. Doc. No. 46, 35th Cong., 2nd Sess., 1859; H. R. Rep. No. 104, 36th Cong., 2nd Sess., 1861; H. R. Misc. Doc. No. 47, 40th Cong., 3rd Sess., 1869; H. R. Rep. No. 77, 41st Cong., 2nd Sess., 1870; H. R. Misc. Doc. No. 39, 41st Cong., 3rd Sess., 1871.

143. See Mullis, *Peacekeeping*, 243–244.

144. While the general status of U.S. territories was the topic of much discussion, the power of Congress to pass "needful rules and regulations" to govern territories was not. The clause originated, again, with Madison. See Farrand, *Records of the Convention*, 2:324.

145. See *Dred Scott v. Sandford* 60 U.S. 393 (1857), at 432–452 (Taney); Don E. Fehrenbacher, *The Dred Scott Case: Its Significance in American Law and Politics* (New York: Oxford University Press, 1978), chaps. 16–17. Two of the four Northern associate justices, Benjamin Curtis and John McLean, also found Taney's position untenable. The other two Northern justices either simply concurred in Taney's opinion (Robert Grier) or (mostly) avoided the territories issue in his own opinion (Samuel Nelson). See *Dred Scott*, at 457–469 (Nelson), 469 (Grier), 538–547 (McLean), 604–633 (Curtis).

146. See Joshua R. Giddings, *The Exiles of Florida: The Crimes Committed By Our Government against the Maroons Who Fled from South Carolina and Other Slave States* (1858; reprint, Baltimore: Swallow, 1997), 314–315.

147. See *Congressional Globe*, 26th Cong., 1st Sess., 1840, 659–667; *Congressional Globe*, 26th Cong., 2nd Sess., 1841, 155, 158.

148. President Jefferson first articulated the vision of Native American removals west of the Mississippi River; Calhoun, serving as Monroe's Secretary of War, was the architect of the policy. See Garrison, "Indian Policy," 101, 104; Reginald Horsman, *Expansion and American Indian Policy, 1783–1812* (1967; reprint, Norman: University of Oklahoma Press, 1992), 103–104, 139–140, 162; Satz, *Indian Policy*, 6.

149. See Alisse Portnoy, *Their Right to Speak: Women's Activism in the Indian and Slave Debates* (Cambridge, MA: Harvard University Press, 2005), 165–166. Tim Garrison cites the sectional division on the southeast removals as evidence that slavery was not the only issue threatening the union, overlooking the strong interrelationship between the two issues. See Garrison, "Indian Policy," 98, 123. Portnoy, in contrast, stresses that interrelationship. See Portnoy, *Right to Speak*, 4–6, 90–91, 158.

150. See *Congressional Globe*, 25th Cong., 3rd Sess., 1839, 321–323.

151. See Missall and Missall, *Seminole Wars*, 173, 191; Twyman, *Black Seminole Legacy*, 148.

152. See Stanley W. Campbell, *The Slave Catchers: Enforcement of the Fugitive Slave Law, 1850–1860* (Chapel Hill: University of North Carolina Press, 1968), 104–105.

153. See William W. Freehling, *The Road to Disunion*, vol. 2, *Secessionists Triumphant* (New York: Oxford University Press, 2007), 79–84, 138–139.

154. See Fehrenbacher, *Slaveholding Republic*, 280–283.

155. See Alison Goodyear Freehling, *Drift toward Dissolution: The Virginia Slavery Debate of 1831–1832* (Baton Rouge: Louisiana State University Press, 1982), chap. 5.

156. See Sullivan, "Charleston, the Vesey Conspiracy," 73–74. Associate Supreme Court Justice William Johnson (South Carolina) had suggested that the acts were unconstitutional in an 1823 circuit opinion, an opinion for which he was widely excoriated in his own state. See Sullivan, "Vesey Conspiracy," 71–72; 8 *Fed. Cas.* 493 (No. 4366; C.C. D.S.C. 1823). When he replaced Berrien as Jackson's Attorney General, Taney brushed aside a British protest to North Carolina's similar black-sailor legislation. See Fehrenbacher, *Dred Scott*, 70.

157. Campbell's population of 332 fugitive-slaves cases includes only fifteen cases from the upper North, six from Massachusetts, seven from upstate New York, and one each from Michigan and Wisconsin. See Campbell, *The Slave Catchers*, 199–206 (Tables 1–11).

158. See Roy B. Basler, ed., *The Collected Works of Abraham Lincoln* (New Brunswick, NJ: Rutgers University Press, 1953), 4:262–263 ("First Inaugural Address—Final Text," March 4, 1861).

159. In coercing Border Ruffians, the federal government was acting against the individual, short-term interests of some slaveholders in order to protect the aggregate, long-term interests of most slaveholders. I would frame Jesup's Black Seminole removal strategy in similar terms.

160. See Andrew R. L. Cayton, "Radicals in the 'Western World': The Federalist Conquest of Trans-Appalachian North America," in *Federalists Reconsidered*, ed. Doron Ben-Atar and Barbara B. Oberg (Charlottesville: University Press of Virginia, 1998), 86, 89; Cayton, "Separate Interests," 39–67; Andrew R. L. Cayton, "'When Shall We Cease to Have Judases?' The Blount Conspiracy and the Limits of the 'Extended Republic,'" in *Launching the "Extended Republic": The Federalist Era*, ed. Ronald Hoffman and Peter J. Albert (Charlottesville: University Press of Virginia, 1996), 156–189.

161. See Hammond, *Slavery, Freedom, and Expansion*, 14, 24–25, 31, 40, 45–46, 48–50, 53, 57; John Craig Hammond, "'They Are Very Much Interested in Obtaining an Unlimited Slavery': Rethinking the Expansion of Slavery in the Louisiana Purchase Territories, 1803–1805," *Journal of the Early Republic* 23, no. 3 (Fall 2003): 356–358, 363–365, 374–375, 378–379.

162. See Coakley, *Role of the Military,* 128–137; Young, "Army in the South," chaps. 9–10.

163. See Freehling, *Secessionists Triumphant,* 140–141; Weingast, "Political Stability," 178–180. The defection of five border-state congressmen was also crucial to the defeat of the bill in the House by a narrow 120–112 margin. Despite Douglas's opposition, the bill had passed the Senate by a relatively comfortable 33–25 margin.

164. See Mahon, *Second Seminole War,* 326–327; Mullis, *Peacekeeping,* 243–244.

165. See Bensel, *Yankee Leviathan,* 98–99.

166. See Skelton, *American Profession,* 359–361; Wilson, "Politics of Procurement," 46–48, 56, 59–60, 62–63. The Union also benefited from the development of the navy through its efforts to suppress American participation in the slave trade.

167. See Mullis, *Peacekeeping,* 248.

168. See Balogh, *Government Out of Sight,* 210–211; Katznelson, "Flexible Capacity," 90.

169. Ironically, Smith had seen action in the Second Seminole War as the commander of a Louisiana volunteer unit. See Canter Brown, Jr., "Persifor F. Smith, the Louisiana Volunteers, and Florida's Second Seminole War," *Louisiana History* 34, no. 4 (Fall 1993): 389–410. Smith died in 1858, but Sprague's career took an interesting twist at the beginning of the Civil War. He was first assigned to lead the army's recruiting efforts in Albany, New York. When Governor Edwin D. Morgan appointed him head of the 113th Regiment of New York Volunteers, Secretary of War Simon Cameron (Pennsylvania) rejected the appointment. Soon thereafter, Sprague was appointed adjutant general of New York. See Ben E. Pingenot, "Sprague, John Titcomb," *Handbook of Texas Online,* http://www.tshaonline.org/handbook/online/articles/fsp30.

170. See Lancaster, "Sherman's Introduction to War," 65–66; Young, "Army in the South," 520–521.

171. Quoted in James M. Merrill, *William Tecumseh Sherman* (Chicago: Rand McNally, 1971), 47. See also Lancaster, "Sherman's Introduction to War," 62, 65–66, 72.

172. The other three policy areas, though, also had covert aspects, such as the indirect nature of the ACS's federal support.

173. Interestingly, Jesup had moved from the center to the periphery to take command of the war effort in Florida and then back to the center after stepping down as military commander.

174. Again, Brian Balogh's *Government Out of Sight* fails to discuss how the presence of slavery was one factor that strongly encouraged the federal government to operate "out of sight," on the periphery.

CHAPTER 6. FREE LABOR NOT PREFERRED

1. See Morris J. MacGregor and Bernard C. Nalty, ed., *Blacks in the United States Armed Forces: Basic Documents,* vol. 1, *A Time of Slavery* (Wilmington, DE: Scholarly Resources, 1977), 218.

2. Ibid., 187. As we will see below, the army had also adopted regulations against free-black enlistments, while the navy had established quotas on such enlistments.

3. See Reports of Persons and Articles Hired, 1818–1905, Boxes 14–15; Office of the Quartermaster General; Record Group 92; Entry 238; National Archives, Washington, DC.

4. See *Historical Statistics of the United States Millennial Edition Online,* Tables Ea894–903; Ed26–47, http://hsus.cambridge.org. Even then, the military probably remained the largest federal employer if one counts its slave rentals and other temporary hires.

5. See *American State Papers, Post Office* 1:9 ("Further Provision for Transporting the Mail," March 30, 1802), 22.

6. On Southern Indian agents as slaveholders, see R. Halliburton, Jr., *Red over Black: Black Slavery among the Cherokee Indians* (Westport, CT: Greenwood, 1977), 117, 143; George Klos, "Blacks and the Seminole Removal Debates, 1821–1835," *Florida Historical Quarterly* 68, no. 1 (July 1989): 55, 63–65; William G. McLoughlin, "Red Indians, Black Slavery and White Racism: America's Slaveholding Indians," *American Quarterly* 26, no. 4 (December 1974): 375; Theda Perdue, *Slavery and the Evolution of Cherokee Society, 1540–1866* (Knoxville: University of Tennessee Press, 1979), 54.

7. See Accounts of the Commissioners of the City of Washington, 1794–1802, Boxes 43–50; Records of the Account Officers of the Department of Treasury; Fred Manning Collection of Documents from Various Series in Record Group 217; UD Entry 104; National Archives, College Park, MD.

8. As we will also see below, the federal government occasionally employed slaves in Northern states and territories.

9. See John Lauritz Larson, *Internal Improvement: National Public Works and the Promise of Popular Government in the Early United States* (Chapel Hill: University of North Carolina Press, 2001), 125–126, 143–144.

10. Ibid., 162–173.

11. See Donald L. Robinson, *Slavery in the Structure of American Politics, 1765–1820* (New York: Harcourt Brace Jovanovich, 1971), 402.

12. See William W. Freehling, *Prelude to Civil War: The Nullification Controversy in South Carolina, 1816–1836* (New York: Harper & Row, 1965), 131–133, 143–144.

13. See Persons and Articles Hired; Record Group 92; National Archives. Free labor would be, in almost all cases, white labor. Free black laborers generally fell through the cracks of federal employment data from this period, as did, in fact, many slaves. In my examination of several "persons and articles hired" record collections at the National Archives, I found only a handful of cases in which the person hired was clearly identified as a free black. The paucity of such cases was probably the result of a combination of factors: sloppy record-keeping, very few free black hires, and free black hires identified as slaves or not identified as blacks.

14. Job shifting was, of course, not confined to slave labor.

15. Unfortunately, this data does not exist in the capital construction case or in any of the other cases I discuss in this chapter. My assumption is that overseers spent more time supervising slave labor than free labor because of the different incentive structures involved, but that is only an assumption. The debate over whether slave labor was cheaper than free labor in the private sector is a longstanding one. Cf. Robert W. Fogel and Stanley L. Engerman, *Time on the Cross: The Economics of American Negro Slavery* (Boston: Little, Brown, 1974); Gavin Wright, *The Political Economy of the Cotton South: Households, Markets, and Wealth in the Nineteenth Century* (New York: Norton, 1978).

16. The federal government temporarily owned slaves, as when U.S. marshals confiscated imprisoned slaves to cover their maintenance costs or when navy crews seized Africans from suspected slave ships, but only until they were auctioned or transported to Liberia.

17. See Records Relating to Personnel Pay Rolls, 1844–1899, Box 136; Records of the Office of the Chief of the Bureau; Navy Record Collection; Record Group 71; Entry 32; National Archives, Washington, DC.

18. See *Senate Journal*, 37th Cong., 2nd Sess., June 16, 1862, 653. The Naval Academy had been moved out of harm's way to Newport, Rhode Island, the previous month. In Annapolis, it had employed slaves as attendants. See Charles Todorich, *The Spirited Years: The History of the Antebellum Naval Academy* (Annapolis, MD: Naval Institute Press, 1984), 126, 156.

19. Thirteen of the twenty-one Republican senators who voted on the amendment voted in its favor. Conversely, ten of the fourteen opposition senators who voted on the amendment voted against it, as did all five of the senators from the non-seceding slave states (Delaware, Kentucky, Maryland, and Missouri) who voted on the amendment and one of the two Virginia unionist senators. See *Senate Journal*, 37th Cong., 2nd Sess., June 16, 1862, 653.

20. See Thomas Reid, *America's Fortress: A History of Fort Jefferson, Dry Tortugas, Florida* (Gainesville: University Press of Florida, 2006), 69.

21. In Appendix C, I list three major ($100,000+) slave-labor expenditures. They total almost $1 million. Unfortunately, the lack of documentation also prevents most finer-grained comparisons, such as between the federal government's use of slave labor and free labor within given years, at specific facilities, or in different regions, or, alternatively, between the federal government's use of slave labor and its use by other levels of government or by private firms in comparable economic sectors.

22. See MacGregor and Nalty, *Time of Slavery*, 219.

23. See Robert S. Starobin, *Industrial Slavery in the Old South* (New York: Oxford University Press, 1970), 32. I discuss the Dancy scandal further below.

24. See MacGregor and Nalty, *Time of Slavery*, 220–221.

25. Ibid., 222–223. According to this data, 96.5 percent of the black employees of the army in August 1842 were slaves.

26. Ibid., 222.

27. Ibid., 221. Jesup adds that the navy actually employed some of the reported slaves. He had been the commanding officer in Florida from December 1836 to May 1838.

28. Ibid., 222–223. George Bomford (New York) was actually the Ordnance Office head; Talcott was acting in that capacity.

29. I base this $15.25 monthly average on the average in my 1843 selection of quartermaster reports discussed immediately below.

30. See *Historical Statistics of the United States*, Table Ea894–903. This table lists the federal civilian-employment totals only at ten-year intervals from 1821 to 1871. The 1841 figure is 18,038.

31. Most disappointingly, I did not find any longitudinal data for the Office of the Chief of Engineers, which undoubtedly employed the most slaves during the period.

32. I selected August because the 1842 employment data discussed above is from August.

33. It is distinctly possible that some army facilities are not represented because their quartermasters did not file any monthly reports for the year or that the reports they did file are not in the record collection for the various reasons stated in the text. In any case, the record collection is too incomplete to make any facility-by-facility or region-by-region comparison of the use of slave labor, especially because most of the reporting facilities were temporary ones.

34. See Persons and Articles Hired, Boxes 1–2; Record Group 92; National Archives. Box 1 is labeled 1818–1821 and contains very few reports, almost all from 1821. Box 2 is labeled 1822–1823 and also contains very few reports, including some from 1821. For the record, I found monthly reports with six slaves employed (five at Charleston posts and one in New Orleans) in Box 1 for 1821 at a total monthly cost of $41.50 and two slaves employed (both at Fort Moultrie in Charleston) in Box 2 for 1823 at a total monthly cost of $70.

35. See Persons and Articles Hired, Box 5; Record Group 92; National Archives.

36. The Savannah slaves were probably helping build Fort Pulaski. See Julia Floyd Smith, *Slavery Rice Culture: Low Country Georgia, 1750–1860* (Knoxville: University of Tennessee Press, 1991), 59–60.

37. See Persons and Articles Hired, Boxes 8–9; Record Group 92; National Archives. One of the reports (Fort Monroe, Virginia) is for September.

38. See Persons and Articles Hired, Boxes 14–15; Record Group 92; National Archives. Probably because of the dislocations of the Second Seminole War, the 1838 monthly reports are very incomplete and my selected months ranged over a number of months.

39. See Persons and Articles Hired, Boxes 26–27; Record Group 92; National Archives. One report (Fort Stansbury, Florida) is for January, one (Cedar Keys, Florida) for February, and one (Baton Rouge) for March.

40. As we have seen, the official end of the Second Seminole War was somewhat premature.

41. The quartermaster identifies the two slaves employed at Fort Washita as the slaves of Native Americans, presumably Choctaw. For the army's use of the slaves of Native Americans at its southwestern forts, see Jane F. Lancaster, *Removal Aftershock: The Seminoles' Struggles to Survive in the West, 1836–1866* (Knoxville: University of Tennessee Press, 1994), 69; Daniel F. Littlefield, Jr., *Africans and Creeks: From the Colonial Period to the Civil War* (Westport, CT: Greenwood Press, 1979), 181–182, 186.

42. See Persons and Articles Hired, Boxes 33–34; Record Group 92; National Archives. One of the reports (New Orleans barracks) is for June.

43. The last U.S. troops left Mexico in June 1848.

44. See Persons and Articles Hired, Boxes 45–47; Record Group 92; National Archives. One of the reports (Indianola, Texas) is for June and one (Pensacola) is for December.

45. See Persons and Articles Hired, Boxes 64–71; Record Group 92; National Archives. The quartermaster identifies one of the three slaves employed at Fort Smith as the slave of a Native American.

46. See H. R. Doc. No. 111, 17th Cong., 2nd Sess., 1823. The slave-labor costs at the New Orleans armory represent 88 percent of the total. Slaves also helped construct the new arsenal at Harpers Ferry in 1819 and thereafter worked there, though apparently, because of its relatively isolated location in western Virginia, they were always few in number and predominantly the slaves of army officers. See Merritt Roe Smith, *Harper's Ferry Armory and the New Technology: The Challenge of Change* (Ithaca, NY: Cornell University Press, 1977), 44.

47. See Payrolls of Workers at Ft. Jefferson, Fla., 1860–62; Box 1; Records of the Office of the Chief of Engineers; Record Group 77; Entry 268; National Archives, Washington, DC. I tallied the costs only through June 1861 because it was the last month of FY1861.

48. See "Memorandum to State Department," May 7, 1861; Box 166 (S8683); Letters Received by the Office of the Chief of Engineers; U.S. Army; Record Group 77; Entry 18; National Archives, Washington, DC; Reid, *America's Fortress*, 45–46.

49. See Reid, *America's Fortress*, 69.

50. See Letters Received by the Chief of Engineers, Boxes 117–118, Record Group 77; National Archives.

51. See Letters Received by the Chief of Engineers, Box 91; Record Group 77; National Archives.

52. See "Captain E. B. Hunt to Colonel [Renee Edward] De Russy," October 13, 1859; Letters Received by the Chief of Engineers; Box 91 (H1295); Record Group 77; National Archives. I was unable to find any De Russy response or any direct indication of why Hunt either stopped or started recording the number of his black workers. Based on my examination of several "persons and articles hired" record collections at the National Archives, there seems to have been no general policy on reporting the race and status of temporary hires, or if there was, it was not generally followed.

53. See MacGregor and Nalty, *Time of Slavery*, 219. While the departmental regulations had a caveat that allowed navy officers to employ blacks at navy yards with the permission of either the secretary of navy or the Board of Navy Commissioners, the reported cases strongly suggest that local navy officers employed blacks without seeking such permission and that neither the secretary nor the board monitored their compliance. Indeed, Congress abolished the board in 1842. See *Statutes at Large* 5 (1842): 579.

54. See Ernest F. Dibble, "Slave Rentals to the Military: Pensacola and the Gulf Coast," *Civil War History* 23, no. 2 (June 1977): 107.

55. My examination of the (incomplete) payroll abstracts for the Pensacola navy yard supports this estimate. As noted above, the June 1855 abstract lists 137 slaves. See Records Relating to Personnel Pay Rolls, 1844–1899, Box 136; Record Group 71; National Archives.

56. See Records Relating to Personnel Pay Rolls, 1844–1899, Boxes 135–137; Record Group 71; National Archives.

57. See Yuval Taylor, ed., *I Was Born a Slave: An Anthology of Classic Slave Narratives,* vol. 1, *1772–1849* (Chicago: Lawrence Hill Books, 1999), 271.

58. See "The Diary of Michael Shiner Relating to the History of the Washington Navy Yard, 1813–1869," 1 (preface), www.history.navy.mil/library/online/shinerdiary.html (edited and transcribed by John G. Sharp; dated October 14, 2007). Preface page citations are from my printout of this document. The document itself includes only diary page numbers.

59. See "Shiner Diary," 6–7 (preface), n5. (The editor's notes appear on an unnumbered page at the end of the document.) In this case, Hull or one of his predecessors may well have sought special permission; if so, it was probably because of the yard's location near the seat of government.

60. See MacGregor and Nalty, *Time of Slavery*, 218; Bernard C. Nalty, *Strength for the Fight: A History of Black Americans in the Military* (New York: Free Press, 1986), 26. One or more of the slaves involved in several celebrated escapes or attempted escapes worked at navy yards, including in the *Pearl* (Washington) and Minkins (Norfolk) cases. See Gary Collison, *Shadrach Minkins: From Fugitive Slave to Citizen* (Cambridge, MA: Harvard University Press, 1997), 32; Josephine F. Pacheco, *The Pearl: A Failed Slave Escape on the Potomac* (Chapel Hill: University of North Carolina Press, 2005), 115.

61. See MacGregor and Nalty, *Time of Slavery*, 219. See also Christopher McKee, *A Gentlemanly and Honorable Profession: The Creation of the U.S. Naval Officer Corps, 1794–1815* (Annapolis, MD: Naval Institute Press, 1991), 333, 561n11.

62. Army officers could supplement their incomes by using slaves as their personal servants because they then received the army rate for the pay, rations, and clothing of personal servants. Of course, they had to devote at least some of that money to the upkeep of their slaves, but the supposition is that they profited from the practice. See Edward M. Coffman, *The Old Army: A Portrait of the American Army in Peacetime, 1784–1898* (New York: Oxford University Press, 1986), 430n.120.

63. Ibid., 94.

64. Ibid., 94; William Cooper, Jr., *Jefferson Davis, American* (New York: Knopf, 2000), 49.

65. See Coffman, *Old Army*, 95; Bernard C. Nalty, "The Black Serviceman and the Constitution," in *The United States Military under the Constitution of the United States, 1789–1989*, ed. Richard H. Kohn (New York: New York University Press, 1991), 156; "Rachael, A Woman of Color v. Walker," *Reports of Cases Argued and Decided in the Supreme Court of the State of Missouri, from 1835 to 1837* (Fayette, MO: Boon's Lick Democrat, 1837), 350–354.

66. See Zachary Taylor, *Papers*, Series 2, *General Correspondence, 1814–1850* (Washington, DC: Library of Congress, 1958), Reel 1 ("Taylor to Dr. Thomas Lawson, surgeon, U.S. Army, Pensacola," August 28, 1828). Taylor's letters do not record the result of his inquiry. Though the Jackson administration was more sympathetic to the concerns of slaveholders—Jackson had himself been a slaveholding army officer—the order was not rescinded. See William B. Skelton, *An American Profession of Arms: The Army Officer Corps, 1784–1861* (Lawrence: University Press of Kansas, 1992), 443n7. For a later case at the Augusta arsenal, see Capt. [Edward] Harding to [Henry] Stanton (acting quartermaster general), July 1, 1839; Box 1041; Consolidated Correspondence; Department of War; Record Group 92; Entry 225; National Archives, Washington, DC.

67. Following Barbour, seven of the thirteen secretaries of war were from Southern states, including all five from 1849 to 1861.

68. See "Lt. Wright to Gen. Totten," August 18, 1851 (Box 185; W1074); "Phelps to Totten," October 9, 1851; "Mallory to Phelps," December 23, 1851; "Totten to Controller's Office," December 27, 1851 (Box 48; C2936); Letters Received by the Chief of Engineers; Record Group 77; National Archives.

69. See *American State Papers, Military Affairs*, 2:267 ("Fortification on Dauphin Island," February 9, 1825), 331. The assessor added that the contractors still would have lost money on the project. It was finally completed in 1861 and named Fort Gaines.

70. See Dibble, "Slavery Rentals," 103–105, 107–108, 110–113.

71. See Christopher L. Tomlins, "Nat Turner's Shadow: Reflections on the Norfolk Dry Dock Affair of 1830–1831," *Labor History* 33, no. 4 (Fall 1992): 513.

72. See Tomlins, "Turner's Shadow," 498–499. A group of skilled white workers from Pennsylvania who had earlier been recruited to help construct a hospital at the navy yard initiated this first protest. Later, Baldwin recruited white masons and stone cutters from Massachusetts who had worked on the construction of new dry docks at the Charlestown (Boston) navy yard. Baldwin was simultaneously the chief engineer for both projects. The Norfolk project cost $950,000, almost $300,000 more than the Boston project. Tomlins claims that the higher cost was largely the result of Baldwin's reliance on out-of-state labor. Ibid., 498.

73. Ibid., 500. Ten cents of the slaves' daily pay went to the slaves themselves as a work incentive.

74. Ibid., 505.

75. Southampton County is just west of Norfolk.

76. See Tomlins, "Turner's Shadow," 511, 514.

77. Ibid., 516. Tomlins tracks only the number and percentage of slaves working on the project until October 1832, in order to show that the protest did not affect those figures. At $.72 per day and 26 working days per month, it would have cost $49,402 to employ 91 slaves for the 29 months from May 1830 through October 1832. (The prevailing norm was 26 working days per month. See Robert A. Margo, *Wages and Labor Markets in the United States, 1820–1860* [Chicago: University of Chicago Press, 2000], 169n15.)

78. See Linda Upham-Bornstein, "'Men of Families': The Intersection of Labor Conflict and Race in the Norfolk Dry Dock Affair, 1829–1831," *Labor: Studies in Working-Class History of the Americas* 4, no. 1 (Spring 2007): 90. The petition may be referring to the total workforce at the navy yard, but in either case the numbers seem inflated for rhetorical effect, as does, obviously, the characterization of the black workers.

79. Ibid., 76–77, 87. Baldwin's own salary, which covered his supervision of both the Norfolk and Boston projects, was $4,000 per year plus $80 per month in expenses. Johnson had previously trained black convicts to cut stone on the Boston project. See ibid., 72, 76.

80. Ibid., 75, 81.

81. See Tomlins, "Turner's Shadow," 517–518.

82. See Mark F. Boyd, "The First American Road in Florida: Papers Relating to the Survey and Construction of the Pensacola–St. Augustine Highway, Part I," *Florida Historical Society Quarterly* 14, no. 2 (October 1935): 73–106, and "The First American Road in Florida: Papers Relating to the Survey and Construction of the Pensacola–St. Augustine Highway, Part II," *Florida Historical Society Quarterly* 15, no. 1 (January 1936): 139–192.

83. The first roads in new territories were typically military roads. See Carter Goodrich, *Government Promotion of American Canals and Railroads, 1800–1890* (New York: Columbia University Press, 1960), 174, 268–269; Andrew C. Isenberg, "The Market Revolution in the Borderlands: George Champlin Sibley in Missouri and New Mexico, 1808–1826," *Journal of the Early Republic* 21, no. 2 (Autumn 2001): 464; Laurence J. Malone, *Opening the West: Federal Internal Improvements before 1860* (Westport, CT: Greenwood, 1998), 25, 52–72; Yancey M. Quinn, Jr., "Jackson's Military Road," *Journal of Mississippi History* 41, no. 4 (November 1979): 335–350. The Federal Road, which eventually connected New Orleans to western Georgia, was an earlier case of a military road that was built with slave labor. Slaves also helped maintain roads in Southern states and territories because state and local governments imposed levies on slaveholders for that purpose. In the case of the Federal Road, the federal government paid the maintenance costs, thus again indirectly subsidizing slave labor. See Henry DeLeon Southerland, Jr., and Jerry Elijah Brown, *The Federal Road through Georgia, the Creek Nation, and Alabama, 1806–1836* (Tuscaloosa: University of Alabama Press, 1989), 52–56.

84. See H. R. Doc. No. 201, 26th Cong., 1st Sess., 1840, 13–16.

85. See "[illegible] to Jesup," June 11, 1840; "[George C.] Whiting [Treasury Department clerk] to Jesup," June 23, 1841; Box 1041; Record Group 92; Entry 225; National Archives.

86. See H. R. Doc. No. 201, 26th Cong., 1st Sess., 1840, 116, 118.

87. The exceptions were cases in which slaveholders allowed slaves to rent themselves out. Otherwise, slaves had no monetary incentive to enforce a labor contract or arrangement to which they were not a party. They also could not testify in court to legally enforce such agreements.

88. See Dibble, "Slave Rentals," 110. The Shiner diary records racial violence against blacks who worked at the Washington navy yard, including against Shiner himself. See "Shiner Diary," 6 (preface), 60–63 (diary).

89. See D. L. Robinson, *Slavery in American Politics,* 114. Washington later relaxed the policy to allow free blacks who had enlisted to re-enlist. It was also the case that the states had generally proscribed black enlistments. Even the New England states had, though they did not enforce the policy. Virginia actually had the most liberal policy at the beginning of the war in at least permitting free blacks to enlist in its militia. Ibid., 113, 480n36.

90. See Robinson, *Slavery in American Politics,* 480nn36, 40. Because of chronic manpower shortages, all these states, except for Virginia, had liberalized their policies during the war to permit even slaves to enlist in their militias.

91. See Lorenzo Johnston Greene, "Some Observations on the Black Regiment of Rhode Island in the American Revolution," *Journal of Negro History* 27, no. 2 (April 1952): 166; D. L. Robinson, *Slavery in American Politics,* 115–116. Despite its name, the unit also included white soldiers and within the year permitted only white enlistments.

92. See D. L. Robinson, *Slavery in American Politics,* 118–119. The incentives were $1,000 for the slaveholder, while the slave received freedom and $50 at the end of his enlistment. The idea had originated with Laurens's son, John, who was on Washington's staff. John Laurens continued to lobby for the idea until his battlefield death in 1782. Ibid., 121–122.

262   NOTES TO PAGES 152–153

93. Ibid., 118. As we have seen, slaves later worked in these Charleston fortifications.

94. See Laura Jensen, *Patriots, Settlers, and the Origins of American Social Policy* (Cambridge: Cambridge University Press, 2003), chaps. 2–5.

95. See MacGregor and Nalty, *Time of Slavery*, 156–183. The Department of War did not disclose who requested the search. Bernard Nalty estimates that as many as 5,000 blacks served in the U.S. military during the war. See Nalty, *Strength for the Fight*, 18.

96. See MacGregor and Nalty, *Time of Slavery*, 181–182; H. R. Rep. No. 289, 27th Cong., 2nd Sess., 1842; H. R. No. 640, 26th Cong., 2nd Sess., 1841; H. R. No. 257, 27th Cong., 2nd Sess., 1842; *Senate Journal*, 27th Cong., 2nd Sess., August 29, 1842, 637. Tatton's claim was originally denied because she had remarried. Wells' last name was also listed as Saunders and the years he served from 1777 or 1778 to 1783.

97. See MacGregor and Nalty, *Time of Slavery*, 187; Nalty, *Strength for the Fight*, 19–20.

98. See David S. Heidler and Jeanne T. Heidler, ed., *Encyclopedia of the War of 1812* (Annapolis, MD: Naval Institute Press, 2004), 4–5; Lorenzo J. Greene, "The Negro in the War of 1812 and the Civil War," *Negro History Bulletin* 14, no. 1 (March 1951): 133; Harold D. Langley, *Social Reform in the United States Navy, 1798–1862* (Urbana: University of Illinois Press, 1967), 93; MacGregor and Nalty, *Time of Slavery*, 213; Nalty, *Strength for the Fight*, 21; Dennis Denmark Nelson, "The Integration of the Negro into the United States Navy" (M.A. thesis, Howard University, 1947), 9–14. This permission was only to last until the end of the war.

99. See Greene, "The Negro in the War of 1812," 133; James M. Guthrie, *Camp-Fires of the Afro-American; or, The Colored Man as a Patriot* (1899; reprint, New York: Johnson Reprint, 1970), 66; MacGregor and Nalty, *Time of Slavery*, 213–214; Nalty, *Strength for the Fight*, 23; William C. Nell, *The Colored Patriots of the American Revolution* (1855; reprint, New York: Arno Press and the New York Times, 1968), 205, 208. New York's 1800 gradual emancipation act left many African Americans in slavery until the state legislature finally enacted a new law in 1817 that emancipated (almost) all the state's remaining slaves as of July 4, 1827. The number of slaves in the state plunged from 10,088 to 75 between the 1820 and 1830 censuses. See Campbell Gibson and Kay Jung, "Historical Census Statistics on Population Totals by Race, 1790 to 1990, and by Hispanic Origin, 1970 to 1990, for the United States, Regions, Divisions, and States" (Washington, DC: U.S. Census Bureau, 2002), Table 47, http://www.census.gov/population/www/documentation/ twps0056/twps0056.html; Arthur Zilversmit, *The First Emancipation: The Abolition of Slavery in the North* (Chicago: University of Chicago Press, 1967), 213–214.

100. See Y. Taylor, *Born a Slave*, 463–468.

101. See MacGregor and Nalty, *Time of Slavery*, 215–216; Nalty, *Strength for the Fight*, 24–25. When the New Orleans free-black militia helped win the Battle of New Orleans, General Jackson recommended that the members of the militia receive full army pay and benefits, despite the existing regulations against mustering blacks into the U.S. military, but they never received such compensation. See MacGregor and Nalty, *Time of Slavery*, 217; Nalty, *Strength for the Fight*, 25–26.

102. See H. R. Rep. No. 78, 21st Cong., 2nd Sess., 1831. The report notes that Jackson had already received Gammon's back pay of $37.42.

103. See H. R. Rep. No. 184, 22nd Cong., 1st Sess., 1832; *House Journal*, 22nd Cong., 2nd Sess., December 29, 1832, 117; *Senate Journal*, 22nd Cong., 2nd Sess., February 20, 1833, 200.

104. See H. R. Rep. No. 111, 23rd Cong., 1st Sess., 1833. The committee also notes that slaves could not legally hold title to real estate and that, as a result, Frederick could not have profited from a land bounty even if his military service had entitled him to one.

105. See H. R. Rep. No. 392, 23rd Cong., 1st Sess., 1834.

106. See H. R. Rep. No. 425, 24th Cong., 1st Sess., 1836.

107. See *American State Papers, Claims,* 1:278 ("Claim for a Slave and Clothing Lost in Military Service," December 29, 1815), 453; *Miscellaneous* 1:300 ("Slave Lost in the Hospital Service," February 24, 1816), 468; *Claims* 1:382 ("Slave Killed in Military Service," February 3, 1818), 548; *Claims* 1:478 ("Loss of a Slave Impressed into the Public Service," January 20, 1819), 669–670; *Claims* 1:496 ("Slave Killed in Military Service," December 31, 1819), 679; *Claims* 1:503 ("Loss of a Slave Impressed into the Public Service," January 6, 1820), 686; *Claims* 1:552 ("Slave Lost in the Public Service," January 29, 1821), 776; *Claims* 1:590 ("Slave Lost in the Public Service, and Final Settlement Certificates," February 22, 1822), 838.

108. See MacGregor and Nalty, *Time of Slavery,* 218. As we have seen, the new navy regulations also barred both slaves and free blacks from working at navy yards.

109. See Langley, *Social Reform,* 92–93; MacGregor and Nalty, *Time of Slavery,* 219; Nalty, *Strength for the Fight,* 26–27.

110. See *House Journal,* August 13, 1842, 1282; Nalty, *Strength for the Fight,* 27; *Senate Journal,* 27th Cong., 2nd Sess., July 29, 1842, 514; *Senate Journal,* July 30, 1842, 519.

111. See Kevin Mulroy, *Freedom on the Border: The Seminole Maroons in Florida, the Indian Territory, Coahuila, and Texas* (Lubbock: Texas Tech University Press, 1993), 28. Like many of the blacks who worked for the army during the war, Pacheco had at one time lived among the Seminoles; hence, both his potential usefulness and subversiveness from the army's perspective.

112. See *Congressional Globe,* 30th Cong., 1st Sess., 1849, 303. Antonio Pacheco was to receive $25 per month from the army for Louis's services. He asked for $1,000 as compensation for the loss of those services.

113. Ibid., 174.

114. Ibid., 176. Giddings contended that both he and John Quincy Adams had intended to speak against the bill.

115. See H. R. Rep. No. 146, 27th Cong., 3rd Sess., 1843; *Statutes at Large* 6 (1844): 920. De Peyster and Cruger owned one of the largest sugar plantations in Florida.

116. See Guthrie, *Camp-Fires,* 230; Robert E. May, "Invisible Men: Blacks and the U.S. Army in the Mexican War," *Historian* 49, no. 4 (August 1987): 465–466; Nell, *Colored Patriots,* 390–391. Scott, Taylor, and Worth had each been commanding officers in Florida during the Second Seminole War, while Butler had been one of its strongest congressional defenders. Coincidentally, Davis had married Taylor's second daughter, Sarah, against Taylor's wishes in 1835. Sarah died of malaria shortly thereafter. The two men reconciled during the Mexican-American War. May notes that navy officers also employed slaves as personal servants during the war. See May, "Invisible Men," 464n.4.

117. See Rhoda van Bibber Tanner Doubleday, ed., *Journals of Major Philip Norbourne Barbour and His Wife Isabella Hopkins Barbour* (New York: G. P. Putnam's Sons, 1936), 28.

118. For a recent reexamination of this alleged quid pro quo, see Joshua D. Clinton and Adam Meirowitz, "Testing Explanations of Strategic Voting in Legislatures: A Reexamination of the Compromise of 1790," *American Journal of Political Science* 48, no. 4 (October 2004): 675–689.

119. See William C. Allen, "History of Slave Laborers in the Construction of the United States Capitol," 3, http://clerk.house.gov/art_history/art_artifacts/slave_labor_reportl.pdf (dated June 1, 2005); Bob Arnebeck, *Through a Fiery Trial: Building Washington, 1790–1800* (Lanham, MD: Madison Books, 1991), 34–35. The members of the commission underwent substantial turnover during the eleven years of its existence, but apparently all the commissioners either were

slaveholders or became slaveholders soon after assuming their duties. See Bob Arnebeck, "The Use of Slaves to Build and [*sic*] Capitol and White House, 1791–1801," pt. 5, 2, www.geocities.com/bo barnebeck/slaves.html. Page citations are from my printouts of the five parts of this document.

120. See Allen, "Slave Laborers," 3–5, 18; Arnebeck, *Fiery Trial*, 117, 138, 245, 291–92; Arnebeck, "Use of Slaves," http://www.geocities.com/bobarnebeck/slaves.html, pt. 1, 2–3, 22–24; pt. 3, 2–3, 7–8, 23–24, 31. The commissioners decided to begin employing slave labor in April 1792. Most of the initial construction work, which included the Capitol and White House, occurred between 1794 and 1800. See Arnebeck, *Fiery Trial*, 117, 520; Arnebeck, "Use of Slaves," pt. 1, 18; http://www .geocities.com/bobarnebeck/slaves.html, pt. 3, 17–18, 51; pt. 5, 9. As we will see, several of the commissioners' own slaves worked on the project.

121. See Accounts of the Commissioners of the City of Washington, 1794–1802, Boxes 43–50; Record Group 217; National Archives. Many of the vouchers were in English pounds, others in dollars, and some in both. Based on the latter, the commission's conversion rate fluctuated around $2.80 per pound, which was the rate I used to convert pound payments to dollar payments. Total construction were $1,047,267. See Annals of Congress, 6th Cong., 2nd Sess., 1355–1356 (Appendix).

122. The commission records contain only one 1793 voucher, only a few 1794 vouchers, and three large gaps thereafter, August 1797–February 1798, March–December 1799, and September 1800–October 1801.

123. See *Accounts of the Commissioners*, Box 44, voucher 981, 1st series, December 9, 1795.

124. Bob Arnebeck has identified only three free blacks who worked on the project. See Arnebeck, "Use of Slaves," http://www.geocities.com/bobarnebeck/slaves.html,pt. 3, 46.

125. See Arnebeck, "Use of Slaves," pt. 1, 2, 18–20, 24; pt. 3, 6, 44–45.

126. See Allen, "Slave Laborers," 5, 9–13. Arnebeck is much more skeptical than Allen and even in his own earlier work that many slaves actually performed skilled labor; in most of the relevant cases, they are listed as "assistants" on the voucher. See Arnebeck, "Use of Slaves," http:// www.geocities.com/bobarnebeck/slaves.html, pt. 1, 29; pt. 2, 6, 26, 38, 41; pt. 3, 1; pt. 4, 3, 24–25, 28; pt. 5, 26.

127. See *Accounts of the Commissioners*, Box 48, unnumbered voucher, 4th series, January 1, 1799; Box 49, voucher 1603, 4th series, January 3, 1800; Arnebeck, "Use of Slaves," pt. 2, 8.

128. See *Accounts of the Commissioners*, Box 47, voucher 308, 3rd series, [for May] 1797; Box 50, voucher 2114, 4th series, August 9, 1800; Arnebeck, "Use of Slaves," pt. 3, 23–24, 30; pt. 4, 23.

129. See *Accounts of the Commissioners*, Box 46, voucher 96, 3rd series, April 1, 1797; Box 49, voucher 1673, 4th series, September 23, 1800; Allen, "Slave Laborers," 18; Arnebeck, "Use of Slaves,"http://www.geocities.com/bobarnebeck/slaves.html, pt. 3, 31. Thornton, who remained on the commission the longest, received a salary increase to $666.66 per quarter in 1802. See *Accounts of the Commissioners*, Box 50, voucher 2908, 4th series, June 1, 1802.

130. In some cases, "their" slaves were literally their slaves.

131. See Arnebeck, "Use of Slaves," pt. 1, 10, 14; pt. 3, 6.

132. See Pacheco, *The Pearl*, 21. Even during the initial construction of the capital, slaves cleaned streets. See *Accounts of the Commissioners*, Box 44, unnumbered voucher, 1st series, August 4, 1795; Arnebeck, "Use of Slaves," http://www.geocities.com/bobarnebeck/slaves.html,pt. 3, 15. Almost all the 1800–1802 payments for slave labor were for custodial work.

133. See Allen, "Slave Laborers," 9, 14–15; Arnebeck, "Use of Slaves," http://www.geocities .com/bobarnebeck/slaves.html, pt. 2, 2; pt. 3, 56–57; Sarah Luria, *Capital Speculations: Writing and Building Washington, D.C.* (Hanover, NH: University Press of New England, 2005), 32. Dissatisfied with the commission's supervision of the construction of the capital, a cabinet committee

took control of the project in 1800 and supervised the completion of its first phase. Congress formally disbanded the commission in 1802. See Arnebeck, *Fiery Trial*, 553, 612; Arnebeck, "Use of Slaves," http://www.geocities.com/bobarnebeck/slaves.html, pt. 2, 2; pt. 3, 51–52.

134. See Minutes, List of Petitions and Awards, and Final Report, April 12, 1862–January 14, 1863 (National Archives Microfilm Publication), M520; roll 1, 29; Records of the Board of Commissioners for the Emancipation of Slaves in the District of Columbia; Record Group 217; National Archives, Washington, DC. Slaveholders received a maximum of $300 per slave and freed slaves, $100 if they emigrated outside the United States. In August 1862, Lincoln met with a delegation of the city's African American leaders to discuss the virtues of colonization, vaguely referring to a possible Central American site (Chiriqui, Panama) and making no mention of Liberia. The most palpable results of the meeting were an enraged group of black abolitionists (Frederick Douglass) and Radical Republicans (Thaddeus Stevens), a derisive Northern press, and a chagrined ACS Board of Managers. In the end, only ten freed slaves from the District of Columbia emigrated to Liberia. See *Annual Reports of the American Colonization Society* (1818–1910; reprint, New York: Negro Universities Press, 1969), 46 (1863): 15; 50 (1867): 189; Hans L. Trefousse, *Thaddeus Stevens: Nineteenth-Century Egalitarian* (Chapel Hill: University of North Carolina Press, 1997), 124–125; Michael Vorenberg, "Abraham Lincoln and the Politics of Black Colonization," *Journal of the Abraham Lincoln Association* 14, no. 2 (Winter 1993): 33–35.

135. See H. R. Rep. No. 81, 33rd Cong., 1st Sess., 1854; H. R. No. 235, 33rd Cong., 1st Sess., 1854; *House Journal*, 33rd Cong., 1st Sess., May 8, 1854, 725. Baker's mission was a prelude to the Gadsden Purchase. New Mexico was the closest contemporaneous case to Kansas in terms of the formation of proslavery and antislavery factions but no extraordinary violence or federal expenses resulted. Baker headed the proslavery faction. Most of the slaves in New Mexico were, however, Native, not African, Americans. See H. R. Rep. No. 508, 36th Cong., 1st Sess., 1860; Robert W. Larson, *New Mexico's Quest for Statehood, 1846–1912* (Albuquerque: University of New Mexico Press, 1968), 69; Alvin R. Sunrise, "Indian Slave Trade in New Mexico, 1846–1861," *Indian Historian* 6, no. 4 (Fall 1973): 20–22.

136. See Richard R. John, *Spreading the News: The American Postal System from Franklin to Morse* (Cambridge, MA: Harvard University Press, 1995), 73, 303n44.

137. Ibid., 141.

138. Ibid., 140, 315n114.

139. See *American State Papers, Post Office*, 1:9 ("Further Provision for Transporting the Mail," March 30, 1802), 22.

140. See John, *Spreading the News*, 141.

141. See H. R. Doc. No. 138, 25th Cong., 2nd Sess., 1838, 3, 31; H. R. Doc. No. 84, 26th Cong., 1st Sess., 1841, 31, 67; H. R. Doc. Ex., No. 112, 34th Cong., 1st Sess., 1856, 28, 62; H. R. Ex. Doc. No. 40, 36th Cong., 1st Sess., 1860, 49, 72; H. R. Ex. Doc. No. 32, 37th Cong., 2nd Sess., 1862, 95. Congressional records lack reports from 1839–1840, 1844, and 1847–1853. For an early case in Illinois territory, see Clarence Edwin Carter, ed., *The Territorial Papers of the United States* (Washington, DC: Government Printing Office, 1934–1969), 16:112 (The Postmaster General [Granger] to John McArthur, August 17, 1810).

142. See Carter, *Territorial Papers*, 25:62 (Wiley Thompson to [Bureau of Indian Affairs superintendent] Elbert Herring, October 28, 1834).

143. See Carter, *Territorial Papers*, 5:63 (Presentment of the Grand Jury of Adams County [Mississippi], June 6, 1799); Charles J. Kappler, *Indian Affairs: Laws and Treaties*, vol. 2, *Treaties* (Washington, DC: Government Printing Office, 1904), 342, 344. See also James R. Atkinson, *Splendid Land, Splendid People: The Chickasaw Indians to Removal* (Tuscaloosa: University of

Alabama Press, 2004), 200; Klos, "Seminole Removal Debates," 69–70, 76, 77n85; Littlefield, *Africans and Creeks*, 45; Kenneth W. Porter, *The Black Seminoles: History of a Freedom-Seeking People* (Gainesville: University of Florida Press, 1996), 32.

144. See John E. Sunder, *Joshua Pilcher: Fur Trader and Indian Agent* (Norman: University of Oklahoma Press, 1968), 145.

145. See Larry E. Morris, *The Fate of the Corps: What Became of the Lewis and Clark Explorers after the Expedition* (New Haven, CT: Yale University Press, 2004), chap. 14. As regional Indian superintendent, Clark played a key role in the Platte purchase. Pilchur was a longtime Clark associate and also helped negotiate the purchase. See H. Jason Combs, "The Platte Purchase and Native American Removal," *Plains Anthropologist* 47, no. 182 (August 2002): 272–273; Kappler, *Indian Affairs*, 468, 479.

146. See J. G. de Roulhac Hamilton, ed., *The Papers of William Alexander Graham* (Raleigh, NC: State Department of Archives and History, 1961), 4:138 (Robert G. Rankin to C. W. Rockwell, March 15, 1851). On this policy episode, see Starobin, *Industrial Slavery*, 33.

147. See Graham, *Papers*, 4:61–64 (C. W. Rockwell to Thomas Corwin, March 29, 1851).

148. Ibid., 4:138–139 (C. W. Rockwell to Robert G. Rankin, March 22, 1851).

149. Ibid., 4:139 (Robert G. Rankin to C. W. Rockwell, April 17, 1851).

150. See *Senate Journal*, 27th Cong., 2nd Sess., July 29, 1842, 514.

151. See *Globe*, 30th Cong., 1st Sess., 1849, 303. There was one early American Party member of the 30th Congress, Lewis Charles Levin (Pennsylvania), who voted for the bill. Lincoln (Illinois Whig), serving his only House term, voted against it.

152. No one factor can explain the failure of federal employers to report the full extent of their slave rentals. One factor was undoubtedly general bureaucratic sloppiness. But another factor was the efforts of middle- and low-level officials to disguise violations of federal policies against the employment of slave labor, apparently with the connivance of cabinet-level officials. Though I would not discount the extent to which the latter were unaware of the violations or unaware that they were violations, they still seemed wedded to an unofficial policy of, as much as possible, keeping its use out of sight. For whatever reason, Upshur provides Congress with patently false information about the navy's use of slave labor in his 1842 report.

153. The complaint of a disgruntled slave dealer also precipitated Giddings's inquiry into the true causes and costs of the Second Seminole War.

154. On the illiberal nature of many forms of labor at this time, see Karen Orren, *Belated Feudalism: Labor, the Law, and Liberal Development in the United States* (Cambridge: Cambridge University Press, 1991); Seth Rockman, "The Unfree Origins of American Capitalism," in *The Economy of Early America: Historical Perspectives and New Directions*, ed. Cathy Matson (University Park: Pennsylvania State University Press, 2006), 351–355; Christopher L. Tomlins, *Law, Labor, and Ideology in the Early American Republic* (New York: Cambridge University Press, 1993).

155. See Eric Foner, *Free Soil, Free Labor, Free Men: The Ideology of the Republican Party before the Civil War* (New York: Oxford University Press, 1970), chap. 2.

156. Given the fact that the total slave population in the United States had reached nearly four million people by 1860, the federal government would have had to employ hundreds of thousands of slaves—which it clearly did not—to have had much of an aggregate effect. See Gibson and Jung, "Historical Census Statistics," Table 1.

157. See Foner, *Free Soil, Free Labor*, 117. Antislavery politicians made a similar argument with respect to the continued existence of slavery in the nation's capital. See Fehrenbacher, *Slaveholding Republic*, 67, 77.

CHAPTER 7. THE "HOUSE DIVIDED" REVISITED

1. See Robert W. Johannsen, ed., *The Lincoln-Douglas Debates of 1858* (New York: Oxford University Press, 1965), 14.

2. The impermanency of such a union was precisely what Douglas denied in his Senate campaign debates with Lincoln. Ibid., 44, 125–131, 197, 288, 326.

3. Of course, some opinion leaders, in both the North and South, proposed permanently dividing the house.

4. Lincoln left open exactly when and how slavery would be abolished in the Southern states. Ibid., 55, 200.

5. See Louis Hartz, *The Liberal Tradition in America: An Interpretation of American Political Thought since the Revolution* (New York: Harcourt Brace, 1955).

6. This understanding would complement Lincoln's "slave power conspiracy" rhetoric. See Johannsen, *Lincoln-Douglas Debates*, 15–19. On this Republican trope, see David Brion Davis, *The Slave Power Conspiracy and the Paranoid Style* (Baton Rouge: Louisiana State University Press, 1969); Larry Gara, "Slavery and the Slave Power Theme: A Crucial Distinction," *Civil War History* 15, no. 1 (March 1969): 5–18; Michael William Pfau, *The Political Style of Conspiracy: Chase, Sumner, and Lincoln* (East Lansing: Michigan State University Press, 2005); Leonard L. Richards, *The Slave Power: The Free North and Southern Domination, 1780–1860* (Baton Rouge: Louisiana University Press, 2001); David Zarefsky, *Lincoln, Douglas and Slavery: In the Crucible of Public Debate* (Chicago: University of Chicago Press, 1990), chap. 3.

7. See Roy B. Basler, ed., *The Collected Works of Abraham Lincoln* (New Brunswick, NJ: Rutgers University Press, 1953), 7:23 ("Address Delivered at the Dedication of the Cemetery at Gettysburg," November 19, 1863).

8. See Robin L. Einhorn, *American Taxation, American Slavery* (Chicago: University of Chicago Press, 2006), 22, 211; Don E. Fehrenbacher, *The Slaveholding Republic: An Account of the United States Government's Relations to Slavery* (New York: Oxford University Press, 2001), 10–12.

9. See Appendix C.

10. See *Historical Statistics of the United States Millennial Edition Online*, Table Ea636–643, http://hsus.cambridge.org.

11. See Laurence J. Malone, *Opening the West: Federal Internal Improvements before 1860* (Westport, CT: Greenwood, 1998), 17 (Tables 2.1, 2.2).

12. From 1789 to 1861, post office expenditures were $222,372,000, 12.4 percent of total federal expenditures. See *Historical Statistics of the United States,* Table Ea636–643; *The Statistical History of the United States: From Colonial Times to the Present* (New York: Basic Books, 1976), 805 (Series R163–171).

13. See Richard R. John, *Spreading the News: The American Postal System from Franklin to Morse* (Cambridge, MA: Harvard University Press, 1995), chap. 7.

14. See Judd Scott Harmon, "Suppress and Protest: The United States Navy, the African Slave Trade, and Maritime Commerce, 1794–1862" (Ph.D. diss., College of William and Mary, 1977), 233–237 (Appendix D); *Historical Statistics of the United States,* Table Ed26–47; Paul H. Silverstone, *The Sailing Navy, 1775–1854* (Annapolis, MD: Naval Institute Press, 2001), 26, 36, 38, 40, 42–44, 49–50, 53, 56, 62–63, 75; Paul H. Silverstone, *Civil War Navies, 1855–1883* (Annapolis, MD: Naval Institute Press, 2001), 15, 17, 22, 45–46.

15. See Robert W. Coakley, *The Role of Federal Military Forces in Domestic Disorders, 1789–1878* (Washington, DC: Government Printing Office, 1998), 136–137; *Historical Statistics of the United States,* Table Ed26–47.

16. See John K. Mahon, *History of the Second Seminole War, 1835–1842* (Gainesville: University of Florida Press, 1967), 226, 325.

17. See *Historical Statistics of the United States,* Table Ed26–476; Sheldon D. Pollack, *War, Revenue, and State Building: Financing the Development of the American State* (Ithaca, NY: Cornell University Press, 2008), 96.

18. See *Historical Statistics of the United States,* Table Ea894–903; Morris J. MacGregor and Bernard C. Nalty, ed., *Blacks in the United States Armed Forces: Basic Documents,* vol. 1, *A Time of Slavery* (Wilmington, DE: Scholarly Resources, 1977), 219–223.

19. See Mahon, *Second Seminole War,* 325.

20. In the Nathaniel Gordon case, the federal government paid for his incarceration until he was executed.

21. See Samuel J. May, *The Fugitive Slave Law and Its Victims* (New York: American Anti-Slavery Society, 1861), 54.

22. See *Historical Statistics of the United States,* Tables Ea894–903; Ed26–47; U.S. Office of Personnel Management (OPM), "Total Government Employment since 1962," http://www.opm.gov/feddata/HistoricalTables/TotalGovernmentSince1962.asp. The fact that the federal civilian-employment table in *Historical Statistics* begins only in 1816 and then lists the totals at ten-year intervals from 1821 to 1871 dictates the 1816–1851 time frame. (The last pre–Civil War year on the table is 1851.) The OPM figures are for 2010.

23. See Lawrence Delbert Cress, *Citizens in Arms: The Army and the Militia in American Society to the War of 1812* (Chapel Hill: University of North Carolina Press, 1982); Richard H. Kohn, *Eagle and Sword: The Federalists and the Creation of the Military Establishment in America, 1783–1802* (New York: The Free Press, 1975). One indication of this early professionalization was the increasing reluctance of army regulars to engage in filibustering themselves as well as their growing opposition to private filibusterers. See Robert E. May, "Young American Males and Filibustering in the Age of Manifest Destiny: The United States Army as a Cultural Mirror," *Journal of American History* 78, 3 (December 1991): 857–886; William B. Skelton, *An American Profession of Arms: The Army Officer Corps, 1784–1861* (Lawrence: University Press of Kansas, 1992), 333–338; Samuel J. Watson, "The Uncertain Road to Manifest Destiny: Army Officers and the Course of American Territorial Expansionism, 1815–1846," in *Manifest Destiny and Empire: American Antebellum Expansionism,* ed. Sam W. Haynes and Christopher Morris (College Station: Texas A&M University Press, 1997), 115–145.

24. Since it is unclear whether Ryan was ever paid, his efforts did not necessarily add to the costs of the Booth prosecution.

25. See John T. Noonan, Jr., *The Antelope: The Ordeal of the Recaptured Africans in the Administrations of James Monroe and John Quincy Adams* (Berkeley: University of California Press, 1977), 6–7, 81–82, 85. At the time, Attorney Generals were, however, expected to retain private practices to supplement their relatively meager $3,500 annual salaries. Other cabinet salaries had been equalized at $6,000 in 1820. Only in 1853 were all cabinet salaries equalized at $8,000, which prompted then-Attorney General Caleb Cushing to become the office's first full-time occupant. See Nancy V. Baker, *Law and Politics in the Attorney General's Office, 1789–1990* (Lawrence: University Press of Kansas, 1992), 56–58.

26. The "new governance" may even be reversing the trend toward less federal reliance on private agents to perform state functions. See Kathleen Sullivan and Patricia Strach, "Inclusion, Exclusion, and Citizenship," in *The Politics of Inclusion and Exclusion: Identity Politics in Twenty-First Century America,* ed. David F. Ericson (New York: Routledge, 2011), 91–109.

27. See Robert J. Kaczorowski, "The Inverted Constitution: Enforcing Constitutional Rights in the Nineteenth Century," in *Constitutionalism and American Culture: Writing the New Constitutional History,* ed. Sandra F. VanBurkleo, Kermit Hall, and Robert J. Kaczorowski (Lawrence: University Press of Kansas, 2002), 46–50; Richard M. Valelly, *The Two Reconstructions: The Struggle for Black Enfranchisement* (Chicago: University of Chicago Press, 2004), 109–110, 200, 231.

28. While local constituency demands precipitated the Second Seminole War, the army asserted its independence thereafter by sloughing off its auxiliary forces and retrenching on its civilian support services. In Kansas, the territorial militia was, of course, federalized.

29. This federal assistance was mostly delivered through the policy connection between African colonization and slave-trade suppression.

30. Cf. Daniel R. Carpenter, *The Forging of Bureaucratic Autonomy: Reputation, Networks, and Policy Innovation in Executive Agencies, 1862–1920* (Princeton, NJ: Princeton University Press, 2001), 65–70; Mark R. Wilson, "The Politics of Procurement: Military Origins of Bureaucratic Autonomy," in *Ruling Passions: Political Economy in Nineteenth-Century America,* ed. Richard R. John (University Park: Penn State University Press, 2006), 45–46. Wilson also argues that the army led all public and private organizations in organizational innovation. See M. R. Wilson, "Politics of Procurement," 46, 56–57, 61–62. Both Richard John, relative to the United States Post Office, and Prince and Keller, to the United States Customs Service, sketch a more checkered history of the growth of bureaucratic autonomy within "their" institutions. See John, *Spreading the News,* 3–6; Carl E. Prince and Mollie Keller, *The U.S. Customs Service: A Bicentennial History* (Washington, DC: Department of Treasury, 1989), 36, 71, 97.

31. As we saw in chapter four, Southern congressmen had sought a more active federal role in this policy area as early as 1793.

32. The sectional division in this policy area was tempered by the initial lower South–upper South division on banning slave imports, by the relative lack of resistance to the enforcement of the ban in the lower South after its enactment, as well as by the relative lack of criticism of the lax enforcement of the nation's slave-trade laws in the North.

33. See Richard Franklin Bensel, *Yankee Leviathan: The Origins of Central State Authority in America, 1859–1877* (Cambridge: Cambridge University Press, 1990), chap. 3.

34. Over time, a state would presumably build up a reservoir of legitimacy, but the sustenance of that reservoir would still depend on the specific actions it did or did not perform.

35. See Leonard A. Carlson and Mark A. Roberts, "Indian Lands, 'Squatterism' and Slavery: Economic Interests and the Passage of the Indian Removal Act of 1830," *Explorations in Economic History,* 43, 3 (July 2006): 500–501.

36. See Andrew R. L. Cayton, "'When Shall We Cease to Have Judases?': The Blount Conspiracy and the Limits of the 'Extended Republic,'" in *Launching the 'Extended Republic': The Federalist Era,* ed. Ronald Hoffman and Peter J. Albert (Charlottesville: University Press of Virginia, 1996), 162–168, 171, 187, 189; Andrew R. L. Cayton, "Radicals in the 'Western World': The Federalist Conquest of Trans-Appalachian North America," in *Federalists Reconsidered,* ed. Doron Ben-Atar and Barbara B. Oberg (Charlottesville: University Press of Virginia, 1998), 86, 89; Andrew R. L. Cayton, "'Separate Interests' and the Nation-State: The Washington Administration and the Origins of Regionalism in the Trans-Appalachian West," *Journal of American History* 79, 1 (June 1992): 42, 54–55, 64–65. See also Adam Rothman, *Slave Country: American Expansion and the Origins of the Deep South* (Cambridge, MA: Harvard University Press, 2005), 11–13, 39–42, 166, 219.

37. See Alisse Portnoy, *Their Right to Speak: Women's Activism in the Indian and Slave Debates* (Cambridge, MA: Harvard University Press, 2005), chap. 1.

38. See Cayton, "Blount Conspiracy," 170; Cayton, "Radicals in the Western World," 89; Cayton, "Separate Interests," 47–49. See also Patrick Griffin, *American Leviathan: Empire, Nation, and Revolutionary Frontier* (New York: Hill and Wang, 2007), chap. 9.

39. See Carlson and Roberts, "Indian Lands and Slavery," 501.

40. See Wendell Phillips, "Speech at the Worcester Disunion Convention, January 15, 1857," in vol. 1, *Pamphlets on Slavery in the United States* (Regenstein Library, University of Chicago, n.d.). Of course, in neither case was the fugitive-slave issue their only rationale for disunion.

41. Again, this total does not include the thousands of Native Americans who self-removed. Tim Garrison estimates that a total of 90,000 Native Americans moved or were moved across the Mississippi River from 1830 to 1843. See Tim Allen Garrison, "United States Indian Policy in Sectional Crisis: Georgia's Exploitation of the Compact of 1802," in *Congress and the Emergence of Sectionalism: From the Missouri Compromise to the Age of Jackson*, ed. Paul Finkelman and Donald R. Kennon (Akron: Ohio University Press, 2008), 123.

42. On African American resistance to fugitive-slave renditions, see Jean Richardson, "Buffalo's Antebellum African-American Community and the Fugitive Slave Law of 1850," *Afro-Americans in New York Life and History* 27, no. 2 (July 2003): 29–46; Carol Wilson, "Active Vigilance Is the Price of Liberty: Black Self-Defense against Fugitive Slave Recapture and Kidnapping of Free Blacks," in *Antislavery Violence: Sectional, Racial, and Cultural Conflict in Antebellum America*, ed. John R. McKivigan and Stanley Harrold (Knoxville: University of Tennessee Press, 1999), 108–127.

43. When federal officials rented slave labor, they also sometimes coerced free white laborers and even slaveholders.

44. The emergence of the Republican Party changed these dynamics considerably.

45. See Max Farrand, ed., *The Records of the Federal Convention of 1787* (1911; reprint, New Haven, CT: Yale University Press, 1937), 2:370.

46. See Jeffrey Rogers Hummel and Barry R. Weingast, "The Fugitive Slave Act of 1850: An Instrumental Interpretation," in *Party, Process, and Political Change in Congress*, vol. 2, *Further New Perspectives on the History of Congress*, ed. David W. Brady and Matthew D. McCubbins (Stanford, CA: Stanford University Press, 2007), 385–386.

47. See Stanley W. Campbell, *The Slave Catchers: Enforcement of the Fugitive Slave Law, 1850–1860* (Chapel Hill: University of North Carolina Press, 1968), 167–168, 199–206 (Tables 1–11); Robert F. Dalzell, *Daniel Webster and the Trial of American Nationalism, 1843–1852* (Boston: Houghton Mifflin, 1973), chap. 3; John L. Myers, *Henry Wilson and the Coming of the Civil War* (Lanham, MD: University Press of America, 2005), chap. 4.

48. See *Annals of Congress*, 9th Cong., 2nd Sess., 243; Farrand, *Records of the Convention*, 3:161. Varnum was a Massachusetts Democratic Republican.

49. See *Annual Reports of the American Colonization Society* (1818–1910; reprint, New York: Negro Universities Press, 1969), 16 (1833): xv–xvii (Finley); 17 (1834): xiii (Frelinghuysen); 19 (1835): 7–9 (Gurley); 19 (1835): 10–11 (Clay).

50. See J. G. de Roulhac Hamilton, ed., *The Papers of William Alexander Graham* (Raleigh, NC: State Department of Archives and History, 1961), 4:61–64 (C. W. Rockwell to Thomas Corwin, March 29, 1851); MacGregor and Nalty, *Time of Slavery*, 222–223.

51. See Coakley, *Role of the Military*, 171–172.

52. See Farrand, *Records of the Convention*, 2:371.

53. See ACS, "Annual Reports," 35 (1852): 11–21 (Stanton), quote at 13–14; 35 (1852): 21–26 (Slaughter). Stanton later served as Kansas territorial secretary.

54. See *American State Papers, Post Office* 1:9 ("Further Provision for Transporting the Mail," March 30, 1802), 22.

55. See Coakley, *Role of the Military,* 171.

56. See Fehrenbacher, *Slaveholding Republic,* 272; Hummel and Weingast, "Fugitive Slave Act," 380–383.

57. On the importance of time as a political variable, see Karen Orren and Stephen Skowronek, *The Search for American Political Development* (Cambridge: Cambridge University Press, 2004), 12–13, 195–196; Paul Pierson, *Politics in Time: History, Institutions, and Social Analysis* (Princeton, NJ: Princeton University Press, 2004).

58. See Donald L. Robinson, *Slavery in the Structure of American Politics, 1765–1820* (New York: Harcourt Brace Jovanovich, 1971), 233; William M. Wiecek, "'The Witch at the Christening': Slavery and the Constitution's Origins," in *The Framing and Ratification of the Constitution,* ed. Leonard W. Levy and Dennis J. Mahoney (New York: Macmillan, 1987), 179.

59. See Bensel, *Yankee Leviathan,* x, 13, 95–96, 191, 233–236.

60. See Kaczorowski, "Inverted Constitution," 46–50.

61. See Tony R. Mullis, *Peacekeeping on the Plains: Army Operations in Bleeding Kansas* (Columbia: University of Missouri Press, 2004), 248–249.

62. See Mahon, *Second Seminole War,* 322.

63. See M. R. Wilson, "Politics of Procurement," 61–64. See also Pollack, *War and State Building,* chap. 7.

64. See Donald L. Canney, *Lincoln's Navy: The Ships, Men and Organization, 1861–65* (Annapolis, MD: Naval Institute Press, 1998), 1.

65. See Joseph L. Grabill, "The 'Invisible' Missionary: A Study in American Foreign Relations," *Journal of Church and State,* 14, 1 (Winter 1972): 99–103; Colin D. Moore, "State Building through Partnership: Delegation, Public-Private Partnerships, and the Political Development of American Imperialism, 1898–1916," *Studies in American Political Development* 25, no. 1 (April 2011): 27–55.

66. See Brian Balogh, *A Government Out of Sight: The Mystery of National Authority in Nineteenth-Century America* (New York: Cambridge University Press, 2009), 398–399.

67. See Seth Rockman, "The Unfree Origins of American Capitalism," in *The Economy of Early America: Historical Perspectives and New Directions,* ed. Cathy Matson (University Park: Pennsylvania State University Press, 2006), 351–353.

68. See James M. McPherson, *Abraham Lincoln and the Second American Revolution* (New York: Oxford University Press, 1991), chaps. 2, 7.

69. See Anthony W. Marx, *Making Race and Nation: A Comparison of the United States, South Africa, and Brazil* (Cambridge: Cambridge University Press, 1998), chap. 6. But cf. Richard Franklin Bensel, *Sectionalism and American Political Development, 1880–1980* (Madison: University of Wisconsin Press, 1984).

70. This list is obviously not exhaustive. For examples of these other narratives, see Paula Baker, "The Domestication of Politics: Women and American Political Society, 1780–1920," *American Historical Review* 89, 3 (June 1984): 620–647; Mary P. Ryan, *Civic Wars: Democracy and Public Life in the American City during the Nineteenth Century* (Berkeley: University of California Press, 1997); David Montgomery, *Citizen Worker: The Experience of Workers in the United States with Democracy and the Free Market during the Nineteenth Century* (Cambridge: Cambridge University Press, 1993); Sean Wilentz, *Chants Democratic: New York City and the Rise of the American Working Class, 1788–1850* (New York: Oxford University Press, 1984).

71. See, for example, Pollack, *War and State Building*, chap. 8; Gretchen Ritter; *The Constitution as Social Design: Gender and Civic Membership in the American Constitutional Order* (Palo Alto, CA: Stanford University Press, 2006); Aristide Zollberg, "How Many Exceptionalisms?" in *Working Class Formation: Nineteenth Century Patterns in Western Europe and the United States*, ed. Ira Katznelson and Aristide Zollberg (Princeton, NJ: Princeton University Press, 1986), 397–455.

72. See Alexis de Tocqueville, *Democracy in America*, ed. J. P. Mayer, trans. George Lawrence (Garden City, NY: Doubleday, 1969), vol. 1, chap. 18.

73. See Charles M. Wiltse, ed., *The Papers of Daniel Webster: Speeches and Formal Writings* (Hanover, NH: University Press of New England, 1988), 2:473 ("Objects of the Mexican War," March 23, 1848).

74. See Kevin Mulroy, *Freedom on the Border: The Seminole Maroons in Florida, the Indian Territory, Coahuila, and Texas* (Lubbock: Texas Tech University Press, 1993), chaps. 2–3; Kenneth W. Porter, *The Negro on the American Frontier* (New York: Arno, 1971), 425–458. When the other Seminoles left these borderland communities to return to Indian territory after the United States finally recognized the Seminoles as a separate nation in 1856, the Black Seminoles remained in Mexico. On borderland communities, see Jeremy Adelman and Stephen Aron, "From Borderlands to Borders: Empires, Nation-States, and the People In Between in North American History," *American Historical Review* 104, 3 (June 1999): 814–841.

75. On the history of immigration policy during this period, see Daniel J. Tichenor, *Dividing Lines: The Politics of Immigration Control in America* (Princeton, NJ: Princeton University Press, 2002).

76. The agency went through a number of name and departmental changes until it became the Immigration and Naturalization Service within the Department of Labor in 1933. It became part of the Department of Justice in 1940.

77. See Campbell Gibson and Kay Jung, "Historical Census Statistics on Population Totals by Race, 1790 to 1990, and by Hispanic Origin, 1970 to 1990, for the United States, Regions, Divisions, and States" (Washington, DC: U.S. Census Bureau, 2002), Table 1, http://www.census.gov/population/www/documentation/twps0056/twps0056.html.

78. See John B. Trevor, "An Analysis of the American Immigration Act of 1924," *International Conciliation*, 202 (September 1924): 58–59 (Appendix B). Filipinos were not subject to quotas because they were "insular" American citizens. The quotas for the other "permitted" Asian groups were 100 each. The quotas were also originally skewed toward northern and western over eastern and southern Europeans because they were based on the 1890 census. After the 1930 census, they were updated to remove that bias.

79. The new system still contained some geographic biases because it allowed exemptions for family reunification, special skills, and political refugee status. At the time, the last exemption substantially boosted immigration from southeast Asia.

80. The agency is, however, pressed from the other side by employer demands for cheap, immigrant labor.

81. On the history of Native American policy during this period, see Kevin Bruyneel, *The Third Space of Sovereignty: The Postcolonial Politics of U.S.-Indigenous Relations* (Minneapolis: University of Minnesota Press, 2007).

82. Congress created the agency in 1824. Originally located in the Department of War, it moved to the new Department of Interior in 1849.

83. See Valelly, *Two Reconstructions,* chap. 6. Just as they had during the antebellum period, the Northern states also pursued racially exclusionary policies but less explicit ones and, in any

case, most African Americans initially remained in the South. See Eric Foner, *Reconstruction: America's Unfinished Revolution, 1863–1877* (New York: Harper & Row, 1988), chap. 10.

84. See Ira Katznelson, *When Affirmative Action Was White: An Untold History of Racial Inequality in Twentieth-Century America* (New York: Norton, 2005), chaps. 2–3.

85. See Valelly, *Two Reconstructions,* chaps. 7–9.

86. Interestingly, Congress created the department to reduce the costs of hiring private attorneys to adjudicate Civil War claims; a powerful indication of the early American state's reliance on private agents to perform state functions. See Nancy V. Baker, *Law and Politics,* 61–62.

87. See Valelly, *Two Reconstructions,* chap. 10.

88. See Julie Novkov, "Toward a Legal Genealogy of Color Blindness," in *Politics of Inclusion and Exclusion,* 177–206.

INDEX

Abert, John James, 141, 170, 178
Ableman v. Booth, 91–92, 103, 235n74
Abolition, "early," 199n91
Abolitionists
    the American Colonization Society and, 63
    mailings controversy, 15, 166
    slave escapes and, 88
Adams, John Quincy
    Adams-Onís Treaty, 199n100
    Amistad case and, 96
    Antelope case and, 95
    elected president, 61
    Native American removals and, 129
    support of slave interests, 102, 111
    Treaty of Ghent and, 93
Adams-Onís Treaty, 35, 94, 102, 199n100,
    208n65, 209n70
African Americans
    attitudes toward the ACS and African
        colonization, 18, 64
    1790 census figures, 199n99
    the civil rights revolution and, 184
    enlistment in the U.S. navy, 152, 153–154
    exclusion laws, 184, 219n42
    federal employment of free black laborers,
        256n13
    "personal liberty" laws and, 232n33
    poverty rate in 2009, 202n129
    race relations in the U.S. and, 182–183,
        247n77
    in the Revolutionary War, 151–152
    slave rescues by, 125
    U.S. navy policy against employing,
        197n76
African colonization
    ambiguous intentions and effects, 177–178
    American Colonization Society and, 18,
        59–60, 169, 218n35
    "Americanizing" Africa, 55
    anticipation of American colonialism, 181

attitude of free blacks and slaves toward,
    18, 64
James Buchanan and, 72–73
coercion and, 199n98
compared to Native American removal,
    249n94
constitutional defenses of, 70, 225n115
continued presence of slavery in the U.S.
    and, 57
counterfactual history, 18–19, 75
critics of, 56, 61–62, 63
executive policy-making and, 78, 173
federal expenditures on, 26, 37, 188
federal support for, 60
funding from state governments, 69, 72,
    220n52, 224n102
impact on American state development,
    57, 77–78
impact on federal authority, 172
impact on state legitimacy, 174–175
intent of, 79
interpenetration of state and society in, 77
Lincoln and, 265n134
as a public-private partnership, 1, 23, 57, 76
racist attitudes to black emigration and, 77
recent major studies of, 218n29
sectional differences over, 177
significance of, 75–76
slavery-related institutional development
    and, 170
slave trade suppression and, 54, 71, 74, 78
See also American Colonization Society;
    Liberia
African immigrants, 77, 183, 202n122
African Squadron (U.S. Navy)
    in the Civil War, 26–27, 48
    compared to the British West African
        Squadron, 26, 42
    effectiveness of, 26, 27, 42
    the *Erie* seizure, 46

African Squadron, *continued*
   expanded by Pres. Buchanan, 6, 44, 71, 72
   federal expenditures on, 27, 46
   federal resources allocated to, 54, 166, 170, 203n9
   mission to protect American commerce, 42
   navy secretaries for, 212n119
   operating costs, 41–42, 46
   protection of Liberia, 67–68
   relocation of base of operations, 214n144
   seizures from 1860 to 1861, 46, 73–74
   in slave trade suppression, 72, 73–74
   Webster-Ashburton Treaty and the establishment of, 26, 40, 67
Aiken, James, 48
Alabama, 97
Alien Act of 1798, 216n165
Alligator (USS), 37, 67
Amelia Island, 35, 38, 110, 243n22
American Anti-Slavery Society (AASS), 63
American colonialism, 181
American Colonization Society (ACS)
   abolitionists and, 63
   African colonization and, 1, 18, 59–60, 169, 177–178, 218n35, 249n94 (*see also* African colonization)
   "Americanizing" Africa, 55
   appeals for federal support, 55–56
   attitudes of African Americans toward, 18, 64
   the "benevolent empire" and, 222n76
   categories of emigrants to Liberia, 227n155
   chartered by Maryland in 1831, 220n54
   colonial agents in Liberia, 166, 223n83, 223n84
   critics of, 63, 64
   defense of conditions in Liberia, 221n69
   different measures of success, 55
   emancipation and, 59, 70–71
   federal expenditures on, 26, 37, 56
   federal financing of resettlement efforts in Liberia and, 71, 72, 73–75
   first trajectory of federal support, 53–54, 56–57, 58–65
   founding of Liberia, 26, 53
   goals of, 55, 59, 199n99, 217n14
   impact on American state development, 57

Kendall's 1830 audit of, 56, 61–62, 71
last federal payment to, 226n141
Liberia's colonial government and, 75–76
Native Americans and, 219n42
official name of, 216n1
positions on slavery, 59, 70–71, 219n38
as a public-private enterprise, 1, 53, 57, 76
purpose of, 18
racist attitudes to black emigration and, 77
"rescue" of recaptured Africans in Georgia, 60
second trajectory of federal support, 54, 57, 65–71
state auxiliaries, 72, 225–226n132
third trajectory of federal support, 54–55, 57, 71–75
type of federal support received by, 56–57
vice presidents of, 53, 58, 62–63, 220n48
"Washington Community" supporters, 53, 58, 69
See also Liberia
American exceptionalism, 2, 107–108, 242n7
"Americanizing" Africa, 55
American state development
   comparison of society-centered models, 7–17
   counterfactual history of, 17–21
   cross-national comparisons, 2–3
   federal employment of slave labor and, 161–162
   frontier thesis of, 8
   impact of ACS and African colonization on, 57
   impact of fugitive-slave disputes on, 81, 83, 96
   impact of fugitive-slave policy on, 101–106
   impact of peacetime military activities on, 108
   impact of race on, 23, 182–185
   impact of slavery on, 1–2, 6–7, 11–17, 179–180
   impact of slavery-related military activities on, 107, 109, 131, 133
   impact of slave trade suppression on, 25, 30, 49–52
   impact of war on, 9–10, 22, 108
   internal-improvements narrative, 12, 13
   "market revolution" narrative, 8–9

society-centered model of, 6
Southern direction of, 184–185
"American System," 9
Amistad (Spanish slave ship), 95–96
Anderson, Richard Clough, 85
Anderson, Walker, 88
Anglo-American relations
fugitive-slave recoveries and, 92, 93, 94
mutual search and seizure treaty of 1862, 48
slave-trade policy and, 30, 40–41, 51, 52
Antelope (Spanish slave ship), 37–38, 95, 169, 210n83
Anti-abolitionist riots, 89
Anti-Federalists, 32
Antislavery "mobs," 125
Antislavery petitions, 32
Anti-slave trade sentiment, 29–30
Arkansas, 100
Army engineers, 147, 194n37
Army officers, use of slaves as personal servants, 135, 146, 154–155, 259n62
Ashmead, John W., 234n69
Ashmore, Margaret, 86
Ashmun, Jehudi, 67
Asian immigrants, 183, 272n78
Assimilation policy, 184
Ayres, Eli, 67

Baker, Grafton, 157, 265n135
Baker, Pamela, 12
Baldwin, Abraham, 31, 176, 206n43
Baldwin, Loammi, 14–15, 147–149, 161, 260–261n79, 260n72
Ball, Charles, 145, 152
Balogh, Brian, 255n174
Bancroft, George, 212n119
Barbour, James, 100, 146
Barbour, Maj. Phillip Norbourne, 154–155
Bassa Cove settlement, 224n102
Batchelder, James, 125
Bayard, James A., 236n85
Beecher, Philemon, 85
Belden, George W., 235n72
Bell, Capt. John R., 80–81, 98
Bell, Mary and Daniel, 88, 232n45, 232n48
Bellamy, John, 149
Beloved (Morrison), 234n67

"Benevolent empire" organizations, 222n76
Bennett, Thomas, 123, 124
Bensel, Richard, 2, 3, 5, 10, 11, 108, 132, 180
Berrien, John M., 38, 130
Birney, James, 63
Black, Edward Junius, 129
Black, Jeremiah S., 43, 47
"Black Dirt" (Foc-te-luc-te-harjoe), 116, 246n68
"Black Dirt" treaty, 249n95
Black Hawk War of 1832, 117
"Black Militia" law of 1792, 152, 162
Black Regiment of Rhode Island, 261n91
Black Seminoles
American claims to be fugitive or "stolen" slaves, 243n20
"Black Dirt" treaty, 249n95
fear of (re-)enslavement and, 20
fear of the Creeks, 112, 113
federal efforts to remove, 112
numbers prior to the Second Seminole War, 118
overview of, 195n50
the "Patriot War" and, 110
reasons for resisting removal, 10, 113
Second Seminole War and, 99, 112, 113–114, 120
Seminole removal and, 175
slave revolts and, 249n103
during the War of 1812, 111
the Watson case, 99–100
Blake, Luther, 116
"Bleeding Kansas," 7, 128, 130, 132, 178, 181
Board of Navy Commissioners, 259n53
Bomford, George, 171, 257n28
Booth, Sherman, 91–92, 169, 235n74
Booth case. *See* Ableman v. Booth
Border control
effect of slave trade suppression on, 30, 36, 49
effect of the slave-import ban on, 1
Border Ruffians, 128, 254n159
Bounties, 27, 38, 40, 98, 152–153, 203n10
Bowie, Jim, 35
Boyd, Mark, 149
Bracero Program, 183
Bradley, Joseph H., 232–233n53
Bragg, Braxton, 108, 132

Branch, John, 148
Brandt, Nat, 235n72
Brazil, 210n90
Brearley, David, 100
Bribery, 28, 203n14
British West Indies, 241n145
Brooks, Preston, 130
Brown, John, 123, 253n140
Brown, Michael, 23
Buchanan, James
    African colonization and, 72–73
    the Booth case pardon, 235n74
    "doughface" reputation, 45
    the *Echo* Africans and, 72
    executive decision-making in slavery-
        related policies, 173
    Edward Loring and, 252n129
    refusal to recognize Liberia, 225n120
    resettlement of recaptured Africans in
        Liberia and, 54
    slave trade suppression and, 26, 30, 44,
        45–46, 49, 71, 72–73
Buchanan, Thomas, 66, 223n80, 223n81
Burbank, Capt. Sidney, 95
Burch, Lt. Daniel E., 149
Bureau of Indian Affairs (BIA), 184, 195n45
Bureau of Pensions, 152
Bureau of Topographical Engineers (U.S.
    Army), 140–141
Burin, Eric, 219n45, 226n132
Burnham, Walter Dean, 5
Burns, Anthony, 90–91, 125, 167, 233n65,
    251n125, 251n127, 251n128
Burr, Aaron, 92
Bush, George W., 23, 76
Bushnell, Simon, 235n72
Butler, Andrew Pickens, 241n152
Butler, Pierce, 83, 101
Butler, William O., 129, 154

C. *Perkins* seizure case, 48, 215n158
Calhoun, John C.
    amendment to exclude African Americans
        from the navy, 153–154, 159
    authorization of slave payments, 98
    conversion from nationalist to states-
        rightist, 137

federal use of slave labor and, 147, 172
fugitive-slave renditions and, 86
Giddings' proposed resolution on
    runaway slaves and, 89
Native American removals and, 254n148
opposition to the Mexican-American War,
    199–200n102
proposed ACS charter and, 62
response to slave conspiracies, 123, 130–131
support for internal improvements, 12
California, 127
Call, Richard K., 113
Callahan, James Hughes, 95
Cameron, Simon, 255n169
Campbell, Hugh, 110, 133
Campbell, Stanley, 80, 90, 91, 234n68
Canada, 94, 241n145
Cape Palmas colony, 220n52, 228n160
Caribbean black immigration, 216n165
Carlson, Leonard, 8, 174
Carpenter, Daniel, 3–4
Carpenter, David, 170
Carr, John, 153
Carroll, Charles, 220n54
Cass, Lewis, 123
Categorical grants, 57
Cayton, Andrew, 131, 174
Census Bureau, 22, 202n129
Census of 1790, 199n99
Census of 1820, 227n157
Census of 1860, 197n72
Chambers, George, 153
Chaplain, William L., 88, 232n45
Chase, Salmon P., 89, 90, 162, 172, 177
Cherokee Indians, 80
Cherokee Nation v. Georgia, 119
Cherokees
    preremoval census, 117–118
    removal, 116–117, 119
    self-removal, 248n87
    slave disputes, 100
    slaveholding and, 21, 96
    slave-related removal expenses, 120
Chickasaws
    army estimate of removal costs, 248n90
    emancipation of slaves, 200n104
    preremoval census, 118

removal, 116–117, 119–120
slaveholding and, 21, 80, 96, 248n88
slave-related removal expenses, 120
Chinese immigrants, 183, 215–216n165
Choctaw Indians, 80
Choctaws
    emancipation of slaves, 200n104
    non-emigrants, 248n91
    preremoval census, 118
    removal, 116–117, 119, 120
    in the Second Seminole War, 246n56
    slave disputes, 100
    slaveholding and, 21, 80, 96
    slave-related removal expenses, 120
    treaty of 1825, 111
    during the War of 1812, 111
Christiana slave rescue, 91, 125, 234n69
"Civilized" Native American nations
    binary relation with European Americans,
        120
    preremoval census, 117–118
    removals, 116–117, 118–122
    slave disputes and, 116
    slaveholding and, 21, 80, 96, 228–229n2
    social structure, 118
    See also individual nations
Civil Rights Act of 1866, 104, 181
Civil rights revolution, 184
Civil War
    African Squadron during, 26–27, 48
    creation of two American states and, 22,
        180
    federal employment of slave labor during,
        139
    impact on American state development,
        22, 108
    nonseceding slave states, 201n114
    race-driven state development following,
        23
Clagett, Clifton, 85
Claiborne, William C. C., 35, 94, 122
Clark, Charles, 48
Clark, William, 158, 266n145
Clay, Henry
    the American Colonization Society and,
        53, 58, 59, 60, 61, 62, 63–64, 69, 76,
        217n14

attitude toward African colonization, 178
    criticism of Jackson's removal policies, 129
    support for internal improvements, 12
    Treaty of Ghent and, 236n85
Cleve, George William van, 22
Cleveland, Charles, 232n46
Clinch, Col. Duncan L., 111
Clotilda (American slave ship), 215n155
Coakley, Robert, 126
Cobb, Howell, 43, 52
Cobb, Thomas Wills, 85
Collins, Nathaniel F., 99
Colonial agents, in Liberia, 54, 65, 66, 67, 75,
    166, 223n83, 223n84
Columbia (American slave ship), 210n83
Comet (seized American ship), 236n86
Commercial agents, in Liberia, 54, 66, 70, 166
Commissioners of the City of Washington,
    136, 138, 155–156, 264n119, 264n120, 264n121,
    265n133
Committee of Claims, 40, 99
Committee of Detail, 30
Committee of the Whole, 33
Compromise of 1850, 90, 127, 178
Compromise of 1877, 181
Confederate state, 180
Connor, James, 43, 44
Constitutional Convention
    ambiguous intentions and effects of the
        slave-trade clause, 177
    "dirty compromise," 31
    effect of slavery on, 15
    fugitive-slave clause, 81, 83–84
    slave revolts issue, 123–124
    slave trade issue, 25, 30–31, 176–177
Constitutional rights
    fugitive-slave cases and, 23–24, 104–105
    protection for freed slaves, 181
Constitution (American slave ship), 35–36,
    209n67, 209n70
Constructionism, 12–13, 137
Continental Army, 151, 152
Cooper, Mark Alexander, 129
Corrie, William C., 43, 213n131
Corwin, Thomas, 69, 158, 224n109
Cotton exports, 194n40
Couper, Hamilton, 43, 44

Crawford, William, 53, 58, 60
Creeks
    army preestimate of removal costs, 248n83
    Black Seminoles' fear of, 112, 113
    bounty money received for surrendering
        African Americans, 98
    emancipation of slaves, 200n104
    First Seminole War and, 98
    preremoval census, 118
    Red Stick War, 97
    removal, 116–117, 118–119
    resistance to removal, 118, 200n104
    in the Second Seminole War, 99, 246n56
    Seminoles and, 238n114, 244n35
    slave disputes, 97, 99
    slaveholding and, 21, 80, 96
    slave-related removal expenses, 120
    during the War of 1812, 111
Creek War of 1836, 118, 120, 200n104
Creole (seized American ship), 93, 236n86
Criminal extraditions, 84
Crittenden, John, 69, 224n109
Crocker, John, 155
Cross-national comparisons, 2–3, 191n6
Cruger, Henry N., 154, 263n115
Crummell, Alexander, 64, 222n70
Cuba, 210n83, 210n90
Cuffee, Paul, 64
Curtis, Benjamin, 253n145
Cushing, Caleb, 92, 130, 251n127, 268n25
Cyane (USS), 37, 66, 67

Dade, Maj. Francis L., 112, 154
Dade's Massacre, 245n54
Dallas (revenue cutter), 37–38
Dancy, Francis L., 140
Dancy scandal, 140, 149–150, 161
Daniel, John R., 99
Davis, David Brion, 11
Davis, Jefferson, 89, 128, 130, 146, 154, 178,
    263n116
Davis, John, 84, 231n19
Dawes Act of 1887, 184
Dayton, William L., 89, 90, 101
Delaney, Martin, 64
Delawares, 246n56
Denmark, 207n58

Department of Homeland Security, 184
Department of Justice, 184
Department of the Interior, 73, 78
    Haitian colonization project, 219–220n45
    the Mexican-American War and, 195n45
Department of the Navy, 36, 145, 147
    See also United States Navy
Department of Treasury, 36, 158, 183
Department of War, 122–123, 152, 168–169
De Peyster, Capt. William, 154, 263n115
Deputy marshals, 166–167
Derrick, William S., 125
Devans, Charles, 125, 251n123
Dew, Thomas R., 63, 172
Dibble, Ernest, 144, 145, 147
Dickinson, Charles, 21
Diouf, Sylvainie, 215n155
Direct taxation, 11–12, 196n61
"Dirty compromise," 31
District of Columbia, 86, 88
    See also Washington, D.C.
Dix Bill of 1854, 222n78
Dodge, Henry, 127
Dolphin (USS), 43
Domestic violence clause, 123, 171–172,
    250n110, 250n115
Dormon, James, 249n104
Dorr, Ebenezer, 88
Douglas, Stephen A., 69, 71, 130
Douglass, Frederick, 64, 265n134
Drayton, Daniel, 88, 232n49
Dred Scott case, 82, 128–129, 133, 253n145
Du Bois, W. E. B., 42, 51, 202n1, 203n6
Duties, on slave imports, 32, 205n34, 207n54
Dutton, Capt. George W., 151
Du Val, Marcellus M., 100, 240n131
Du Val, William, 86, 98

"Early" abolition, 199n91
Eaton, John H., 123, 130–131
Echo Africans, 72, 73, 74, 227n150, 227n152
Echo (American slave ship), 26, 27, 43, 72, 73
Edling, Max, 9, 107
Edwards, Ninian, 127
Einhorn, Robin, 11–12, 165, 196n57
Elizabeth (American ship), 66
Ellicott, Andrew, 126

Emancipation
    the American Colonization Society and,
        59, 70–71
    by the Creeks, Choctaws, Chickasaws, and
        Seminoles, 200n104
    in New York, 262n99
Emory, William H., 132
Encomium (seized American ship), 236n86
Engerman, Stanley, 249n103
English, Chester, 88
Enterprise (seized American ship), 236n86
Enterprise (USS), 35
Epps, Gen. Richard, 122
Erie (American slave ship), 46
Espionage. *See* Slave-smuggling espionage
Etheridge, Emerson, 45
Europe, impact of war on state development,
    107
European Americans, race relations in the
    U.S. and, 182–183, 247n77
Everett, Edward, 69, 217n13
Everett, Horace, 130, 177
Excise taxes, 196n58
Exclusionary policies and laws, 184, 219n42
Executions, 46–47
Executive authority
    African colonization and, 78, 173
    federal employment of slave labor and,
        162–163
    impact of slavery-related policies on, 104,
        172, 173

"Faith-based initiative," 23
Fanning, Maj. Alexander C. W., 98
Farnum, J. Egbert, 43, 44, 47, 213n130
Federal employees
    civil rights policies and, 184
    effectiveness of regular and temporary
        employees, 169
    effects of the presence of slavery on,
        166–169
    involved in slave trade suppression, 50
    number of, 168
Federal employers
    authority of, 138–139
    employment of slave labor and, 135–136
    as slaveholders, 136

Federal employment policy and practices
    decentralization in, 136
    role of middle- and low-level officials in
        the making of, 15
    slave labor and, 14–15, 136–139
Federal expenditures
    on African colonization, 26, 37, 188
    on the African Squadron, 27, 46
    on the American Colonization Society,
        26, 37, 56
    associated with violence in Kansas, 128
    on fugitive-slave recoveries and
        renditions, 82, 90–91
    on the Home Squadron, 46
    on internal improvements, 166
    on Native American removals, 118, 119, 120
    on the Post Office, 166, 267n12
    related to slave rescues, 91
    in the Second Seminole War, 16, 109, 113,
        114–115, 116, 120, 165
    slavery-related total, 165–166, 189
    on slave trade suppression, 27–28, 40, 46,
        187, 203n7
    See also Military expenditures
Federal government
    activity in fugitive-slave disputes, 80, 82–83
    ambiguous intentions and effects of
        slavery-related policies, 177–180
    ban on slave imports, 23
    cabinet salaries, 268n25
    coercion related to slavery, 175–176
    direct taxation and, 11–12
    employment of private agents to perform
        state functions, 6–7, 50, 167–169 (*see
        also* Private agents)
    employment of slave labor (*see* Slave
        labor)
    fugitive-slave recoveries involving Native
        Americans, 96–101
    fugitive-slave renditions, 83–92
    immigration policies, 23, 49, 183–184,
        215–216n165
    impact of fugitive-slave disputes on, 81, 83
    impact of slave-related policies on the
        governing authority of, 171–173
    impact of slavery on state legitimacy,
        173–175

Federal government, *continued*
 impact of slave trade suppression on, 51–52
 land grants, 218n26, 222n78
 land sales, 196n58
 protection of the institution of slavery, 9,
  178–179
 slavery-related institutional development,
  170–171
 slave trade suppression (*see* Slave trade
  suppression)
 support and financing of Liberia, 54, 65,
  66–68, 71, 72, 73–75
 temporary ownership of slaves, 256n16
 See also American state; United States;
  United States Congress
Federalists, 32, 58
Federal justices, in slave trade suppression, 39,
 44, 46, 50
Federal law enforcement
 enforcing the rights of slaveholders and, 24
 impact of fugitive-slave policy on, 1, 6, 81
 impact of the Fugitive Slave Law of 1850
  on, 6, 90, 102–103, 105, 166–167, 170
 protection of the constitutional rights of
  freed slaves, 181
Federal Road, 261n83
Federal-state comparison, 3
Federal subsidies, to the American
 Colonization Society, 56–57
Fehrenbacher, Don, 13–14, 42, 96, 165, 202n1
Fenix (Spanish slave ship), 39, 72
Filibusters and filibustering, 110, 111, 243n19,
 268n23
Fillmore, Millard, 69, 88, 125, 130, 224n108,
 234n69
Finkelman, Paul, 31
Finley, Rev. Robert S., 177–178
First Seminole War, 98, 111, 209n66
Florida
 army employment of slave labor in, 142,
  143, 144, 149
 fugitive-slave renditions, 86
 Andrew Jackson suppresses slave
  smuggling in, 208n65
 slave-catching expeditions in, 167
 slave disputes between Native Americans
  and European Americans, 98–99
 slavery-related military activities in,
  109–116 (*See also* First Seminole War;
  Second Seminole War)
 slaves in military service, 154
 "slave stealing" and, 88
 U.S. acquisition of, 98, 112
 See also Spanish East Florida
Floyd, John B., 122, 123, 124
Foc-te-luc-te-harjoe ("Black Dirt"), 116,
 246n68
Foner, Eric, 23
Foot, Solomon, 222n78
Foote, Henry, 89
Foreman, Grant, 248n83
Formissano, Ronald, 11
Fort Duncan, 95
Forten, James, 64
Fort Gadsden, 98
Fort Gaines, 260n69
Fort Jackson, 142
Fort Jefferson, 143, 144, 146–147, 151
Fort Monroe, 122
Fort Moultrie, 152
Fort Pickens, 143, 147
Fort Pulaski, 258n36
Fort Scott, 142
Fort Taylor, 143, 144
Fort Washita, 142, 258n41
Foster, Abiel, 32
Foster, Winslow, 110
Franklin, Benjamin, 206n43, 235n78
Free blacks. *See* African Americans
Freehling, William, 230n7
Freeman, Watson, 125
Frelinghuysen, Theodore, 62, 129, 178
French slave ships, 37, 238n108
Frontier thesis, 8, 108
Fugitive-slave cases/disputes
 enforcement of constitutional rights and,
  23–24, 104–105
 federal coercion in, 175–176
 federal use of private agents in, 7, 81, 103
 impact on international relations, 81
 impact on the federal government and
  state development, 81
 international (*see* International fugitive-
  slave disputes)

role of the federal government in, 80, 82–83
"runaways" held in Washington County
     prison, 86
sectional differences over, 177
Fugitive-slave clause(s)
   in treaties with Native American nations,
     82, 96
   in the U.S. Constitution, 81, 83–84, 86, 101,
     102, 171
   the U.S. Congress and, 205n36
Fugitive Slave Law of 1793, 84–85, 86, 87, 89, 101
Fugitive Slave Law of 1850
   civil rights acts and, 181
   creation of, 89–90
   enforcement of, 90, 92, 105
   federal activity in fugitive-slave renditions
     and, 80
   federal authority and, 81, 92, 171
   federal employment of private agents
     and, 103
   federal enforcement of constitutional
     rights and, 104–105
   federal expenditures related to, 90–91
   impact of enforcement on state legitimacy,
     174
   impact on African American emigration,
     69
   impact on federal law enforcement, 6, 90,
     102–103, 105, 166–167, 170
   legal nationalization inherent in, 126
   as part of a *quid pro quo,* 178
   provisions of, 90, 233n61
   repeal of, 235n79
   sectional divide over, 130
   Southern slaveholders and, 11
   use of the army to enforce, 125, 126
Fugitive-slave laws
   army enforcement of, 125–126
   constitutionality of "fair" laws, 101–102
   federal employment of private agents in
     the enforcement of, 167–168
   impact of enforcement on state legitimacy,
     174
   impact on federal employment, 166–167
   impact on federal legitimacy in the North
     and South, 103–104
   impact on the federal government, 1, 6

intent of, 79
Southern law and, 82
Fugitive-slave policy
   federal support of slave interests and, 80, 102
   1817 fugitive slave debate, 85, 231n24
   Fugitive Slave Law of 1793, 84–85, 86, 87,
     89, 101
   Fugitive Slave Law of 1850 (*see* Fugitive
     Slave Law of 1850)
   fugitive-slave renditions, 83–92
   impact on American state development,
     101–106
   impact on executive-legislative balance, 104
   impact on federal authority, 171
   impact on federal institutional
     development, 170
   impact on federal legitimacy in the North
     and South, 103–104
   impact on federal-state balance, 104
   impact on the judiciary, 105–106
   international fugitive-slave recoveries,
     92–96
   Native American fugitive-slave recoveries,
     96–101
   parallel on enforcing the constitutional
     rights of freed slaves, 181
   partisan and sectional differences in,
     101–102
   role of the Congress in, 173
   Southern slaveholders and, 81–82
Fugitive-slave recoveries
   federal activity in, 80
   federal expenditures on, 82
   impact on the federal government and
     American state development, 83
   international cases, 92–96
   Native American nations and, 80–81, 96–101
Fugitive-slave renditions
   army assistance in, 125, 126
   federal activity in, 80
   federal expenditures on, 82, 90–91
   history of, 83–92
   impact on the federal government and
     American state development, 83
   legal nationalization of, 103
Fugitive slaves
   origins in the South, 230n7

Fugitive slaves, *continued*
    "personal liberty" laws and, 87
    "runaways" held in Washington County
        prison, 86
    See also Slave rescues
Fuller, Philo Case, 40

Gabriel conspiracy, 157, 250n108
Gag rule, 15
Gaines, Gen. Edmund P., 124
Gallatin, Albert, 33, 236n85
Gammons, James, 153
Ganahl, Joseph, 43
Garner, Margaret, 91, 168, 233–234n67
Garnet, Henry Highland, 64
Garrison, Tim, 254n149
Garrison, William Lloyd, 63, 64, 172
Geary, John W., 178
General Land Office, 195n45
General Survey Act of 1824, 12, 13
Georgia
    disputes and conflicts with Spanish East
        Florida, 94, 98, 110
    restriction on slave imports, 205n32
    sale of recaptured Africans into slavery, 60
    Treaty of Indian Springs and, 97
German Coast slave revolt, 122, 208n60,
    249n104
Gettysburg Address, 165
Gibson, George, 141, 170
Giddings, Joshua R.
    antislavery stance, 172, 177
    House censure of, 238n106
    indictment of the Second Seminole War, 154
    monograph on U.S. Seminole policy,
        239n126
    the Pacheco case and, 154
    the *Pearl* case and, 89
    the Watson case and, 99
Gilmer, Thomas W., 211n108
Glover, Joshua, 91, 169
Goodrich, Carter, 13
Gordon, Nathaniel, 46–47, 214n148, 214n150
Gorsuch, Edward, 234n69
Gosport navy yard, 14, 147–149, 160
Grampus (USS), 39
Granger, Gideon, 157, 163, 178

Grant, Ulysses S., 154
Great Britain
    American slave claims and, 92, 93, 236n86
    ban on slave imports into colonies, 207n58
    "bribing" other nations in slave-trade
        treaties, 28, 203n14
    naval assistance to Liberia, 67
    recognition of Liberia, 224n104
    refusal to extradite slaves to Florida, 94
    in slave trade suppression, 26, 28–29, 34, 40
    See also Anglo-American relations
Grier, Robert, 253n145
Grimes, Leonard, 251n127
Grimké, Thomas S., 220n48
Guerero (Spanish slave ship), 40, 211n97
Gurley, Rev. Ralph R., 178

Habeas corpus rights, 91, 235n74
Habersham, Richard Wylly, 210n84, 210n87
Hackett, Nelson, 94
Haidee seizure case, 48, 215n158
Haiti, 219–220n45
Haitian colonization project, 219–220n45
Haitian refugees, 208n60
Haitian Revolution, 216n165
Hale, John Parker, 89
Hallett, Benjamin Franklin, 251n125
Hamilton, Alexander, 155
Hamilton, Daniel, 43, 212n122
Hammond, James Henry, 137
Hammond, John Craig, 22, 126
Hampton, Brig. Gen. Wade, 122
Hanway, Castner, 91, 234n69
Harmon, Judd, 42, 212n113
Harper, Robert Goodloe, 58, 76
Harpers Ferry arsenal, 258n46
Harpers Ferry raid, 123
Hartley, Thomas, 88
Hartz, Louis, 164
Hayes, Isaac W., 43
Henshaw, David, 212n119
Herbert, John Carlyle, 58
Hermosa (seized American ship), 236n86
Herring, Elbert, 98
Hoban, James, 156
Holmes, Capt. Andrew Hunter, 35, 207–
    208n60

Holmes, John, 231n24
Holmes David, 207n60
Holt, John E., 122
Holt, Michael, 11
Home Squadron (U.S. Navy)
    capture of the *Echo*, 26, 43, 72
    expanded by Pres. Buchanan, 6, 44, 71, 72
    federal expenditures on, 46
    federal resources allocated to, 166
    seizures by, 46, 73, 212n113
    in slave trade suppression, 72, 73
Hornet (USS), 37
Horseshoe Bend, Battle of, 97
Horton, Carol, 23
House Committee on Commerce, 68
House Committee on Foreign Affairs, 70
House Committee on Private Land Claims,
    152–153
"House Divided" metaphor, 1, 22, 164–165,
    191n1
"House Divided" speech (Lincoln), 22, 164, 165
House Select Committee on the Colonization
    of Free People of Colour, 60
Howard, John E., 58
Hull, Isaac, 145
Hulse, Isaac, 147
Hummel, Jeffrey, 230n7, 235n78
Humphreys, Gad, 240n131
Hunt, Capt. Edward Bissell, 144
Huston, James, 11

Immigration and Naturalization Service
    (INS), 183–184, 272n76
Immigration policies
    effect of slave trade suppression on, 49
    federal ban on slave imports and, 23
    post-Civil War period, 183–184, 215–
        216n165
Immigration quotas, 183, 272n78
Indian agents, employment of slave labor,
    135–136, 157–158
Indian Removal Act of 1830, 8, 11, 112, 113, 117,
    129, 174
Indian Springs, Treaty of, 97
Indian territory, 127
Indirect subsidies, 78
In-kind subsidies, 57, 68

Insurrections clause, 172, 250n110
Intercurrences, 4, 192n21, 229n3
Internal improvements
    American state development and, 12–13
    army engineers and, 194n37
    federal expenditures on, 166
    military employment of slave labor in,
        149–150
    reaction of Southern slaveholders to,
        136–137
International fugitive-slave disputes
    federal reliance on private agents in, 103
    impact on American state development, 96
    impact on federal legitimacy in the South,
        104
    impact on international relations, 80, 81
    rejections of federal authority in, 104
    review of, 92–96
International relations
    impact of fugitive-slave disputes on, 80, 81
    See also Anglo-American relations

Jackson, Andrew
    acquisition of Florida and, 244n27
    the American Colonization Society and,
        53, 54, 58, 60, 61, 72
    counterfactual history, 21
    federal support for Liberia and, 65
    First Seminole War and, 111
    incursion into Florida during the War of
        1812, 110–111
    internal improvements and, 13
    Maysville Road veto, 12, 13
    Native American removals and, 129
    New Orleans free black militia and,
        262n101
    as provisional governor of Florida, 208n65
    Red Stick War and, 97
Jackson, Archibald, 153
Jackson, Henry Rootes, 43, 44, 213n127
Jackson, James, 157, 172
Jackson, John, 38
Jay, John, 81–82, 92
Jay, William, 63
"Jayhawkers," 128
Jay Treaty, 81–82, 92, 102, 235–236n82
Jefferson, Thomas, 33–34, 155, 235n80, 254n148

Jensen, Laura, 108
Jesup, Gen. Thomas S.
  Creek slave disputes and, 99
  on military employment of slave labor, 141
  period as commanding officer in Florida,
    257n27
  Second Seminole War and, 20, 112, 113–114,
    133, 173, 244n41, 255n169
  tenure as Quartermaster General, 170
Job shifting, 137–138
John, Richard, 11, 15
Johnson, Cave, 153
Johnson, June, 91, 234n72
Johnson, Samuel, 149
Johnson, William, 254n156
Johnston, Joseph E., 108, 132
Jones, Roger, 140, 170
Jones, Walter, 232–233n53
Jones v. Van Zandt, 89
Judicial policy-making, 173

Kaczorowski, Robert, 181
Kansas, 132, 176, 253n140
  See also "Bleeding Kansas"
Kansas-Nebraska Act, 71, 127, 128
Kansas Territory, 128
Katznelson, Ira, 2–3, 23, 184
Kendall, Amos, 56, 61–62, 71
Kendall report, 56, 61–62, 71, 78
Kennedy, John Pendleton, 68–69
Kennedy Report, 68–69, 224n101
Kentucky v. Dennison, 235n74
Key, Francis Scott, 53, 217n13
Key, Phillip Barton, 88, 89, 232n48, 232n52,
  232n53
Key West Africans, 74, 226n144, 227n150
King, Desmond, 23
King, Rufus, 123, 172
Kline, Henry H., 234n69
Klinkner, Philip, 23
Knox, Charles, 125
Kremlin (American ship), 39
Kryder, Daniel, 23

Lafitte, Jean, 35
La Jeune Eugénie (French slave ship), 37
Lamar, Charles, 43, 213n125, 213n126, 213n130

Land grants, 218n26, 222n78
Land sales, federal, 196n58
Lane, William Carr, 157
Lane Seminary, 63
Langdon, John, 205n25
Lanston, Charles H., 235n72
La Pensée (French slave ship), 37
Larson, John Lauritz, 13
Latin American immigrants, 183
Laurens, Henry, 151
Laurens, John, 262n92
Laval, Maj. Jacint, 110, 243n21
Law enforcement. *See* Federal law
  enforcement
Lawrence, Abbott, 177
Lawson, Thomas, 146
Lee, Robert Bland, 58
Lee, Col. Robert E., 123
Legal nationalization, 126
Levin, Lewis Charles, 266n151
Liberal state development, 2–5
"Liberator nation" competition, 207n58
Liberia
  ACS defense of conditions in, 221n69
  ACS's appeals for federal support and,
    55–56
  American colonialism and, 77
  assistance and protection from the U.S.
    navy, 54, 66, 67–68
  attacks on, 67
  attitude of free blacks and slaves toward, 64
  British recognition of, 224n104
  categories of emigrants to, 222n75, 227n155
  colonial agents, 54, 65, 66, 67, 75, 166,
    223n83, 223n84
  colonial government, 75–76
  colonial status, 53, 54
  commercial agents, 54, 66, 70, 166
  compared to the Dutch colonization of
    South Africa, 228n163
  constitution of, 76
  critics of, 56, 61–62
  federal employment of private agents
    and, 168
  federal support and financing of, 54, 65,
    66–68, 71, 72, 73–75
  first black governor, 223n81

founding of, 26
impact on American state development, 78
incorporation of the Cape Palmas colony,
    228n160
independence, 69
the Kennedy Report on, 68–69
last payment of the ACS to, 226n141
Lincoln's recognition of, 71, 219n45
public-private enterprise and, 1, 23
relationship with the U.S., 76–77
resettlement of recaptured Africans, 38, 39,
    40, 43, 55
securing a colonial site in, 66–67
John Seys's monitoring of, 75
significance of, 75–76
U.S. refusal to recognize, 70, 225n120
See also African colonization; American
    Colonization Society
Lieberman, Robert, 23
Lincoln, Abraham
    African colonization and, 265n134
    fugitive-slave laws and, 102
    Gettysburg Address, 165
    "House Divided" speech, 22, 164, 165
    protection of slavery and, 131
    recognition of Haiti, 219n45
    recognition of Liberia, 71, 219n45
    slavery and, 130, 230n9
    understanding of "union," 164, 165
Livermore, Arthur, 85
Logan, James, 100, 240n131
Log-rolling policy, 13
Loring, Edward G., 125, 212n123, 251–252n129
Louisa (American slave ship), 35, 36, 209n67,
    209n70
Louisiana
    Pointe Coupée slave revolt, 249n104
    slave smuggling and, 207–208n60
Louisiana Purchase, 13, 33, 127, 207n53
Louisiana Territory, 33, 207n53
Lovejoy, Owen, 162, 172
Lundy, Benjamin, 221n58

Macon, Nathaniel, 12, 137
Madison, James
    compromise proposal on the antislavery
        petitions, 33

fugitive-slave clause and, 84
location of the capital and, 155
opposition to constructionism, 12
the "Patriot War" and, 110
president of the American Colonization
    Society, 220n54
slave-trade clause and, 32
U.S. occupation of Spanish West Florida
    and, 243n19
Magrath, Andrew G., 44
Mahon, John, 108, 181
Mail delivery. See Post Office
Mallory, Stephen R., 143, 146–147, 151
Malone, Laurence, 108
Mann, Horace, 232n52
Marcy, William, 69
"Market revolution" thesis, 8–9
Maroon communities, 111, 240n129
Marsh, Charles, 58
Marshall, John, 58
Marshall, Thomas Alexander, 153
Martin, Luther, 31, 123–124, 176
Marx, Anthony, 11, 23, 196n55
Maryland, 220n52, 220n54
Mason, George, 31, 176–177
Mason, John M., 89–90, 101
Mason, John Y., 42
Mason, Jonathan, 231n24
Mason, Matthew, 22, 244n27
Massachusetts, 174
Mathews, Brig. Gen. George, 243n19
May, Samuel J., 233–234n67
Mayhew, David, 9, 108
Maysville Road veto, 12, 13
McFarland, Capt. Walter, 144
McHenry, Jerry, 91
McKenney, Thomas L., 98, 240n131
McKim, Isaac, 58
McLane, Louis, 63
McLean, John, 87, 232n36, 253n145
Meade, George, 108, 132
Mercer, Charles Fenton, 56, 58, 60, 62, 218n33
Mercer, Charles Francis, 39, 210n93
Mercer report, 60, 61
Merino (American slave ship), 35, 36, 209n67,
    209n70
Metcalfe, Thomas, 80

Mettler, Suzanne, 192n12
Mexican Americans, 183
Mexican-American War
  cost in lives, 108, 242n8, 245n54
  counterfactual history of, 19–20
  impact on American state development,
    108
  institutional effects of, 195n45
  opponents of, 199–200n102
  slavery and, 9, 10
  slaves as personal servants of officers,
    154–155
Mexico
  abolishment of slavery in, 199n101
  maroon communities, 240n129
  Seminole colonies, 183
  slave disputes with Texas and the U.S., 94,
    95, 199n100
  slave-extradition treaty with the U.S.,
    238n103
  slave smuggling and, 208n60
  underground railroad and, 241n145
Mexico cession, 127
Mifflin, Thomas, 84
Military-driven development, 9–10, 22
Military expenditures
  by the federal government, 109
  on incursions into Florida, 111
  in the Second Seminole War, 109, 113, 114
Military roads, 149, 261n83
Military slaves
  construction of military roads, 149, 261n83
  employed by the army, 140–144, 146–147,
    149–150, 151, 154–155, 167
  employed by the navy, 144–146, 147–149
  in military service, 151–155
  pay range of, 144–145
Militias
  in the Second Seminole War, 246n61
  slave and free black enlistees, 151, 152,
    261n89, 261n90, 262n101
  the U.S. army and, 133
Miller, Caleb, 72
Millstein, Andrew, 192n12
Minicucci, Stephen, 13
Minkins, Shadrach, 91, 125, 130, 251n121
Mississippi Choctaws, 248n91

Mississippi territorial constitution, 33
Mississippi Territory, 126
Missouri Compromise, 127, 128
Missouri crisis, 39, 49
Missouri Supreme Court, 146
Mitchell, David B., 35, 110
"Mixed enterprise" model, 181
Mobile Point (Alabama), 147
"Mongrel" people, 183
Monroe, James
  the American Colonization Society and,
    37, 53, 54, 60
  the Antelope case and, 95
  executive decision-making in slavery-
    related policies, 173
  First Seminole War and, 111
  Gabriel conspiracy and, 250n108
  interpretation of the slave-trade law of
    1819, 75
  David Mitchell and, 35
  Native American removals and, 129
  opposition to constructionism, 12
Morel, John, 38, 210n87
Morel, William, 169
Morgan, Edward D., 255n169
Morgan, Margarette, 86
Morril, David Lawrence, 85
Morris, Gouverneur, 123, 172
Morris, Thomas, 80
Morrison, Toni, 234n67
Moultrie Creek, Treaty of, 112
Mullis, Tony, 181
Mulroy, Kevin, 249n95
Murray, Robert, 48

Nash, Gary, 199n91
Nassau, 94
Natchitoches (Mexico), 208n60
Native American removals
  compared to African colonization, 249n94
  critics of, 129–130
  effect on federal legitimacy, 131
  federal coercion, 175
  federal efforts to remove the Seminoles,
    112, 113 (see also First Seminole War;
    Second Seminole War)
  federal expenditures on, 118, 119, 120

impact on state legitimacy, 174
impact on the U.S. army, 121–122
Indian Removal Act of 1830, 8, 11, 112, 113,
    117, 129, 174
Thomas Jefferson and, 254n148
motives for, 8, 100, 101
as "multi-tiered," 248n89
numbers moved from 1830 to 1843, 270n41
removal of southeastern "civilized"
    nations, 116–122
role of slaveholders in, 8, 117, 121
role of the military in, 108
slave-related removal expenses, 120
slavery as a factor in, 117, 120
as a state-driven process, 246n73
use of army contractors and
    subcontractors in, 132
Native Americans
    the American Colonization Society and,
        219n42
    federal relocation and assimilation
        policies, 184
    fugitive-slave clauses in treaties with, 82, 96
    fugitive-slave recoveries and, 80–81, 92–96
    race relations in the U.S. and, 120, 182–183,
        247n77
    renting of slaves to the army, 258n41
    slaveholding nations, 21, 80, 96, 117,
        228–229n2
    triangulation of race relations in the U.S.
        and, 182–183
    See also "Civilized" Native American
        nations; Native American removals;
        Second Seminole War
Nat Turner slave revolt, 122
Nautilus (American ship), 66
Naval Academy, 256–257n18
Navy yards
    employment of African Americans in,
        197n76
    employment of slave labor in, 144–146,
        147–149
"Negro Fort," 111, 244n25
Negro Seamen Act, 124, 130, 250–251n118,
    254n156
Nelson, Samuel, 253n145
"New institutionalists," 3, 192n15

Newman, Richard, 15, 206n46
New Mexico, 127, 157, 265n135
New Orleans, Battle of, 111, 262n101
New Orleans armory, 258n46
New Orleans (Louisiana), 143, 210n89,
    250n105, 262n101
New York State, 224n102, 262n99
Nicholas I (Tsar of Russia), 93
Nimble (HMS), 40
Norfolk navy yard. See Gosport navy yard
North Carolina, 205n33
Northwest Ordinance, 83, 86, 126, 127, 252n136
Novak, William, 3, 4

Obama, Barack Hussein, 185
Oden, Benjamin, 153
Office of Commissary General of Subsistence
    (U.S. Army), 141
Office of the Chief of Engineers (U.S. Army),
    141, 143, 149–150, 159
Office of the Quartermaster General (U.S.
    Army), 141–143
Office of the Superintendent of Immigration,
    183
"Old Republicans," 12–13
Ordnance Office (U.S. Army), 141, 170–171
Orleans territory, 122, 207n55
Orr, James L., 45
Orren, Karen, 2, 3, 4, 5–6, 11, 80
Overseers, 136, 138
Over-time comparisons, 6

Pacheco, Antonio, 154, 159, 263n111, 263n112
Pacheco, Louis, 154
Pacific Squadron (U.S. Navy), 39, 41, 67
Palfrey, John Gorham, 89
Panic of 1837, 197n69
Parker, Josiah, 32
Parker, Theodore, 251n125
Parramore, Thomas, 250n106
"Patriot War," 110, 133
Patterson, Thomas, 58
Payne's Landing, Treaty of, 112
Pearl case, 88–89, 232n47
Pemberton, James, 146, 154
Pennsylvania, 224n102, 231–232n33
Pennsylvania antislavery society, 32, 206n42

Pensacola (Florida), 111, 209n66
Pensacola navy yard, 145, 147, 259n55
Perry, Lt. Matthew, 67
"Personal liberty" laws, 87, 91, 231–232n33, 235n74
Personal servants, slaves employed as, 135, 146, 154–155, 259n62
Peter, George, 58
Peyton, Lucien, 44, 47
Phelps, Amos, 63
Phelps, Edward, 147
Phillips, Wendell, 126, 174, 251n125
Pickering, Timothy, 252n133
Pierce, Franklin, 69, 130, 178, 222n78
Pierson, Paul, 4, 5
Pilchur, Joshua, 158, 266n145
Pinckney, Charles, 31, 176, 205n28
Pinckney, Charles Cotesworth, 31, 32, 84, 176, 178, 205n28, 205n31
Pindall, James, 85, 101
Pine Island (Florida), 86
Piracy, 37, 43
Platte region, 127, 128, 253n137, 266n145
Pointe Coupée slave revolt, 249n104
Point Peter battery, 110
Polk, James K., 20, 89, 95
Pollack, Sheldon, 4, 107
Pons (American slave ship), 26, 27, 42, 72
Porter, Bruce, 107
Portnoy, Alisse, 174, 249n94
Portugal, 95
Post Office
    abolitionist mailings controversy, 15, 166
    federal expenditures on, 166, 267n12
    slave labor and, 135, 157, 163
Poverty rates, 202n129
Pratt, Thomas G., 233n58
Price, John, 91, 235n72
Prigg, Edward, 86, 87, 232n36
Prigg v. Pennsylvania, 86–87, 102, 106, 133
Private agents
    employed in fugitive-slave cases and disputes, 7, 81, 103
    employed to enforce fugitive-slave laws, 167–168
    employed to perform state functions, 6–7, 50, 167–169

federal employment of slave labor, 161
Private investigators, 50
Prosser conspiracy. *See* Gabriel conspiracy
Prucha, Francis Paul, 9
Public-private partnerships
    African colonization and, 1, 23, 57, 76
    the American Colonization Society and, 1, 53, 57, 76

Quakers, 32, 206n42, 206n43

Race
    American state development and, 23, 182–185
    triangulation of relations in the U.S., 182–183
Race control, 23
Randolph, Beverley, 84
Randolph, John, 12, 34, 53, 58, 59–60, 137
Rankin, Robert G., 158, 163
Reconstruction, 11, 104, 105, 181
"Red" Seminoles, 120
Red Stick War, 97, 120
Rented slave labor. *See* Slave rentals
Revenue cutters, 37–38, 158
"Reverse" slave raids, 98
Revolutionary War, 242n4
    American slave claims from, 92–93
    free blacks and slaves in, 151–152, 261n89, 262n95
Rhea, John, 85
Rhode Island militia, 151, 261n91
Rich, Charles, 85, 101
Richard Cobden (American ship), 43
Right to Speak (Portnoy), 249n94
Riley, Patrick, 251n121
Ringgold, Tench, 86, 231n31
Rives, William C., 62
Roberts, Joseph Jenkins, 66, 70, 223n81
Roberts, Mark, 8, 174
Robinson, Hiram H., 168
Rockwell, Charles William, 158, 163, 178
Rodgers, Daniel, 2
Rothman, Adam, 8, 250n105
Rush, Richard, 53, 58
Russell, Capt. John B. F., 98–99
Russell, Jonathan, 236n85

Rutledge, Edward, 151, 152
Rutledge, John, 30, 31, 151, 176
Ryan, Edward V., 91–92, 169
Ryecraft, Ryan, 91

Saint Augustine (Florida), 110, 140, 149–150
Sanderson, Samuel, 40
Sauks, 117
Sayres, Edward, 88
Scott, Dred, 146
    See also Dred Scott case
Scott, Gustav, 156
Scott, Capt. Martin, 146
Scott, Winfield, 154
Search and seizure, 27, 41, 48, 240n139
Second Seminole War
    army employment of slave labor in, 135, 167
    army policy toward Black Seminoles in, 99
    auxiliary army forces, 245–246n56
    benefits to slaveholders, 114
    causes of, 113, 167
    concept of military-driven state development and, 9
    cost in lives, 108, 115, 242n8
    counterfactual history of, 20–21
    critics of, 129, 130
    decision-making in the periphery during, 172–173
    development of the U.S. Army and, 1, 6, 108, 115–116, 132, 167, 168–169
    distinct features of, 114
    executive decision-making in, 172
    federal expenditures in, 16, 109, 113, 114–115, 116, 120, 165
    government triangulation of parties in, 120
    Gen. Jesup recommends ending "early," 244n41
    length of, 113
    militia and volunteers in, 246n61
    as a "negro war," 113–114
    overview of, 112–113
    post-war expenditures, 116
    relationship to slavery, 10
    secrecy and, 133
    William T. Sherman and, 133
    as a slave revolt, 249n103
    slaves in military service, 154

    supporters of, 129
    the Watson case, 99–100
Sellers, Charles Grier, 8–9, 11
Seminole maroon community, 111
Seminoles
    Creeks and, 97, 238n114, 244n35
    emancipation of slaves, 200n104
    federal efforts to remove, 112
    First Seminole War, 98, 111, 209n66
    navy transportation to New Orleans, 248n86
    preremoval census, 118
    reasons for resisting removal, 113
    recognized by the U.S., 240n132
    removal, 175
    Second Seminole War (*see* Second Seminole War)
    slave disputes and, 97, 98
    slaveholding and, 80, 81, 96, 246n72
    slave-related removal expenses, 120
    Third Seminole War, 116, 143
    during the War of 1812, 111
Senate Committee on Foreign Relations, 61, 213n134
Seward, William, 45, 130, 251n125
Seys, John, 72, 73, 75, 227n156
Shadd, Abraham D., 64
Shannon, Wilson, 253n142
Shaperstein, John, 169
Shark (USS), 67
Shawnees, 246n56
Sherman, Roger, 83, 101
Sherman, William Tecumseh, 133
Shick, Tom, 228n163
Shiner, Michael, 145
Shipman, William Davis, 46
Sims, Thomas, 91, 125, 233–234n67, 251n123
Singleton, Henry, 149
Sinoe settlement, 224n102
Sioux, 117
Skocpol, Theda, 2, 108
Skowronek, Stephen, 2, 3, 4, 5–6, 11
Slaughter, Rev. Philip, 70–71, 178
Slave-catching expeditions, 94, 95, 167
Slave disputes
    cases involving Native Americans, 96–101
    See also Fugitive-slave cases/disputes

Slave-extradition treaties, 94, 238n103
Slaveholders
    benefits of the Second Seminole War to, 114
    claims to Black Seminoles, 20
    constitutional rights and the return of
        fugitive slaves, 23–24, 104–105
    dominance in the executive departments
        of the federal government, 14
    fugitive-slave disputes and, 80
    fugitive-slave policy and, 81–82
    Native American removals and, 8, 117, 121
    relationship to the government when
        renting slave labor, 160–161
    response to federal internal
        improvements, 136–137
    states rights and, 11
    threat to regime stability, 11
Slaveholding Republic, The (Fehrenbacher),
    13–14
Slave import bans
    effect on the federal government, 1
    federal, 23
    by Great Britain, 207n58
    South Carolina and, 205n28
Slave imports
    duties on, 32, 205n34, 207n54
    restricted by Brazil, 210n90
    restricted by Cuba, 210n90
Slave labor
    ambiguous intentions and effects of, 178
    authority of federal employers over,
        138–139
    during the Civil War, 139, 181
    coercion and, 176
    congressional policy on, 162, 163
    distributive and symbolic effects of, 162
    employed by the federal government,
        14–15, 135–136, 155–158
    executive decision-making and, 162–163
    favoring of slaveholders in federal policy,
        162
    federal employment practices and, 136–139
    impact on American state development,
        161–162
    impact on bureaucratic autonomy in the
        periphery, 140, 163, 170–171, 173
    impact on federal authority, 172

    impact on the federal government, 1, 7,
        14–15, 135
    job shifting and, 137–138
    labor contracts and arrangements in,
        261n87
    micromanagement structures, 156
    military slaves, 140–151 (see also Military
        slaves)
    overseers, 136, 138
    pay rates, 137, 138
    relationship between the government and
        slaveholders in, 160–161
    sectional and partisan differences in
        Congress over, 159–160
    substitution effect, 167
Slave markets, 9
Slave raids, "reverse," 98
Slave rentals
    coercion and, 176
    impact on the federal government, 1, 14–15
    See also Slave labor
Slave reparations, 24
Slave rescues
    abolitionists and, 88
    the Booth case, 91–92
    federal expenditures related to, 91
    local support for in the North, 103
    the Pearl case, 88–89
    use of the army in preventing, 125
    the Walker case, 87–88
Slave revolts
    army coercion and, 175
    the Black Seminoles and, 249n103
    German Coast slave revolt, 122, 208n60,
        249n104
    government suppression of, 122–124, 126
    number of, 249n103
    Pointe Coupée revolt, 249n104
    the Second Seminole War as, 249n103
    Southampton revolt, 122, 124, 130, 131, 148,
        250n106
Slavery
    abolished in Mexico, 199n101
    the American Colonization Society on,
        70–71
    American state development and, 1–2, 6–7,
        11–17, 179–180

Compromise of 1850 and, 127
in a counterfactual history of American
    state development, 17–21
"early" abolition, 199n91
as a factor in Native American removals, 120
federal ban on slave imports, 23
federal coercion and, 175–176
federal protection of, 9, 178–179
impact on American state capacities,
    165–169
impact on federal governing authority,
    171–173
impact on federal institutional autonomy,
    170–171
impact on state legitimacy, 173–175
impact on the market revolution, 9
Lincoln and, 130, 230n9
military-driven state development and, 9, 10
Missouri Compromise and, 127
in the territories, 126–129, 130
the U.S. as a "house divided," 1, 22, 164–
    165, 191n1
Slavery-centered narrative
    American state development and, 1–2, 6–7,
        13–17
    counterfactual history of, 17–21
    historical and contemporary significance
        of, 22–24
Slavery-related military activities
    American state development and, 107, 109,
        131, 133
    commitment of federal officials to, 130–131
    enforcement of federal fugitive-slave laws,
        125–126
    in Florida, 109–116
    impact on federal authority, 171–172
    impact on federal legitimacy in the South,
        131–132
    impact on state legitimacy, 173–174
    impact on the U.S. army, 132–133
    interregional differences over, 130
    partisan and sectional differences over,
        129–130
    protection of slavery and, 131
    removal of southeastern "civilized"
        nations, 116–122
    secrecy and, 133–134

slave revolts, 122–124
slavery in the territories and, 126–129
Slaves
    in military service, 151–155
    temporary ownership by the federal
        government, 256n16
Slave smuggling
    the Antelope case, 37–38, 95, 169
    decrease between 1819 and 1842, 37–39
    Andrew Jackson suppresses in Florida,
        208n65
    by Jean Lafitte and Jim Bowie, 35
    in Louisiana, 207–208n60
    Louisiana Purchase and, 33
    Mexico and, 208n60
    in New Orleans, 210n89
    suppression of (see Slave trade
        suppression)
    the Wanderer case, 43–44, 47
Slave-smuggling espionage, 47–48
"Slave stealing," 88
Slave trade
    American participation in, 39
    debated during the Constitutional
        Convention, 25, 30–31
    1856 House resolution condemning, 45
    the Louisa, Merino, and Constitution cases,
        35–36
    partisan and sectional differences over,
        176–177
    suppression of (see Slave trade
        suppression)
Slave-trade cases
    federal use of private agents in, 7
    government payments to witnesses, 48
Slave-trade clause, 24, 177
Slave-trade law of 1819, 36–37, 39, 60, 75
Slave-trade law of 1820, 37
Slave-trade laws
    development of the U.S. navy and, 181
    execution of Nathaniel Gordon, 46–47
    impact of enforcement on state legitimacy,
        174
    intent of, 79
    "nullification," 214n140
    politics and the enforcement of, 44–45, 47
    state commitment to implement, 52

Slave-trade policy
    Anglo-American relations and, 30, 40–41,
        51, 52
    compared to African colonization policies,
        78
    executive policy-making and, 173
    growth of federal powers and, 51–52
    impact on federal authority, 171
    interpenetration of state and society in, 77
    racist attitudes to black emigration and, 77
Slave-trade revival movement, 45, 47
Slave trade suppression
    African colonization and, 54, 71, 74, 78
    American state development and, 25, 30,
        49–52
    James Buchanan and, 26, 30, 44, 45–46, 49,
        71, 72–73
    counterfactual history, 29–30
    factors affecting American commitment
        to, 52
    federal expenditures on, 27–28, 40, 46, 187,
        203n7
    Great Britain and, 26, 28–29, 34, 40
    impact on the U.S. navy, 166
    overview of federal activity in, 25–27, 48–49
    role of the U.S. navy in, 6, 26–27, 28–29,
        33, 36, 37, 39, 40–43, 46, 48 (see also
        African Squadron; Home Squadron)
    state functions and capacities involved in,
        49–51
    from 1791 to 1807, 25, 30–34
    from 1808 to 1819, 25–26, 34–36
    from 1819 to 1842, 26, 36–41
    from 1843 to 1859, 26, 41–46
    from 1860 to 1861, 26–27, 46–48
    U.S. and British efforts compared, 28–29,
        42
Slidell, John, 44–45
Sloan, James, 34
Slocumb, Benjamin F., 47
Smallwood, Samuel, 156
Smith, Caleb B., 47–48
Smith, E. Delafield, 47
Smith, Gerrit, 63, 88, 232n46
Smith, John, 38, 210n83, 210n84
Smith, Joseph L., 98
Smith, Brig. Gen. Persifor F., 128, 132, 178,
    255n169

Smith, Rogers, 23
Smith, Samuel, 58
Smith, Col. Thomas Adam, 110, 133, 243n21
Smith, Waters, 40
Smith, William, 85
Smith, William Loughton, 32, 85
Social-welfare programs, 184
Society-centered models, 7–17
Southampton slave revolt, 122, 124, 130, 131,
    148, 250n106
Southard, Samuel, 62, 220n56
South Carolina
    slave import bans, 205n28
    slave revolts, 123, 124
    slave-trade article of the Webster-
        Ashburton Treaty and, 214n140
    the Vesey conspiracy and, 130
Southern Democratic Republicans, 12
Southern Indian agents, 135–136, 157–158
Southern slaveholders. See Slaveholders
Spain, 95–96, 208n65
Spanish East Florida
    slave disputes between Native Americans
        and European Americans, 97
    slave-smuggling and, 35, 38
    U.S. incursions into, 35, 94, 98, 110, 111,
        209n66
    U.S. occupation of, 26
Spanish slave ships, 37–38, 39, 40
Spanish West Florida, 243n19
Spence, Capt. Robert T., 67
Spencer, John C., 140
Sprague, Maj. John T., 114, 115, 132, 133, 246n62,
    255n169
Spratt, Leonidas, 212n122
Spullock, James, 213n126
St. Clair, Arthur, 127
Stanton, Frederick P., 178, 225n115
State, definitions of, 3–5
State development
    approaches to the measure of, 5–6
    concepts of, 4–5
    impact of war on, 107
    society-centered models of, 6
    See also American state development
State governments
    funding of African colonization, 69, 72,
        220n52, 224n102

responsibility for slave trade suppression, 25

sectional differences over African colonization, 177

State legitimacy, 173–175

States rights, 11

Stephens, Alexander, 89

Sterigere, John Benton, 153

Stevens, Thaddeus, 265n134

Stockton, Lt. Robert T., 67, 68

Stockton, Lt. Thomas B. W., 146

Storrs, Henry, 231n24

Story, Joseph, 37, 86, 101, 102, 106

Strange, Robert, 62

Stuart, Alexander H. H., 88, 127

Substitution effect, 167

Sullivan, Kathleen, 124

Sumner, Charles, 88, 130, 172, 177, 251n125

Surprise (USS), 35

Suttle, Charles F., 125

Sylla, Richard, 196n58

Takaki, Ronald, 45, 47

Talcott, George, 141, 257n28

Taney, Roger B.
  Ableman v. Booth decision, 91, 235n74
  Dred Scott decision, 128–129
  Negro Seamen Act and, 254n156
  Prigg v. Pennsylvania decision, 86–87, 101, 102, 106

Taney Court, 89, 173

Tappan, Arthur, 63

Tariffs, 12

Tatton, Phillis, 152, 262n96

Taxation
  direct, 196n61
  excise taxes, 196n58
  the federal government and, 11–12

Taylor, John, 53, 58

Taylor, Sarah, 263n116

Taylor, Gen. Zachary, 146, 154, 263n116

Tazewell, Littleton Waller, 61, 172

Tazewell report, 61, 77, 78, 224n103

Temporary employees, 169

Tennessee volunteers, 97, 111

Territorial constitutions, 33

Territorial militia, 7, 128

Territories

Congress and the governing of, 253n144

handling of fugitive-slave renditions in, 86

slavery and, 126–129, 130

Territories clause, 128–129

Texas
  Adams-Onís Treaty and, 199n100
  army employment of slave labor in, 142
  ceding of New Mexican lands, 178
  counterfactual history of, 19–20
  declares independence, 95
  international slave disputes and, 94–95
  Mexico's efforts to restrict slavery in, 199n100, 199n101
  U.S. annexation of, 95, 114

Third Seminole War, 116, 143

Thomas, George H., 108, 132

Thompson, Jacob, 47, 52

Thompson, Smith, 38, 67, 210n84

Thompson, Wiley, 98, 157–158

Thornton, William, 156, 264n129

Three-fifths clause, 205n33

Tilly, Charles, 9, 107

Tocqueville, Alexis de, 182, 201n119

Tomlins, Christopher, 147–149

Tompkins, Daniel D., 85

Totten, Joseph G., 141, 146, 147, 170

Toucey, Isaac, 44, 73

Townsend, Edward N., 43, 212n123

Trail of Tears, 119

Treaty of Ghent, 34, 93, 102, 236n85

Treaty of Indian Springs, 97

Treaty of Moultrie Creek, 112

Treaty of New Echota, 248n87

Treaty of Paris, 92

Treaty of Payne's Landing, 112, 239n121

Treaty with the Choctaw (1825), 111

Trumbull, Lyman, 104–105, 181

Turner, Frederick Jackson, 108

Turner, Nat, 122

Tyler, John, 42, 67, 68, 95, 211n109

Tyler-McGraw, Marie, 221n69

Underground railroad, 94, 104, 241n145

United States
  American exceptionalism, 107–108
  annexation of Texas, 95
  anti-slave trade sentiment in, 29–30
  census of 1790, 199n99

United States, *continued*
  census of 1820, 227n157
  census of 1860, 197n72
  continuity and change in the pre- and
    post–Civil War periods, 180–182
  demographics, 197n72, 199n99
  division into free and slave states, 22
  employment of private agents to perform
    state functions, 6–7, 50, 167–169
  "House Divided" metaphor, 1, 22, 164–165,
    191n1
  as a "house united" on racial supremacy,
    181–182
  impact of slavery on the foreign policy
    of, 96
  international fugitive-slave and slave-loss
    cases, 92–96
  poverty rates in 2009, 202n129
  relationship with Liberia, 76–77
  slave-extradition treaties, 94, 238n103
  slave trade suppression (*see* Slave trade
    suppression)
  triangulation of race relations in, 182–183
  See also American state development;
    Federal government
United States Army
  coercive policies, 175–176
  deployment to suppress domestic
    violence, 126
  employment of slave labor, 140–144, 146–
    147, 149–150, 151, 154–155, 167
  fugitive-slave law enforcement, 105,
    125–126
  impact of Native American removals on,
    121–122
  impact of peacetime activities on
    American state development, 108
  impact of slave labor on "mezzo-level"
    autonomy in, 170–171, 173
  impact of slavery-related military
    activities on, 132–133
  impact of the Second Seminole War on, 1,
    6, 108, 115–116, 132, 167, 168–169
  intervention in Kansas Territory, 128
  local militia and, 133
  in Native American removals, 118, 119, 184
  prevention of slave rescues, 125

slavery-related institutional development,
  1, 170–171
in slave trade suppression, 35
stationed around New Orleans, 250n105
suppression of slave revolts, 122–123
use of auxiliary forces, 7
United States Citizenship and Immigration
  Services (USCIS), 184
United States Congress
  ambiguous intentions and effects of
    slavery-related policies, 177, 178
  "Black Militia" law of 1792, 152
  Committee of Claims, 40, 99
  development of slave trade policy, 32–34
  effective beginning of, 21–22
  the fugitive-slave clause and, 205n36
  1817 fugitive slave debate, 85, 231n24
  Fugitive Slave Law of 1793, 84–85
  governing of U.S. territories, 253n144
  House Committee on Commerce, 68
  House Committee on Foreign Affairs, 70
  House Committee on Private Land
    Claims, 152–153
  1856 House resolution condemning the
    slave trade, 45
  House Select Committee on the
    Colonization of Free People of Colour,
    60
  land grants, 218n26
  origins of the gag rule, 15
  partisan and sectional differences on
    slave-related issues, 176, 177
  post–Civil War period immigration
    policies, 183–184
  Revolutionary War slave claims and, 92–93
  role in fugitive-slave policy area, 173
  sectional and partisan differences over
    slave labor, 159–160
  Senate Committee on Foreign Relations,
    61, 213n134
  social-welfare programs, 184
United States Constitution
  domestic violence clause, 123, 171–172
  fugitive-slave clause, 81, 86, 101, 102, 171
  insurrection clause, 172
  slave-trade clause, 24
  territories clause, 128–129

three-fifths clause, 205n23
See also Constitutional Convention
United States military
  number of employees, 168
  slavery-related institutional development,
    170–171
  slaves in military service, 135, 151–155 (*see
    also* Military slaves)
United States Navy
  assistance to and protection of Liberia, 54,
    66, 67–68
  bounties paid to crews in slave-trade
    cases, 203n10
  coercive actions, 176
  costs of the Second Seminole War, 114
  employment of slave labor, 14–15, 144–146,
    147–149
  enforcement of slave-trade laws and, 181
  enlistment of free blacks in, 152, 153–154
  impact of African colonization on the
    development of, 77–78
  impact of slave trade suppression on, 25,
    49, 51, 166
  number of ships in 1842 and 1859, 211n111
  Pacific Squadron, 39, 41, 67
  in the "Patriot War," 110
  patrols off the coast of Africa, 39
  policy against employing African
    Americans, 197n76
  slavery-related institutional development,
    170
  in slave trade suppression, 6, 26–27, 28–29,
    33, 35–36, 37, 39, 40–43, 46, 48, 71–72
  See also African Squadron; Home
    Squadron
United States Supreme Court
  Ableman v. Booth, 91–92, 103, 235n74
  the *Antelope* case, 38
  on the capture of the *Constitution*, 35
  Dred Scott, 82, 128–129, 133, 253n145
  Jones v. Van Zandt, 89
  judicial policy-making, 173
  Kentucky v. Dennison, 235n74
  Native American removal cases, 119
  Prigg v. Pennsylvania, 86–87, 102, 106, 133
  United States v. Amistad, 95–96
United States v. Amistad, 95–96

Upham-Bornstein, Linda, 148, 149
Upper Louisiana territory, 207n55
Upshur, Abel P.
  the African Squadron and, 41, 42
  the American Colonization Society and, 67
  on black navy enlistees, 154
  navy employment of slave labor and, 144,
    146
  as Secretary of State, 211n108
  slave disputes with Great Britain and, 94
  in Tyler's cabinet, 211n107
U.S. attorneys
  civil rights policies and, 184
  hiring of private agents, 168
U.S. attorneys general
  impact of fugitive-slave policy on, 81
  involvement in slave trade suppression,
    43, 47, 50
  private practice and, 268n25
U.S. commissioners, 81, 167
U.S. custom officials, 50
U.S. marshals
  civil rights policies and, 184
  Fugitive Slave Law of 1850 and, 81, 166–167
  hiring of private agents, 167–168
  interccurence, 229n3
  involvement in slave trade suppression, 36,
    38, 40, 43, 50
  prevention of slave rescues, 125
  in slave-smuggling espionage, 48
  as unsalaried employees, 209n69

Valelly, Richard, 23
Valliere, Kenneth, 247n82
Van Buren, Martin, 40, 68, 127, 130
van Cleve, George William, 22
Varnum, Joseph P., 177
Vesey, Denmark, 123
Vesey conspiracy, 123, 124, 130
Veterans
  African American, 152
  benefit programs, 108
Virginia, 130, 157, 250n108

W. R. Kirby (American slave ship), 214n143,
  227n152
Walker, David, 64, 172

Walker, Jonathan, 87–88, 232n40, 232n44

Walker, Robert J., 69, 253n142

Wanderer (American slave ship), 43–44, 47, 213n126, 213n127

War, state development and, 9–10, 22, 107, 108

War of 1812
  American slave claims from, 93
  "American System" and, 9
  Creek Indians and, 97
  federal taxation and, 12
  impact of slavery on, 10
  impact on American state development, 108
  incursions into Florida, 110–111
  slaves in military service, 152–153

Washington, Bushrod, 35, 53, 58, 209n66

Washington, D.C.
  anti-abolitionist riots, 89
  federal employment of slave labor in, 136, 138, 155–157, 264n120, 264n132
  See also District of Columbia

Washington, George, 84, 151, 155, 162, 261n89

Washington county prison, 86, 231n31

Washington navy yard, 145

Watson, James C., 99, 154

Wayne, James, 69, 70, 225n114

Weber, Max, 4

Webster, Daniel
  African Squadron and, 40
  the American Colonization Society and, 53, 58, 62, 67, 69, 220–221n57
  fugitive-slave issues and, 177
  on Mexican Americans, 183
  opposition to the Mexican-American War, 200n102
  slave rescues and, 251n122
  as Tyler's Secretary of State, 211n108
  use of the military to enforce federal fugitive-slave law, 130

Webster-Ashburton Treaty
  establishment of the African Squadron, 26, 40, 67
  fugitive-slave extraditions and, 94
  slave-trade article, 211n109, 214n140
  slave-trade politics and, 44–45
  slave trade suppression and, 41
  U.S. boundary with Canada and, 215n163

Weingast, Barry, 15, 230n7, 235n78

Weld, Theodore, 63

Wells, Cuff, 152, 262n96

Wendover, Peter Hercules, 58

West African Squadron (Great Britain), 26, 28, 34

Westward expansion, 8

Wharton, Francis, 234n69

Wheldon, Mrs. L. E., 150

Whigs, 62

Whiskey Rebellion, 126, 196n58

White House, 156

Wigg, Maj. William Hazard, 93

Wilde, Richard, 38

Williamson, Passmore, 234n72

Wilmot, David, 177

Wilson, Henry, 45, 177

Wilson, James, 32, 83, 177

Wilson, Mark, 170, 181

Winthrop, Robert, 90

Wirt, William, 130, 169

Wisconsin, 235n74

Wood, Thomas J., 132

Worcester v. Georgia, 119

Worth, Col. William J., 113, 133, 154, 246n62

Wright, Lt. Horatio G., 146

Wright, Robert, 53

Yarbrough, Fay A., 247n81

Yell, Archibald, 94

Young, Tommy Richard, II, 122